Mastering the World of Selling

Mastering the World of Selling

The Ultimate Training Resource from the Biggest Names in Sales

ERIC TAYLOR
DAVID RIKLAN

WILEY

John Wiley & Sons, Inc.

Published by John Wiley & Sons, Inc., Hoboken, New Jersey.
Published simultaneously in Canada.

For general information on our other products and services or for technical support, please contact our Customer Care Department within the United States at (800) 762-2974, outside the United States at (317) 572-3993 or fax (317) 572-4002.

Wiley also publishes its books in a variety of electronic formats. Some content that appears in print may not be available in electronic books. For more information about Wiley products, visit our web site at www.wiley.com.

ISBN 978-0-470-61786-1 (paper)
ISBN 978-0-470-65106-3 (ebk)
ISBN 978-0-470-65149-0 (ebk)
ISBN 978-0-470-65150-6 (ebk)

Printed in the United States of America

10 9 8 7 6 5 4 3 2 1

This book is dedicated to our families:
our wives, Michelle Riklan and Clare Taylor,
and our eight wonderful children,
Joshua, Jonathan, Rachel, Kelly,
Mark, Zachary, Luke, and Jake.

Contents

Acknowledgments   xxi

Foreword   JEFFREY GITOMER   xxiii

Introduction   xxv

Your Past and Present Hold the
     Key to Your Future   JEFFREY GITOMER   xxvii

Chapter 1   Collaboration: Changing the World   1
               Randall K. Murphy

               Collaboration, client retention, negotiation,
               relationship building

Chapter 2   Living Your Vows in a Whirlwind Economy   4
               Seleste Lunsford

               Customer relationships, customer loyalty,
               CRM, sales strategy

Chapter 3   Ninety Percent of All Sales Force Training Fails   8
               Duane Sparks

               Relationships, sales call planning, questioning skills,
               presentation skills, and commitment

Chapter 4   Eleven Telephone Tips to Effectively Reach
               Out and Touch Others   13
               Dr. Tony Alessandra

               Effective communication, telephone etiquette,
               call strategy, productivity

Chapter 5   The "At-Leaster" Phenomenon   16
Brian Azar

*Attitude, beliefs, self-confidence, mind-set,
motivation, failing*

Chapter 6   Confronting the CRM Challenge   22
Walter Rogers

*Sales 2.0, customer relationship management,
sales management, sales process*

Chapter 7   Rethinking Sales Success: Storytelling   26
Mike Bosworth

*Client communication, storytelling, bonding,
rapport building, engagement*

Chapter 8   Selling for the Independent Professional   30
Ian Brodie

*Consultative selling, sales methodology,
questioning strategies, closing*

Chapter 9   Ten Tips for Convincing the Buyer to Pay More   35
Ed Brodow

*Effective negotiation, pricing, closing,
qualifying, buyer's remorse*

Chapter 10   How to Sell a Pencil—and Your Product
or Service   40
Mike Brooks

*Sales process, presentation skills,
questioning skills, sales scripts*

Chapter 11   Cultivating Endless Referrals: An Introduction   43
Bob Burg

*Referrals, prospecting, networking, relationship
development, building trust, likeability*

Chapter 12   Twenty-One Ways to Increase Sales This Year   46
Jim Cathcart

*Relationship development, improving sales skills,
prospecting, brand identity, closing*

Chapter 13   The Psychology of Persuasion   50
              Robert Cialdini

              Persuasion, manipulation, business etiquette,
              principle of scarcity

Chapter 14   The Virtual Presentation: Mastering the Medium   55
              Bill Rosenthal

              Presentation skills, PowerPoint, communication
              skills, public speaking

Chapter 15   Do You Have an Effective Closing Strategy?   60
              Tim Connor

              Closing strategies, prospecting,
              questioning strategies, sales competency

Chapter 16   Sales Manager or Administrator?   64
              John Holland

              Sales management, pipeline, proposals,
              sales cycle, sales behavior and activity

Chapter 17   Uncover Sales Opportunities   68
              Dale Carnegie

              Sales meetings, prospecting, lead generation,
              sales pipeline, account management,
              centers of influence, networking

Chapter 18   How Can I Wow the Audience When Speaking?   72
              Sam Deep

              Public speaking, presentation skills, audience
              analysis, proper language, articulation,
              body language, PowerPoint, confidence

Chapter 19   The Good Life Rules   76
              Bryan J. Dodge

              Belief, confidence, motivation, inspiration,
              professional selling

Chapter 20   Five Traits of a Great Sales Leader   79
              Barry Farber

              Sales management, recruiting, accountability,
              sales coaching, leadership

Chapter 21   Reconstructing the Pieces of the Sales Puzzle   82
Jonathan Farrington

Attitude, sales skills, sales process,
sales knowledge, sales best practices

Chapter 22   Manage Salespeople as You Would Invest   87
Jeffrey Fox

Sales management, sales coaching,
sales training, sales accountability

Chapter 23   The Amazing Power of Testimonials   89
Colleen Francis

Testimonials, relationship building, networking,
social media

Chapter 24   Want More Sales? Stop "Selling" and
Start Helping Clients Succeed   93
Mahan Khalsa

Setting expectations, why people buy,
building trust, sales intentions

Chapter 25   Your Next Job Interview   98
Thomas A. Freese

Buying decisions, creating value, selling yourself,
personal branding, character traits, differentiation,
building credibility

Chapter 26   Nine Biggest Mistakes Salespeople Make in
Their Presentations   101
Patricia Fripp

Presentation skills, focus, communicating
effectively, using testimonials, connecting with
the audience, using technology to present

Chapter 27   Seven Cold-Calling Secrets Even the
Sales Gurus Don't Know   105
Ari Galper

Cold calling, mental focus, mind-set, overcoming
fear, communication and questioning strategy,
building confidence

Chapter 28   Learn More, Sell More   110
              Daniel Miller

              Product knowledge, social media, qualifying,
              personal brand, professional development,
              market analysis

Chapter 29   Are You a Sales Rock Star, or Just a
              Member of the Band?   112
              Jeffrey Gitomer

              Sales excellence, self-confidence, passion,
              internal drive

Chapter 30   Selling Professional Services   115
              Charles H. Green

              Sales perception, trusted advisor, client service,
              sales purpose

Chapter 31   Dealing with Unreturned Phone Calls   120
              Ford Harding

              Handling rejection, building self-confidence,
              self-belief, persistence, creativity

Chapter 32   Engaging and Defeating Competition:
              Competitive Strategy and Political Alignment
              in World-Class Selling   122
              Holden International

              Creating value, sales process, sales strategy,
              client relations, competitive advantage

Chapter 33   How to Double Sales in 12 Months Flat   126
              Chet Holmes

              Increasing market share, persistence, marketing,
              prospecting, qualifying, selling strategy

Chapter 34   Developing the Thank-You Note Habit   129
              Tom Hopkins

              Client retention, cultivating referrals, building
              relationships, customer communication

Chapter 35 Escaping the Price-Driven Sale Selling to
            Clients at a Premium   132
            John Golden

            *Closing, creating value, differentiation, diagnosis
            of problem, understanding buying behaviors*

Chapter 36 Creating Client Value: A Practical, Modern
            Approach to Building Business   137
            Richard Barkey

            *Creating value, relationship development,
            effective sales behaviors, targeted prospecting*

Chapter 37 Selling through the Eye of the Buyer   143
            Steve Maul

            *Buying process, client expectations, Web 2.0,
            marketing and sales integration, becoming a
            solution provider*

Chapter 38 Building a Bridge between Service and Selling 148
            Walt Zeglinski and Bill Kowalski

            *Commoditizing, customer service, transformational
            change, creating value, creating a service-selling team*

Chapter 39 Developing and Implementing a Structured
            Sales Process   152
            Justin Zappulla

            *Designing a sales process, clarifying your sales
            philosophy, creating customer profiles, benchmarking
            winning sales behaviors*

Chapter 40 How to Present with Mastery, So People
            Take Action   156
            Tony Jeary

            *Presentation practices, engaging the audience,
            influencing the audience, developing confidence,
            understanding the audience, customizing
            the presentation*

Chapter 41 Biggest Time Wasters for Salespeople   159
            Dave Kahle

            *Time management, prioritizing, embracing
            technology, delegation, communication,
            overcoming procrastination*

Chapter 42 The Key to Growing Your Sales: Work on Your Openings, Not Your Closings! **163**
Ron Karr

Client engagement, rapport skills, questioning strategies, leading with outcomes, differentiation, closing

Chapter 43 How, What, and Why Projects Fail **167**
Dave Allman

Sales cycle, follow-up, creating a value proposition, understanding client initiatives, organizational alignment and priorities

Chapter 44 Making a Difference **171**
Jill Konrath

Differentiation, client analysis, questioning strategies, quantifying your value

Chapter 45 How to Overachieve **174**
Dave Kurlan

Goals, motivation, pipeline, personal initiative, desire, personal weaknesses

Chapter 46 How to Make Successful Cold Calls **177**
Ron La Vine

Cold calling, appointment setting, gatekeepers, decision makers, qualifying, listening skills, establishing call objectives, asking permission

Chapter 47 Create E-Mail Subject Lines That Draw Prospects In **182**
Kendra Lee

E-mail prospecting, creating a compelling message, personalization, making specific requests, getting appointments

Chapter 48 The Sales Funnel **185**
Ray Leone

Sales funnel, qualifying, closing, questioning strategies, uncovering pain, educating the buyer, eliminating objections

Chapter 49   Having a "Great Meeting" Is Not the Objective   188
              Chris Lytle

              *Sales management, accountability, specific
              language, questioning strategy, appointment setting,
              understanding the engagement metric*

Chapter 50   "Referrals" Are a Waste—Introductions
              Are Golden   192
              Paul McCord

              *Referrals, introductions, prospecting,
              lead generation, relationship building,
              appointment setting*

Chapter 51   Increasing Sales Quickly   196
              Charles Newby

              *Sales activity, account management, client
              communication, qualifying opportunities,
              increasing sales conversions*

Chapter 52   Seven Myths and Misconceptions about
              Top-Performing Salespeople   200
              Sam Reese

              *Sales execution, assessing top salespeople,
              behaviors of top sales professionals, how top
              sales performers think, characteristics of top
              sales professionals*

Chapter 53   Magic Moments in Selling: Subtle Yet Crucial
              Actions to Advance the Sale   205
              Anne Miller

              *Advancing the sale, gaining rapport, building
              trust, client engagement*

Chapter 54   Truth or Delusion: Busting Networking's
              Biggest Myths   208
              Dr. Ivan Misner and Mike Macedonio

              *Referral process, selling yourself, referral
              marketing, client development*

Chapter 55   **Buying Decisions: What Happens behind the Scenes?**   **211**
Sharon Drew Morgen

Sales process, buying decisions, closing the sale, shortening the sale cycle

Chapter 56   **Your "Needs" May Not Be Your "Rights"**   **216**
Napoleon Hill

Overdelivering, personal accountability, entitlement, self-improvement

Chapter 57   **The *Real* Secret to Effectively Enrolling and Selling**   **219**
Michael Oliver

Network marketing, direct sales, recruiting, enrolling, questioning strategies

Chapter 58   **Qualifying Your Sales Process**   **223**
Rick Page

The complex sale, sales process, qualifying

Chapter 59   **Selling to VITOs (Very Important Top Officers)**   **226**
Anthony Parinello

Sales process, c-suite selling, prospecting

Chapter 60   **The " Book Yourself Solid" Simple Selling System**   **231**
Michael Port

Relationship development, building client trust, creating value

Chapter 61   **Managing Sales Success: 10 Critical Performance Factors That Drive Revenue and Sales Team Growth—A System for Improving Both Sales Manager and Sales Team Performance**   **235**
Warren Kurzrock

Sales management, accountability, sales success factors, sales performance indicators

Chapter 62   Value Clarity: The Optimal Source of
Differentiation   241

Jeff Thull

*Complex sale, creating value, value clarity,
diagnostic process, facilitating change*

Chapter 63   Selling in Harder Times   245

Neil Rackham

*Creating trust, evaluating sales opportunities,
buying cycles, competing*

Chapter 64   Advanced Questioning Techniques:
Utilization of Questioning Techniques for
Consultative Selling   249

LaVon Koerner

*Advanced listening techniques, questioning
techniques, building rapport*

Chapter 65   Sales Coaching Increases Sales Performance   257

Linda Richardson

*Sales management, sales coaching, developing
sales teams, coaching strategies*

Chapter 66   Mismanaging Expectations: Are You Preparing
Your Sales Team for Change?   262

Keith Rosen

*Sales management, executive sales coaching,
coaching process, sales assessment*

Chapter 67   Use Social Dynamics to Control Sales
Appointments   266

Frank Rumbauskas

*Nonverbal subcommunication, body language,
vocal tone, eye contact, building confidence,
gaining rapport*

Chapter 68   The Successful Sales Formula: Why 50 Percent
of Deals Fail to Close   269

Keith M. Eades

*Sales forecasting, qualifying, sales formula,
uncovering pain, creating value*

Chapter 69   The Up-Front Contract: Adding Control and
              Predictability to Your Sales Calls   274
              David H. Sandler

              *Sales systems, establishing rapport, uncovering pain,
              discussing money, dealing with buyer's remorse*

Chapter 70   How to Write a Winning Proposal   278
              Dr. Tom Sant

              *Proposal writing, needs analysis, value proposition,
              solutions, deliverability*

Chapter 71   The 11 Biggest Sales Lies   282
              Stephan Schiffman

              *Sales sabotage, sales lies, sales myths, humility,
              sales misconceptions*

Chapter 72   One Great Opening Is Worth
              10,000 Closes   285
              Dan Seidman

              *Communication, building rapport,
              questioning strategies*

Chapter 73   Life = Sales   287
              Blair Singer

              *Mind-set, attitude, self-esteem, confidence,
              sales philosophy*

Chapter 74   What Are the Biggest Sales Presentation
              Mistakes That Professionals Make and
              How Can You Avoid Them?   290
              Terri L. Sjodin

              *Presentation skills, preparation, content,
              using visual aids*

Chapter 75   It's *Not* a Numbers Game, It's a Game
              of Numbers   293
              Art Sobczak

              *Sales strategy, questioning strategies,
              selling over the phone, sales language*

Chapter 76   Optimizing Sales Leads: Moving Quickly
from Inquiry to Lead to Closure   296
Drew Stevens

Lead generation, qualifying, Sales 2.0,
sales funnel, marketing, closing

Chapter 77   Unmanaged, Telling Tensions Cost You Sales   300
Conrad Elnes

Managing tension, sales pressure, controlling
anger, communication

Chapter 78   Twelve Things Your Buyers Want Other
Than Lowest Price   304
Bill Brooks

Negotiating, building client trust, service, handling
price objections, relationship development

Chapter 79   No Thanks, I'm Just Looking!: Professional
Retail Sales Techniques for Turning Shoppers
into Buyers   308
Harry J. Friedman

Retail sales, rapport building, questioning strategies,
opening lines, continuing dialogue

Chapter 80   The Keys to Successful Pipeline Management   312
Donal Daly

Sales process, pipeline, lead generation, Sales 2.0

Chapter 81   Superior Sales Management   316
Brian Tracy

Sales management, salesperson activity,
prospecting, presenting, closing, sales success

Chapter 82   Jump-Starting a Stalled Sales Opportunity   320
Julie Thomas

Decision-making process, sales cycle,
account management

Chapter 83   All Salespeople Use Scripts   323
Wendy Weiss

Cold calling, sales scripts, prospecting by phone,
elevator speech, setting appointments

Chapter 84   Top 10 Reasons Sales Managers Fail and
              What to Do about It   326
              Jacques Werth

              *Sales management, sales process, best sales
              practices, sales coaching*

Chapter 85   Become the Duke or Duchess of Dialogue:
              Three Keys to Successful Dialogue Selling   329
              Floyd Wickman

              *Effective communication, dialogue selling,
              methodology, presentation skills, persuasion*

Chapter 86   Is Your Customer Base at Risk?: Protecting Your
              Existing Business in Tough Times   334
              Ed Emde

              *Account management, customer service, creating
              customer loyalty, relationship development*

Chapter 87   Become a Champion Performer   338
              Dirk Zeller

              *Real estate sales, accountability, sales process,
              sales goals, self-discipline*

Chapter 88   Timeless Truths in a 2.0 Sales World:
              Ownership, Integrity, and Amplification   341
              Zig Ziglar and Tom Ziglar

              *Self-belief, trust, communication, personal
              values, behavior*

Chapter 89   Your Best Sales Year Ever!   345
              Eric Taylor and David Riklan

              *Personal energy, self-belief, goals, time
              management, communication*

Chapter 90   More World-Class Sales Training Resources   352

About the Authors   365
Index   367

Acknowledgments

Each and every one of us wants to increase sales and revenue for our associated business. In our journey toward optimum sales results, we frequently find that reaching our goals is a team effort. We rely on others to provide quality products for us to sell, enhanced by attractive marketing materials and superior customer support.

Similarly, the writing of this book was also a group effort. This book was truly created by a dedicated team that spent countless hours writing, revising, and updating. It could not have been created alone.

We'd like to acknowledge each and every author who contributed to this book—in fact, there would be no book without the inspiring wisdom and words of each of our contributing authors.

In addition to all of the contributors to the book, we would like to thank all of the amazing individuals at John Wiley & Sons, Inc., who enthusiastically brought this project to life, including Matt Holt, Shannon Vargo, Beth Zipko, and Lauren Freestone.

Thanks to our agent, John Willig, who is the real "Jerry Maguire."

Finally, heartfelt thanks to our friends and family, who have provided much-needed support, encouragement, and patience throughout the process. A special thanks to our wives, Michelle and Clare, who are a continual source of motivation for everything that we do.

Foreword

I have been a student of sales since November 11, 1971. I was listening to a brand-new technology called a cassette tape when a guy named Jay Douglas Edwards uttered the sales tip, "If the customer says, 'Do these come in green?' you say, 'Would you like them in green?'" And I thought—cool.

That's the day I realized that there was a science to selling. I wanted to learn more.

I have read all or portions of hundreds of sales books over the past 40 years, but most of what I have learned has come from the spark of an idea gleaned from a book and then somewhat altered once I got out into the field and had to actually apply the strategy. Kind of like you.

All sales books—as well as sales experts—offer some form of valuable information. As a student, it's your job to determine how that information fits into your skill set, environment, marketplace, and customer interactions.

Mastering the World of Selling is loaded with sales experts and business experts offering some of their best ideas and their best strategies and their best tips and their best information.

Eric Taylor cold-called me in 2002, claiming he could put on a public seminar in my home state of New Jersey. He told me that he would fill the hall with people and sponsors and was willing to pay my fee in order to make that happen.

I had worked with many public seminar promoters, most of whom had failed miserably, and at that time it was my decision not to work with any public promoter, but rather to do the seminars myself. But there was something about Eric that I liked—his spirit, his ideas, his self-confidence, his ability to convey a message; so I decided to say okay.

Eric filled the hall that day, and my new friend Matt Holt—an editor from John Wiley & Sons, Inc.—came to see me.

Matt has risen much higher in the company and is publishing this book along with his talented editor Shannon Vargo. (It all comes full circle.) Eric filled the hall again in 2003, 2004, 2005, 2006, and 2007. In 2008, we did an event called "Jersey Boys" where I partnered with two other sales experts who had grown up in New Jersey like I had.

Eric Taylor has done it again, this time with David Riklan, the founder of SelfGrowth.com. Eric is a world-class student, participant, and all-around father. In compiling this twenty-first-century best-of sales book, he has used his connections, his wisdom, and his moxie to create a book that contains way more than reading material. Study it, highlight it, implement it, and bank it.

How to read the book: Learning sales skills is a matter of understanding, adoption, application, and a bit of tweaking. I have found that unless the tip or strategy is comfortable to me, I won't use it. It has to fit with my personality and be in the framework of my comfortable conversation and ethics.

As a reader myself, I am challenging you to look at the ideas you encounter here with an open mind and strike from your mind the phrase "I know that." Most salespeople already know everything; the problem is that they don't do it. Rather, ask yourself, "How good at that am I on a scale of 1 to 10?"

Then ask yourself:

How does this information apply to me?

Do I agree with this?

Am I comfortable with this?

Does it fit my personality?

Is this me?

If the answer to all of those questions is yes, then ask yourself the following questions:

Is this in the best interest of the customer?

Will this lead me to a long-term relationship with the customer?

And finally the true self-test question:

Will this make my mother proud?

This book is all about *what is working now.* It looks at business, sales, service, and personal development for the second decade of the twenty-first century. The messages offered are from experts in their field who have actually used these methods and strategies to build their own success. And your job is to adopt them, adapt them, and turn them into money.

—Jeffrey Gitomer, author of
The Little Red Book of Selling

Introduction

"Nothing happens until somebody sells something."
— Arthur H. (Red) Motley (1900–1984), Master Salesman

Everyone Sells

Since you most likely sell something for a living, you know the value of self-improvement and building your sales skills. Like you, we are selling in the trenches every day, fighting to gain more market share and to keep our existing client base. Just one good idea from the hundreds in this book can give you a competitive advantage and repay your investment many times over.

The goal of *Mastering the World of Selling* is simple, clear, and focused; we want this book to become your ultimate sales resource.

This book was created to help *you* to sell something better . . . faster . . . smarter . . . and with more profit!

What's in This Book for You?

➤ Over 400 sales tips from the top sales training companies in the world.

➤ More than 85 powerful sales articles you can use for sales meetings, to prep for a sales call, or to coach your sales team.

➤ Detailed profiles and contact information to over 150 of the world's greatest sales training resources.

➤ Access to hundreds of products and services, online resources, associations, and sales communities you can learn from and contribute to.

The current economic climate has created new opportunities but has also made the competitive landscape fierce. Whether you are just starting your sales career today or have been closing complex sales transactions for decades, this book has sales answers that can help you sell more.

Selling is one of the most rewarding and noble professions in the world.

Thank you for investing in this book and in your sales success!

Mastering the World of Selling enables *you* to sell more, more easily.

Your Past and Present Hold the Key to Your Future

Where are you going?

No, I'm not asking where you are going on your next appointment or where you are going out to dinner. And I'm not asking where you are going when you get to the mall. I'm asking "Where are you going in life?" That's a pretty big question because it's about your future.

Did you miss your quota last month? Last year? How come? Blaming it on the economy again? Blaming it on the competition again? What is a quota, anyway? A quota is a goal that *someone else* sets for you. I'm asking: What have you set for yourself? When someone gives you a quota, why not double it? That way you'll make the number with ease. It's all in how you look at things.

Guess what? You create barriers or you jump over them.

Once a year I try to predict the future. I do it on the anniversary of the beginning of my writing career. This week marks my fifteenth anniversary. It's always a cause for deep reflection because writing and being published is the fulcrum point of my success. It's not only about how I've made a name for myself, it's also about the legacy that I will leave salespeople worldwide—and, of course, my children and grandchildren.

Writing is about more than creating new sales information each week that salespeople like you can benefit from. It's about being self-disciplined so I can clarify my own ideas, which form the basis for the speeches that I give and the books that I write.

If you really want to know where you're going, you have to understand where you've been and recognize where you are. Where you've been, or the past, provides you with knowledge and experiences, successes and failures, as well as opportunities and obstacles. Where you are, or the present, is what happened during the past 30 days, what's happening today, as well as what's going to happen within the next 30 days. Where you'll be, or the future, is a combination of your experience, your being open to opportunity, your goals and dreams, your tolerance for risk, as well as your determination and focus.

Let me clarify that and break it down into three-and-a-half easy-to-digest categories.

1. Once was.
2. As is.
3. Can be.
3.5 Become.

Once was is the history of your life. It's the sum total of your knowledge, your wisdom, your experience, your victories, and your defeats. If you look closely at the history of your life, you can see some things that you wanted with all your heart but you didn't get. At the time you were devastated, but in retrospect it seems silly that you ever wanted those things. You can also see some things that you were given or that you earned, but once you got them, you quickly lost interest. More important, you see the things you loved and how they have affected you. You look at the risks you took and think that if you had the opportunity to take them again, you might not. And all of that brings you to *as is*.

As is is where you are today. Are you where you want to be? Are you happy with your lot in life? Are you blaming your lack of success on someone else? Have you found what you are looking for? Do you even know what it is?

Some of us haven't found what we are looking for, but that doesn't mean to stop looking. I didn't start writing until I was 45 years old. If you're younger than that and you start writing tomorrow, in 13 years you'll be ahead of me.

I'm teaching my granddaughter to write. She'll be 50 years ahead of me.

As is provides you with your greatest single opportunity. It's about how you decide to invest your time and money. The time to take action is now. The time to take a risk is now. The time to go for what you want is now. The time to educate yourself and study is now. If you do, you may be able to achieve the success you are looking for later.

Many people think that once they're done with high school or college, they have essentially finished their studies. That may be okay if you aspire to ask clients "Will that be paper or plastic?"

Success doesn't simply show up in the now. Success comes as a result of hard work and focus in the now. It's what you are willing to "do" in the now. But that elusive brass ring you are looking for lies within. It's the *can be.*

Can be is full of dreams, full of goals, and full of serendipity. Some things are not goals. Some things just evolve. And in that evolution, you can find what you really love. If you love something, you don't have to make it a goal. Instead, you just work your butt off, and it becomes reality.

What you *can be* is going to be a result of your hard work, your positive attitude, your passion, your focus on achievement, and your drive not to let little things stand in your way—even if it means risking what you've got.

Many people in their struggles will come to me and say, "Jeffrey, you don't understand." And then they go on to say something about their personal situation, their money, their luck, their spouse, or their kids.

I understand just fine. People are afraid to risk what they have in order to go for what they really want. The worst part of not risking is lamenting—lamenting that you didn't try it, that you didn't go for it, or that you should have done it.

Maybe it's time for you to read or watch *The Wizard of Oz* again and see how it relates to your life. Remember what Dorothy's companions were searching for? Courage, brains, and heart. You've always known the formula—you just haven't used it. And with very few exceptions, you're not in Kansas anymore.

And when you combine *once was, as is,* and *can be,* the sum of that is what you *will become.* One of the most valuable lessons I have ever learned was from a friend, Dr. Paul Homoly, who said to me, "Make all decisions based on the person you would like to become." That wisdom is so powerful that I think of it every day. It's been a big part of my success. It makes me think "long term" as I decide. It makes me think "best" as I decide. Perhaps you can use it in your quest to be your best.

Allow me to throw some words at you: Educate yourself, try your best, risk failure, seize the opportunity, develop self-discipline, dedicate yourself to becoming a winner, and make a commitment that it's for you first and everybody else second.

It's not a formula—it's a philosophy. And philosophy is the secret to getting you from where you are to where you want to be.

My philosophy is simple.

I give value first.

I help other people.

I strive to be my *best* at what I *love* to do.

I establish long-term relationships with everyone.

I have fun—every day.

I don't just "have" a philosophy—I live it.

And I found out a secret: When you love what you do, all of your days are the same—they are holidays! And I wish the same for you: a safe, fun, and successful journey.

—Jeffrey Gitomer

Jeffrey Gitomer is the author of The Little Red Book of Selling. *president of Charlotte-based Buy Gitomer, he gives seminars, runs annual sales meetings, and conducts Internet training programs on selling and customer service at www.trainone.com. He can be reached at 704-333-1112, or e-mail salesman@gitomer.com.*

Chapter 1

Collaboration

Changing the World

Randall K. Murphy
Acclivus R3 Solutions

Collaboration. What do we mean by collaboration, and why would a book on sales training start with a chapter on collaboration?

The reason is simple. Collaboration is all around us. Frequently still in the concept stage, often not fully understood, and sometimes awkwardly situated between rhetoric and reality, collaboration is nonetheless steadily emerging as the new model or paradigm for individuals and groups working productively together. It is becoming the preferred method for successful sales and customer relationships.

From *Newsweek* and *Time* to *Harvard Business Review* and *Fortune* to *The Futurist*, articles abound promoting collaboration, "the collaborative mind-set," and "the collaborative advantage." Collaboration is being recommended for applications ranging from relationships between individuals to relationships between organizations to relationships between and among nations.

What is collaboration? Where does it come from? What does it mean? Where is it going?

Collaboration is the most promising approach for building productive, long-term relationships, both personal and professional. As an approach, collaboration is based upon interdependent needs. To be interdependent, the needs of one individual do not have to be exactly the same as the needs of another; they must, however, be so aligned that when one individual benefits, both benefit, and if one individual is harmed, the other is also harmed.

The perception of interdependent needs allows for (1) a driving motivation to achieve an optimal return for both, or all, parties involved; (2) a high level of implicit trust; and (3) a sharing of power. The seller and the buyer must have this collaborative mind-set to be successful.

Where did collaboration come from as a term, as a concept, and as an approach for building productive, long-term relationships? If you search through books and articles from 20 years ago, you will find no mention of collaboration other than in reference to musical composers. Under the headings of conflict resolution, negotiation, interpersonal communication, professional selling, management, and leadership, there is no mention of sharing power, no mention of interdependent needs, and no mention of collaboration.

Twenty years ago Acclivus R3 Solutions launched an intensive, ongoing study of relationships in the workplace. The initial focus for this study was the process of negotiation, particularly business-to-business negotiation, between a sales or consulting professional and a customer or client. The study evolved into an effort to determine (1) the optimal form of a working relationship and how to build it, (2) methods for preventing damage to the relationship during negotiation and conflict resolution, and (3) approaches for strengthening the relationship through the negotiating process.

What Acclivus R3 Solutions discovered was a form of working relationship vastly more productive than competition, and with potential considerably beyond that of simple cooperation. We discovered collaboration—a higher level of relationship, communication, and negotiation.

Collaboration is the best approach, not for every individual or organization and not for every relationship, but for those individuals and organizations that want to work together as partners toward the achievement of optimal results.

Collaborative relationships are built, not simply formed, and alignment of needs requires continuing effort. Most of us have more experience as competitors than as collaborators, and there is a strong tendency to follow our competitive instincts—especially under pressure. Because collaboration is a relatively new way, it is not always the most comfortable or natural way.

Collaboration, though, provides us with the opportunity to escape the bounds and limitations of the traditional supplier/ customer, consultant/client, and manager/individual contributor relationships. Collaboration is truly working together. In order for salespeople, sales teams, and companies to be successful in this new environment, we must focus on building and achieving a true collaboration between ourselves and our customers. With this mind-set, instead of being perceived as one of many vendors, you are seen as a collaborative partner, changing the way you do business.

Name: Randall K. Murphy

Company: Acclivus R3 Solutions

Web Site: www.acclivus.com

Biography: Randall K. Murphy is the founder and president of Acclivus R3 Solutions, a global performance development and consulting organization. He is the primary author and architect of the 17-program integrated curriculum utilized by clients of Acclivus R3 Solutions. He introduced the concept and application of the word *cocreate* and gave the word *collaboration* meaning in the organizational workplace. He conceived the Consultative Approach and has taught more than 30,000 professionals and managers in workshops worldwide.

Leading organizations in more than 80 countries worldwide rely on Acclivus R3 Solutions to assist them with the training of their sales, support, and service professionals, managers, and executives.

Selling Philosophy: The Consultative Approach

Target Industries: Computer hardware and software, consulting and financial, telecommunications, medical equipment, manufacturing, consumer products

Best Sellers: R3 Sales Excellence, Inside R3 Sales, Acclivus Sales Negotiation, R3 Service, R3 Strategic Sales Presentations, Acclivus Coaching, R3 Interaction, MAPS (Major Account Planning and Strategy) TP&M (Territory Planning & Management), AIM Services

Sales Tip One: First diagnose, then prescribe.

Sales Tip Two: Plan your opening; the opening sets the stage for the entire meeting.

Sales Tip Three: Qualifying is forever; anything and everything can change.

Product One: R3 Sales Excellence

Product Two: R3 Service

Product Three: Acclivus Sales Negotiation and Dr. Azul (online follow-through)

Chapter 2

Living Your Vows in a Whirlwind Economy

Seleste Lunsford

AchieveGlobal

In today's economy, selling needs to be more like a marriage and less like a whirlwind romance.

The concept is fairly basic: Predictable long-term revenue growth requires enduring, mutually beneficial customer relationships.

The challenge lies neither in grasping that point, nor in popping the question, but in doing what it takes to live up to your vows.

■ FIND THE RIGHT CUSTOMERS

To reach and exceed their revenue goals, salespeople need customers who value what you sell—which is ideally expressed in a clear value proposition. Whether product-centered ("We sell world-class widgets") or service-centered ("We grow your business"), a value proposition—like a marriage proposal—frames the kind of relationship you want.

Yet a recent AchieveGlobal study found at least two trends that complicate your customer relationships. Increased competition has made commodities of many products and services, and savvy customers now rely on arm's-length buying models—requests for proposal (RFPs), reverse auctions, procurement teams, and others. To weather these challenges, it's important to segment and prioritize customers based on the value they find in you, not just the value you find in them. Then sift this data for the specific customers most likely to value what you sell.

■ DEFINE A RELATIONSHIP PROCESS

Even among organizations that sell on price or convenience, few realize long-term success without equally long-term relationships. Our study found that leading sales organizations now support these relationships by matching salespeople to specific market segments, allocating resources to the best opportunities, and leveraging multiple sales channels, such as distributors and e-commerce.

In addition, these organizations often tailor a relationship process for each customer segment. As a result, they're far more likely to send the right salesperson to the right customer to generate the right return.

Relationships thrive or fail based on defining moments in every customer interaction. Make these moments positive with a relationship process that matches your activities and resources to the buying patterns and expectations of each market segment. A tailored process benefits customers through your solution, of course, and equally through the expert counsel of your salespeople. The process benefits you through longer-term revenue streams and protection from competitors and price pressures.

■ BUILD A WELCOMING HOME

Customers tend to stick around when your house is in order. A welcoming home begins with a coherent sales strategy that tells everyone what to sell, to whom, and how to sell it. A mismatched sales culture or support system can sabotage even the best-laid strategy.

At the heart of your sales culture, values and beliefs drive decisions, activities, motivation, performance, and turnover. Even so, our research found that mergers, acquisitions, other big changes, and related short-term thinking can crush the effort to maintain long-term customer relationships.

Promote the needed values and practices by making relationships a strategic centerpiece and by making learning and development a cultural norm. Once your team agrees on the beliefs that guide decisions, reward information sharing and celebrate success.

Like cultural challenges, overwrought systems and policies can weaken customer relationships. For example, if you think your customer relationship management (CRM) or sales force automation (SFA) software hasn't lived up to the hype, perhaps people simply don't know how to use it.

To remove systemic obstacles, streamline your market, territory, account, opportunity, and sales-call planning. Align compensation and incentives to strategy. Recalibrate coaching and performance management to support desired behaviors. Find and use effective CRM or SFA software. Finally, select or create essential collateral, return-on-investment (ROI) calculators, and other selling tools—and deep-six the rest.

■ LEARN FROM EACH OTHER

Strategy, culture, and systems support customer relationships. Building relationships requires salespeople who can demonstrate knowledge in a number of areas that affect the customer's perception of them and of your organization:

➤ Global and national business issues

➤ Industry trends and events affecting you and your customers

➤ Product features and benefits

➤ Customers—both organizations and people

➤ Each stage of your relationship processes

➤ Politics in the customer's organization

Help everyone see the wider context and nitty-gritty details for each market segment. The payoff is nothing less than mutual understanding, without which no customer relationship can survive. Besides applying this knowledge, salespeople need to be obsessive about maintaining each customer relationship. Support that daily effort by giving salespeople the "why" behind your expectations. Provide frequent developmental opportunities, and then recognize and reward the desired behaviors. Just as critical, give people the skills to cultivate long-term relationships—not only in-the-moment sales skills, but prospecting, presentation, negotiation, service, strategic, and other skills as well.

■ TO HAVE AND TO HOLD

While it's mainly salespeople who interact directly with customers, a customer marries your entire family. The truth is, everyone in the sales organization plays a role in every long-term customer relationship:

➤ Senior executives define the sales strategy and cascade it to others.

➤ Divisional or regional VPs communicate the strategy, oversee its execution, and develop sales leaders.

➤ Sales managers communicate and apply the strategy as they coach and develop their teams.

➤ Salespeople, service reps, technicians, and other frontline people acquire, grow, and retain individual customer relationships.

So, to retain your valued customers, people at every level—even executives—need to demonstrate your shared values as well as level-specific knowledge and skills.

Like any partner, a customer can change as reflected needs and expectations evolve. That's why at least one marriage cliché applies equally to sales: Never stop working on your relationship. Stay in touch with market trends. Revisit and adjust your strategy.

Refine your culture. Restructure systems to support your strategy. Provide opportunities for all to learn and grow.

Only then will your customers sustain you, even in the toughest economy.

Name: Sharon Daniels

Company: AchieveGlobal

Web Site: www.achieveglobal.com

Biography: AchieveGlobal helps organizations translate business strategies into results by improving the performance of their people. AchieveGlobal has proven expertise in leadership development, customer service, and sales effectiveness.

AchieveGlobal is led by Chief Executive Officer Sharon Daniels.

Ms. Daniels worked in banking prior to joining the training industry. She has held numerous roles in operations, mergers and acquisitions, branch management, and training and consulting.

She holds a bachelor of education degree from the University of Florida and a Master's in training and organizational development from the University of South Florida and has over 25 years of experience in general management and sales leadership.

Selling Philosophy: Relationship-building skills

Best Sellers: PSS: Professional Selling Skills; SCW: Selling in a Competitive World; PPS: Professional Prospecting Skills; PSC: Professional Sales Coaching

Sales Tip One: Clarify the value you offer your customers.

Sales Tip Two: Find and engage the customers who will value your services.

Sales Tip Three: Develop a consistent relationship process that matters to these customers.

Book One: *Strategies That Win Sales*

Book Two: *Secrets of Top-Performing Salespeople*

Book Three: *Achieving a Triple Win: Human Capital Management of the Employee Lifecycle*

Product One: Professional Selling Skills

Chapter 3

Ninety Percent of All Sales Force Training Fails

Duane Sparks
Action Selling

"Here's the problem—and the solution."

■ SALES TRAINING'S DIRTY LITTLE SECRET

Investing in training for your sales force seems like a perfectly sensible business practice. It must be a smart thing to do; after all, sales training is estimated to be a billion-dollar industry.

Here's the problem: 90 percent of the training that salespeople receive fails to produce meaningful, long-term performance gains.

A billion-dollar industry with a 90 percent failure rate? Even I'm disgusted with that.

■ BUT YOU STILL NEED TO PROVIDE TRAINING

With the ever-accelerating speed of change in both knowledge and technology, it is clear that we have a choice: We either continue to learn, or we allow our skills and knowledge to become obsolete.

I can't tell you how many times I've heard "We hire only experienced salespeople," as if that were a solution. The idea that sales experience is a "living textbook" has two major pitfalls:

1. As the world changes, our methods for dealing with situations lag behind. Therefore, we continue to make the same selling errors time and time again.

2. In a sales career spanning 30 years, the same one year's worth of experience can be repeated 30 times.

Aberdeen Group, a highly regarded research firm, reports that even in a constricted economy, best-in-class companies are increasing revenues by 20 percent more than laggard firms, through the use of sales training. So, how do the top 10 percent of companies leverage sales training while others waste their time and money?

■ WHY DOES SALES TRAINING FAIL?

Everyone has experienced a great seminar. You laughed, you cheered, you took notes. But a month later, I'll bet you could barely recall the name of the speaker, much less the things you "learned." Research shows that 87 percent of the information delivered in seminars and workshops is forgotten within 30 days. After that, the retention rate gets worse.

The following sections outline the three biggest reasons why any given training program will fail to produce lasting performance improvements.

➤ A. Wrong Content

First, you have to teach the right content. Many skills, traits, and qualities contribute to sales success. For example, personality and motivation definitely have an impact on performance. The trouble is, you can't teach personality and motivation—and salespeople can't "learn" it! Training has to focus on skills that can be taught, learned, mastered, and measured.

There might be a hundred skills that are teachable and learnable and that contribute to sales success. But you can't teach anyone how to do a hundred things well. Instead, you must focus on the skills that are most likely to lead to high performance in a sales role: the Five Critical Selling Skills™.

1. **Buyer/Seller Relationship:** When sellers understand the series and sequence of sub-decisions that customers go through when making a major buying decision, and skillfully match their sales process with the buyer's decision-making process, success rates improve dramatically.

2. **Sales Call Planning:** What is your Commitment Objective for this sales call? That is, what do you want the customer to agree to do next? Failure to have a Commitment Objective is the most frequent mistake made by salespeople. That's followed by failure to devise a questioning plan for the sales call and failure to prepare a Company Story. Poor planning skills often result from the lack of a clearly defined sales process to follow.

3. **Questioning Skills:** The impact of poor questioning skills is horrendous. Eighty-six percent of salespeople ask the wrong types of questions. The question is the number-one tool in the salesperson's kit. Unfortunately, it's either used improperly or it's rusty.

4. **Presentation Skills:** Most salespeople think that they are fantastic presenters. They can spew large quantities of data about their products. The problem is, customers don't want that. They want you to zero in on specific solutions based on their unique needs for your product or service.

5. **Gaining Commitment:** Most salespeople agree that this is the skill they most need to improve. If a salesperson is not good at gaining commitment from the client, why is he or she on anyone's payroll? Yet research shows that 62 percent of salespeople don't ask for commitment consistently on their sales calls.

➤ B. Rejected by Salespeople

You've seen them—the sales reps who come to a training session with the attitude that they already know it all. Their body language alone speaks volumes: arms crossed, eyes rolling, virtually daring the instructor to say something that might interest them. These people were not properly prepared to come to your training. And without motivation, there can be no learning at all.

Salespeople need to be sold on the need for training and the benefits it offers them. And I mean they have to be sold on the need for this particular program—not on the idea of training in the abstract or on learning as a swell thing.

This sale is no different from any other sale. The buyers (your salespeople) must see the program as a solution to needs that they agree exist. If they don't recognize and agree on the need, the training will be a waste of time. The benefits of using and mastering the skills have to be perceived as far greater than the investment of time and effort required.

➤ C. Ineffective Transfer

Transfer is a term we use when learning is actually applied in the field. It's the only reason why a business organization would want to do training in the first place.

Most people mistakenly think of transfer as a synonym for follow-up or reinforcement—events that happen after the training program is over. Sure, that's part of what needs to be done. But other factors play into the transfer process as well.

The following are the five critical elements that determine whether learning will transfer from the classroom to the job:

1. Students must be actively involved in the entire learning process.

2. Early in the training process, students need to connect the learning to their life experiences. It has to make sense in the world they know. They need to see relevance right away.

3. They must know that there will be follow-up activities and assessments that measure what they learned and how well they are applying the new skills in their day-to-day work.

4. They must be held accountable by their managers to demonstrate the use of new skills and knowledge in the field. This cements the message that management believes that learning was important.

5. Managers must minimize the transfer distance by helping learners apply new skills and knowledge on the job—quickly.

■ LOTS OF TALK AND FAILED ATTEMPTS

Corporate trainers, including sales trainers, have discussed these issues for decades. And companies that create their own sales training or buy it from sales training companies are certainly aware of the questionable benefits they usually get. Why, then, does the problem persist? My answer is that most sales training does produce an immediate result. It just doesn't last.

Most sales training programs contain *some* useful information. Immediately following a training session, some salespeople will pick up an idea, take it to the field, and score a sale that they wouldn't have gotten before. Instant return on investment! Terrific! But a few months later, they're back to their old behaviors. It's called relapse.

Let's talk about the solution.

■ THE VISION FOR EFFECTIVE SALES TRAINING

The following table describes the problems and three solutions for each one.

Problem	Solution	Solution	Solution
A. Poor or wrong content	1. Well-documented sales process	2. Focus on critical selling skills	3. Custom-tailored content to your company's needs
B. Rejected by your salespeople	1. Student and manager are properly prepared	2. Needs for training must be agreed upon	3. Student involvement in best sales practices
C. Ineffective transfer system	1. Implement field coaching procedure	2. Install systematic reinforcement	3. Measure learning and application

Note: If these capabilities are present in your sales training methodology, you'll escape the 90 percent failure rate.

No doubt this table makes effective sales training sound like a daunting proposition, difficult to pull off. Sorry, but it is. I've invested 20 years in the development of content and systems for student motivation and transfer. I wouldn't suggest that you try to duplicate this effort when the results are available from my company for a very affordable price.

I know what other companies in the sales training industry are providing. Some of their content is very good. The problem is simply this: The reason for the 90 percent failure rate of sales training courses has to do with *all* of the factors I've described. You can't cover only one or two bases and expect to get long-term results.

All of us in sales have developed certain habits, no matter if our careers span 5 days or 50 years. Some of those habits work against us; they're dead wrong. Changing habits is the hardest thing that a human being is ever asked to do. But when sales organizations approach training in the way I have described, it works every time. And with Action Selling, it's not that hard to do.

Name: Duane Sparks

Company: The Sales Board—Action Selling

Web Site: www.ActionSelling.com

Biography: Duane Sparks is chairman of The Sales Board and author of *Action Selling*. His company has trained and certified more than 350,000 salespeople in the skills of Action Selling. Duane has personally facilitated over 300 Action Selling training sessions and has written five best-selling books: *Action Selling: How to Sell Like a Professional, Even If You Think You Are One*; *Selling Your Price: How to Escape the Race to the Bargain Basement*; *Questions: The Answer to Sales*; *Masters of Loyalty: How to Turn Your Sales Force into a Loyalty Force*; and *Sales Strategy from the Inside Out: How Complex Selling Really Works*.

Selling Philosophy: Sustainable results from superior sales training

Target Industries: Manufacturing, distribution, medical, services

Best Sellers: *Action Selling Sales Training*

Sales Tip One: Focus on improving the five critical selling skills: (1) buyer/seller relationship, (2) sales call planning, (3) questioning, (4) presenting, and (5) gaining commitment.

Sales Tip Two: Without reinforcement and measurement, 87 percent of learning is forgotten in 30 days. What gets measured gets learned.

Sales Tip Three: Set a commitment objective for every call: A goal that you set for yourself to gain agreement from the customer that moves the sales process forward.

Book One: *Action Selling: How to Sell Like a Professional, Even If You Think You Are One*

Book Two: *Selling Your Price: How to Escape the Race to the Bargain Basement*

Book Three: *Questions: The Answer to Sales*

Product One: Action Selling

Product Two: Selling Your Price

Product Three: Questions: The Answer to Sales

Chapter 4

Eleven Telephone Tips to Effectively Reach Out and Touch Others

Dr. Tony Alessandra
Platinum Rule Group

We tend to take our telephones and cell phones for granted, but salespeople must demonstrate appropriate telephone behavior when talking to clients and other business contacts. Courtesy and thoughtfulness are the basic components of telephone etiquette. The knowledge of etiquette makes telephoning easier because if you creatively obey the rules, you can be confident that you will behave in the most appropriate, productive way.

With this in mind, here are 11 guidelines for polite and effective telephone usage:

1. When answering the phone in the office, immediately identify your company, department, and name. If you are self-employed with a home office, answer by stating your name.

2. When talking to customers, call them by name. Not only will the customer be pleased, but by repeating the name, you're more likely to remember it. Be sure not to overuse this courtesy though, as it can become annoying. This also applies when talking to an executive assistant: First ask for the name of the assistant, and then you can begin using their name in all future correspondence.

3. Know yourself and how you sound to others. You can find this out by recording your voice. Then critique your tone, manners, friendliness, and vocal quality. This is even more helpful if you ask others to critique you.

4. Always use the hold button if you must temporarily leave the phone. It's surprising what the person on the line can hear, and you may inadvertently embarrass yourself—or the other person.

5. When placing a customer on hold, make sure you reassure the customer every 20 to 30 seconds that you haven't forgotten him or her. If you must do this more than twice, it's probably better to call back when you're able to talk.

6. Know your customers. Know not only their names, but also how they prefer to be treated. Then deal with them in their preferred mode. Do they like a fast or slow pace? Do they want just the facts or do they prefer to chat first before getting down to business?

7. Know your product or service. Your product mastery should shine through. Then you'll be able to match customer needs (benefits) with your product knowledge (features).

8. Keep a telephone notepad and pen handy so you can quickly write messages or notes. We've all waited for what seems to be 10 minutes while the harried message taker searches for a pencil or paper.

9. Plan your calls ahead. Try writing a summary of everything you need to know before making the call. Every sales call you make should have an objective (goal).

10. Let the customer hang up first. Have you ever concluded a conversation with someone and just as they were hanging up, you thought of one more thing to say? To avoid cutting off your customer's thoughts, let them hang up first.

11. Choose your words carefully. On the telephone, your words and vocal quality carry your message. In person, if there is any doubt as to the meaning, you can sense it from the person's nonverbal feedback. Over the phone, however, you may unintentionally insult your customer and never know it. For example, when you say, "As I said . . ." or "To put it another way . . . ," you imply that the other person did not understand you the first time. Another common phrase is, "Let me ask you a question." It may be a subtle difference, but notice that this is a command, not a question. A command immediately puts someone on the defensive. A better way to say this is, "May I ask you a question?" or "Do you mind if I ask you some questions?" This involves them in the conversation and makes them want to talk to you instead of resentfully following your orders.

Name: Tony Alessandra

Company: Platinum Rule Group, LLC

Web Site: www.PlatinumRule.com

Biography: Dr. Tony Alessandra has a streetwise, college-smart perspective on business, having been raised in the housing projects of New York City and eventually realizing success as a graduate professor of marketing, entrepreneur, business author, and hall-of-fame keynote speaker.

In addition to being president of the Assessment Business Center, Tony is a founding partner in The Cyrano Group and Platinum Rule Group. He has written 18 best-selling books, including *The New Art of Managing People, Charisma, The Platinum Rule, Collaborative Selling,* and *Communicating at Work*. He is featured in over 50 audio/video programs and films and originated the Platinum Rule.

Selling Philosophy: Collaborative (nonmanipulative) selling

Target Industries: Financial services, medical/pharmaceuticals, hardware/software companies

Best Sellers: *Platinum Rule, Collaborative Selling, Charisma, Customer Loyalty, The Power of Listening*

Sales Tip One: Prescription before diagnosis is malpractice—any salesperson who attempts to sell a solution before fully understanding the customer's needs, from the customer's point of view, is engaging in sales malpractice.

Sales Tip Two: The Platinum Rule of Selling: Adjust your selling style to fit the customer's buying style.

Sales Tip Three: People don't buy because they're made to understand; they buy because they feel understood.

Book One: *The Platinum Rule for Sales Mastery*

Book Two: *Charisma*

Book Three: *Collaborative Selling*

Product One: *The Platinum Rule* (two-hour DVD)

Product Two: *Astounding Customer Service* (DVD)

Product Three: *The Platinum Rule* (video training DVD)

Chapter 5

The "At-Leaster" Phenomenon

Brian Azar
The Sales Catalyst

If you've ever watched the opening of ABC's *Wide World of Sports*, then you've seen the winning runner break through the finish line, arms upraised in triumph, elated by the "thrill of victory." Of course, you've also seen the championship skier as he miscalculates and goes tumbling down the slopes into the "agony of defeat."

Victory and defeat. Winning and losing. Good and bad. All similar concepts—right? The thing is, both these people are winners. Why? Because only winners enter the race in the first place.

Whether it's business, professional life, athletics—or even love—only those who are ready to risk losing, willing to accept the consequences, and able to profit from their losses will ever know the taste of victory.

The risk involved in becoming a winner is a tall order for a salesperson, and the reason so many sales forces are suffering is not that they don't have winners on their teams, but because too many of their players won't enter the race. While the "thrill of victory" is undeniably seductive, the "agony of defeat" is often more intimidating.

Just what makes the fear of losing so immobilizing? The reasons are buried in our social conscience, where attitudes we hardly understand and barely acknowledge shape our thinking and actions. Perhaps the most powerful mixed message we receive as children is the belief we hold about winning and losing. "It's not whether you win or lose, it's how you play the game," we learn to say. But what we really believe is the dictum of coach Vince Lombardi: "Winning isn't everything, it's the only thing." Is it any wonder, then, that most people would rather forego the "thrill of victory" than risk the "agony of defeat"?

■ THE COMFORT ZONE

Most people tend to be nonriskers. Their tombstones could easily read: "Died at 30 . . . buried at 80." They're men and women who've settled at an early age into the comfort zone of mediocrity. As justification for the grayness of their lives, they tell themselves: "Well, I may not have won, but at least I didn't lose."

In years of working with sales organizations, we've found that 60 percent of the nation's sales force is made up of these "At-Leasters." Stymied by their fears, hung up between failure and world-class success, occasionally actualizing their potential (but sure to fall back), At-Leasters, with their seesaw sales-performance records, are a mysterious drain on their companies' sales records, representing a major hidden loss and often infecting the entire corporation with At-Leastitus.

More than most other professions, salespeople are judged, by themselves and by others, on "measurable results," which makes them particularly susceptible to At-Leastism. For managers, the challenge becomes one of how to revitalize this group—to turn those mushy "50 Percenters" into true winners.

In their attempt to put solid ground under their psyches, salespeople define themselves in one of three ways, all based on "measurable results." They are either Losers, Winners, or something in between. How each one sees himself or herself, the internal picture, becomes the face that looks back in the corporate washroom mirror.

"Loser" salespeople see themselves inescapably hedged in by their limitations. Lifelong low self-esteem chronically inhibits their sales ability. They blame themselves when something goes wrong, unable to examine the circumstances or analyze the situation. Loser salespeople occupy 20 percent of the sales jobs in this country, but since they almost never make quota, they eventually move on, making room for a new crop of underachievers.

At the same time, the infamous 80/20 rule tells us that 20 percent of the sales force is making 80 percent of the sales. This 20 percent is naturally made up of "Winner" salespeople. Despite the fact that we may all be "born winners," after a good dose of mixed messages, eroded confidence, daily pessimism, and fear of failure, most "born winners" metamorphose into something else. Those who do survive are the ones who've developed the tools they need to keep their high self-esteem intact. Winners see themselves as winners and deliver like pros—even when they fail, lose, and lose again. They're self-motivated, they believe in themselves, and they know they make a difference. In major-league baseball, the leading home-run hitter often leads the league in strikeouts as well, but that doesn't keep him from going up to the plate and taking a swing.

Winners also take full responsibility for what went wrong; but they don't simply blame themselves. They feel good about themselves no matter how they perform on any one day or in any one role. Winners know you can't win if you're afraid to lose, and that's where they differ from At-Leasters.

At-Leasters look in the mirror and see confusion. They define a string of successes as a "run of luck." When they do extremely well (for instance, closing 10 for 10 on a given day), At-Leasters worry they really aren't as good as they may appear. Initial elation quickly gives way to secret fears: exposure, expectation, inability to repeat their success, and, ultimately, failure. They quickly retreat back into that gray area of mediocrity, where they hug their lucky win and say: "At least I didn't lose."

And when At-Leasters strike out, they deny responsibility for their failures. "It wasn't my fault in the first place," they cry. "Hey, I'm really not that bad." They do whatever it takes to get back to that comfort zone between success and failure. Most significantly, whether winning or losing, they forfeit the opportunity to learn from their experiences. They won't risk failure, and because of this, they never grow into Winners.

■ REVERSING THE IMAGE

It's paradoxical that so many companies, while investing in state-of-the-art business technology, remain in the Dark Ages when it comes to incorporating modern behavioral knowledge into their sales-training structure. They're big on drilling their salespeople on technique, but at the same time, they neglect to address their workers' negative self-images. Make no mistake, At-Leasters are smart and skilled. They learn new techniques quickly enough, but their lack of internal reprogramming negates all this packaging. The result: More seesaw sales performance, more new salespeople added to the staff, more training programs, more money spent, and few positive results.

Without the proper inner resources, even the best skills in the world won't make a sale, and all this fine-tuning simply shackles the organization with a disproportionate share of unhappy At-Leasters. Given the fact that At-Leasters are a common product of the way we're brought up, how can a sales organization convert them into Winners?

A profile of Winners shows that these people have internal resources that outside negativity just won't erode. Here are a few examples:

> Winners are self-motivated; they believe in themselves and feel they make a difference. They're driven by a "fire in the belly" and won't be

discouraged by naysayers. They've got their priorities straight. Winners have the tools that keep their internal belief systems running, repairing and revitalizing themselves every day, every hour.

➤ When Winners don't feel good, they act as if they do. This isn't brainwashing or denial; it's purely a technique for getting over the hump until that original spontaneity comes back.

➤ Winners prepare for a challenge by thinking positively. They focus their minds on instances in their lives where they truly wanted something and got it.

➤ Winners literally keep their heads up. They keep smiling no matter how hard their opponent is trying to beat them down. Just try feeling lousy while looking up at the sky. Tough, isn't it?

➤ Winners build a support group of positive people around them, even though their background, circumstances, or social circle may not have given them that support when they were growing up. Winners know they can't change the past, but they can create a healthy environment in the present, which carries them into the future with optimism and positive feelings.

Management can help guide employees toward these winning goals by introducing workshops for self-growth into the job curriculum. Such programs assist salespeople in building internal strengths to reinforce their external selling skills.

And it's up to the company to create that healthy environment— to become the support system, mentor, and guide that its salespeople need. Here are a few basic suggestions on how to acknowledge your salespeople and treat them like the precious resource they are:

➤ Begin each day with positive interaction. Listen. Let the worker be the talker here. Similarly, end the day on an upbeat note. Get rid of any negative energy in the office.

➤ After a sale, or the loss of one, talk about what went right. Always start positively, and encourage your people to think that way too. Next, get your salespeople to feel good about those things that went right. Congratulate them. Make sure they acknowledge themselves and feel positive about their accomplishments.

➤ Teach them to "disassociate" themselves from the sale. Have your people separate, step back from the actual situation, and put some space between themselves and the sale. Have them look at themselves in the "role" they were playing as salespeople.

➤ Using this same technique, analyze the sale. Separated from their roles as salespeople, workers are in a much better position to analyze their own performance for learning and improvement. Have them ask themselves what they could have done differently. Encourage them to come up with several variables. Then, change the scenario and play it again. Let them ask you for ideas. Be available, but keep listening; the more your salespeople discover their own strategies for success, the more success they'll have.

➤ Teach them to ask for help, and not only from you. If you were the coach of a sports team, you could see your players in progress and analyze their performance firsthand. But your salespeople win or lose the sale in their prospect's office, not yours. Have them go back to the very prospects or clients they didn't close with and ask them: "What did I do wrong? What could I have done differently?"

➤ Be available. Getting feedback will help your salespeople solidify their feelings, so encourage your staff to ask you for help. Build a team. Hearing a member of your staff ask, "Can you help me?" will become music to your ears.

➤ Finally, teach your salespeople to fail. Send them out to get nos and praise them for each one they come back with. The mere fact that they went out again and again—like that winning home-run hitter—means that they deserve your praise. As At-Leasters, they'll never know the "thrill of victory" until they realize that the willingness to risk the "agony of defeat" is just as praiseworthy, and that defeat doesn't mean disaster.

Name: Brian Azar

Company: The Sales Catalyst, Inc.

Web Site: www.Salesdoctor.com

Biography: For more than 35 years, Brian Azar's sales training and coaching methods have changed the way people do business. As president of The Sales Catalyst, Inc., for the past 29 years, he has conducted sales training, management, and workforce development seminars around the world.

As a former record-breaking sales representative and sales manager for Xerox Corporation, he has a unique viewpoint on both large and small businesses.

Today, Brian utilizes his legendary Sales Doctor methods to teach individual workers how to sell and bring out the best in themselves in every situation, and teach business teams how to work together to overcome any hurdle.

Selling Philosophy: Utilizing personal development and rapport skills to break down barriers preventing individual success

Target Industries: Brian's training is universal and is unique because it can be custom-tailored for each specific industry. His main focus is sales training, rapport building, and workforce development for any industry in need.

Best Sellers: *Your Successful Sales Career*, *Sales Professional Certification Program*, *Future Selling: The 10-Step Sales Interview*, *The Ten Laws of Business Success*, and *The Sales Doctor: Selling from the Inside Out*

Sales Tip One: Light Up Your Network by continuing to forge relationships across and outside your firm. Successful networks and alliances are key to making things happen and will give you unprecedented power and connections.

Sales Tip Two: Expand Your Group of Mentors by contacting older and newly retired professionals to help you understand where your company is on its journey, help you understand the motivations of the lead characters, and give you a powerful endorsement.

Sales Tip Three: Become a scout by asking and listening to your customers and vendors in the right way. Schedule time with them to share information and find out who they see as succeeding or struggling so you can determine how your company can continue on its path to success.

Book One: *Your Successful Sales Career*

Book Two: *The Sales Doctor: Selling from the Inside Out*

Book Three: *The Ten Rules for Sales Success*

Chapter 6

Confronting the CRM Challenge

Walter Rogers
Baker Communications

For the last couple of years now, all of the buzz in business has been about the Sales 2.0 revolution. By Sales 2.0, I am referring to the way technology—especially Web-based strategies and applications—has transformed the way sales and marketing organizations can and must interact with customers, track information, implement solutions, and manage sales teams.

For the most part, this revolution is driven by the simple reality that customers are empowered and inspired by the advantages they gain through using the Web and its sophisticated interactive features to control the buying process and customize solutions to fit their needs. In response to this demand from customers, countless developers of business applications have jumped into the market with products to help sales organizations leverage the Sales 2.0 revolution to more successfully interact with customers and drive revenue. At any rate, that is the stated goal, which brings us to the CRM Challenge.

CRM—an acronym for Customer Relationship Management—broadly refers to a vast array of software applications (including many Web-based strategies) purportedly offering sales organizations the "silver bullets" they need to more effectively manage all the processes it takes to connect with customers and grow revenue in the intensely competitive, rapidly shifting market conditions we all deal with these days. The theory is that CRM systems, and other processes related to Sales Force Automation (SFA), can help sales teams collect and manage huge chunks of data faster and more efficiently, more accurately forecast the product pipeline, better target the solutions that customers need, shorten the sales cycle, create more revenue, and provide sales managers with better snapshots of what is going on across the organization at any given time.

The potential upside that CRMs promise to provide to sales organizations is fantastic. Billions of dollars have been invested by very smart people to create very complex and highly customizable systems that can scale to any type of process or organization. At this point, you won't find a credible, successful sales organization on the planet that hasn't invested a lot of money in some sort of CRM program. The problem is, you will also find most of them soon scratching their heads, mystified over the fact that the systems aren't delivering nearly the bang for the buck they had hoped for, mostly because the level of adoption and functionality on the part of their sales teams is distressingly low. Why, in spite of all of the hype and hope, are CRMs missing the mark for most organizations?

Over the years, we have built a deep repository of expertise in helping companies significantly boost their level of CRM adoption, and we can trace the difficulty to a handful of issues:

Failure to gain executive leadership and sponsorship. Extracting the true value from a CRM starts at the very top of any organization. CRMs are intended to streamline workflow and increase sales throughput. The executive leadership team is responsible for helping the organization make the transition to a new way of business, one that eliminates as many friction points as possible in the customer presales and support cycle. If executive leadership continues to require old reports, support nonoptimized workflows, and resist new technology, then CRM efforts will surely fail.

Failure to focus on sales management. Just as important as executive leadership, sales managers are the key change agents or change resistors. Sales reps will only follow what the managers will ask them to do. If sales managers don't utilize the CRM as the communication platform for coaching, best practices, and team communications, then the sales reps will resist any CRM.

Failure to focus on generating revenue. The purpose of implementing a CRM is not to have a sales accounting system; it is to have a sales enablement system that helps eliminate choke points and bottlenecks that prevent revenue from occurring, ultimately increasing sales throughput. Most CRM implementations focus on pipeline visibility, which helps management but does little to help the sales representative retire quota.

Failure to include users in the design or deployment of the system. Too often, CRM systems are thrust upon sales teams, presenting them with lots of fancy menus and buttons that look cool but have no immediate perceived relevance to what the salesperson does every day. If the users are the last to know about a change like this, they will not be enthusiastic about using it.

Failure to align CRM processes with sales team processes. Deploying a CRM represents a massive change in workflow. Sales teams already have a process they are comfortable with, including order management, pricing and approval systems, and document management. The CRM may interrupt or hinder those processes and tools, if it is not aligned with what the team is already doing. Either the CRM must track with the present process and support other tools, or the sales team must be retasked to follow a different process that incorporates existing tools into the CRM, in order for true and lasting benefit to be realized. Sadly, they are often allowed to exist in conflict with each other.

Failure to build trust with the sales team. A high percentage of the sales team may perceive a CRM to be another tool of the "Big Sales Manager" watching over them, using the data entered by the reps against them during performance reviews or force reductions.

Failure to get buy-in from the users. This is really a by-product of all the above. If users feel the system has been thrust upon them without taking their needs into consideration, or that it is only creating more work for them by requiring them to enter copious amounts of useless data, and especially if the data are going to be used against them, users will only do the minimum, if that much. Usually they will claim they are just too busy with real work to spend time with the CRM.

Failure to include nonsales facing functions. Finance, human resources, support, operations, and other functions all impact customer experience. Not connecting other functions into a CRM decreases the opportunity to eliminate redundant work processes and ultimately affects the customer's experience. If an organization is leveraging a CRM for a subset of its customer interactions but asking nonsales groups to use different tools that contain redundant or potentially conflicting information, then a disconnect on where, when, and how to leverage a CRM to improve the customers' experiences will persist.

Failure to integrate sales and marketing workstreams. Sales and marketing are often at odds with each other. Even though both sales and marketing are ultimately responsible for driving revenue, they often report to different executives with conflicting measurement objectives. As a result, 75 percent of leads generated by marketing for sales never receive a phone call, wasting the time and energy of both groups. Both sales and marketing processes should come to "life" inside integrated workstreams enabled by the CRM.

Failure to deliver effective training. CRMs can be highly complex and intricate. The training and tutorials provided by most organizations during the deployment of the system focus on what the buttons do but provide very little reinforcement regarding why reps should really care, or what is in it for them if they start using those buttons. It can be overwhelming; for these reasons, reps often end up using CRMs as nothing more than hugely expensive address books to manage their customer contacts and record their sales. This leads to the ultimate reason sales teams' CRM adoption rates are so low, as follows.

Failure to help reps see how the CRM will drive revenue and benefit them. If the CRM doesn't drive more revenue for the rep, the team, and the company, it is truly a colossal waste of time and money. Because communication from upper management is often poor and training is generally insufficient or irrelevant, sales team members never get the vision or the skills to leverage the CRM for its ultimate purpose: driving more sales and improving productivity! With the right strategic alignment that includes processes, skills, and tools for the entire sales team (including sales managers and senior executives), CRMs really do drive revenue. Once sales reps discover the power at their fingertips and learn how to use it, sales numbers begin to climb, enthusiasm for the process builds, adoption increases, and the CRM finally becomes the valuable tool it was always intended to be.

Name: Walter Rogers

Company: Baker Communications, Inc.

Web Site: http://BakerCommunications.com

Biography: Walter Rogers is president and CEO of Baker Communications. He has created and led businesses in 13 countries on three continents. He was a finalist for the 2000 and 2001 Texas eCommerce Awards; is a guest instructor on the topics of entrepreneurship, sales, and marketing at the University of Texas; and has been interviewed about sales and marketing integration on *ABC News,* CNN, Sales Rep Radio, and WF. He currently hosts a sales effectiveness and CRM segment on CNN650 Radio. During his time with Baker Communications he has increased sales by over 1,000 percent and pushed the organization into new products, services, and markets.

Selling Philosophy: Lasting improvement is achieved through measurable and repeatable execution of integrated sales and marketing processes.

Target Industries: Technology, energy, finance, government, manufacturing, education

Best Sellers: *Sales Effectiveness, Revenue Generation Plays (RevGen), Clearview Plays (Clearview), STORM Methodology,* and *CRM Adoption*

Sales Tip One: Align sales transformation with executive metrics.

Sales Tip Two: Field sales managers are your number-one priority.

Sales Tip Three: Coach the deals, not the numbers.

Book One: *Intersections* (in development)

Product One: CNN Live Radio: Selling in the Eye of the Storm (airs every Wednesday morning on CNN radio)

Product Two: *Consultative Selling Skills* (audio recording)

Product Three: *Sales Negotiations* (audio recording)

Chapter 7

Rethinking Sales Success

Storytelling

Mike Bosworth
Story Leaders

This is Mike Bosworth, and I'd like to share with you the journey along the winding road that brought me to offering you these sales tips.

My journey in training salespeople began in 1976, while working for Xerox Computer Services. I was 29 years old when the executive team asked me to train others to do the things that had come naturally to me. The first thing Xerox wanted from me before I was to teach other salespeople was to learn the corporate sales methodology, PSS (Professional Selling Skills), inside and out. One thing that stuck from my studies was the thought, *you can't teach rapport*. Rapport is "chemistry," and the chemistry between every two humans is unique.

Since then, through my Solution Selling and Customer Centric Selling days, one area I avoided as a sales trainer was teaching sellers how to "establish rapport." I would spend literally 30 minutes out of a four-day workshop on the basics of not *blowing* your first impression: using eye contact, avoiding stereotypical sales language, avoiding the trophies and props in the buyer's office, silence up front so the buyer can lead in either getting right down to business or having some "small talk." That was it. I stayed away from the "rapport" issue because I had it in my head that it was not *teachable*. Instead, I taught people a system for managing complex sales cycles.

I know that the selling systems I created have dramatically improved the effectiveness of thousands of sellers since 1983. Our clients have told us so. But at the back of my mind, I knew something was still missing.

In 2008, Sales Benchmark Index published a finding about the "80/20 rule." (A small percentage of the sellers in an organization rack up the lion's share of the sales.) Of 1,100 companies indexed, it was actually 87/13. This hit me like a ton of bricks. Despite all my personal efforts and the efforts of the entire sales training industry, with all the CRM systems, sales processes, and sales manager training, and with all the marketing messaging and all the coaching, *13 percent of salespeople brought in 87 percent of the revenue*. I can only conclude that the top 13 percent are doing something *very* different than the bottom 87 percent.

This discovery led me to seriously rethink sales success. I began to revisit the dynamics between buyers and sellers. Even though I have been asking myself these questions since 1976, I did it again with a different focus: Which sellers were being selected by buyers, and why? What happens in the buyer's brain when they make a buying decision? What happens in the brain during *any* decision? What do top sellers do *differently* to influence those decisions?

I have come to realize that we can do a lot more than teach sellers to manage a complex sales process. We can *also* teach sellers to emotionally connect with their buyers. With a strong emotional connection with their buyers and customers, sellers can inspire change, relax their buyers, and ultimately, influence decisions.

We can teach sellers how they can more effectively influence change by better connecting with their buyers' natural human behavior through *storytelling*.

Storytelling is a powerful tool for expressing ideas, helping people learn and change, and allowing sellers to emotionally connect with their customers and buyers.

We are now teaching sales professionals how to better connect with and influence the people they wish to do business with. We are creating new methods for sellers (initially) to learn how to organize, convey, and share ideas through storytelling. We will then expand our audience to anyone who has the need to connect and inspire: teachers, entrepreneurs, leaders, mentors, parents, coaches, executives, and so on.

The question I am being asked these days is "Why storytelling?" For the past 190,000 years, humans have used stories to lead, to communicate, to educate, to warn, to persuade, to engage others, to inspire, to celebrate success, and to *connect emotionally*. Why are the leaders in virtually all professions good storytellers? Storytelling is in our DNA.

Why use stories to sell? A good story can have a profound effect on the emotional connection with the seller and therefore the buying process. People respond *unconsciously* to stories. When people hear the phrase "Once upon a time . . . ," a part of their brain tells them that what comes next is *safe*, it's just a story, and I don't have to *do* anything. I can relax and enjoy the story. Paradoxically, at the same time, we also respond with *more and better attention*, with the thought, *I might need to remember this, it could be important.* Long after we forget data, we remember stories.

Here's why. In addition to our "lizard" brain (fight or flight) and limbic brain (emotions), our brain is also composed of two hemispheres, left and right.

When we anticipate a story, our limbic or emotional brain begins to create an altered state of awareness. It relaxes and quiets the left side of the brain. Why is that important?

Our left brain responds to numbers, examples, facts, figures, and logic. It never gets enough information. The more information it gets, the more it wants, leading to procrastination. The left brain sees things in black and white, as a series of single items; it *demands certainty* and remains emotionally *neutral*.

A story-opening phrase "fixates" the left brain and frees up the right. Our right brain responds to images, takes in the "whole" picture, and can imagine the future. Our right brain will fill in gaps with *intuition*, with "gut" feelings, can tolerate shades of gray, and sees overall patterns. Our right brain is *decisive*, decides to *trust*, decides to take *action,* and most importantly, *connects emotionally*.

When ideas are conveyed in a story, the buyer's right brain is activated. They are able to visualize, to imagine, to trust, to be hopeful, to retain, and to *act*.

Most corporate marketing departments are creating messages for the buyer's left-brain needs, delivered by sellers trained to ask logical questions and make left-brain presentations. Most sales training companies (including two I founded) are teaching sellers to satisfy the buyer's left-brain needs.

The top 13 percent of salespeople use their selling methodology to sell to the buyer's left brain, but they *also* use their own intuitive skills to emotionally connect (with the right brain), and therefore they are satisfying the buyer's whole brain. Story is the perfect complement to virtually any selling methodology by enabling all sellers to sell to the buyer's whole brain.

The best sellers use stories to answer four questions in the buyer's mind: Who is this person? Who does she represent? How has she helped other people like me? How can I use her product in my world?

Stories create anticipation, enhance attention, and increase *retention*. Stories help sellers take people from where they are now to where they need to be. The best way to get a buyer to take decisive action is to make the future desirable by creating a vision in their imagination.

Name: Mike Bosworth

Company: Story Leaders, LLC

Web Site: www.storyleaders.com

Biography: Mike Bosworth founded Solution Selling in 1993, cofounded CustomerCentric Selling in 2001, and is a founding partner of Story Leaders, LLC.

Bosworth has a degree in business management and marketing from California State Polytechnic University. He is the author of *Solution Selling: Creating Buyers in Difficult Selling Markets*, and coauthor of *Customer Centric Selling: The Message-Driven Sales Process*. He has lectured at the Stanford Graduate School of Business, The Stanford Program on Market Strategy for Technology-Based Companies, and numerous professional organizations. Bosworth serves on advisory boards of five early-stage technology companies.

Selling Philosophy: Emotionally connect and facilitate the buying process.

Target Industries: All industries

Sales Tip One: People need to know your story.

Sales Tip Two: People need to know the story of the organization you represent.

Sales Tip Three: People need to know stories of other people who are like themselves and who have benefited from your offering.

Book One: *Solution Selling: Creating Buyers in Difficult Selling Markets*

Book Two: *CustomerCentric Selling: The Message-Driven Sales Process*

Chapter 8

Selling for the Independent Professional

Ian Brodie

We're a funny bunch, we sole practitioners—but an important one.

Nearly half the lawyers in private practice in the United States are sole practitioners. The ranks of consultants, coaches, trainers, architects, and engineers are dominated by the independent professional.

We're hugely diverse: We come from different ethnic, religious, and social backgrounds, and we have different personality types, different experience bases, and different lifestyles.

Yet we almost all share one universal characteristic: a hatred of selling.

Our mantra is well practiced: "I didn't spend five years in training because I wanted to do selling," "I didn't get all those years of experience because I wanted to sell myself," or "I didn't set up my own business because I wanted to sell."

Yet sell we must, if we want to survive, let alone prosper.

Sure, a small minority of professionals have such rare and in-demand skills, or such a brilliant contact network, that they never need to actively sell themselves.

But the rest of us have to live in the real world. We have to "suck it up" and learn how to sell effectively.

Now that doesn't mean we have to become professional salespeople. For the independent professional, selling will always be an adjunct to their day job of actually delivering their services. And of course, they have to run their businesses, too.

And our clients don't really want to buy from professional salespeople either. They want to buy from the people who will be doing the job for them. They want to be sure that they "know their stuff" and that they can get along with and work with them.

So we need to learn how to sell in a way that works for us in our professional role as a lawyer, accountant, consultant, or coach.

Most professionals feel uncomfortable in sales situations. And it's no wonder: The dominant stereotype we have of salespeople is of aggressive extroverts—pushy, manipulative Ricky Roma types.

But that type of selling just doesn't work for independent professionals. You can't push or manipulate someone into buying a highly expensive service that is likely to impact some of the most critical areas of their business. Before they buy they'll need a high degree of confidence that you understand their challenge, that you know what you're doing, and that they'll be able to work with you.

That confidence won't be built by the pushy tactics of the typical salesperson. It will only come from a constructive dialogue with a knowledgeable professional who puts the client's best interests at heart.

That doesn't mean you need to be a "pushover." An effective professional is a peer-level partner to their client. And that's the role you need to adopt when selling.

Clients will make major judgments about what it will be like to work with a professional based on their experiences during the sales process. They want someone who will act as a trusted advisor and partner to them, and so you must behave in that way right from the first meeting.

In my role both as an independent professional and as someone who has trained and coached a huge number of professionals to improve their selling skills, I have determined that there are three main areas that most professionals need to focus on:

1. Developing a positive mind-set toward sales
2. Becoming adept at an effective sales methodology
3. Growing the confidence and capability to close

■ DEVELOPING A POSITIVE MIND-SET

Many professionals view selling as manipulative, and they're uncomfortable doing it. Others view selling as somehow "beneath them." They worry about their image as a professional and what others will think of them if they engage in sales activities. Others fear the inherent rejection that comes with sales.

Sometimes these issues can be addressed by challenging professionals' assumptions about what selling actually is, and helping them to see that selling is very similar to what they do when they help clients solve their problems as a professional anyway. For others, role-playing and practicing their skills on friendly clients can give them the confidence they need to take a more active role.

Whatever approach is used, having a positive attitude toward sales is an absolute necessity to doing it well.

■ BECOMING SKILLED AT A SALES METHODOLOGY

A number of methodologies have been developed that are appropriate for independent professionals, for example, SPIN Selling, Solution Selling, or my own Breakthrough Selling System.

For professionals, the key to selling is questioning. Through smart questions, the professional learns about the client's problems or opportunites, is able to clarify the size of the issue, and finds out enough to propose a compelling solution to the problem.

But questioning is about much more than merely finding out information:

➤ Smart questions focus in on the key topics and establish a professional's knowledge and credibility much more than any unfounded claims or monologues could.

➤ A question-based approach shows the client that you are interested in them and their issues. It shows you'll try to understand them, and develop solutions tailored to their needs, rather than respond reactively with canned answers.

➤ Asking good questions brings new insights to the client's mind. Ideally, they should come out of the meeting with you inspired by new ideas and fresh thinking. In essence, you're giving them a free sample of what it would be like to work with you.

Perhaps the most important thing questioning does from a sales perspective is to motivate the client to buy.

For most professionals, their number-one competitor is not another firm: It's simply a client not doing anything, or trying to muddle through by himself or herself.

Why do clients do this? Although they know they have a problem or opportunity, they're not convinced it's important enough to warrant hiring an expensive professional to address it.

Typically this happens because as soon as professionals hear clients talk about their problems or opportunities, they jump straight to the solution they can provide. It's an almost Pavlovian reaction. Talking about their solutions, their methodologies, and their results is comfortable and safe ground for professionals. And it feels as though they're adding value and demonstrating their expertise.

But if they do this before they've explored with the client the full impact of their problem or opportunity, then the chances are that the client won't see just how big it is. And that means they won't buy.

■ GROW THE CONFIDENCE AND CAPABILITY TO CLOSE

Most salespeople try to close too early, too often, and too hard.

They've read too many "27 Surefire Closing Secrets"–type books and have come to believe that by using clever language or manipulative methods and attempting to close at least five times in a call, they can somehow win more business.

In fact, for anything other than small sales, trying to manipulate people into signing up backfires. If people aren't yet convinced that they really need a product or service, and they're not sure that your particular one is right for them, then using closing techniques such as asking if they'd like delivery on Tuesday or Thursday will push them further away.

The evidence on methods of closing is clear. The optimum number of closes per meeting is *one*.

However, for professionals, the challenge is a different one.

Whereas product salespeople try to close too often, most professionals don't even attempt to close once. Some get so tied up in the client's business problems that the meeting overruns and they end weakly. Others don't want to sound pushy, or simply don't know what to say to progress to the next step.

Effective closing is much more than something you tag on at the end of a sales meeting. To close effectively at the end, you need to make sure that through your whole sales discussion, the client is growing in confidence that their problem needs a solution urgently, that you understand them, that you know what you're doing, and that they will be able to work with you.

To that end, effective closing is much more about a natural continuation and conclusion of the discussion you were having with the client. The key steps must be built in throughout your sales methodology rather than a technique you use at the end.

■ MY ONE BEST PIECE OF ADVICE

Being able to sell effectively is well within the reach of almost all independent professionals, so long as they take a positive approach to it.

The most important thing to remember, however, is that selling is a *skill*. Unlike most of our professional competencies, which can be built by research or classroom study, if you want to get better at selling, you need to practice. You need to focus on one element of selling at a time, go out and practice that skill, get feedback, reflect on it, and improve.

At the end of the day, the most effective independent professionals at selling are those who have the courage to go out and do it, and also the humility to listen to feedback and learn.

Make sure you're one of them.

Name: Ian Brodie

Web Site: www.ianbrodie.com

Biography: Ian Brodie helps lawyers, accountants, consultants, coaches, and other service professionals get better at attracting clients and winning new business. He's been helping some of the world's leading organizations with their marketing and sales challenges for over 16 years.

Ian has sold multimillion-dollar consulting engagements across multiple countries and cultures.

Through study, experience, and having some of the best rainmakers in the field as his mentors, he's learned what it takes for even the most reluctant of professionals to become highly effective at marketing and sales, and that's what he now teaches his clients.

Selling Philosophy: Breakthrough selling

Target Industries: Independent professionals, such as lawyers, accountants, consultants, architects, coaches, and trainers

Best Sellers: *The Client Breakthrough System: Seven Steps to Attract and Win as Much New Business as You Can Handle*; *More Referrals, More Business: How to Grow Your Professional Practice by Harnessing the Power of Referrals*; *Get Clients with Twitter*; *Get Clients with LinkedIn*

Sales Tip One: Build a positive attitude to selling. It's not about manipulating clients—it's about helping them find solutions to their challenges.

Sales Tip Two: Adopt a proven sales methodology: learn it, use it, get good at it.

Sales Tip Three: Get the confidence to close. Your whole approach should lead up to asking for commitment.

Book One: *The Client Breakthrough System: Seven Steps to Attract and Win as Much New Business as You Can Handle*

Book Two: *More Referrals, More Business: How to Grow Your Professional Practice by Harnessing the Power of Referrals*

Chapter 9

Ten Tips for Convincing the Buyer to Pay More

Ed Brodow
Negotiation Boot Camp

Every salesperson eventually must confront the following situation:

➤ You want the deal badly.
➤ You need the business.
➤ You've been suspecting that your price is too high to begin with.

So what do you do? You lower your price rather than negotiate. Many salespeople are afraid to stand by their price structure because of a single mistaken assumption: "If I refuse to negotiate my price, I'll lose all my customers." The reality is just the opposite. If you aren't prepared to defend your price, your customers will lose respect for you.

Here are 10 tips that will help you to negotiate the price you deserve:

Tip Number One: You are entitled to reasonable compensation. Just as your doctor, your accountant, and your plumber are entitled to a reasonable compensation for their services, you are entitled to a reasonable compensation for your product or service. What is reasonable? Whatever you can convince your buyer that your product or service is worth. The operative principle here is value. No buyer will begrudge you a price that is reasonable relative to the perceived value of the product or service.

Tip Number Two: Don't sell yourself short. Do you believe that what you are selling is worth the price? If the answer is yes, and I certainly hope it is, then you should expect to receive a worthy price. If you lack

35

confidence about your product or service, buyers will become aware of your doubts. Have you noticed the range of prices for similar products and services? It fascinates me when some salespeople are able to bring in the order at a premium price while others can't seem to get by without discounting. What accounts for this? One salesperson gets up in the morning and says, "My product is great and my customers are happy to pay my price!" Another salesperson gets up and says, "My product is great, but the buyer will never pay me such-and-such!" Don't sell yourself short.

Tip Number Three: Don't apologize. Once you have established the value of your product or service, present your price with confidence. Never apologize for your price. If you believe your price is correct, just assume that your customers will agree.

Tip Number Four: Always be willing to walk away. I call this Brodow's Law. You must be prepared to say "Next!" or your customers will sense your uncertainty. The willingness to walk away from a sale comes from having options. It is crucial to have other potential sales in the line-up. When you know that your sales career doesn't hinge on this one deal, you can exude confidence. And buyers will bow to confidence.

Tip Number Five: How to justify your price. Once you have decided on your price, you must provide reasonable justification so your buyer will say, "Okay, that makes sense. I can accept that." Here are three methods to justifying your price:

1. Give your price legitimacy. "My price is reasonable for the marketplace. This is the going price for this product or service." If your buyers are doing their homework, they will know you are telling the truth. And remember you are entitled to a reasonable compensation.

2. Focus on the value of your product or service, not on the price. Buyers will pay for value. Sell features and benefits.

3. Show them that you'd like to help them out, but you can't because you can't lower your price for one customer without lowering your price for everybody.

Tip Number Six: When to negotiate your price. Obviously, there are exceptions. You want to leave yourself the option of negotiating a lower price if it is in your best interest to do so. The operative principle here is called "saving face." In other words, you will lower your price only if you can save face, that is, maintain the integrity of your basic pricing structure. So you tell your customer, "I accept a lower price only under the following circumstances . . ."

What are those circumstances?

You might consider offering a discount if the customer will buy more than one, or if the merchandise is flawed. I recently gave a keynote speech at a reduced fee for a client who had already booked six two-day seminars. My face-saver: the multiple bookings. (As a result of the interest generated by the keynote, the client booked another six seminars.)

Tip Number Seven: Make the buyer work for concessions. If you appear too anxious to negotiate your price or terms downward, the buyer will perceive you as worth less (or worthless). One of my favorite price negotiations was with a client who received a proposal from a competitor of mine who wanted the job so badly that they offered to do a negotiation seminar for nothing (just to break into the account). My client tried to convince me that I should lower my fee, but I politely refused. In the end, my clients booked me because they viewed my competitor's presentation as worth the price—namely, zero. My seminar was perceived to be more valuable due to my confident negotiating posture. If you do lower your price, be sure you made your buyer earn the concession. Don't give in right away. Ask for concessions in return, such as additional business.

Tip Number Eight: Qualify your prospective buyers. There are occasions when you may be wasting your time negotiating with a customer. If you think a buyer may be out of your price range (either below it or above it), ask: "What kind of budget are we looking at?" or "What range are we looking at here?" You may want to let them know that you are not in the same range. You may want to sell them a more or less expensive item. Or you may want to fit them into an exception category—provided you can save face.

Tip Number Nine: How to deal with three typical buyer tactics.

1. The Flinch: The buyer says, "Your price is what!" and they start choking. Your response: silence. They just wanted to see if they could get a reaction out of you. Don't react. It's a test. Be persistent. Repeat your price and justify it as in Tip Number Five.

2. The Squeeze: The buyer tells you, "You have to do better!" or "I can get it for less." Your response:

   a. Sell your unique qualifications. Take the focus off the price. Get them to agree that yours is the one they want, and that the price is only a technicality. If they really want yours, they will find a way to pay for it. Remember my story of the competitor who offered to speak for nothing. Just because the buyer has a potential vendor with a lower price doesn't mean that they want that vendor.

   b. Tie a string. Offer to reduce your price only in return for additional volume or a commitment to purchase other products at full price.

3. The Sob Story: They cry, "All I have in my budget is . . ." or "All we can afford is . . ." Your response:

   a. Don't budge. Call their bluff. They may be testing to see how firm your price is.

    b. Ask "Are there any other budgets you can draw from?" Their budget for your product or service may not be the only one available to them.

Tip Number Ten: Leave the customer feeling satisfied. Whatever you do, remember that your objective is to create a satisfied customer. The following are ways to satisfy your customers without lowering your price:

1. Be a good listener. Allow the client to gripe about your price and get it off his or her chest. The client will thank you for being patient.

2. Help the client to accept your fee by providing reasonable justification.

3. Sell your unique strengths. Believe in yourself. The major obstacle that prevents salespeople from receiving the price they want is the fear of rejection. One way of dealing with this fear is to lower your price. A better way is to overcome your fear by schooling yourself in assertive negotiation techniques. When you do it right, both you and your customer will feel a sense of satisfaction. Ultimately, your belief in yourself and your product or service will be your best weapon. Your confidence will be rewarded.

Name: Ed Brodow

Company: Negotiation Boot Camp

Web Site: www.brodow.com

Biography: Ed Brodow is an internationally renowned expert on the art of negotiation. SEC Chairman Harvey Pitt dubbed Ed the "King of Negotiators." *Forbes* magazine agreed, ranking Ed as one of the nation's leading dealmakers. Ed is negotiating consultant to some of the world's most prominent organizations, including Microsoft, Goldman Sachs, Starbucks, Learjet, Raytheon, Philips, Hyatt, The Gap, Revlon, Zurich Insurance, Mobil Oil, the IRS, and the Pentagon. He is the best-selling author of four books, including *Negotiation Boot Camp: How to Resolve Conflict, Satisfy Customers, and Make Better Deals.* Ed has appeared as a negotiation guru on PBS, ABC *National News, Fox News, Inside Edition,* and *Fortune Business Report.*

Selling Philosophy: Negotiation

Target Industries: All industries

Best Sellers: Seminar: Negotiation Boot Camp; *Negotiation Boot Camp: How to Resolve Conflict, Satisfy Customers, and Make Better Deals* (Doubleday)

Sales Tip One: To be an effective listener, follow the 70/30 Rule (let the buyer do most of the talking) and ask open-ended questions so the buyer will tell you which problems they want you to solve.

Sales Tip Two: Follow Brodow's Law of Negotiation: Always be willing to walk away from a sale. In other words, never negotiate without having other potential buyers in the wings.

Sales Tip Three: The key to selling your product or service at higher prices is to focus on value. A buyer who perceives the value of your product, which means they understand how your product/service will solve their problem, will pay any price you ask.

Book One: *Negotiation Boot Camp: How to Resolve Conflict, Satisfy Customers, and Make Better Deals* (Doubleday)

Book Two: *Beating the Success Trap: Negotiating for the Life You Really Want and the Rewards You Deserve* (HarperCollins)

Book Three: *Negotiate with Confidence* (American Media)

Product One: *Negotiation Boot Camp* audio book (CD; Random House Audio)

Product Two: *The Three Rules for Win-Win Negotiating* (video)

Product Three: *The Six Essentials of Effective Listening* (video)

Chapter 10

How to Sell a Pencil—and Your Product or Service

Mike Brooks
Mr. Inside Sales

If I gave you a pencil and asked you to sell it, how would you go about it? Better yet, if you gave your sales team this test and went around the room asking each rep to sell you the pencil, how do you think they would do at it?

This is one of the most basic ways of assessing the sales skills of your reps, and the answers you'll get will reveal a lot about their previous training, their understanding of the sales process, and ultimately about where the work for you is in terms of turning underperformers into competent sales producers.

So, you may be wondering, what *is* the most effective way to sell a pencil? Well, first let's look at how most sales reps go about doing it. Whenever I'm working with a new sales team (or interviewing sales reps—a great way to assess previous training!), I automatically use this technique. After letting a rep tell me what a good closer they are, I pull out a pencil, hand it to them, and tell them to sell it to me. And off they go!

If you do this with your sales team, I'll bet that 80 percent of them will start the same way: They'll start pitching. "This pencil is brand new, never used. It has grade 2 lead and a bright yellow color, so it's easy to find. It comes with a built-in eraser," and so forth.

You'll be surprised and dismayed to see that some of your sales reps can (and do!) talk about it for five minutes or more before they even *think* to ask a question or ask for an order. To make a point, as your sales rep rambles on, try yawning or rolling your eyes to see what happens. Amazingly, most of the time, this will just make them talk even more!

Now let's look at how the top 20 percent go about selling a pencil. As you move down the line to your best producers, you'll probably notice a distinct difference in how they go about selling the pencil. Usually, when I give a top rep the pencil, they pause, and then they begin asking me questions (rather than pitching):

"So, how often do you use a pencil?" the rep will ask me.

"How many do you go through in a month?" Another great qualifying question.

"What other locations does your company use pencils in, and how often do they order them?" Great for setting up multiple orders.

"What quantity do you usually order them in?" An assumptive question here is always the best way to ask a buying question.

"Besides yourself, who else is involved in the buying decision?" Again, assumptive questions, especially when they involve discovering the decision makers, will often eliminate the common smoke-screen objections later on.

Quite a difference here, isn't it? If you're like me, then you probably listen to hundreds of sales presentations in a month, and they can easily be separated into these two groups: Those who pitch, pitch, pitch, and those who take the time to understand their prospect's unique buying motives and properly qualify to understand the entire selling process.

Now let's see which category your sales team fits into. When they speak with a prospect for the first time, how much of their scripts are focused on describing and pitching your product or service as opposed to questioning and uncovering buying motives?

If your sales presentation is like most of the scripts I review, then it's filled with descriptions of what you do and how your product or service helps people. Most scripts attack the prospect with a barrage of "value statements" that turn people off and make them want to get your sales team off the phone as quickly as possible.

Want a better way? Then take a tip from some of the best "pencil sales reps" and change your script and opening to focus more on questioning and discovering whether you're dealing with a qualified buyer and what it might take to actually sell them.

Without knowing this, you'll just end up with a lot of frustrated sales reps and a lot of unsold pencils at the end of the month!

Name: Mike Brooks

Company: Mr. Inside Sales

Web Site: www.MrInsideSales.com

Biography: Mike Brook is the best-selling author of *The Real Secrets of the Top 20 Percent: How to Double Your Income Selling over the Phone*, and is the founder and principel of Mr. Inside Sales, a Los Angeles–based inside sales consulting and training firm.

Mike specializes in working with business owners who have underperforming outbound or inbound inside sales teams, either business-to-business or business-to-consumer. He offers free closing scripts and a free audio program designed to help salespeople double their income selling over the phone. If you want to close business like a top 20 percent producer, then learn how at www.MrInsideSales.com.

Selling Philosophy: Teaching proven top 20 percent skills, techniques, and strategies

Target Industries: Inside sales, telesales, and telemarketing

Best Sellers: Five-CD series: *Secrets of the Top 20 Percent: How to Double Your Income Selling over the Phone*; Teleseminar Boot Camp: How to Open and Close Sales Like the Top 20 Percent; Executive Coaching: Taking Your Business to the Next Level; speaking and keynotes: "Ten Techniques of Top 20 Percent Performance"; inside sales book: *Secrets of the Top 20 Percent*

Sales Tip One: Leads never get better! Eighty Percent of your competition fails because they are chasing unqualified leads who will never buy.

Sales Tip Two: The top 20 percent are more interested in disqualifying leads than in trying to stuff unqualified leads into their pipeline.

Sales Tip Three: Practice doesn't make perfect, it only makes permanent. The top 20 percent use proven and effective techniques on every call so they can practice perfection and get the results they want.

Book One: *Secrets of the Top 20 Percent: How to Double Your Income Selling over the Phone*

Book Two: *35 Techniques to Make You Closer of the Month*

Chapter 11

Cultivating Endless Referrals

An Introduction

Bob Burg
Burg Communications

How do we make the prospecting process both fun and profitable? By developing what I call "Personal Walking Ambassadors." These are typically "Centers of Influence" (those people who already have large, prestigious personal spheres of influence and have lots of credibility within those spheres) who will enthusiastically connect us with those people who are ready, willing, and able to buy what we sell. In other words, these referred prospects cross the "Marketing Bridge" of "need it, want it, and can afford it."

Picture a rainbow. At the end of that rainbow is the proverbial pot of gold. In a sense, we could say that the pot of gold is "where the money is" . . . where those who can and will buy are located. Much more importantly, these are the people we have the best opportunity to serve, and the lives to which we can add the most value.

Too many salespeople spend the majority of their time at the beginning of the rainbow, doing work that is hard, unsatisfying, and often not particularly profitable. They cold call, send out literature to the percentage-wise few who are interested (or "say" they are), and follow up, follow up, follow up.

While this, of course, is certainly a legitimate part of selling, it's also the most difficult, the most time consuming, and the least profitable.

The answer is to cultivate a network of endless referral business. The two key words are "Network" and "Referrals."

Networking continues to be a much used but very misunderstood concept.

So, let's define our terms, first by describing what Networking is *not*!

As one who spends much of his life speaking on this very topic, I've been exposed to just about every false premise and preconceived notion regarding Networking that there is. It seems as though many people still see Networking as personified by the stereotypical, fast-walkin', slick-talkin' sales type; the one who aggressively sticks a business card into the face of everyone they meet and says such *clever* things as, "Hey, give me a call—I'll cut you a deal."

In my opinion, that's not Networking.

I define Networking as "the cultivation of mutually beneficial, *give* and take, win/win relationships." The emphasis is most definitely on the "give" aspect.

But is that "real-world" type of thinking? Yes, it is. Why? Because "all things being equal, people will do business with, and refer business to, those people whom they know, like, and trust." And part of developing these feelings toward you in others is to first add value—and lots of it—to their lives in a significant way.

When you Network according to our definition, with a genuine concern for someone (regardless of whether he or she is a direct prospect) and a sincere determination to help that person fulfill their wants, needs, and desires, it becomes a very effective way for you to do business.

It also becomes very profitable, as you'll find yourself developing a list of people who want to do the same for you. As you do this consistently, on an everyday basis, you'll find that not only will the quality of names on your list continue to improve, but they will multiply geometrically.

The reason is that these people with whom you are developing relationships know many others to whom they can eventually refer you. (In fact, it's been documented that the typical person knows 250 other people—thus every time you develop a solid relationship with one new person, you increase your own personal "sphere of influence" by a potential 250 people, every . . . single . . . time.)

In a sense, you could say that the ultimate goal of Networking is the building, cultivating, and developing of a very large and diverse list of people who will gladly and continually refer to you lots and lots of business, while, of course, you do the same for them.

You're dramatically increasing your referral business, without spending significantly more time or money in order to accomplish that goal.

In other words, you'll be hanging out by the "pot of gold" at the end of the rainbow, working only with people who are qualified to buy (and/or refer) and have the desire to do so. At that point, your business will become a lot *more* fun, a lot *less* stressful, and a lot *more* profitable.

Remember, the key is that:

"All things being equal, people will do business with, and refer business to, those people whom they know, like, and trust."

If you can keep that thought at the very top level of your consciousness every time you meet someone new, you will be 9 steps ahead in the game . . . in a 10-step game.

Name: Bob Burg

Company: Burg Communications

Web Site: www.burg.com

Biography: Bob speaks on "How to Cultivate a Network of Endless Referrals." He is best known as author of the underground best seller *Endless Referrals: Network Your Everyday Contacts into Sales* (over 200,000 sold!). Bob's method of teaching assures that attendees are equipped with the necessary skills and the confidence to enact them.

Bob has shared the platform with some of America's best-known speakers and celebrities, including Zig Ziglar, Jim Rohn, Tom Hopkins, Larry King, Loral Langemeier, Mary Lou Retton, cookie magnate Debbie Fields, Brian Tracy, Dr. Denis Waitley, Mark Victor Hansen, T. Harv Eker, Og Mandino, former president Gerald Ford, and many others.

Selling Philosophy: All things being equal, people will do business with, and refer business to, those people whom they know, like, and trust.

Target Industries: Financial services/life insurance, MLM/direct sales, general sales

Best Sellers: *The Go-Giver* and *Endless Referrals: Network Your Everyday Contacts into Sales*

Speaking Program "How to Cultivate a Network of Endless Referrals: The Go-Giver"

Sales Tip One: All things being equal, people will do business with, and refer business to, those people whom they know, like, and trust. Your job is to cultivate these types of relationships and develop an army of "Personal Walking Ambassadors."

Sales Tip Two: Posture can be defined as "the lack of emotional attachment to a desired result." The amount of posture you'll have and the amount of posture you'll display is directly proportional to the number of quality names on your prospect list.

Sales Tip Three: A great way to quickly establish rapport is to ask Feel-Good Questions. These are questions that are neither saleslike nor intrusive, and are enjoyable for your new networking prospect to answer.

Book One: *Endless Referrals: Network Your Everyday Contacts into Sales*

Book Two: *The Go-Giver* (coauthored with John David Mann)

Book Three: *Go-Givers Sell More* (coauthored with John David Mann)

Book Four: *The Success Formula*

Product One: "How to Cultivate a Network of Endless Referrals"

Product Two: "The Referral Mind-set"

Product Three: "Winning without Intimidation"

Product Four: "Master Your Traits—Master Yourself"

Chapter 12

Twenty-One Ways to Increase Sales This Year

Jim Cathcart
Cathcart Institute

The relationship between buyer and seller is probably the one that most impacts your success as a salesperson. Too often, however, salespeople neglect this relationship, focusing mainly on presentations or the desire to make the best offer. While these aspects do play a major part in sales, in the long run, the sales process involves humans interacting with other humans. The tips I've outlined below show you not only how to *persuade* your customers, but how overall to *work with* them.

1. **Prepare Yourself to Excel.** Use a checklist to prepare your attitude, appearance, customer information, company and product information, and the selling environment, so you can be at your best on every call.

2. **Notice What Is Working.** Study yourself, your product or service, and your company to know what is working now. Reinforce the actions and tools that are generating results. Learn from your successes as well as your failures.

3. **Know Your Competitive Advantage.** Study your company and your products and services in relation to what your competitors offer. Know where and how you stand out and where you don't. Be prepared to discuss these comparisons at any moment.

4. **Improve Your Sales Skills, Not Just Your Product Knowledge.** Don't rely on product knowledge to make you more persuasive. Sharpen your skills in reading people, describing your offer in compelling ways, and asking for the order at the right time.

5. **Target the People Who Are Your Best Prospects.** Best customers have patterns. Most will fit the same pattern, so prospect among those who fit the pattern. Calling on people with similar needs, circumstances, and interests makes you more likely to create another best customer.

6. **Know What to Be Curious About.** Know in advance what questions to ask by knowing what answers you need. Cultivate a strategic curiosity. Learn to be curious about the things that will advance your chance of making a sale.

7. **Realize Who Is in Your Market.** Create a profile of the ideal market for what you offer. Define who they are, where they can be reached, what they care about, what they fear, what they read, whom they admire, and more. Know them well.

8. **Understand the Person and His or Her Situation.** Create an awareness of the psychological needs of your prospects as well as knowing what their technical needs are. Sometimes the way people *want* to feel has more influence on their decision to buy than what they actually need.

9. **Find the Diamonds in Your Own Backyard.** More business exists around you than you know. Look among your friends, neighbors, existing customers, past customers, colleagues, competitors, and coworkers for the opportunities that others overlook.

10. **Ask for Specific Referrals.** Tell people what your ideal customer or prospect looks like. Ask them who they know who fits this description. Then ask them to take a specific action to help you meet the prospect: a telephone introduction, a testimonial letter, a luncheon or coffee shop meeting, and so forth.

11. **Manage Your Sales Reputation.** Determine today how you want to be thought of tomorrow. Specify the reputation you want within each group of which you are a part, and then work a plan to earn it piece by piece.

12. **Grow Your Brand Identity.** Get yourself and your company known within your market area. Write articles and letters to editors, offer expert input for reporters and publishers, conduct surveys, provide free services to key people, donate your time to worthy causes, put your photo on your business card, and share valuable ideas via e-mail. Create a broad awareness of yourself as an authority on what you do.

13. **Build a Fortress of Great Relationships.** It is not only who you know that determines the value of your relationships, it is whether they know you as a valuable business resource. Define who you need to know today and five years from today. Start now to cultivate the relationships and the reputation that will expand your possibilities.

14. **Learn to Manage Points of View.** Half your job is keeping yourself and others in the right frame of mind. Cultivate your ability to keep

the focus on the things that matter most. Become a person who can put everything in perspective for others.

15. **Manage Tension throughout the Sales Process.** As tension rises, trust falls. Be aware of the ebb and flow of tension as the sale unfolds. Learn to reduce it when it gets in the way and to momentarily increase it to add urgency to the decision process.

16. **Look Like Good News to Your Customer.** The way you are perceived by your customer determines how much resistance you will encounter as you sell. Learn to project a positive feeling among those you communicate with. Become a partner in problem solving, not a sales persuader.

17. **Cultivate a Selling Style That Uses Your Sales Strengths.** Use the combination of online communication, in-person calls, telephone contacts, trade show attendance, and public speaking that allows you to shine. Build a mix of activities to diminish your sales weaknesses and amplify your strengths.

18. **Give Samples of the Experience You Represent.** A movie ticket doesn't simply buy you a seat in the theater; it buys you the experience of enjoying the movie. What experience does your product or service bring to people? Give them a way to sample that experience through your presentation.

19. **Stay Conscious of the Meaning in What You Do.** When people don't find much meaning in what they do, they don't bring much value to what they do. Write down specifically how your product or service makes life better for those who buy it. Read this description every day briefly to keep in mind the reason behind the purchase. It's not about buying; it's about benefiting from buying.

20. **Know When and How to Ask for the Order.** Learn to recognize buying signals, how to ask in different ways with different people, when to let the customers sell themselves, how to negotiate details, and when to walk away. If you don't ask, you don't get. But how you ask often determines success or failure.

21. **Deserve to Have Loyal Customers.** Know how to cultivate dedicated clients. Become competition-proof by delivering more than people expect. Overfill your client's needs and be their business friend, even when they are not buying from you. Be the kind of person people rave about.

Name: Jim Cathcart

Company: Cathcart Institute, Inc.

Address: Speakers Office, 5927 Balfour Court, Suite 103, Carlsbad, CA 92008

Biography: Jim Cathcart popularized the concept of "Relationship Selling." His book, *Relationship Selling*, has been audio recorded, video recorded, and published worldwide. Its concept is simple yet profound: "Relationships should be treated as Assets!"

Jim serves on the boards of advisors for Pepperdine University and California Lutheran University business schools. He has delivered over 2,600 speeches and seminars and was inducted into the Professional Speaker Hall of Fame in 1986. He was president of the National Speakers Association and recipient of both the Cavett Award and the Golden Gavel. His television shows are broadcast under the title *The Purpose of Selling (Building Profitable Business Friendships)*.

Selling Philosophy: Relationship selling, relationships as assets

Target Industries: Hospitality, financial services, information services, coaching and consulting, training and development, health care, real estate

Best Sellers: Books: *The Acorn Principle* (know yourself and grow yourself) and *Relationship Selling* (the eight competencies of top sales producers); most popular speech and seminar topics: "All Leadership Begins with Self-Leadership," "Relationship Selling in a New Era," "Lifetime Customer Loyalty," "Teaching Others to Lead"; most meaningful role for Jim: Serving as the ongoing motivational advisor to managers and sales teams through periodic seminars and individual coaching.

Sales Tip One: Every relationship has a value or a cost. Treat relationships as assets and your business will grow.

Sales Tip Two: The purpose of selling is building profitable business friendships. If someone has a lifetime need to buy what you sell, then you should go after *all* of the business, not just today's portion.

Sales Tip Three: Build professional equity. Consider your professional assets and grow each one: credentials, relationships, reputation, experiences, skills, habits, and beliefs.

Book One: *Relationship Selling*

Book Two: *The Acorn Principle*

Book Three: *The Relationship Selling Series* (e-books for digital learning)

Product One: Relationship Selling—Sales Excellence Series (150 audio messages on CD and online)

Product Two: All Leadership Begins with Self-Leadership (motivational keynote video and audio: DVD, CD, and online)

Product Three: Leadership Communication: The Vital Skills for Meeting with Success (audio CDs and online)

Chapter

13

The Psychology of Persuasion

Robert Cialdini
Influence at Work

Why is the psychology of persuasion an important concept for salespeople and managers to understand?

Just saying "I'm the boss" doesn't work in a world where cross-functional teams, joint ventures, and intercompany partnerships have blurred the lines of authority. In such an environment, persuasion skills exert far more influence over others' behavior than formal power structures do. Influence is best exerted horizontally, not vertically. We all need to be influencers at some point or another, no matter what position we occupy in a company.

What is the difference between persuasion and manipulation?

Manipulation involves the unethical use of the principles of persuasion, and some of those involve brute force or coercion to achieve a goal. Persuasion involves the use of principles that exist in the situation and that allow us to inform people into *yes*, to educate them into *yes*, by giving them a view of reality as we see it. It involves moving them in a direction that we desire, on the basis of valid information.

American culture likes to celebrate the hero who fights authority, the individual who bucks a crooked system. Are all the scandals over the past few years, from Enron to Tyco to now AIG, proving that managers often still go along with what an authority figure says, even when they feel uneasy about it?

I'm not sure the managers and employees know that what they are doing is wrong really. When an authority figure speaks, people presume there is some legitimacy there. Part of the definition of "an authority" is a legitimately constituted expert in some sense, a person who has been given a place at the top of the hierarchy because of some special knowledge, wisdom, or experience. So we defer to these individuals as a shortcut on what to do in these situations.

Shortcuts are useful in our daily lives. When I am going through the supermarket and I need a tube of toothpaste, I don't want to first have to go to the library and research the properties and benefits of a good dentifrice. I want to see on the box that a product has been approved by the American Council on Dental Health. Bang, it's in my basket, and I'm on to the next decision in my decision-overloaded day. I need some decisions to be made by legitimately constituted experts in order to get through my day. Most of the time that works, but sometimes the expert is wrong.

Your books talk a lot about verbal cues and body language and how that ties into the important emotional pull of liking someone. In a business environment where so much communication is now "virtual" and spanning the globe, is it more difficult to influence someone?

That question really requires two levels of answers, one involving electronic communication and the other having to do with the global nature of it. There are differences in susceptibility of certain psychological principles of influence depending on the culture and the nationality of the audience. It's not just that the messages are sent electronically, it's also that they are being sent across cultural boundaries.

First, it *is* possible to deal with the problem of purely electronic communication. There was a study done at the Stanford Business School having to do with negotiation undertaken by students at Stanford and Northwestern. They had students negotiate either face to face or by e-mail. They found that when using e-mail, there were far more stymied negotiations where nobody benefited and the parties simply walked away from the discussion. However, some of the subjects were told to "get to know each other" first, exchanging personal information and even photos. After doing that, the number of stymied negotiations between these subjects fell to close to that of the subjects in face-to-face meetings. So it is possible to conquer the difficulties of electronic exchanges by infusing into those exchanges the kinds of elements that exist in a personal meeting.

On the cultural side, my books have been translated into 26 languages and have sold well in some cultures that are very different from the United States, so it is fair to assume the overall elements of persuasion and influence are somewhat universal. Having said that, different cultures give different weight to these principles.

For example, there was a Citibank survey done with global employees. One question was, "If someone within your organization came to ask you for help on a project and this project would take you away from your own duties, under what circumstances would you feel most obligated to help?" In the United States and similar cultures, the issue was about reciprocity. People asked themselves:

"What has this person done for me? Have they helped me in the past?" If the answer is yes, the person feels obligated to reciprocate.

In Hong Kong, the question people asked themselves was about the authority principle. "Is this person connected to my small group, especially a senior member of my small group? If so, I am obligated to help."

In Spain, the question was, "Is this person connected to my friends? If so, I am obligated to help." So that is the liking principle. You must be loyal to your friends.

In Germany it was different still, and related to consistency. The answers were along the lines of "According to the rules and regulations of this organization, am I supposed to say yes? If so, I am obligated."

So you can see how you would strategically craft a communication to a colleague in Berlin as opposed to one that you would draft for one in New York, Madrid, or Hong Kong. If you understand the difference in weights, in emphasis for the various persuasion principles, you can incorporate those levers into your messaging.

What persuasion advice would you give to a leader who faces the task of totally turning around a company or division and doing things very differently from how they were done in the past? A company such as Kodak or General Motors, for instance?

I would advise leaders to use the principle of scarcity. People are attracted to opportunities that are scarce, rare, or dwindling. If the CEO can describe what will be lost to everyone if the organization fails to move in this direction, rather than what will be gained if they do, he or she will be more successful. There is a lot of evidence to support this. One of the recent Nobel Prize winners in economics, Daniel Kahneman, found in a study that people are more affected by the prospect of losing something than they are by the prospect of gaining something equivalent. I also read another study lately showing that CEOs weigh information about possible losses more carefully than they weigh information about possible gains. These leaders should also remember that the people they are leading have this same bias, so the leaders have to focus in their communications on what will be lost more than on what will be gained.

The other recommendation I would make is that a CEO not try to be the sole voice of change. Multiple individuals within an organization need to be tapped for this task. People are powerfully influenced by the opinions of people like them. This has to do with the concept of social proof or consensus that I discuss in my book. The best communicators know when they are not the best communicators in a situation; they give voice to those individuals who are. If there are long-time employees who are resisting a change, the best strategy would not be to keep sending messages from on high. The best strategy would be to find those other long-term employees who can serve as champions of change and give them a voice. You let them speak in employee meetings, in newsletters, and in informal gatherings. When the message comes from people who are like those who are resisting, the influence is coming in from the side to make the change happen, not from above, and it's likely to have more impact.

You make the statement that "Public commitments tend to be lasting commitments." How can managers or team leaders best capitalize on that with their coworkers?

One of the best things we can do is use the process of writing things down, even if it is only in a preliminary meeting. Often you have a meeting in which certain things are agreed, and then when you come back a week later, nothing has been done. It's because people didn't commit themselves to anything. What we've learned in research is that people live up to what they write down. So my advice would be to assign individuals to summarize in writing what they understand to be their agreements and responsibilities and to send them around to the other attendees. Even if these things are decided in a preliminary way, people will be more loyal to the issues if they have made them public in some written form.

I also suggest salespeople do this with clients, by sending out a quick e-mail summary of what was discussed and asking for written confirmation from the client. "Here is my understanding of what we agreed on—is this your understanding as well?" That way you either have an agreement and understanding that is public and committed, or you get any problem areas out in the open immediately.

How do MBA students make the most of these extra few letters they are going to be able to tack onto the end of their names when they graduate?

That's about the authority principle and how they can capitalize on it. These students need to communicate to potential employers that they have been tested in two ways. One is that they have demonstrated competence in a variety of dimensions that are important to business. That is what the MBA program is about. But another aspect that is important to emphasize is that they have the conscientiousness and the resolve to finish difficult programs of work that they started. That is very valuable to employers.

Name: Robert Cialdini

Company: Influence at Work

Web Site: www.influenceatwork.com

Biography: Dr. Robert Cialdini has spent more than 30 years researching and publishing on the ethical business applications of the science of influence, earning him an international reputation as the seminal expert in the fields of persuasion, compliance, and negotiation.

His book, *Influence*, has sold over two million copies. His most recent coauthored book, *Yes! 50 Scientifically Proven Ways to Be Persuasive*, was on the *New York Times*, *USA Today*, and *Wall Street Journal* best-seller lists.

Currently, Dr. Cialdini is Regents' Professor Emeritus of Psychology and Marketing at Arizona State University.

His clients include Google, Microsoft, Coca-Cola, Kodak, Merrill Lynch, and NATO.

Selling Philosophy: When the science is available, why use anything else?

Target Industries: Pharmaceuticals, health care, insurance, financial, and professional services

Best Sellers: *Influence: Science and Practice, Influence: The Psychology of Persuasion*, and *Yes! 50 Surprises from the Secret Science of Persuasion* (now in paperback)

Sales Tip One: It's not what you do. It's what you do *before* you do what you do that counts. Just as any good gardener understands, before you can plant a seed and expect it to grow, you have to cultivate the earth first.

Sales Tip Two: It's not enough to tell the client what he or she has to gain. It's also important to tell the client what he or she honestly stands to lose as well.

Sales Tip Three: If the information you are providing a client is new or exclusive, it is very important to say so before you present that information.

Book One: *Influence: Science and Practice*

Book Two: *Influence: The Psychology of Persuasion*

Book Three: *Yes! 50 Surprises from the Secret Science of Persuasion* (now in paperback)

Product One: The Principles of Persuasion (POP) Workshop (two-day customized, in-house interactive workshop)

Product Two: *Influence—Principles of Ethical Influence* (CD set)

Chapter 14

The Virtual Presentation

Mastering the Medium

Bill Rosenthal
Communispond

People still tell a story, perhaps apocryphal, about the early days of automobiles. At that tentative beginning of the transportation revolution, there were only two horseless carriages in the entire city of Topeka, Kansas. Somehow, improbably, they managed to crash into each other. The townsfolk who witnessed the collision displayed a mixture of apprehension and relief. They were fearful to see a new-fangled technology they didn't know how to use and for which they didn't even perceive a need. And they were relieved that the wreck of these two noisily belching, self-propelled vehicles seemed to validate their reliance on the known, horse-drawn method of getting around.

According to many, the Internet rivals the automobile in its transformational effects on our world. And perhaps by now, people are getting used to the lightning speed at which new technologies appear and become integrated into our lives. Certainly anyone with a teenager sees the ease—and speed—with which new gadgets and new technologies spread (are you "twittering" yet?).

Web-based technology for meetings, presentations, demonstrations, or training isn't even new anymore. If you're a business person, you've surely experienced it. But have you prepared a Web-based presentation? Have you facilitated an Internet-based meeting in your company? Have you been the teleconferenced presenter to dozens or even hundreds of potential customers?

If you haven't, you will. Web-based events are becoming a dominant means of communication—just as the automobile supplanted the buggy. The growth of virtual business communication has been exponential, and there's every indication it will remain that way.

By most estimates and the reports of virtual meeting technology vendors, Web-based conferencing represents at minimum a $3 billion business with a growth rate of more than 20 percent. And the growth rate is likely to accelerate for a number of reasons, including economic imperatives.

One reason is that many people not only accept, but prefer, the Internet as a method of keeping in touch. This latest generation of new hires into the workforce communicates virtually—both synchronously and asynchronously—as a matter of course, whether by texting, instant messaging, or staying connected through Facebook. They have grown up with these technologies and expect to find them in their workplace.

During the current economic downturn, travel budgets have been cut, even by as much as 50 percent in some companies. Many organizations have had to find alternatives to face-to-face meetings, conferences, and training sessions.

And costs for those alternatives are now reasonable. There's no need to buy special software or equipment for virtual events. Service providers are commonplace, and pricing is highly competitive.

No company can imagine doing business without the Internet; the same is now becoming the norm for Internet-based meetings.

■ APPLYING THE FUNDAMENTALS

Marshall McLuhan had it wrong, at least when it comes to conducting a virtual meeting. The medium is not the message—not entirely, anyhow. The medium certainly creates considerations that you must factor into the crafting of your message. Overall, however, the message is the message; that is, the "what" of your presentation is more important than the "how."

Internet technology simply provides the stage for your content. Staging it well can strongly support your message, while staging it poorly can undermine it. For those reasons, you must give careful consideration to the technology. Just don't forget your message.

In revolutionizing transportation, cars may have replaced horse-drawn carriages, but they didn't eliminate the need for roads. Likewise, virtual meetings do not reduce the need for good presentation skills. Presenting via the Internet may demand a sharpening or adaptation of skills in certain areas, but the basics of facilitating pertain whether you're face-to-face or virtual.

■ ASSUME YOUR AUDIENCE IS BORED AND DISTRACTED

In one sense, hosting a Web-based event is just like facilitating any other meeting. Holding your audience's interest is of paramount importance. It's the one consideration that must precede all others. The most information-packed presentation is, after all, only as informative as your ability to command your listeners' attention so that they will remember your message.

In a virtual meeting you must work even harder to seize and keep that attention. In a face-to-face setting, you can "read the room." You can gauge the reactions of those around you and adjust accordingly. Web-based events offer infinitely greater possibilities for distraction. Instead of sitting in front of you, the audience is sitting in front of a screen. As a result, they will inevitably be more tempted to multitask—to scan their e-mails or play solitaire. The added challenge of ensuring you have the full attention of the participants should inform all of your decisions as you plan a virtual meeting. Your voice, the pace of your speaking, and the amount of information you decide to convey—all must be passed through the filter of holding the audience's attention.

■ IDENTIFY YOUR GOAL AND SCOPE OUT YOUR AUDIENCE

Before you do anything else, write down your goals for the event. Identify what you seek to accomplish.

Consider what you want your audience to take away from the meeting or to do in response. Also ask yourself who the audience will be. What's their point of view on your subject? What preconceptions will they bring to the event? How important is your message to them? These questions—simple as they are—are the ones most often overlooked in planning any presentation. But they are probably the most important.

Once you have identified your goal, determine exactly what you will need to support it. What visual support will you require? Do you need to include a question-and-answer period, or allow time for comments following the presentation? Does the content (such as a training session) dictate that participants should be able to interject with questions at any time? In planning your event, you'll have to think through a host of such questions.

Try not to give in to the temptation of cramming as much as possible into the meeting, on the always dubious theory that more is better. That's why, in Web-based events, it is particularly important to follow the Twain/Poe rule.

■ WHAT'S THE TWAIN/POE RULE?

Edgar Allan Poe developed a distinctive formula for writing short stories. He believed that every single word should support either the story's theme or help create its tone. Every word had to pull its own weight. Mark Twain followed a likeminded approach. After writing his drafts, he would go back and delete every redundant or extraneous word he could find. A day or two later, he would sit down again and delete every unnecessary word from the revised draft. Later, he would return with fresh eyes and purge words again—and again and again and again. Even on the sixth or seventh drafts, Twain would spot wasteful words that weighed down his prose.

The same discipline that contributed to the prose of Poe and Twain is essential to any good presentation—especially a virtual one. Considering the limited time available and the limited attention span of the audience, virtual meetings demand even greater focus than those conducted in person. Plan to present only what is absolutely vital to reinforcing your goal. Delete everything else. And conduct this reality check more than once. Sometimes, the idea that seemed so brilliant at 9 PM looks very different by the light of the next morning.

At the same time, being focused doesn't mean you should be a minimalist. A short unengaging presentation is just as ineffective as a long unengaging one. Make your visuals interesting and use the power of any interactivity afforded by your technology, such as online polling and document sharing. Just make sure everything you do supports your goal and is designed to hold the audience's attention.

■ PRACTICE, PRACTICE, PRACTICE

There is simply no substitute for practice. That's true with any presentation. It is even more critical with virtual events that depend so heavily on technology. One of the most common mistakes made by presenters and facilitators of virtual meetings is failing to rehearse beforehand. You may be accustomed to going over your notes and reviewing your visual aids, but have you practiced with the system you will be using for the live event? Do you know how slowly you'll need to talk? How loudly? Do you understand how participants will flag you for questions? Have you decided when in your presentation you will take questions? If your event involves multiple presenters, have you figured out how the handoff from one speaker to the next will happen? If you haven't practiced, you risk fumbling with the technology and your words during the live event, which can instantly sap the energy your meeting.

■ READY OR NOT, HERE IT IS

You probably have been in the audience of a virtual meeting or training session. If you have to make presentations as part of your job, then you may have already facilitated a virtual event. If you haven't, you will probably have to do it soon enough.

As with any task, you can learn the skills of virtual presenting. You can practice to get comfortable with it; you can learn to become good at it. Don't be like the townspeople of Topeka witnessing the first car crash, caught between feelings of apprehension at seeing something new and the relief that you haven't had to master it yet. Be proactive about gaining the skills. Take advantage of opportunities to learn and to practice.

After all, when's the last time you saw a horse-drawn carriage on your street?

Name: Bill Rosenthal

Company: Communispond, Inc.

Web Site: www.communispond.com

Biography: Celebrating its 41st anniversary in 2010, Communispond has been responsible for training more than 600,000 people worldwide on how to respond skillfully to any communications situation. Written by founder Kevin Daley, the book *Socratic Selling* was heralded by Ken Blanchard and scores of sales VPs as a powerful new methodology for partnering with customers. *The Full Force of Your Ideas: Mastering the Science of Persuasion*, coauthored by Kevin Daley and other Communispond senior faculty, is a standard on the art and science of communicating to influence.

Selling Philosophy: Socratic Selling Skills

Target Industries: Fortune 500

Best Sellers: Since 1969, Communispond's Socratic Selling Skills and Executive Presentation Skills have been the gold standard in instructed training. Additionally, the book *Socratic Selling* has been a huge success.

Sales Tip One: Don't rush to solve objections too quickly. Ask questions to ensure that (1) you've identified the true objection, and (2) isolated it to make sure there is nothing else you have to do, and then (3) resolve the issue.

Sales Tip Two: Rather than list features and benefits, always create a "Value Link," which is an explicit explanation of how your product or service will meet a customer's stated needs.

Sales Tip Three: Always open the conversation by inviting the customer to speak first and move the focus from your sales agenda to their needs.

Book One: *Talk Your Way to the Top*

Book Two: *Socratic Selling*

Book Three: *The Full Force of Your Ideas: Mastering the Science of Persuasion*

Product One: ProSpeak—iPhone/iPod Touch App: Tips & techniques for delivering high-impact presentations, including patent-pending "coaches" that give you feedback on your vocal and physical energy as you practice a presentation.

Product Two: The Full Force of Your Ideas: Mastering the Science of Persuasion (audio book, available at audiable.com, amazon.com, and so on)

Chapter 15

Do You Have an Effective Closing Strategy?

Tim Connor
Connor Resource Group

Closing the sale is not an event. It is

➤ Having effective prospecting skills.

➤ Based on an accurate understanding of the customer's real needs, desires, or problems.

➤ Developing professional probing skills.

➤ Having a closing awareness or attitude.

➤ Based on the desire to help your customer solve a problem.

➤ Related to everything that you have done up to the final close.

➤ A function of a positive relationship with this customer.

➤ Based on the ability to come from the customer's perspective.

➤ Grounded in the ability to create a high level of trust.

Attempting to close a sale without all of the above criteria is to invite a "no sale" result.

Most poor prospects attempt to get the salesperson to move to the close quickly and then base their decision not to buy on price or some other stalling tactic that most salespeople can't effectively handle. Therefore the entire sales process comes down to a nickel or some differential that you can't control.

Few salespeople have a "closing strategy"—a process that they follow with each and every sales opportunity. They ask a few questions, jump into the presentation (too soon, I might add), try to overcome any objections, and go for the close. The successful salespeople know the outcome long before they get to the end of this routine process, and they learn it by ensuring that each of the above items is in place before they ask their closing question.

People generally don't like to make buying decisions. The primary reason is that they don't want to make a poor or wrong decision. Traditional sales closing methods for years have been to ask people to make a decision. For example: Do you want it in green or red? (alternative choice). Do you want to use your pen or mine? (action close). Can we write up an order now? (direct close). Each of these closing techniques, even though it can work, has two fundamental problems: (1) It asks the prospect to make a decision and (2) the average salesperson is uncomfortable using it.

Since people don't like to make decisions, I suggest you stop asking them to. Here is a simple close that I have been using for over 30 years. Make the buying decision for the prospect, and ask the prospect to agree with the decision you have made. It goes like this. Let's do this, is that okay? Let's arrange for delivery on the 15th, is that okay? Let's get together on Thursday at 10 AM, is that okay?

This close works for three reasons: (1) It gets a decision made, but the prospect doesn't have to make it. By agreeing with you, the prospect, prospect in essence, makes the decision. I have found that people want decisions to be made, but don't want to make them. (2) It is common language. I guarantee in the next two to three days you will either say to someone or hear from someone "Let's go to the movie, okay?" "Let's go out to dinner tonight, okay?" (3) It is easy to remember and use, and it gets the job done.

When you use this close, the prospect has only three options: (1) They can go along with both your decision for them and your recommendation or (2) they can go along with your decision, but don't like your recommendation. In both cases, you have a close. (3) They go along with neither your decision nor your recommendation. No sale. However, using this with a qualified prospect gives you a two out of three closing percentage.

Trust me, it works. Try it and find out for yourself. Keep in mind that it can be used in any area of the sales process from getting appointments to confirming sales. Any time you want a decision from a prospect, you use the sentence beginning with "Let's . . ." and watch your sales skyrocket.

■ ARE YOU ASKING YOURSELF ENOUGH OF THE RIGHT QUESTIONS?

In life, if you fail to ask yourself the right questions, you may often find that you are living a delusional life. It is just as vital in your sales career that you also ask yourself the right questions if you hope to improve your performance, results, and income.

Thought-provoking and often difficult questions are the only way to get to any degree of self-truth and understanding. This self-knowledge is important if you are committed to changing behavior or improving any aspect of your sales effectiveness.

In selling I teach that the key to effective prospecting is the ability to ask the right questions, in the right way, and at the right time. In personal and career development this skill is just as critical. If you hope to discover the prospect's real buying motive or passion, you will learn it only by asking questions. If you hope to discover your own true weaknesses, you must be willing to identify your own blind spots and then work to eliminate them.

I would like to get you started with some of my favorite questions. I hope you find these helpful. Remember these are just a very small sampling of the questions you need to ask yourself periodically. I'll start with some more general ones and then get more specific. Again, keep in mind that these are just the tip of the iceberg.

➤ What is the one area of the sales process that you need to improve the most, for example, prospecting, presentations, time management, and so forth? Why?

➤ What are three habits you have that may be sabotaging your sales success?

➤ If you could start your sales career over again, knowing what you know now, what would you do differently? Why?

➤ What causes you the most discouragement in your sales career? Why?

➤ When you lose a sale after a great deal of time and effort, what is your typical reaction? Why?

➤ Do you feel you adequately prepare yourself for each new prospect encounter? If not, why not?

➤ Do you spend regular time each week in self-improvement activities? If yes, what? If no, why not?

➤ How do you handle price as a sales objection? Is what you are doing working?

➤ Where or how do you tend to waste the most time each week?

➤ Have you improved or changed any area of your sales skills in the past month? What? How? Why?

There are hundreds of additional questions you could ask yourself, so get to it!

I have a new sales development tool that you might want to consider. I use it with my personal coaching clients. It is called The Sales Competence Evaluation and Assessment Tool. It is 55 pages of questions that cover every aspect of the sales process to help you identify strengths and weaknesses. It is $49.00. If you want to order one, give me a call.

All of the successful people I know regardless of their career position or tenure have formed the habit of asking themselves the right questions, or they have hired a personal coach who helps them through this often difficult, yet necessary process. You cannot become successful in anything unless you are willing to grow, learn, and change. The right questions help you change for the right reasons and in the right ways, and before it is too late!

Name: Tim Connor

Company: Connor Resource Group

Web Site: www.timconnor.com

Biography: Tim is the president and CEO of Connor Resource Group and Peak Performance Institute and founder and CEO of Grow Charlotte. He has been a professional speaker, trainer, coach, consultant, and best-selling author for over 35 years. Since 1973 he has given over 4,000 presentations in 21 countries around the world.

Tim is a member of the National Speakers and is one of only 400 Certified Speaking Professionals in the world.

He is the best-selling author of over 75 books, including several international best sellers: *Soft Sell*, *81 Management Challenges*, *Your First Year in Sales*, and *91 Mistakes Smart Salespeople Make*.

Selling Philosophy: Focus on building relationships and not only on the transaction.

Target Industries: Food, manufacturing, housing and construction, high tech, financial

Best Sellers: Books: *Soft Sell*, in 18 languages with sales of over 750,000 copies since 1981; *Your First Year in Sales*, with sales of over 50,000 copies since 2005; *91 Mistakes Smart Salespeople Make* (2007); *81 Mistakes Smart Managers Make* (2007); *Success Is a Decision* (2007); CDs: 25 Sales Principles to Grow Your Business (2-CD set); 25 Motivation Principles to Find Peace and Happiness (2-CD set); 25 Success Principles to Achieve Your Dreams (2-CD set); Soft Sell (4-CD set); Success Is a Decision; Seminars: Two-Day Public Sales Boot Camps, custom in-house sales development programs

Sales Tip One: Make a sale and you will make a living. Sell a relationship and you will make a fortune. Successful salespeople focus on selling the relationship while poor salespeople focus on closing the transaction.

Sales Tip Two: Prospects buy when they are ready to buy, not when you need to sell. Just the fact that you or your company need to sell your products or services is not going get the sale closed.

Sales Tip Three: The biggest mistake poor salespeople make is that they talk too much. Your prospect will tell you what you need to tell them to sell them. Get information before you give information, and you will sell more every time.

Book One: *Soft Sell*

Book Two: *Your First Year in Sales*

Book Three: *91 Mistakes Smart Salespeople Make*

Product One: 25 Sales Principles to Grow Your Business (2-CD set)

Product Two: Soft Sell (4-CD set)

Product Three: 25 Success Principles to Achieve Your Dreams (2-CD set)

Sales Manager or Administrator?

John Holland
CustomerCentric Selling

In your sales career, have you reported to sales managers or sales administrators? Of the managers you've reported to, is there one you wish your son or daughter could work for in their first sales job? My first manager assigned quota, signed my expense reports, told me what to do, and frightened me into doing it. Subsequent managers left me alone. All were sales administrators, simply trying to deliver the revenue expected of them.

Titles containing the word *manager* imply assessment and development of staff. Most salespeople are motivated to succeed. Sub par performance is due to a shortage of activity or skill deficiencies. Sales administrators tell salespeople the *quantity* of activity (what and how much to do), but are unable to influence the *quality* of their efforts. The definition of insanity is doing the same thing repeatedly and expecting a different result. I'd like to suggest a few ways to address both the quantity and quality of a salesperson's activity.

■ AVOIDING TRAIN WRECKS

Bad years occur a month at a time. By the time a manager or salesperson realizes things are bad (18 percent year-to-date [YTD] in May?), it may be too late to salvage the year. Consider taking a salesperson's monthly quota and multiplying it by the length of an average sales cycle. Each month the manager can evaluate where the seller is YTD and apply an estimated historical close rate to his or her pipeline to get a sense of where they will be one sales cycle out. If they are behind, prospecting activity must be increased.

■ REMOVING THE ROSE-COLORED GLASSES

Another reason sellers fall behind is because their pipelines are full of stale opportunities. Totaling the line items yields a result larger than the GDP of many small countries. Sellers lack a sense of urgency to prospect when they apply unrealistically high probabilities to their pipeline and convince themselves things will be fine. A closer look may reveal that many are low-probability opportunities. One easy suggestion is to remove all proposals more than 45 days old, unless there are specific circumstances indicating that the opportunity is still viable. Getting the pipeline to more closely resemble reality is a critical step in determining how much effort must be placed on prospecting.

■ SPRING CLEANING

For stale proposals, consider having the salesperson inform prospects either in writing or verbally that the proposal or quote is being withdrawn because no action has been taken. I suggest sending a registered letter. One of two things will happen:

1. You don't hear back from the prospect, an indication that you should delete the prospect from the pipeline.
2. The prospect calls back, in which case you can attempt to resell the opportunity.

If the prospect wants to talk about reviving the proposal, the manager can make a joint call or conference call to determine if the opportunity is salvageable and show how to get things back on track.

■ QUALITY OF ACTIVITY

Once sellers understand they must find new opportunities, they stare at the phone and realize they not only despise cold telephone prospecting, they aren't good at it. Studies show the telephone is not the most effective way to contact businesspeople. The odds of reaching them improve with an initial letter or fax. Why not work with the seller to identify a vertical industry and likely title of a decision maker and help draft a one-page fax with a menu of likely business issues that title may be facing? The biggest challenge in making initial contacts is having executives understand the potential value of talking with a salesperson. A one-page fax or letter provides a basis to start a conversation with an executive or their assistant in order to schedule a call.

■ AVOID THE RFP TRAP

Salespeople like to put off prospecting, and those below quota want to add new opportunities to their pipelines. Unsolicited requests for proposal (RFPs) address both desires. Consider for a moment your win rate on RFPs that you didn't influence. Many of our clients discover their success rate is below 5 percent in such cases, because a vendor has already "wired" the requirements.

One technique to avoid the RFP trap is to contact the person issuing the RFP (seldom a decision maker), and request interviews with two or three titles that would be involved in the decision. Most likely, the salesperson will get pushback because the requirements are all listed within the document. At this point, the seller can explain that to do a professional job and justify the hours it will take to respond, the perspective of the other people is necessary. These interviews may also uncover some unique features or capabilities that could further improve the cost versus benefit.

When you consider that RFPs can take 20 or more hours to respond to, this is a perfectly reasonable request. If granted the interviews, attempt to bring out differentiators that will change the requirements. If denied access to the people you ask to talk to, consider sending a letter indicating you cannot respond. If the issuer of the RFP wants you to bid, you will do so provided you are granted access to the people requested.

This approach is counterintuitive, but consider your *competitors'* win rate on RFPs that *you* wire. The majority of RFPs have been wired, and other vendors are invited to bid only to provide leverage in negotiating the best possible terms and price with the preferred vendor.

■ PROACTIVE SALES MANAGEMENT

While sellers want to qualify opportunities, part of a manager's role is to disqualify those having a low probability of closing. Your salespersons' chance of success will be enhanced if you look one sales cycle ahead, and try to focus on not only how *much* to do, but also *how* to do it.

Name: John Holland

Company: CustomerCentric Selling

Web Site: http://customercentric.com

Biography: Leveraging over 20 years of experience in sales, sales management, and consulting, John Holland coauthored and cofounded *CustomerCentric Selling* (CCS) in 2002. His primary responsibility is evolving CCS intellectual property to reflect ongoing changes in how people and organizations buy.

As a sales consultant prior to launching CCS, Holland helped organizations design and implement standardized sales processes in such diverse sectors as professional services, technology, leasing, overnight delivery, logistics, language localization, office equipment, temporary housing, and financial services.

In 2007, Holland coauthored *Relational Capital* with Ed Wallace, and in 2009 coauthored *Rethinking the Sales Cycle* with Tim Young.

Selling Philosophy: Tactical selling to empower buyers

Target Industries: High technology, professional services, services

Best Sellers: CustomerCentric Selling workshops; Sales Ready Messaging workshops; consulting services

Sales Tip One: Change your definition of selling from convincing and persuading buyers to empowering them to understand how to use your offerings to achieve a goal or solve a problem.

Sales Tip Two: A buying cycle begins when a buyer shares a goal, a problem, or a need that can be addressed through the use of your offering.

Sales Tip Three: Executive buyers want to learn about business outcomes that can be achieved through the use of your offerings. Few want to learn all about your offerings.

Book One: *CustomerCentric Selling*

Book Two: *Rethinking the Sales Cycle*

Book Three: *Creating Relational Capital*

Product One: *CustomerCentric Selling* (audio book)

Chapter 17

Uncover Sales Opportunities

Dale Carnegie
Dale Carnegie & Associates

As sales leaders in our organizations, planning and conducting sales meetings can be one of the best uses of our time. Well-run sales meetings keep our sales teams focused and motivated. A relevant, well-planned sales meeting has the potential for being some of the most productive time in the sales week and an event that the team wants to attend every time. In order to get that productivity and enthusiasm out of our sales meetings, we need to ensure that the meeting is relevant to the salespeople and that the meeting is participatory. Salespeople are always hungry for ideas that work, and they are eager to share their own good ideas. One topic that is always a winner at sales meetings is how to uncover sales opportunities.

In today's business environment it is critical that sales professionals uncover sales opportunities rather than wait for leads or for customers to come to them. Many salespeople have been less than enthusiastic about prospecting and developing the right habits in this critical part of selling. The top sales professionals have found ways to make prospecting for new opportunities both fun and rewarding.

The best performers recognize that even if there is a lot currently in their sales pipeline, a regular percentage of their time must be focused on uncovering new sales opportunities. To further increase their odds of success, top salespeople have incorporated a varied prospecting approach as an integral part of building and sustaining their business. The best salespeople use an appropriate blend of activities on an ongoing basis. It is critical to determine the blend of prospecting activities that is right for you, based on your strengths, marketplace opportunities, and time management considerations.

Following are four ways to find new opportunities.

■ OPPORTUNITY CHART

Many times our best opportunities for uncovering new sales opportunities are with our existing customer base. Many average salespeople assume that our existing customers already know about everything that we have to offer them. In the past we have given them an overview of our product line or given them brochures that cover everything we do. The best salespeople realize that this is nonsense and opens us up to having our competitors walk into our accounts and service their additional need areas. One tool that addresses this issue is an Opportunity Chart. Create a spreadsheet that has a list of your full range of products and services in the left column. On the top row list your existing accounts. Then simply fill in which products and services each client is using with an A. Place a B in empty boxes that represent good selling opportunities for clients that are *not* using a product or service that could be a good match to their needs. The next step is to call clients to give them an update meeting to better understand their need areas that may match these additional products or services. Remember, we can't expect our existing clients to buy from us what they don't know we offer. The more products and services that our clients are purchasing from us, the more difficult it will be for our competitors to dislodge us from the account.

■ REFERRALS AND CENTERS OF INFLUENCE

Think of your buyers as partners who can refer you to a steady stream of new business. Salespeople quickly discover that using the name of someone the prospect knows, admires, or respects opens doors. Make it a habit at the conclusion of every sale to ask for a referral. Constantly ask your loyal customers whom they know that you should be calling. A key to getting ongoing referrals from your customers is to close the loop with them. Let them know the results of your contact with these referrals. Thank them again for having opened up these opportunities. You might want to take them to lunch or give them an inspirational book that you think is appropriate to their interests. This nurturing of your loyal customers can move them into becoming an ongoing Center of Influence for you. Keep this referral cycle going. Each time you give feedback to your customer by asking for additional referrals.

■ CHAMPIONS

Champions in your existing accounts can be excellent sources of new business opportunities. Look within your existing accounts for individuals who have benefited from your product or services in the past. Research indicates that your ideal choice would be someone who is not just satisfied with your results but believes that you have exceeded their expectations. Your champion should clearly understand what makes your products or services effective. He or she should be someone in an existing account that is well respected within their company, and is able to communicate to other people well. Nurture this relationship by staying in regular contact with them. An easy and nonintrusive way to do this is to e-mail them articles on topics that you know are of interest.

■ NETWORKING

Effective networking is a critical tool for uncovering new sales opportunities. Become involved in organizations that would include your typical prospects. It is important that you become active in a group to maximize your prospecting results. Begin by creating value for other people, even if it has little to do with your product or service. This will give you an opportunity to share your unique abilities and knowledge with others. Be sure to follow through on all of the commitments that you make so that you will build a credibility that will transfer into your sales efforts. Share your own contacts and network with others. To be successful in sales, it's not really who you know: It's who wants to know you. The more value you give, the more new sales opportunities will open up for you.

Name: Dale Carnegie

Company: Dale Carnegie & Associates

Web Site: www.dalecarnegie.com

Biography: Founded in 1912, Dale Carnegie Training has evolved from one man's belief in the power of self-improvement to a performance-based training company with offices worldwide. We focus on giving people in business the opportunity to sharpen their skills and improve their performance in order to build positive, steady, and profitable results.

Dale Carnegie Training is represented in all 50 states of the United States and in over 80 countries. Approximately seven million people have completed Dale Carnegie Training, which emphasizes practical principles and processes by designing programs that offer people the knowledge, skills, and practices they need to add value to their business.

Best Sellers: The Dale Carnegie Course in Effective Speaking and Human Relations, Sales Advantage Course, How to Sell Like a Pro Seminar

Sales Tip One: Start by developing an exciting vision statement for your future. The key is to become excited about your career in sales by establishing personally motivating goals. When developing a vision statement, think about what you would ultimately hope to accomplish as a result of your sales efforts. Take the time to create your own, personal mission statement. Your mission statement is a succinct outline of your implementation of your vision. These two statements should clearly articulate the essence of your beliefs and values, and define your place in the world. They will allow you to establish what is important and enable you to chart a course to your being a success.

Sales Tip Two: Building rapport and trust are critical to achieving sales success. Rapport is developed by having a combination of good people skills, effective listening, credibility, and professionalism. Rapport is a process that builds confidence and establishes a relationship between a customer and a salesperson. The sale will not proceed without establishing rapport with your prospective customer. Take a sincere interest in your customer. Listen and talk in terms of their interests. Focus in on how you can help them to achieve their objectives by using your product or service. Building rapport is something that good salespeople begin from the very first contact with a customer. Rapport building continues with every point of contact, whether it is face-to-face, on the telephone, or even in an e-mail. It is critical that a positive rapport be established within the first two minutes of a sales call, so make rapport building a priority.

Sales Tip Three: Sales professionals master the questioning and information gathering process to achieve greater sales results. The key is to discover customer needs in a natural, nonthreatening way that continues to build trust. Prior to meeting with your customer, make sure that you have reviewed their Web site so that you can speak the language of your customer and adapt your conversation with them to their environment. The most successful sales professionals will be able to master the art of asking effective questions. They will focus their questions to elicit valuable information that will enable the salesperson to ultimately develop a unique solution that will satisfy the client's needs and wants. If we listen carefully, the clients will tell us exactly what products and services we can sell, how we must present them, and how to appeal to their Dominant Buying Motive (why they want it).

18

How Can I Wow the Audience When Speaking?

Sam Deep
Ask Sam Deep

Imagine you just heard the best presentation of your life. Why was it so good? Why did it move you? Why are the ideas that you heard so memorable? It's because the presenter achieved many, if not all, of these 14 voice victories. He or she . . .

1. **Analyzed the audience.** The best presentations are shaped by the answers to these questions. How does the audience feel about you, the topic, and them being there? What hopes, dreams, and expectations do they hold? What are their values, beliefs, politics, and worldview? What about their mood and frame of mind? What prior knowledge do they have? Desire for detail? Attention span? What pleasure would they love to gain from your words? And most importantly, what *pain* do they desire to be set free from?

2. **Knew the speech purpose.** When your audience leaves your presence, what do you want them to think, feel, say, or do differently from when they entered your presence? In other words, what better future do you intend to create for them? This, not any topic or title, is the purpose of a great speech.

3. **Made a confident, decisive, and interest-evoking introduction.** When you read a novel, you often gauge the value of finishing the book while still on the first page. Audiences do the same to you. Let the first words out of your mouth be a quotation, a startling statistic, a strong or surprising statement, a thought-provoking rhetorical question, an immediate connection to a current or historical event, or the first lines of a story. These are far stronger openers than "Welcome to . . . ," "Good morning," or "I am pleased to have the opportunity."

4. **Clearly laid out the direction.** The popularity of automobile GPS systems demonstrates how much people want to know where they're going and *how they're going to get there*. As part of your introduction, show them a map they'll reference while you speak in the form of the three to five main points (generalizations) that will achieve your speech purpose.

5. **Provided well-organized and compelling content.** There's an admonition in the Bible about not casting pearls before swine. More often than we care to admit, what we're casting is more like pods than pearls. Rev up your content with these elements: (1) emotional appeals that tug at the heart or conscience; (2) logical appeals grounded in statistics and other objectively verified information; (3) quotations from experts or historical figures; (4) a selection you read from a page in a notable book; (5) eye-catching audiovisuals; (6) storytelling; (7) examples, analogies, and metaphors; (8) definitions ("Webster defines . . ."); (9) acronyms that help people remember key concepts; and (10) creative transitions from one section to another that give your listeners a smooth and enjoyable ride.

6. **Used correct, appropriate, and eloquent language.** There are many word snobs out there offended by incorrect, inappropriate, mispronounced, or ungrammatical expressions. These listeners long to have memorable and masterful word pictures painted for them. How's your verbal artistry?

7. **Spoke clearly and distinctly.** It's not what you say that counts, but how well you say it. Do you speak it in a way that is easily and enjoyably understood? Listen to your recorded voice. Do you need to work on your enunciation?

8. **Avoided unnecessary utterances.** Perhaps the most common comment written on the critiques I hand to my students following my observation of their presentations is "Too many ahs and ums." Also, stay away from overused words and pet phrases such as "basically," "incidentally," "and," "next," "to be truthful with you," "good question," and "the point I'm trying to make is . . ."

9. **Harnessed voice to good advantage.** By one research study, voice ("vocalics") has *five* times more impact on listeners than words. According to both research and Lowell Thomas, your emphasis, inflection, intonation, dialect, fluency, speed, and volume will determine the valuing of your ideas as much as anything else.

10. **Used influential body language, especially eye contact.** The same study reported in number seven concluded that body language is *eight* times more influential than word choice. Presenters are immeasurably helped or hindered by it. A few tips: (1) look your listeners in the eyes; (2) look at notes or PowerPoint slides as little as possible; (3) smile and keep your eyebrows up much of the time;

(4) maintain an erect posture—don't lean on anything; (5) allow hand gestures to be natural and comfortable for you—one of the few bad hand positions is to put both hands in your pockets at the same time; (6) never point at the audience with your index finger—use an open palm with four fingers together; (7) dress with slightly more formality than your audience, with impeccable grooming; (8) don't do anything repeatedly, such adjusting your glasses or scratching your ear.

11. **Used PowerPoint or other audiovisual aids effectively.** Any form of audiovisual aids can markedly advance the fortunes of your presentations. Unfortunately, the misuse of PowerPoint has so often had the opposite effect on message impact. Adopt these ideas to enhance this medium: (1) use a light-colored sans serif font with shadow background on a dark-colored slide; (2) don't ever have so much information on a slide that you are prompted to say, "I realize you can't read this number, but . . ."; (3) make limited use of "custom animation" for formal business presentations; (4) make limited use of graphic art, and for sophisticated audiences, source your pictures from professional Web sites; (5) darken only the part of the room directly in front of the screen; and (6) view your slides on a computer screen put between you and your audience—turn to look at the screen they're looking at only to single out an idea.

12. **Controlled nervousness.** Some presenters don't have much nervousness to control; most have a lot (you're not alone.) Try one or more of these suggestions: (1) study this list so well that you are confidently educated on the components of great presentations; (2) don't use this list to focus fearfully on what *not* to do the next time you present, but rather excitedly on what you *will* do; (3) recognize that a moderate amount of podium anxiety is actually energizing and positive; (4) prepare so thoroughly that you become the expert in the room on your topic; (5) rehearse just enough to know the first three sentence of your opening and to feel assured about entry into each of your main points, not so much that you sound lifeless; (6) get familiar with the room in advance; if possible, rehearse there; (7) deep breathing, stretching, or a bit of exercise just before you go on will calm you; clenched fists may help as well; (8) when you begin, filling the room with your voice expends nervous energy; (9) look for a friendly (familiar?) face or two in the audience for reassurance; (10) involve the audience in some way on by getting them on their feet, asking you questions, or registering opinions.

13. **Handled questions and the audience with aplomb.** Great presenters actually look forward to questions. They are so knowledgeable on their topic that no matter what the question, their answer can't help but sound good. They also have a plan for handling disruptions

or other audience trouble. When someone says, "I disagree with you!" they know to resolves matters with, "What did I say that you disagree with?" not "Why do you disagree with me?"

14. **Closed confidently and decisively.** Some would argue that the introduction and conclusion are the two most important segments of your presentation. Certainly, they are the two stages during which your energy needs to peak and for which you need to be most thoroughly prepared. They are not the throwaway that too many presenters treat them as.

Martin Luther King Jr. longed for the day that people would be judged by the "content of their character" rather than the color of their skin. In like manner, I wish I could tell you that the content of your speech will determine its success more than how you deliver it. But I can't tell you that. As you've just seen, the "color of your presentation's skin" will trump its content.

Name: Sam Deep

Company: Ask Sam Deep

Web Site: www.asksamdeep.com

Biography: Following 15 years in teaching and administration at the University of Pittsburgh, Sam Deep has worked with over 150,000 people and written *What to Say to Get What You Want, Yes, You Can!, Smart Moves for People in Charge, Close the Deal*, and *Lost and Found*, which have sold over one million copies in 14 languages.

Sam was adjunct professor of leadership in the Business School at Carnegie Mellon University from 1998 to 2006. He hosted "Following the Leader" for eight years—a Pittsburgh radio show on leadership. He is now an executive coach for clients in leadership and sales.

Selling Philosophy: Prospects are the ones who close deals

Target Industries: Not limited

Best Sellers: *Close the Deal*, Executive Coaching, Seminars on Leadership, Emotional Intelligence, Closing More Deals, Providing Exceptional Customer Service, Facilitation of Team Building, and Strategic Execution

Sales Tip One: Keep prospects talking (at least 70 percent of the time) with raised eyebrows, a half-smile, and plenty of questions.

Sales Tip Two: Look for opportunities to discover a "center set"—a deep-seated value that both you and the prospect share.

Sales Tip Three: Ask questions that elicit the pain prospects are experiencing that influenced them to agree to hear your story.

Book One: *Close the Deal*

Book Two: *Yes, You Can!*

Book Three: *Smart Moves for People in Charge*

The Good Life Rules

Bryan J. Dodge
Dodge Development

In the sales profession, the real question is "What is it?" I believe that the sales profession is freedom—freedom to look in the mirror every morning and choose who and how many you want to help today; freedom to choose where you want to go and what you want to have in life. Life is too short not to be happy, and life is too long not to do well. When I ask myself what sales is, I answer that I truly believe it is a wonderful profession that gives you the freedom to choose.

What is the difference between a good sales program and others? Many sales programs talk about what to say, how to say it, and when to say it. Good training is all about the things that will produce the greatest results not only in your sales career, but most important, in your life. A good sales program starts with a clear understanding of the difference between the "how" in life and the "why" in life. Those who focus on the "how" usually end up working for those who focus on the "why." Put another way, those who focus on the "how" are motivated; those who focus on the "why" are inspired for life. A good training program is inspiration-based, not motivation-based. We've all heard this before, and it's true: If you take an idiot and motivate him, all you have is a motivated idiot. I think we can all agree that method might not yield the overall results that you are looking for. It is your focus that will produce the activities needed to produce the greatest results for you and your business. Remember, the sales profession is the highest-paid hard work and the lowest-paid easy work there is. So first you must have a great work ethic; if you don't, you will learn the hard way.

Why did you choose sales? I believe that most people who are in sales didn't go to school to become a sales professional. It became an obvious choice after graduation. In my book *Becoming the Obvious Choice*, I talk about the steps that you have to take to be the obvious choice for potential and current customers. This article focuses on why the sales profession became the obvious choice for you. In most professions, you decide what you want to be and you choose a school based on your aspirations, like being a doctor or lawyer. What were most salespeople doing at that point in their lives? Having fun! We are really good at that. As each of my children went off to college, I reminded them of the three laws: (1) have fun, (2) have fun, and (3) get good grades. Most salespeople are really good at the first two laws; it is the third one that makes us different. That is why the sales profession is the best friend you will ever have in life. It requires that you learn one great lesson in life—to work harder on yourself than you do on your job. When you do that, you can watch how your job will go back to work for you. You are learning not because somebody told you to, but because you want to.

Why is it that some people can do so well in sales while others fail? The true key to success is having a love for why people buy, not how to get them to buy the product. For the past 18 years, I've been amazed at how much money companies put into "how-to" sales training for their sales teams. Very little training covers the "why" regarding a customer's need to buy—the key word being *need*. You may really think you know why they need to buy; however, the focus you have and the agenda you have chosen for yourself will override why the customer wants and needs to buy your product. Keep in mind that you shouldn't sell to every person you give a presentation to. If you want higher ground in the sales profession, you have to be able to say no. Your product or service may not be the obvious choice for that particular customer. If you can't say no, you can't grow. Each time a customer says yes to my product or service, I always thank them and let them know my job has just begun. It is not the sale that I focus on, it is the life-long relationship I'm excited about.

Name: Bryan J. Dodge

Company: Dodge Development, Inc.

Web Site: www.bryandodge.com

Biography: Bryan Dodge has been a keynote speaker for conferences and conventions in corporate America since 1989. He hosts the "Build a Better You" radio show on ABC's premier Dallas/Fort Worth radio station, WBAP 820 AM. Bryan has authored several professional development audio programs and coauthored the book *Becoming the Obvious Choice*, which has sold over 200,000 copies. His new book, *The Good Life Rules: Eight Keys to Being Your Best at Work and at Play*, made Borders Books' best-seller list.

Bryan's programs are designed to accelerate your personal and professional success through the educational truths that will produce the favorable results you're looking for.

Selling Philosophy: Relationship selling

Target Industries: All sales industries

Best Sellers: *How to Build a Better You*, CD on personal and professional development

Sales Tip One: The foundational key to being a good salesperson is a willingness to change. At every level of any company, only a few people are willing to make this commitment to change for success when it comes to sales. If you want to achieve your goals, then you need to escalate and maximize your self-potential. Many people have given a high priority to revitalization or transformation, yet consciously or unconsciously, their efforts are frustrated. Why? Whether they realize it or not, everyone is remarkably resistant to change and growth. Change involves shifting your strategies and thought processes, but it also means something more. You will have to permanently rekindle your individual responsibility and motivation for a lasting positive change in your behavior at work and at home.

Sales Tip Two: Resist the urge to fight against or become completely absorbed by rejection. Instead, find a way to use objections positively and productively. We gain so much more in life by focusing on moving forward rather than looking backward. Rather than getting hung up on how you got into a certain mess or how somebody said no to you or your offer, become enthusiastic about where you can go from here. Remember that the sales profession is the highest-paid hard work or the lowest-paid easy work. Each and every day, start out your day by choosing to give yourself a raise.

Sales Tip Three: There are two questions that determine whether or not a prospect will really listen to what you have to offer. Do they like you? Do they trust you? During my training seminars, I always talk about being versatile and adapting styles without changing the core of what makes us different. We must be consistent with the needs and comfort levels of the prospect. If you learn to manage this task successfully, your prospect will like and trust you. Once you put these two factors into place, positive decisions are made, and objections are only a sign of true interest. If they don't like or trust you, they will find a way to delay. Always remember that salespeople are not born; they learn the skills that make them the best in their field.

Book One: *The Good Life Rules: Eight Keys to Being Your Best at Work and at Play* (coauthored by Bryan Dodge and Matthew Rudy)

Book Two: *Becoming the Obvious Choice* (coauthored by Bryan Dodge and David Cottrell)

Product One: *How to Build a Better You* (CD)

Product Two: *How to Build a Complete Sales Person* (CD and workbook)

Product Three: *How to Build a Purpose-Guided Life* (CD and workbook)

Product Four: "Debtwork," educational online software on debt elimination, coauthored with Keith Phildius

Chapter 20

Five Traits of a Great Sales Leader

Barry Farber
Farber Training Systems

What makes a great sales leader? There is no one remarkable secret. In fact, great sales leaders play many roles, and they play them all well. At various times, a great sales leader is a time management supervisor, a meeting planner, a contest coordinator, a talent scout, a coach, a trainer, and a psychiatrist. All these roles together, well-executed, make for a great leader. However, there are five key areas in which the best sales leaders excel. A great leader:

1. **Is passionate and enthusiastic.** These traits are transferred to the entire sales team. If the leader is negative, everyone else will be pulled down. How do great leaders keep a realistically positive attitude going? Great leaders are great readers; they read everything they can find about their craft and industry. They seek out mentors whose wisdom and experience can help them achieve their goals, and they encourage their reps to do the same. They surround themselves with high-quality people. Which brings us to the fact that a great leader . . .

2. **Recruits great salespeople.** Many managers don't start recruiting until someone is leaving, which means they often settle for second best in order to fill a gap. Great leaders are always on the lookout for talented people. One way they do that is to carry two-sided business cards to give out to people they meet in other businesses who demonstrate great sales and service skills. One side of the card contains the standard name, address, and phone number. On the other side it says, ''I was very impressed with your service and professionalism. Please call me if you're ever looking for a career.'' The success of a sales leader is in direct proportion to the success of the team, which is why it's critical to hire the best people. That, in turn, enables great leaders to . . .

3. **Make their numbers *through* their people, not *for* them.** The greatest difficulty a sales team can have is when a manager closes for all his people. When that happens, the reps never learn the skills they need to move to the highest level of self-sufficiency. It's instinctive for a manager to want to jump in and save a sale, but the message that this sends is that you don't trust your reps. Then, when the reps are on their own, they won't have the experience of handling tough situations themselves. Close a deal for a rep and you've made one sale; teach him or her how to close and you've made a career. Great leaders teach their reps by . . .

4. **Leading by example.** Great sales leaders are out in the field with their people 60 to 80 percent of the time. There's an old saying that goes *"Don't expect what you don't inspect."* If you don't inspect your rep's performance in the field, you can't expect improvement. A day in the field not only shows you how your reps are doing, it gives you first-hand knowledge of what customers are thinking and what their needs are, based on your products and services. Most important, sales reps respect a leader who knows what it's like in the trenches. Surprise your reps every once in a while by saying, "I thought I'd travel with you today and see how you're doing." How was their day planned? How do they do on calls? What prospecting methods are they using? Great leaders don't just know their sales reps; they . . .

5. **Understand their reps' individual strengths and weaknesses.** They're able to ask nondirective questions ("What do you think you could have done differently on that call?" "What was your objective?"). When the reps say it, they own it; when the manager says it, they doubt it. Great leaders know what motivates each rep and how to get the best from everyone. They expect excellence. If your reps know you think they're capable of reaching greater heights, they'll strive for them.

Your role as a leader is to help your people succeed. There may be substantial monetary rewards to being a great sales leader, but the greatest reward is to have helped others reach their goals. When we're gone, our material possessions don't really matter. Our greatest legacy is the people we've helped to improve who are left to help others in the same way.

Name: Barry Farber

Company: Farber Training Systems, Inc.

Web Site: www.BarryFarber.com

Biography: Rated top speaker of the year by *Successful Meetings* magazine, Barry Farber helps industries break through the sales clutter and land more deals.

Clients include AT&T, American Express, ESPN/ABC Sports, Merck, Nestle Waters, State Farm Insurance, UPS, and Verizon.

He is the best-selling author of 11 books in over 25 languages.

Barry's programs highlight real-world applications from his day-to-day activities. He was the broker and agent for the $7 million Evel Knievel Six Flags roller coaster, winner of three Telly Awards, and also nominated for an Emmy as executive producer of the *Jackie Mason Television Show*, and he is co-inventor and marketer of the FoldzFlat Pen.

Selling Philosophy: Break through barriers

Target Industries: Unlimited

Best Sellers: Seminar: Breaking through Barriers in Sales, Business, and Life; Books: *Barry Farber's Guide to Handling Sales Objections, Superstar Sales Manager's Secrets*, and *Diamond in the Rough*; CDs: State of the Art Selling (6-CD program) and Diamond in the Rough (6-CD program)

Sales Tip One: Understand your customers' customers. Understand their competition. Understand their marketplace. This will give you more opportunities to tie in the value of your product and how it impacts their industry challenges.

Sales Tip Two: Listen more than you talk. You can't really start to build a relationship until you're locked into the other person's hot buttons and listening to what makes them tick. Nobody has ever listened themselves out of a sale.

Sales Tip Three: Find common ground. Doing so allows you to connect with contacts on a deeper level, whether it's in sports, hobbies, or family interests. When my customers start talking about their kids and how they are interested in the same activities as my own, the conversation flows.

Product One: State of the Art Selling (6-CD program)

Product Two: Diamond in the Rough (6-CD program)

Reconstructing the Pieces of the Sales Puzzle

Jonathan Farrington
The JF Consultancy

I first began to recognize the need to benchmark sales performance more objectively and more rigorously over 25 years ago. My motivation was strong because I knew I was wasting thousands—if not hundreds of thousands—of dollars on sales skills training programs that failed to provide me with a proper return on my considerable investment. But I needed to prove my theory because without an accurate analysis of my requirements, I would continue to abdicate that responsibility to the training providers, most of whom had only their own interests at heart.

By taking an analytical approach, I arrived at the following equation:

$$\text{Attitude} + \text{Skills} + \text{Process} + \text{Knowledge} = \text{Success}$$

My initial reasoning was this: *Attitude* is fundamental to any achievement, because individuals with the right attitude are far more likely to embrace the essential *Skills*, recognize the control that *Process* brings, and have the desire to continually expand their *Knowledge*.

As the "tools of the trade," *Skills* have to be developed on an ongoing basis. They also need to be specific because too much time can be wasted overburdening employees with inappropriate and irrelevant skills, without any identifiable plan for their future requirements.

Process brings organization, efficiency, and control, both for the individual and for management. Effective process provides objective analysis and indicators that can be benchmarked and accurately measured.

Then there is the need to build in *Knowledge*; knowledge of products, the industry, market sectors, competitors, business, the salesperson's own company, and, last but not least, the salesperson's own self!

So what did my "new breed" of salesperson look like?

For a start, he or she has progressed from the more traditional Lone Ranger approach of selling to a more team-based, consultative style.

Our research shows that a consultative salesperson needs to fulfill three basic roles: Business Consultant, Long-Term Ally, and Strategic Orchestrator.

By combining all three roles, salespeople are better equipped to develop and maintain long-term relationships with clients.

■ BUSINESS CONSULTANT

Gone are the days in which a salesperson could simply walk into an office, establish a good rapport with the client, show that he or she has thorough knowledge of the products and services, and clinch the sale.

Nowadays, the emphasis is on establishing long-term, mutually beneficial relationships. To achieve this, the salesperson needs to earn the right to continue discussions with a client. Before moving ahead to sell products or services, the salesperson needs to reassure the client of his or her integrity, reliability, and ability to understand and recommend the appropriate solution. This can be done by demonstrating:

➤ Up-to-date knowledge of business news and current affairs.

Best practices include reading newspapers, magazines, journals, trade publications, and other sources of business information; maintaining membership in appropriate professional organizations; acknowledging gaps in knowledge and taking steps to fill them; and locating or developing databases with information on customers, their industries, and their own customers. (This is where social media really comes into its own.)

➤ An in-depth understanding of the customer's industry, company, and strategies, as well as an appreciation of "the big picture."

Best practices require gaining an understanding of the issues at all levels of the customer's organization, including strategic, departmental, and individual needs; seeking to understand the customer's perceptions of market trends and company direction; plus recognizing potential product and service needs.

➤ A readiness to exchange information and ideas between the supplier and client organization.

Best practices include familiarizing the customer with your own industry and companies; sharing useful business information even if it does not directly impact the sales effort; and demonstrating the cost-cutting or revenue-producing benefits of your products and services.

➤ The ability to listen and absorb information.

Best practices include refining the way you identify the customer's needs by asking the right questions and listening actively to customer comments; speaking at the listener's level of knowledge; using stories and analogies effectively; and asking for feedback on the clarity of your message. By demonstrating comprehensive knowledge, outstanding communication skills, and the proper attitude, the salesperson earns the right to move beyond the role of supplier to that of a valued business consultant.

■ STRATEGIC ORCHESTRATOR

To fulfill this role, the salesperson needs to be seen as the key person responsible for engineering the appropriate solution. This involves coordinating all of the information, resources, and activities needed to support customers before, during, and after the sale. It means enlisting support from specialist colleagues—hence the move away from the Lone Ranger approach.

According to our research, effective Strategic Orchestrators have mastered the following competencies:

➤ Knowledge of their own company's structure

➤ Expertise in developing and managing a team

➤ Ability to manage priorities and performance

➤ Ability to coordinate delivery and service to customers

➤ Efficiency

➤ Flexibility

Customers of Strategic Orchestrators express a high level of confidence in the salesperson and his or her organization.

This increased confidence can lead to faster buying decisions, more repeat business, and strengthened links between customer and supplier organizations. Working as Strategic Orchestrators, salespeople are also able to develop their organization's capacity for team selling.

■ LONG-TERM ALLY

Since the key to differentiation is in forging closer links with clients, the role of the Long-Term Ally is a crucial one. Once the salesperson has earned the right, it is important to develop and maintain the relationship.

As the term suggests, acting as a Long-Term Ally involves maintaining contact with the client even when there is no immediate prospect for a sale. It also suggests that the salesperson needs to be committed to the long-term development of the relationship. Our research shows that top salespeople demonstrate this commitment by continuously looking for ways to:

➤ Build interpersonal trust

➤ Create and maintain a positive image of the sales organization

➤ Inspire respect for their company

➤ Show genuine concern for their customers' short- and long-term interests

➤ Identify ways to strengthen the quality of their business relationships

➤ Help the customer meet needs within his or her organization

➤ Deal with issues openly and honestly

➤ Deliver on promises

It is also crucial for the salesperson to ensure that the relationship between the organizations is mutually beneficial. In other words, it is essential to build and honor the expectation that reaching agreements will mean good business for both parties.

A long-term approach ultimately proves more profitable since the customer will recognize that the salesperson has a committed interest and is giving honest and open advice. This inevitably encourages the customer to trust the salesperson and to view him or her as a colleague rather than as an opponent.

So there you have it. But you know, all of this was built on a simple platform—a simple formula:

$$Attitude + Skills + Process + Knowledge = Success$$

The pieces of the sales puzzle have now been reconstructed.

Name: Jonathan Farrington

Company: The JF Consultancy

Web Site: www.jonathanfarrington.com

Biography: Jonathan Farrington is a globally recognized business coach, mentor, author, and sales strategist who has guided hundreds of companies and thousands of individuals worldwide toward optimum performance levels.

He is chairman of The JF Corportation, CEO of Top Sales Associates, and senior partner at The JF Consultancy, based in London and Paris.

He is also the creator of Top Sales World, the most significant online sales community, International Sales Strategist for AllBusiness/Hoovers, and writes The JF Blogit, a highly popular daily blog for dedicated business professionals (see www.thejfblogit.co.uk).

Jonathan is the chairman of the Executive Board at Top Sales Experts (www .topsalesexperts.com).

Selling Philosophy: Attitude + Skills + Knowledge + Process = Success

Target Industries: Nonspecific

Best Sellers: *The JF Sales Academy, ASP Profile*

Sales Tip One: The greatest compliment a customer can pay you is to describe you as professional. Don't worry about being liked; be respected! Customers do not buy from you because they like you, but rather because they are prepared to trust you.

Sales Tip Two: Selling on price is simply a cop-out. You must value your expertise, your products, and your services, and price accordingly. Remember the definition of *negotiation*: To arrange forms of business by means of discussion, conference, or meetings; to transact business; to bargain; to exchange security for cash. It doesn't mention giving anything away for less than its real value.

Sales Tip Three: This may seem obvious, but it cannot be emphasized enough: You are not selling to an organization or to a conglomerate, but to actual, real people. It is important to remember that all people are different, so you cannot sell the same way to everyone. Second, no two sales are the same, even if they are made to the same company under similar circumstances.

Chapter 22

Manage Salespeople as You Would Invest

Jeffrey Fox
Fox & Co.

If, as an investor, you had the choice to invest your money in the stock of a growing, high-potential company, or invest in a stodgy, low-performing company, where would you put your money? You would probably invest your money in the company that is a high performer. Yet, every single day business managers and sales managers not only violate the "invest in performance" rule, they do exactly the opposite. Every day bosses spend more time with low-performing, problem employees than they do with their best people. Every day sales managers invest their time with the bottom sales people, and practically ignore their superstars. Every day managers cut the marketing, selling, and training budgets of their strong businesses and growing product lines to "offset" underperforming parts of the company. Just as the smart investor would never knowingly invest in a stodgy business, so, too, should managers not invest their precious time in low performers. Instead, managers should pour the coals to growth opportunities.

Managers should overinvest in businesses and products and people that have big potential. Sales managers should spend 60 percent of their time in the field with their superstar salespeople. They must spend 30 percent of their field time with their high-potential salespeople. They must invest no more that 10 percent of their time with low-performing salespeople. However, studies of sales managers' calendars show that too many managers spend about 50 percent of their time with the problematical reps. Sales managers must be objective and realistic about getting rid of poor performers . . . even if the manager hired the rep, even if the manager feels he or she has a "fatherly or motherly" relationship to the rep, or even if the sales rep is a nice guy.

Some sales managers think that superstars don't need help, or don't want help. Even when superstars say they don't need anything and prefer to go it alone, it is rare that superstars really mean it, and it is always a sales management mistake to believe it. The best salespeople use their managers to close deals, or to give approvals to customer requests that the salesperson can't. The best salespeople are learners. If the sales manager has something important to teach, the good salespeople will learn it. High performers appreciate the recognition of an attentive sales manager.

Invest your company's money where it gets the highest return. Don't cut investments that are giving a good return on that investment. Don't invest in losing situations. Don't let losing situations drain investment from winning situations. Invest your time with winners. Invest your sales management time and your selling time as you would invest your own money.

Then watch that money grow.

Name: Jeffrey Fox

Company: Fox & Co., Inc.

Web Site: http://foxandcompany.com

Biography: Mr. Fox is the founder of Fox & Co., a marketing and selling skills consulting firm in Chester, Connecticut. He has written 11 books on management and selling. His books have been *New York Times*, *Wall Street Journal*, and *BusinessWeek* best sellers and published in over 30 languages, having been number-one best sellers in France, Russia, Turkey, and Hong Kong. Mr. Fox was *Sales and Marketing Magazine*'s "Marketer of the Year," and the American Marketing Association's "Marketer of the Year." He gives workshops and speeches to senior executives and salespeople worldwide. He graduated from Trinity College (where he was Trustee) and has an MBA from Harvard Business School.

Selling Philosophy: Companies don't buy products; they buy money. Fox & Co. developed dollarization, a selling strategy that quantifies any product benefit into dollars and cents.

Target Industries: Business-to-business marketers

Best Sellers: Workshops and books on dollarization, or economic value selling, and on how to become a rainmaker; and case-study-based programs on sales manager leadership.

Sales Tip One: Companies do not buy anything. They invest to get increased revenues, reduced costs, and avoidance of catastrophic events . . . and nothing else.

Sales Tip Two: Salespeople who sell money are partners. People who sell products with a price list are vendors.

Sales Tip Three: A rainmaker's motto is "If you don't do business with me, we both lose."

Book One: *How to Become a Rainmaker*

Book Two: *The Dollarization Discipline*

Book Three: *How to Become CEO*

Product One: All 11 books are available on CD.

The Amazing Power of Testimonials

Colleen Francis
Engage Selling Solutions

If you are interested in selling more to more people in less time, testimonials are a vital part of the formula for success. If you're not using them in your business right now, you are missing out on one of the most profitable sales tools . . . ever!

Why are testimonials so effective? Consider the story of legendary businessman W. Clement Stone. He built what would one day become a multibillion-dollar empire by selling fire-insurance policies door-to-door during the Great Depression.

There's no denying that Clem's knack for people skills was a big part of his success. And he also had a little something extra—a binder overflowing with testimonials from his customers. Legend has it that that binder never left his side when he was knocking on all those doors. There was a good reason for that. It was chock full of stories— and not just happy accounts from people who were satisfied. It also told painful stories about how people had lost houses, husbands, and wives to misfortune . . . and how *relieved* they were that, thanks to Clem, they had signed on the dotted line long ago, and now were covered. Frankly, after reading stories out of that binder, it's hard to imagine how *anyone* could ever say no to him!

That's the amazing power of testimonials. They work because they reaffirm for others what you already know is true. Testimonials back up what you say with social proof. They validate the feelings a prospect has for you, and they do so with a message that is unmistakably authentic and sincere.

Testimonials are a form of communication that, according to a McKinsey & Company study, influences three quarters of all purchasing decisions. W. Clement Stone understood this—and that's precisely the insight that you can get working for you, no matter what you're selling. So let's look at how you can harness the power of your satisfied customers.

■ KEEP YOUR EARS OPEN WIDE

When you're talking to your customers on the phone, does anyone ever share with you a little story about how they were able to make great use of your product or service? Check your e-mail. Has anyone ever sent you a note just to say "thanks for the great work" on that last job you did for them? Or have you ever received glowing feedback from a client who responded to a survey that you sent out? Each of those is a testimonial, just waiting for you to act on it.

■ ASK AND YOU SHALL RECEIVE

Remember our friend W. Clement Stone? He once famously said: *"If there is something to gain and nothing to lose by asking, by all means ask!"* When a client says great things about you, about your work or the products you sell, give them the opportunity to turn that praise into a testimonial. Simply ask: "I'd really love it if I could include what you just said in my client testimonials. Would that be okay?"

■ NEWER CUSTOMERS ARE PASSIONATE

Get on the phone and call your newest customers. No matter which industry you serve, the most passionate praise that you'll receive for your work and the service you sell tends to come from customers with whom you have only recently started doing business.

■ REPEAT CUSTOMERS ARE WISE AND INSIGHTFUL

But by all means don't ignore the wisdom of your repeat customers! Your repeat customers provide people with important insight about what makes your product or service worth coming back to—again and again. So make a point of calling up those clients whom you have been doing business with for a long time and ask them why it is that they call on you.

■ MAKE IT EASY FOR PEOPLE

One of the most common comments you'll hear from clients when asking for testimonials is "Well, I'm really not much of a writer, so it's hard for me to put it in words." The real power of testimonials comes from the fact that they're not polished; instead, they're authentic and from the heart. A client we work with recently shared with me his secret about how he addresses this issue in his business. "When asking a client for a testimonial, I simply say, 'Finish this sentence in 25 words or less: I really like (product/service/person) because . . .' This really works because it gets right to the point about the feelings people have for you, for what you do, and for what you're selling."

■ DO UNTO OTHERS

Write testimonials for others with whom you do business and whose services have impressed you. It's a good thing to do. It also helps to deepen those all-important reciprocal relationships. Plus, the testimonials you write about others send an important message to everyone about the high standards you have, not only as a supplier but also as a buyer. Social networking sites are handy tools for doing this. Not only does it encourage reciprocity, it also helps you become part of a trusted network of professionals.

■ MAKE TESTIMONIALS NOTICEABLE

As you build your collection of testimonials, you'll need to find a place where people can read them. Lucky for you, you have a lot more choices than W. Clement Stone did back in the Depression. Not only can you put them all in a binder to show prospects, you can also include testimonials in other products . . . and most won't cost you much more than a few minutes of your time. Here are some examples. Create a special Web page devoted to testimonials. Consider ways that you can include sample quotes from that collection and feature them in steady rotation on the main page of your site. Another approach is to include a new testimonial on the signature line of every outbound e-mail. The possibilities are endless, and the potential benefits to your sales record can be quite amazing . . . even lucrative!

Name: Colleen Francis

Company: Engage Selling Solutions

Web Site: www.engageselling.com

Biography: A successful sales professional for 20 years, Colleen understands the challenges of selling in today's market and how traditional sales techniques from decades ago often fall short. She has studied the habits of the top 10 percent of sales performers from Fortune 500 companies to small businesses. She has complemented conventional wisdom of the sales process with these proven techniques for a sales approach that gets results today. Colleen is unwavering in her commitment to sales training that makes a lasting and meaningful impact on the corporate bottom line.

Selling Philosophy: Sales strategies proven in today's tough market

Target Industries: Business-to-business

Best Sellers: Keynote speaking and training for organizations, and coaching for sales executives and business owners.

Sales Tip One: This is a question I am asked more than almost any others. How do I capture the prospect's interest on a new introduction call? The best way to get their attention is to share the success story of a company like theirs. Success stories, or client testimonials, or proof . . . whatever you want to call them, they work the best to capture the prospect's interest and make them hungry to hear more.

Sales Tip Two: One of the situations we've all faced is when a client tells you that your price is too high. The best thing you can do in this situation is *nothing*. Pause, and say nothing for a few seconds to see what the prospect does next.

Sales Tip Three: The first thing you should do immediately after completing a sale is to send your customer a thank-you note. This overlooked and undervalued step can be the most profitable thing you do in your business: It helps the buyer feel secure in their decision, it builds a strong relationship with your new client because it shows that you care, and it sets you apart from all the other vendors they use because you actually took the time to thank them personally, while others did not.

Book One: *Honesty Sells* (coauthored with Steven Gaffney)

Book Two: *Prospecting for Profit*

Book Three: *Secrets of the Top 10 Percent*

Want More Sales? Stop "Selling" and Start Helping Clients Succeed

Mahan Khalsa

FranklinCovey Sales Performance Solutions

One of our senior consultants within the FranklinCovey Sales Performance Practice, a former CEO of a clinical research company, has shared the following experience he had when a large pharmaceutical company approached him about being a pivotal trial site for evaluating a new compound. Winning this study with this client would have been significant for our colleague.

After meeting with our colleague and reviewing the compound, the client began discussing expectations for the study, including a fairly short time line. Right away, our colleague could see that the time line would be too short to develop valid data. He raised this concern with the client, emphasizing that the short time line could compromise the quality of the data produced by the study.

The client's response was that our colleague's competitors were claiming they could conduct a valid study within the time line. Still concerned, our colleague responded that he didn't feel like *his* company could do it, and he reiterated that he didn't want to jeopardize the client's data by rushing through the study.

To get a better understanding of what the client was looking at, our colleague respectfully asked if they would share who the competitors were. After hearing who they were, he commented that they were good companies, they did good work, and if they were saying they could conduct the study within the time line, perhaps they could. Our colleague then repeated that he wasn't comfortable committing his company to the time line and having the client invest a great deal of money at the risk of producing less-than-valid results.

The client, however, had made up their minds to go with a competitor. They thanked our colleague for his time, and parted ways.

Could our colleague have fought harder? Changed his pitch? Looked for ways to meet the time line as the competitors claimed they could do? The answer is yes, if his intent was primarily to get what *he* wanted—the sale. But at what cost?

■ THE REASONS PEOPLE BUY

From our work in complex sales and with organizations all over the world, buyers say their top four reasons for selecting a product/service provider are:

1. **Relationship, compatibility, and fit:** They are a good match with our people, processes, and culture.

2. **In-depth understanding of our business:** They work for and demonstrate an in-depth knowledge of our business.

3. **Chemistry of the provider team:** They work well together as a team, and we have confidence they can deliver.

4. **Technical/industry expertise:** They have what it takes to deliver the right solution.

The first three reasons for why buyers buy are all about people. Why? People buy. People sell. People deliver. The cost, though, of delivering a product or service solution without successfully addressing the first three reasons is trust and value. When a belief that just because we *can* offer something overrides considerations about whether the client *should* buy what we offer, we sell to our own interests, often at the expense of the client's interests, our value to them, and ultimately, their trust in us.

For clients to trust us, they have to believe not only that we *can* do something—that we have the expertise—but that we will *only* do something if it's compatible with the client's best interests. For clients to trust us, they have to perceive our intent as one where we help them get what *they* want in a way *they* feel good about.

To have our story end here, with a deal lost—and seemingly lost deliberately—demonstrates the critical role of intent in a way not always as readily discernable with examples of deals won. Our colleague's intent wasn't to sell his solution, per se, but to advocate on behalf of the best solution in the client's interest. If "best" in the client's mind meant "faster," even after pointing out his concerns, then our colleague's intent was to allow the client to go with that decision.

But of course, the story doesn't end there. Three months later, the client called up our colleague; going with the competition wasn't working out (for all the reasons our colleague had pointed out three months ago). Could they revisit having his company conduct the study within a time line our colleague believed would yield valid data? This time, our colleague won the deal.

The client returned not only because of the value they already knew existed in what our colleague's services could offer but also because of the value of trust that colleague had created by focusing his intent on the client's success and being willing to put their success ahead of his own.

The bottom line is that the value of a product or service lies as much in the relationship between buyer and seller as it does in the product or service itself—in all four reasons people buy. At the heart of this value is trust—trust based on the intent of the seller not to sell but to help the client succeed. This intent frees those who sell to truly look at the client's business issues objectively without pushing their solutions—easing the way for open, honest discussion where mutually beneficial possibilities can be explored.

■ INTENT COUNTS MORE THAN TECHNIQUE

Intent counts more than technique, although this is not to say that technique doesn't count. Rather, selling with an eye toward helping clients succeed isn't about using techniques and processes that get clients to say "yes" to us; it's about providing a series of steps that allow clients to make intelligent decisions in their own best interest. When we facilitate such a process, as our colleague did, we engender trust, open the flow of information, and create value.

Because clients will assign us intent whether we want them to or not, we need to do all we can to convey an honest intent to help them succeed. And while a client-focused intent shows in many ways, the following three ways can clearly let clients know where your intent lies.

1. **A clearly perceived intent to help clients succeed creates a container of safety.** The safer a client feels, the more likely they are to open up, engage with us, share information, and explore possibilities for solutions. To create this container of safety, we need to enable open, intelligent dialogue and questions, ask hard questions in a soft way, peel down for answers, and challenge our own thinking. Through this kind of effective communication, clients actually share

what they feel and think to be true, and feel safe and open to exploring mutually beneficial opportunities.

Incidentally—or not so incidentally—this container of safety also means the client feels safe sharing negative thoughts or feelings, such as wanting to go with the competitor because their price is better.

2. **Well-meaning intentions must be supported by demonstrable and credible expertise.** This expertise should be in all four areas behind the four reasons people buy—not just expertise in the product or services we provide, but in our relationship, compatibility, and fit with the client; our in-depth understanding of their business; and the chemistry of our provider team. When we demonstrate expertise around all four areas, clients trust us and are willing to collaborate toward win-win results.

3. **Good intentions should not turn us into pushovers.** Potential clients will push back, ask questions, and object to options. And they should. How you handle these pushbacks should be as congruent with an intent to help them succeed as any other interaction. Consequently, your responses should seek, rather than to defend yourself or your product or service, to openly and honestly examine the client's true concerns and to explore whether or not they can reasonably be resolved.

The whole premise behind intent is this: Don't try to sell your clients—help them succeed. This intent can enable you to successfully address all four reasons people buy by allowing you and potential clients to get real, talk and listen authentically, collaborate, enable clients to make decisions in their own best interests, craft exact solutions, deliver critical business results—and create mutual, long-term success.

Company: FranklinCovey Sales Performance Practice

Web Site: www.franklincovey.com/spg

Biography: FranklinCovey's Sales Performance Practice, founded by Mahan Khalsa, trains and coaches clients to dramatically improve their execution around sales planning, process, development of leadership and selling skills, and winning deals. Mahan is the author of *Let's Get Real or Let's Not Play: The Demise of Dysfunctional Selling and the Advent of Helping Clients Succeed*. This book, which shares a commonsense sales philosophy and methodology for complex sales, is foundational to the work of the Sales Performance Practice.

FranklinCovey's Sales Performance Practice shows clients how to dramatically increase sales by earning the trust and confidence of their clients and sharpening their sales execution.

Selling Philosophy: Value-based, consultative selling. Sales isn't just about selling. It's about Helping Clients Succeed.

Target Industries: Professional services, IT, banking, consulting, insurance, telecommunications, finance

Best Sellers: Helping Clients Succeed Consultative Sales Training, Coaching, and Consulting; *Let's Get Real or Let's Not Play: The Demise of Dysfunctional Selling and the Advent of Helping Clients Succeed*; *Let's Get Real or Let's Not Play: Transforming the Buyer/Seller Relationship*

Sales Tip One: Sales isn't just about selling. It's about Helping Clients Succeed. Get maniacal about helping clients succeed versus "selling" them something.

Sales Tip Two: Intent counts more than technique. Win more sales by concentrating on your client's numbers rather than on your own. Focus your intent on helping clients succeed.

Sales Tip Three: Solutions have no inherent value. Your knowledge, services, and solutions derive value only from the problems they solve or the results they create for your clients. So cocreate value propositions with your clients.

Book One: *Let's Get Real or Let's Not Play: The Demise of Dysfunctional Selling and the Advent of Helping Clients Succeed*

Product One: *Let's Get Real or Let's Not Play* (audiobook CD set)

Product Two: Let's Get Real or Let's Not Play (introduction CD)

Product Three: Helping Clients Succeed (audio CD)

Chapter 25

Your Next Job Interview

Thomas A. Freese
QBS Research

Make no mistake, a job interview is definitely a sales situation. It turns out that the opposite is also true—every sales call is also a job interview. In addition to customers making a decision to buy your product or service, first customers need to buy into you. And, whether you manage a small business, support the organization in a customer service role, or are an executive in a Fortune 500 company, you are selling yourself every day.

The time you spend during an employment interview is probably the closest you will ever come to actually *selling yourself*. It's also a pure sale in which, in addition to being responsible for selling yourself, you are also the product that's being sold.

For too long, sellers have highlighted product features and highlighted company benefits in the hopes that "a good story" would skew the purchase decision in their direction. Given the current business climate, the more likely scenario is that you will encounter competitors who offer alternate solutions that customers perceive as very similar.

For example, what's the real difference between Allstate, State Farm, and Nationwide insurance companies? I suppose it comes down to whether you want to be "in good hands," want a company that is "like a good neighbor," or have Nationwide "on your side." From a pure product perspective, there's not much difference between the three. The same can be said of the entire financial services industry—you can purchase the same hundred shares of Coca-Cola stock from any number of brokerage houses, often located within blocks of each other. Realtors face a similar challenge, in which they are all competing to sell the same inventory of listed homes at the same market price. Even the drug companies face stiffer competition, with an evolving pipeline of new formulary alternatives coming on the market.

When rival companies battle to outdescribe each other, comparable solutions tend to get commoditized and end up sounding the same to the customer. When this occurs, you can no longer count on the product itself for differentiation.

Don't get me wrong, the image of your company and the quality of your product offering is definitely important. But in most industries, the person representing a product or service will have a greater influence on customer perception than the product itself.

I have been beating the drum on the whole notion of *selling yourself* for many years. Your success in business and in life will ultimately hinge on the impressions other people form about *you*. Whether you are interviewing for an employment opportunity, or selling a product or service, the person evaluating you will certainly be forming an impression about a host of intangibles, including your credibility, expertise, knowledge, experience, vision, integrity, customer focus, and follow-up on verbal commitments. The extent to which you possess these character traits is not even the issue. The challenge is being able to effectively convey these intangible qualities in a way that enhances the value you bring to customers, partners, colleagues, and upward, to your management chain.

During your next job interview, what will differentiate you from the previous candidate who was quietly ushered out of the hiring manager's office minutes before you arrived? During a sales call, what separates you from the seven or eight salespeople who called on the customer and delivered their best sales pitch?

Winning the sale when you have a huge product advantage or when the economy is booming is terrific. That's just not the game anymore. Now, your success is going to be more dependent on how to win when the sale comes down to a virtual tie. What are you doing that makes you different, and will give you the nod over other equally qualified options?

Moving forward, salespeople will play a more crucial role in their own success, and it has never been more important for individuals to be seen as invaluable to their company, customers, colleagues, and partners.

Name: Thomas A. Freese

Company: QBS Research, Inc.

Web Site: www.QBSresearch.com

Biography: For seven consecutive years, Tom Freese not only exceeded his sales quota, he doubled it.

After 17-plus years in corporate sales and management, Tom packaged his unique approach into a proven methodology called Question Based Selling. He has since trained thousands of salespeople who have implemented QBS at client corporations all over the world.

As founder and president of QBS Research, Inc., Tom has published five books, been featured in numerous articles, and is now considered to be one of the foremost authorities on sales effectiveness training, buyer motivation, and competitive positioning strategies.

Selling Philosophy: Differentiation through question-based selling

Target Industries: Technology, health care, financial, insurance, real estate, manufactured goods, professional services, automotive, and any other businesses in which value must be perceived by customers and differentiated by the salesperson.

Best Sellers: Books: *Secrets of Question Based Selling, It Only Takes 1 Percent to Have a Competitive Edge in Sales, The New Era of Salesmanship, The Question Based Parent*, and *Selling Yourself in Today's Competitive Marketplace*. QBS Research, Inc., the company that developed and delivers *Question Based Selling*, provides a menu of customized QBS Methodology Training and Advanced QBS Coaching courses to client organizations all over the world. In addition, we offer QBS audio CDs.

Sales Tip One: Much of the sales training that is currently available today was developed 20 or more years ago. Meanwhile, almost everyone agrees that the selling environment has changed dramatically in the past 20 years. Who cares what worked back in 1985? Instead of looking backward, salespeople and managers need to reengineer their approach around proven skills, techniques, and strategies that will give their respective teams an unfair advantage moving forward.

Sales Tip Two: Customers still buy from who they like. That's true. But rather than trying to get customers to like your personality with the hope that they will then purchase your product or service, the playing field has changed. Now, selling is more about conveying value than ever before. If you are indeed a valuable resource and you are perceived as such, you will have tons of friends and buyers within your target list of accounts. If a salesperson today isn't seen as more purposeful, valuable, and relevant compared to the competition, don't be surprised if customers won't want to deal with that sales person at all.

Sales Tip Three: Rather than trying to motivate sellers in the hopes of making them more effective, the real opportunity to boost performance calls for the exact opposite. Teaching sales teams how to be more effective, in ways that directly translate into increased productivity for the company (and higher bonuses for them), is the best way to get people excited!

Book One: See Best Sellers (earlier section)

Product One: QBS Methodology Audio CD Program (6 CDs/12 tracks)

Chapter 26

Nine Biggest Mistakes Salespeople Make in Their Presentations

Patricia Fripp
A Speaker for All Reasons

Salespeople are incredible. Like Hollywood actors, whenever they open their mouths, they are putting themselves and their company on the line, taking a risk in the hope of a favorable outcome. Just like actors, even the best, most experienced salesperson can use some coaching and polishing now and then.

Here are the nine most common mistakes that my sales clients are making at the beginning of our coaching sessions. By the time we're through, they've learned how to avoid them.

1. Unclear Thinking. If you can't describe the objective of your interaction in one sentence, you may be guilty of fuzzy focus: trying to say too much at once. You'll confuse your listener, and that doesn't make the sale. Decide exactly what you want and need to accomplish in this contact. What would be a positive outcome? For example, imagine that a busy executive says, "You have exactly ten minutes of my time to tell me what you want me to know about your company. In one sentence, tell me how I should describe your benefits when I talk to my managers tomorrow." At any stage of the sales process, you should know in advance why you are interacting, what benefits you are offering your prospect or client, and what you'd like the next step to be.

2. No Clear Structure. Make it easy for your prospect to follow what you are saying, whether in a casual conversation or a formal presentation of information and ideas. They'll remember it better—and you will too. Otherwise, you may forget to make a key point. If you waffle or ramble, you lose your listeners. Even for a conversation, mentally outline your objectives.

What key "Points of Wisdom" do you want the prospect to remember? How will you illustrate each point? What colorful examples will your prospect be able to repeat three days later?

3. Talking Too Much. Salespeople often talk too much about themselves and their service or product. They make a speech rather than having an exchange or interaction, otherwise known as conversation. The key to connecting with a client is conversation; the secret of client conversation is to ask questions; the quality of client information received depends on the quality of the questions—and waiting for, and listening to, the *answers*! In fact, a successful encounter early in the sales process should probably be mostly open-ended questions, the kind that require essay answers rather than simply "yes" or "no." And don't rush on with preprogrammed questions that pay no attention to the answer you've just received. Learn to listen, even pausing to wait for further comments. Silence draws people out.

4. No Memorable Stories. People rarely remember your exact words. Instead, they remember the mental images your words inspire. Support your key points with vivid, relevant stories. Help them "make the movie" in their minds by using memorable characters, exciting situations, intriguing dialogue, suspense, and humor.

5. No Third-Person Endorsements. There's a limit to how many bold claims you can make about your company and product results, but there is *no* limit to the words of praise you can put in the mouths of your delighted clients. Use case histories of your clients' success stories about the benefits they received from your service or product. When you are using their actual dialogue, you can say much more glowing things about yourself and your company than you could if the words were your own. Choose clients that your prospects can connect with.

It helps if the star of your story holds a similar position to your prospect. You can't say, "Do business with me, and you'll get promoted," but you can give a specific example of someone who phoned, e-mailed, or wrote you that this happened to them. "Just last week," you might say, "I heard from Mary Smith. She's the Payroll Manager at Amalgamated Systems. She said that changing their payroll system to our company not only made them more efficient, but they cut their costs 10 percent. She told me, 'You made me look good in the eyes of management. Thanks to you, I received a promotion!'" That's an emotional connection.

6. No Emotional Connection. The most powerful communication combines both intellectual and emotional connections. Intellectual means appealing to educated self-interest with data and reasoned arguments. Emotion comes from engaging the listeners' imaginations, involving them in your illustrative stories by frequent use of the word "you" and by answering their unspoken question, "What's in this for me?" Obviously, a customer is going to justify doing business with you for specific analytical reasons. What gives you the edge—what I like to call the "unfair advantage"—is creating an emotional connection too. Build this emotional connection by using stories with characters that they can relate to and by providing a high You/I ratio, using the word "you" as often as possible and talking from their point of view.

My recommendation is that you make telephone appointments with your happiest clients. Tell them you would like to use their stories about working with you as an endorsement, and ask permission to tape-record your conversation. Then just let them talk. The more they say, encouraged now and then by a question from you, the better their stories and quotes will be. Finally, select the best quotes from what they've said.

7. No Pauses. Few sales presentations have enough pauses. Good music and good communication both contain changes of pace, pauses, and full rests. This is when listeners think about important points you've just made. If you rush on at full speed to crowd in as much information as possible, chances are you've left your prospects back at the station. Give them enough time to ask a question or even time to think over what has been said. Pauses allow pondering and understanding.

8. Not Having a Strong Opening and Closing. Engage your audience immediately with a powerful, relevant opening that includes them. For example, "You have an awesome responsibility." Then fill in what it is: increasing sales, reducing errors, cutting overhead, whatever your product can help your prospect do. Another excellent strategy is to do some research. Then you can say, "Congratulations on your company's recent success," and describe it. Or "I love your new commercials." Most salespeople start by talking about their company. Talk about your prospect, instead.

9. Misusing Technology. Too many salespeople rely too much on their PowerPoint and not enough on making an emotional connection. Do not start preparing your presentation with the PowerPoint. Bottom line: Make technology a support, not a crutch.

When you learn to avoid these nine common traps, you're on your way to being a "star" of the sales world, ready to accept an award for your dazzling performance.

Name: Patricia Fripp, CSP, CPAE

Company: A Speaker for All Reasons

Web Site: www.fripp.com

Biography: Patricia Fripp is a Hall of Fame speaker, sales presentation skills trainer, and executive speech coach. *Meetings and Conventions* magazine calls Patricia "one of the country's 10 most electrifying speakers." *Kiplinger's Personal Finance* says "Patricia Fripp's speaking school is the sixth best way you can invest in yourself." She is also the author of *Make It! So You Don't Have to Fake It* and *Get What You Want*.

Selling Philosophy: Don't focus on making a lot of money, focus on becoming the type of person others want to do business with and you will make a lot of money.

Target Industries: High-tech, consulting, financial services, anyone who gives presentations and sells high-price products or services

Best Sellers: *Help, I Have to Give a Speech! . . . or Yippee! I'm Excited to Give a Speech; The Successful Sales Call Value Pack; How to Outline, Design, and Deliver a Dynamic Speech or Sales Presentation; Compelling Stories: The Inside Secrets;* and *Preparing and Presenting Powerful Talks*

Sales Tip One: There's a limit to how many bold claims you can make about your company and product results, but there is no limit to the words of praise you can put in the mouths of your delighted clients. Use case histories of your clients' success stories about the benefits they received from your service or product.

Sales Tip Two: What gives you the edge—what I like to call the "unfair advantage"— is creating an emotional connection. Build this emotional connection by using stories with characters that they can relate to and by providing a high You/I ratio, using the word "you" as often as possible and talking from their point of view.

Sales Tip Three: Get on the same wavelength as your prospects. Are you providing the big picture and generalities when your listeners are hungry for details, facts, and specific how-tos, or are you drowning them in data when they need to position themselves with an overview and find out why they should care?

Book One: *Make It, So You Don't Have to Fake It!*

Book Two: *Get What You Want*

Book Three: *Speaking Secrets of the Masters*

Product One: Compelling Stories: The Inside Secrets

Product Two: The Successful Sales Call Value Pack

Product Three: How to Outline, Design, and Deliver a Dynamic Speech or Sales Presentation

Chapter 27

Seven Cold-Calling Secrets Even the Sales Gurus Don't Know

Ari Galper
Unlock the Game

More and more e-mails are arriving in my in-box from people who hate cold calling. Here's what they're saying:

➤ "Cold calling terrifies me."
➤ "The phone feels like a 10,000-pound weight."
➤ "Every time I have to make a cold call, I freeze up."

Cold calling the old way is a painful struggle.

But you can make it a productive and positive experience by changing your mind-set and cold calling the *new* way.

To show you what I mean, here are seven cold-calling ideas that even the sales gurus don't know.

1. Change Your Mental Objective before You Make the Call. If you're like most people who make cold calls, you're hoping to make a sale—or at least an appointment—before you even pick up the phone.

The problem is, the people you call somehow always pick up on your mind-set immediately.

They sense that you're focused on your goals and interests, rather than on finding out what *they* might need or want.

This short-circuits the whole process of communication and trust building.

Here's the benefit of changing your mental objective before you make the call: It takes away the frenzy of working yourself up mentally to pick up the phone.

All the feelings of rejection and fear come from getting wrapped up in our expectations and hoping for an outcome when it's premature to even be thinking about an outcome.

So try this. Practice shifting your mental focus to thinking, "When I make this call, I'm going to build a conversation so that a level of trust can emerge, allowing us to exchange information back and forth so we can both determine if there's a fit or not."

2. Understand the Mind-Set of the Person You're Calling. Let's say you're at your office and you're working away. Your phone rings and someone says, "Hello, my name's Mark. I'm with Financial Solutions International. We offer a broad array of financial solutions. Do you have a few minutes?"

What would go through your mind?

Probably something like this: "Uh-oh, another salesperson. I'm about to be sold something. How fast can I get this person off the phone?"

In other words, it's basically over at "Hello," and the salesperson ends up rejected.

The moment you use the old cold-calling approach—the traditional pitch about who you are and what you have to offer, which all the sales gurus have been teaching for years—you trigger the negative "salesperson" stereotype in the mind of the person you've called, and that means immediate rejection.

I call it "The Wall."

The problem is with *how* you're selling, not *what* you're selling. This is an area that's been ignored in the world of selling. We've all been trained to try to push prospects into a "yes" response on the first call. But that creates sales pressure.

But, if you learn to really understand and put yourself in the mind-set of the person you call, you'll find it easier to avoid triggering The Wall.

It's that fear of rejection that makes cold calling so frightening. Instead, start thinking about language that will engage people and not language that will trigger rejection.

3. Identify a Core Problem That You Can Solve. We've all learned that when we begin a conversation with a prospect, we should talk about ourselves, our product, and our solution. Then we hope that the person connects with what we've just told them. Right?

But when you offer your pitch or your solution without first involving your prospect by talking about a core problem that they might be having, you're talking about yourself, not them. And that's a problem.

Prospects connect when they feel that you understand their issues before you start to talk about your solutions. When people feel understood, they don't put up The Wall. They remain open to talking with you.

Here's an example based on my own experience. I offer Unlock the Game as a new approach in selling. When I call a vice president of sales, I would never start out with, "Hi, my name is Ari, I'm with Unlock the Game, and I offer the newest technique in selling, and I wonder if you have a few minutes to talk now." Instead, I wouldn't even pick up the phone without first identifying one or more problems that I know VPs often have with their sales teams—problems that Unlock the Game can solve. For example, one common problem is when sales teams and salespeople spend time chasing prospects who have no intention of buying.

So I would start by asking, "Are you grappling with issues around your sales team chasing prospects who lead them on without any intention of buying?" Come up with two or three specific core problems that your product or service solves. (Avoid generic problem phrases like "cut costs" or "increase revenue." They're too vague.)

4. Start with a Dialogue, Not a Presentation. Let's return to the goal of a cold call, which is to create a two-way dialogue, engaging prospects in a conversation. We're not trying to set the person up for a yes or no. That's the *old* way of cold calling.

This new cold-calling approach is designed to engage people in a natural conversation—the kind you might have with a friend. This lets both of you decide whether it's worth your time to pursue the conversation further.

The key here is never to assume beforehand that your prospect should buy what you have to offer, even if they're a 100 percent fit with the profile of the "perfect customer." If you go into the call with that assumption, prospects will pick up on it and The Wall will go up, no matter how sincere you are.

Avoid assuming anything about making a sale before you make a call. For one thing, you have no idea whether prospects can buy what you have because you know nothing about their priorities, their decision-making process, their budget, and so forth.

If you assume that you're going to sell them something on that first call, you're setting yourself up for failure. That's the core problem with traditional old-style cold calling.

Stay focused on opening a dialogue and determining if it makes sense to continue the conversation.

5. Start with Your Core Problem Question. Once you know what problems you solve, you also know exactly what to say when you make a call. It's simple. You begin with, "Hi, my name is Ari. Maybe you can help me out for a moment."

How would you respond if someone said that to you? Probably, "Sure, how can I help you?" or "Sure, what do you need?" That's how most people would respond to a relaxed opening phrase like that. It's a natural reaction.

The thing is, when you ask for help, you're also telling the truth because you don't have any idea whether you can help the prospect or not. That's why this new approach is based on honesty and truthfulness. That's why you're in a very good place to begin with.

When the prospect replies, "Sure, how can I help you?," you don't respond by launching into a pitch about what you have to offer. Instead, you go right into talking about the core problem to find out whether it's a problem for the prospect.

So you say, "I'm just giving you a call to see if you folks are grappling (and the key word here is 'grappling') with any issues around your sales team chasing prospects who turn out to never have any intention of buying."

No pitch, no introduction, nothing about me. I just step directly into their world. The purpose of my question is to open the conversation and develop enough trust so they'll feel comfortable having a conversation.

That's the secret of building trust on calls. It's the missing link in the whole process of cold calling.

6. Recognize and Diffuse Hidden Pressures. Hidden sales pressures that make The Wall go up can take a lot of forms. For example, "enthusiasm" can send the message that you're assuming that what you have is the right fit for the prospect. That can send pressure over the phone to your prospect.

You must be able to engage people in a natural conversation. Think of it as calling a friend. Let your voice be natural, calm, relaxed . . . easygoing. If you show enthusiasm on your initial call, you'll probably trigger the hidden sales pressure that triggers your prospect to reject you.

Another element of hidden pressure is trying to control the call and move it to a "next step." The moment you begin trying to direct your prospect into your "sales process," there is a very high likelihood that you can "turn off" your prospect's willingness to share with you the details of their situation.

It's important to allow the conversation to evolve naturally and to have milestones or checkpoints throughout your call so that you can assess if there is a fit between you and the person you are speaking with.

7. Determine a Fit. Now, suppose that you're on a call and it's going well, with good dialogue going back and forth. You're reaching a natural conclusion . . . and what happens?

In the old method of cold calling, we panic. We feel we're going to lose the opportunity, so we try to close the sale or at least to book an appointment. But this puts pressure on the prospect, and you run the risk of The Wall going up again.

Here's a step that most people miss when they cold call. As soon as they realize that prospects have a need for their solution, they start thinking, "Great, that means they're interested." What they don't ask is, "Is this need a top priority for you or your organization to solve, or is it something that's been on the back burner for a while?"

In other words, even if you both determine that there is a problem you can solve, you have to ask whether solving it is a priority. Sometimes there's no budget, or it isn't the right time. It's important that you find this out, because months later you may regret not knowing this earlier.

Name: Ari Galper

Company: Unlock the Game

Web Site: www.UnlocktheGame.com

Biography: Ari Galper is the creator of Unlock the Game, a new sales mind-set that overturns the notion of selling as we know it today.

With a master's degree in Instructional Design and over a decade of experience creating breakthrough sales strategies for global companies like UPS and QUALCOMM, Ari is the world's leading authority on building trust in the world of selling.

Ari's deep understanding of human communication and how it can be maximized in the sales process has led him to redefine how to connect with people over the phone.

Unlock the Game has helped thousands of people all over the world.

Selling Philosophy: No-pressure telephone selling skills

Target Industries: Insurance, financial, technology, real estate, consultants, services, small businesses

Best Sellers: Unlock the Game Mastery Coaching Program

Sales Tip One: Stop the sales pitch. Start a conversation.

Sales Tip Two: Never chase prospects. Instead, get to the truth of whether there's a fit or not.

Sales Tip Three: Hidden sales pressure causes rejection. Eliminate sales pressure, and you'll never experience rejection.

Product One: Unlock the Game Mastery Coaching Program—(includes DVDs, CDs, e-books, and ongoing personal coaching)

Chapter 28

Learn More, Sell More

Daniel Miller
General Physics Corporation

The importance of knowing your product has never been more critical than it is today—the access to product information, company information, and even your personal background increases every day. Consider how you have personally changed your buying habits in the past decade. In the past, you may have taken a look at a consumer guide magazine for product reviews. If you were evaluating a high-ticket item, you may have even spent a little money to learn the inside information on the product price and margin. You'd then go to competing retail establishments to learn more about the product and evaluate the best deal (often you'd only make it to one place if the salesperson was good). The deal was done.

Today, information (good and bad) can be found quickly and inexpensively through Internet research. A good sales organization understands the importance of information and creates strategies to take advantage of technology.

First, consider how information technology is used, and what type of information is available. Whether you deal with business-to-business sales or retail sales, the customer now uses technology in several ways: product assessment, value assessment, company brand integrity, and to check the reputation of the people with whom they are directly dealing (particularly in B2B sales). This means that it is important for companies to protect information around their company, product, and people. This requires both a technical and professional approach to managing information.

What does this mean to the sales professional? First, your reputation is at risk! As you create professional (or personal) profiles online, consider who will be reading them, who contributes to your profiles, and what message it sends about yourself. If you don't believe you're being checked out online . . . well, you're wrong. That funny posting and photo of that party in college is not what you want your customers to read. Limit access to personal information and even consider who you allow to view and comment on your information. Do join professional groups—just be careful about what you post and what you say.

Second, know what's "out there" about your company and product. Your customer should never have more knowledge about your product than you. Your sales team should be checking out what people say about your product, and you should be sharing that information with your company. Don't feel that you need to personally correct misinformation; it is best that your company manage the message and information that is available on the Internet. But do know what's being said and consider what questions customers may ask based on what they read. Remember, a blog or wiki can be written and (in the case of a wiki) changed by just about anyone. At the company level, the marketing and communications team should be continually keeping information current on the Internet and ensuring its correctness.

Last, take advantage of that same technology that your customers use to close the sale. Learn about your product as well as your competitors' products and services. Understand how you are different and consider the values that your product, service, and company offer over your competitors. Become an advocate of your product, and your passion and energy will be apparent to the customer. As you learn more, you really will sell more!

Name: Daniel Miller

Company: General Physics Corporation

Web Site: www.gpworldwide.com

Biography: Dan Miller, a Senior Vice President of General Physics Corporation (GP), has led new business launches and product sales initiatives at GP for much of his career. In his role, he developed marketing and sales strategies for the development of GP's highly successful training outsourcing practice and custom learning solutions. Using his extensive global experience, he led business development initiatives in North America, Latin America, and, most recently, the Asia-Pacific region, where he headed the establishment of new operations in Shanghai, China; Chennai, India; and Singapore.

Mr. Miller is a graduate of the New School University, holds an MBA from Anderson University, and has earned an Executive Certificate in International Management from Thunderbird University.

Selling Philosophy: Learn more, sell more.

Target Industries: Business-to-business and retail sales

Best Sellers: Custom Sales Solutions: Learning strategies, product sales training, blended learning, custom e-learning, customer-facing solutions, outsourced sales trainers, sales-training program administration

Sales Tip One: Take advantage of technology; create and manage the message your customer receives about your product and services.

Sales Tip Two: Learn to learn and you'll sell more. Learn methodologies, learn your product, and learn about your customer.

Sales Tip Three: Be an advocate of your product, and your passion will be well received by the customer.

29

Are You a Sales Rock Star, or Just a Member of the Band?

Jeffrey Gitomer
Buy Gitomer

When you hear a boss talk about his or her *best* salesperson, he or she often refers to him or her as a "rock star." It's the highest praise your boss can give someone on your team. Every salesperson aspires to be referred to in that manner, but very few make the grade.

Many have the talent. Many get to the top of the charts for a month or two. Many make it to number one, and then burn out. What's your rating on the top 100 chart?

If you're a rock star, it means . . .

You have superior talent—you can play and sing.

You can harmonize with everyone else in the band.

You write song lyrics that others identify with.

Your fans don't just like you—they *love* you!

You have a confidence, a swagger.

You are a leader (at least of your own band).

You are respected by your peers as a talented player.

People write about you.

People will pay to see you play.

People want (and will pay for) your autograph.

You have proven yourself over time with consistent quality.

It also means . . .

You know the business of rock and roll.

You have real wealth, not just money.

You could qualify for the Rock and Roll Hall of Fame.

You could become a legend.

How do you view yourself? Are you like Bruce Springsteen of the E Street Band? Or are you just a roadie?

Most salespeople would like to *think* of themselves as a sales rock star, but don't display the talent to match the definition. The fact is, someone else referring to you as a rock star is more powerful than you calling yourself one.

But there's much more to it than that.

Ever think about what it took for a rock star to become one? To achieve in the face of doubting people or naysayers? To face rejection after rejection? To spend endless hours practicing and rehearsing? To hone their skills and craft—and *then* to achieve the acceptance of others? Make some sales, and some more sales, and finally produce a number-one song and play it at a sellout concert.

That's a lot of work—no wonder so few people make it.

And yes, there is a dark side to the personality of some rock stars. They become self-abusive. Many put their own lights out early. Luckily in sales, there's not that much time to get into trouble.

It's true, not all rock stars are pure—but neither are regular people. Rock stars, like anyone else, have to have discipline, make the right choices, and take consistently good actions . . . kind of like you.

Think about the rock stars that are familiar to you: Elvis, the Beatles, Bruce Springsteen (the real boss), Little Richard, Buddy Holly, Tina Turner, Roy Orbison, Carole King, Stevie Wonder, Paul Simon, and Aretha Franklin. These people (and lots more like them) achieved their status by putting in years of hard work. All of them *love* what they do. They wouldn't trade their position or situation for anything in the world. They rose from humble beginnings to stardom by taking advantage of their talent.

How are you taking advantage of your talent?

How much do you *love* what you do?

How hard are you willing to work?

How positive can you remain in the face of obstacles?

The love of what you do, combined with your belief in what you do, will not determine your success. It will determine how hard you will work and how dedicated you will be to achieve it. Success just shows up from there.

If you want to become a sales rock star, I think that's *great*. If you want others to refer to you as a rock star, I think that's *greater*. And if you are willing to apply the discipline that it takes to emerge as a rock star, I think that's the *greatest*, and I support you in every way.

Note of confidence: For the past 30 years of selling, I have always played rock and roll music on my way to a sale. It sets my own internal positive and upbeat tone.

If you want to become a rock star, the first thing you gotta do is learn how to rock.

If you're interested in a few more ideas on what it takes to become a sales rock star, go to www.gitomer.com, register if you're a first-time visitor, and enter the word "rock" in the GitBit box.

Name: Jeffrey Gitomer

Company: Buy Gitomer, Inc.

Web Site: www.gitomer.com

Biography: Jeffrey gives public and corporate seminars, runs annual sales meetings, and conducts live and Internet training programs on selling, customer loyalty, and personal development. Jeffrey's customers include Coca-Cola, D.R. Horton, Caterpillar, BMW, AT&T Wireless, MacGregor Golf, Ferguson Enterprises, Kimpton Hotels, Hilton, Enterprise Rent-A-Car, AmeriPride, NCR, Stewart Title, Comcast Cable, Time Warner Cable, Liberty Mutual Insurance, Principal Financial Group, Wells Fargo Bank, Baptist Health Care, BlueCross BlueShield, Carlsberg, Wausau Insurance, Northwestern Mutual, MetLife, Sports Authority, GlaxoSmithKline, AC Nielsen, IBM, the *New York Post*, and hundreds of others.

Jeffrey's syndicated column, "Sales Moves," appears in scores of business journals and newspapers in the United States and Europe, and is read by more than four million people every week.

Jeffrey's *WOW!* Web sites at www.gitomer.com and www.trainone.com get more than 100,000 hits per week from readers and seminar attendees. His state-of-the-art presence on the Web and his e-commerce ability have set the standard among peers, and have won huge praise and acceptance from his customers. Online sales training lessons are available at www.trainone.com. The content is pure Jeffrey—fun, pragmatic, real-world—and can be immediately implemented. TrainOne's innovation is leading the way in the field of customized e-learning. Jeffrey's weekly e-zine, *Sales Caffeine*, is a sales wake-up call delivered every Tuesday morning to more than 350,000 subscribers, free of charge. *Sales Caffeine* allows Jeffrey to communicate valuable sales information, strategies, and answers to sales professionals on a timely basis.

Best Sellers: *The Sales Bible, The Little Red Book of Selling, The Little Black Book of Connections*, and *The Little Gold Book of YES! Attitude*

Sales Tip One: People don't like to be sold, but they love to buy.

Sales Tip Two: If you love to serve, your customers will love you. Work on your service skills as much as you work on your sales skills.

Sales Tip Three: If you're in sales, you should spend the majority of your time in front of people who can say "yes" to you. If you're making cold calls, the majority of your time is wasted on people saying "no."

Sales Tip Four: The "buying motive" of a prospect is the reason *behind* the situation that will cause them to purchase or pass.

Book One: *The Little Red Book of Selling*

Selling Professional Services

Charles H. Green
Trusted Advisor Associates

The best sales thinking in industry at large is well researched, based on sound marketing principles, and has proven successful for many businesses. Buying is seen as a rational, linear process of problem definition, alternatives generation, and criteria-based selection. Selling helps buyers clarify information, answers questions, and offers implications.

This is the dominant view of authors, trainers, and business schools. Not surprisingly, many in the professions believe that our clients must buy this way—and that we should sell this way.

Yet many of us have that nagging feeling telling us that *it just doesn't seem to work like that.* We deny the feeling because we think it means we are bad at selling. It doesn't occur to us that the model itself may be wrong!

The truth is, selling professional services *is* different from other selling. It is more psychological and personal. The professional services sale is by no means irrational—but neither can it be described solely in rational terms.

Our instincts are right. It is the Industrial Sales Paradigm that is at fault.

■ HOW THINGS REALLY WORK

Sellers of professional services face several challenges. We are (usually) both seller and deliverer, and always the "expert." The buyer buys us as well as the service. Our services are expensive, have high risk/return ratios, and results aren't guaranteed. These factors are a recipe for complex psychodynamics.

Most sales people are extroverts, focused at a general level. Service professionals are more cautious and precise. Selling puts us at odds with ourselves from the outset.

Because most sellers are deliverers, we face an uncomfortable fact—we must sell ourselves, though we hate to "hype" ourselves. We want to be seen (and to see ourselves) as client-focused, not self-obsessed. We want to be appreciated for our talents, not to beg or boast. Since I am the product, if the client doesn't buy, it feels like personal rejection. The client must believe there is something wrong with me. It all feels very personal—because it is!

So, we must do something we don't enjoy doing (selling), that offends our sense of modesty (hyping ourselves) and may feel vaguely unethical, and that then exposes us to personal rejection as a result of having done it!

Professionals prefer to believe clients buy our expertise and content, but clients buy our character, interpersonal skills, and judgment as well. We infer that either (1) we are in the wrong job (because it requires a skill level we have not achieved), or (2) we are doing the right job wrong (because what we are good at isn't working). Either way, we're uncomfortable.

Clients complicate matters. They face high-risk, unclear-return decisions on intangible issues outside their expertise. They are nervous. Many manage that nervousness by turning to tangible, expertise-based content, rather than dealing directly with real, emotional risks.

Thus client and professional conspire to avoid the real issues, leaving each stressed and in denial. Each party's fears lead them to "objective" criteria and process discussions, in turn reinforcing the other's view that such issues are key. This is a dance of denial—everyone pretending that a complex emotional process is purely "rational" and about content expertise. It's not. It's messy—precisely because it is not about numbers or qualifications or processes, but about people.

■ TRADITIONAL SALES MODELS

Traditional sales models characterize buying as a special form of rational decision making or problem solving. They use a several-step model with three unspoken but critical assumptions:

1. The seller aspires to sell better.
2. The buyer follows a rational process.
3. Selling is different from delivering.

All three are untrue in the case of professional services.

➤ Assumption 1: The Seller Aspires to Sell Better

One leading sales training program focuses on high-performing salespeople. Each module of the training repeats the mantra: "high-performing salespeople are characterized by . . ." The assumed, unspoken message is "and of course you aspire to be one, too."

But professional services folk aren't salespeople. Most aspire to content excellence, not to sales expertise. Many are ambivalent about selling at best. Sales best practices feel to many professionals like manipulation.

➤ Assumption 2: The Buying Process Is Rational

Consider these quotes from books and materials of leading sales models:

1. "Buying is a special case of decision making."
2. "Selling is a series of business transactions in which you are a problem solver."
3. "Customers are always looking for results."

This view sees buying as a subset of cognitive decision making—from needs assessment to problem definition to selection.

But in professional services, much more is involved. The decision to hire a firm invites uncertainty, success, failure, advancement, fear, status, reputation, and risk—for buyer and seller alike.

Smart clients don't just compare and contrast. They know they lack the data, time, and money to outexpert the experts. Buyers do not think in either linear or rational terms alone. They are iterative and emotional. What they *want* is an advisor who can be trusted.

➤ Assumption 3: Selling Is Different from Delivering

In industry, selling is a distinct business process and organization. After the sale event, the customer relationship moves on to others. Title to product passes to the customer at the sale. Sales are closed with complex contracts.

For us, it's different. The seller usually is the doer (or supervises doing). Selling organizations are relatively rare. Contracts are easily cancellable, and title doesn't pass.

In professional services, the best selling looks very much like delivery. Trust builds through real interactions of real people working real issues in real time. A test drive is worth a thousand brochures. The challenge is to integrate sales and delivery, not to isolate them as distinct processes.

■ THE ALTERNATIVE: TRUST-BASED SELLING

The alternative approach is based on the most powerful motivator for clients to buy—a sense that they trust the professional. It implies a different approach to selling—and to the sales process.

Given a choice, buyers overwhelmingly buy what they have to buy anyway from those they trust. It is, simply, the sensible response to the complex, emotional situation facing them.

■ TRUST AND SALES

Most people think that trust is drawn on or used up in the sales process. The reverse is true—trust is actually created in the sales process. A successful trust-based sale ends with more trust than it started with.

The trustworthiness of a professional is described by the Trust Equation: a blend of credibility, reliability, intimacy, and low self-orientation. The client comes to see these elements *during* the sales process. Most professionals assume that the issue is all about the rational—largely credibility and reliability—and thus focus on credentials and track records.

In fact, professional services sales are much more related to the issues of intimacy and low self-orientation. The professional who can demonstrate these factors, while keeping credibility and reliability at acceptable levels, will almost always be more successful.

These factors can be demonstrated in three key ways.

1. **Personal Interactions.** Listening is critical, but not the "listening" usually referred to in sales programs. What's critical is not listening for needs, or for solutions, but simply . . . listening, for the sake of the client being heard. What is *heard* is less important than the fact of the client having been *listened to*. The need to listen extends across all parts of the sales process, including much less reliance on the standard tools of PowerPoint presentations and recitations of references.

2. **Process.** The sales process needs to be designed to mimic the delivery process as closely as possible. The best proposals are written together with the client. Discussions should be about the client's issues, not those of past clients. The idea of "closing" should be dropped in favor of discussions that move toward improvement of the client's real business issues.

3. **Purpose.** Directly contradicting the industrial sales model, the seller must stop believing that the purpose of selling is to make the sale. Instead, adopt the belief that the purpose of sales is to improve the client situation and the client relationship, and that if that is done,

the result will be higher closing rates and high-impact repeat relationships, sufficient to provide better economic results for both seller and client alike.

There is a paradoxical quality about professional services selling. The best form of selling is not to sell, but to continue looking for ways to be of service to the service, becoming trusted by the client along the way.

Name: Charles H. Green

Company: Trusted Advisor Associates

Web Site: www.trustedadvisor.com

Biography: Charles H. Green is a speaker and executive educator on trust-based relationships and trust-based selling in complex businesses. He is author of *Trust-Based Selling*, and coauthor of *The Trusted Advisor*.

He has taught in executive education programs for the Kellogg Graduate School of Business at Northwestern, and for Columbia University Graduate School of Business, as well as through his own firm, Trusted Advisor Associates. He focuses on improving trust-based relationships and business development skills.

He has published articles in *Harvard Business Review, Directorship Magazine, Management Consulting News, CPA Journal, American Lawyer,* and *Commercial Lending Review,* and is a contributing editor at RainToday.com.

Selling Philosophy: Trust-based selling

Target Industries: Complex businesses and intangible services

Sales Tip One: Trust is the most powerful factor affecting sales. People trust those who are trustworthy, that is, worthy of trust. The biggest factor driving trustworthiness is a willingness to consistently do what's right for the customer.

Sales Tip Two: Paradoxically, more sales come when you stop making the sale the objective. If you consistently do right for the customer, sales happen.

Sales Tip Three: Don't always be closing. Closing is about forcing your will. Instead, help customers make decisions—in their time, according to what's best for them.

Book One: *The Trusted Advisor* (coauthor)

Book Two: *Trust-Based Selling*

Dealing with Unreturned Phone Calls

Ford Harding
Harding & Company

Last week my contact management software reminded me to call Lois. She is the logical point of contact at a firm where I would like to do business. I have known Lois for five years, and her boss for six. Over those years I have made 25 calls to one or the other of them, and exactly 5 have been returned. The last time I spoke with Lois, she informed me that they were working with a competitor. That was almost three years ago. Since then all efforts to contact Lois and her boss by phone have gone into a void. A few e-mails lobbed in for variety have also received no response.

What should I do? What would you do?

The answer, of course, depends on the reason my calls have gone unreturned. A little voice inside me says that Lois and her boss want nothing to do with me. But I have learned through many years of experience that it is the voice of my own insecurities. More probably, they find us too expensive and are uncomfortable saying so. Or they realize that my calls are not urgent and treat them as such. Or they are just busy. Still, three years is a long time. Whatever the reason, I have little enthusiasm for making the call. Another little voice inside me says that this is a waste of time, that nothing will ever come of calling these people. Once again, experience responds, cautioning me that one more call will cost me little, to which the first little voice says that a time comes to give up and refocus one's energies elsewhere.

My deliberations were interrupted, and I put off deciding what to do. This is a true story about a client I have been pursuing, except Lois's name came up on my tickler file a couple of months ago, not last week. I did call, and this time Lois called me back to invite me to pitch on some work. There was only one competitor and our chances of winning were good. Today she called to give us the go-ahead.

I have many such stories after 30 years of business development. Over the years I have learned that an unreturned phone call means that someone did not return my call . . . and little more. Others reinforce this belief. Christy Williams, a friend of mine, ran into a contact she had been trying to reach for months, leaving many messages. All her calls went unreturned. When she met the man at a conference, he greeted her enthusiastically, saying that he had recently referred her to a prospective client. She thanked him and said, "Let's stay in touch." "What do you mean?" he responded, "we've been in touch." He equated *her* unreturned phone calls with *their* being in touch.

A big part of rainmaking is persistence. Still, several times a week a name comes up on my tickler system of someone who has not responded to previous calls. And still, after all these years, the little voice inside me says to give up, that it is not worth the effort, that the person doesn't like me and doesn't want to talk to me. It is by learning to override that voice that I have become successful.

Name: Ford Harding

Company: Harding & Company

Web Site: www.HardingCo.com

Biography: Ford Harding has spent 30 years in management consulting and at an architecture firm. He has helped professionals in 15 countries learn to sell. He has assembled a team of trainer/coaches who have worked in seller/doer environments and sold effectively. The firm knows how to deal with time management, call reluctance, and other challenges facing sales professionals.

Harding has conducted extensive research into how rainmakers develop new business for their firms by interviewing over 300 rainmakers and those who have observed them in action. The firm's programs on lead generation, selling, cross selling, and personal brand building are based on this research.

Selling Philosophy: Selling professional services: We work only with seller/doers.

Target Industries: Management consulting, recruiting, engineering, architecture, accounting, law

Best Sellers: Six-Month Rainmaking Program (for six people)

Sales Tip One: Selling requires having many small successes, such as meeting a CFO for the first time, to put you in a position to get a big one, like winning a new client. Celebrate the small successes and let them sustain you until you get the big one.

Sales Tip Two: A client who laughs is half sold.

Sales Tip Three: When a prospective client doesn't return your phone calls, it doesn't mean she doesn't like you. It probably has nothing to do with you. Try again.

Book One: *Creating Rainmakers: The Manager's Guide to Training Professionals to Attract New Clients* (John Wiley & Sons, Inc., 2006)

Book Two: *Rainmaking: Attracting Clients No Matter What Your Field* (Adams, 2008, 2nd ed.)

Book Three: *Cross-Selling Success: A Rainmaker's Guide to Professional Account Development* (Adams, 2002)

Chapter 32

Engaging and Defeating Competition

Competitive Strategy and Political Alignment in World–Class Selling

Holden International

As a leading sales consulting firm, we are often posed the question, "How do you define World-Class Selling?" Many define it as helping your customer be successful. We agree: Delivering customer business value is fundamental to World-Class Selling. Others define World-Class Selling as "achieving your quota and driving profitability for your organization." This is also true. World-Class Selling is about *both* delivering customer business value *and* achieving revenue and profit growth for your sales organization.

If, on one hand, all you do is please your customer, you could end up providing "special pricing" that makes your customer happy and your shareholders furious. But on the other hand, if all you do is focus on achieving your quota, you could end up making your sales manager happy and your customer furious.

There has been much written about how best to deliver customer business value. What has not been studied as much is how to do so in a way that positions you to win the business against competition and grow the profits of your sales organization, which is a key part of World-Class Selling.

Methods such as Formulating Competitive Strategy and Executing Political Alignment are the keys to winning business. It begins with a competitive mind-set. Selling is a process of competing for business, and to be ready to sell, you must be ready to compete. When you are ready to compete, you are prepared and able to engage the competition in the battle for business and defeat them with swift-ness, agility, and a minimal expenditure of resources.

Formulating Competitive Strategy is one of the most difficult tasks that face competitive salespeople today. As an answer to the question, "What are we counting on to win in a specific sales situation?" the response is often a 30-minute dissertation on what is happening in the account. Translation: No strategy exists. Or does it?

Strategy assigns a clear direction and purpose to all sales activities, both in the penetration and development of an account and in defeating competition for an important piece of business. Every sales activity can be assessed in terms of what is directionally correct, as defined by sales strategy. Ask a salesperson, "Why are you doing a particular demo for a specific department within an account?" A tactician will explain that it will confirm that the capability discussed actually exists, reinforcing the credibility of the proposed solution and that of the salesperson. While this is absolutely correct, it is not the reason for doing the demo. The purpose of the demo is to advance the sales strategy, the purpose of which, in turn, is to win the sale.

Often, advancing a Competitive Strategy requires alignment with powerful customer individuals. In our simple example, the demo may gain the salesperson access to just such an individual. Perhaps a Fox is excited about a particular technology that is incorporated in the salesperson's solution. A Fox is a very powerful person who is not necessarily at the top of the department, but who can work in exception of policy and is rarely surprised by events. Alignment with a Fox will often make or break a deal. The demo is not only an opportunity to gain exposure to the Fox, but also to better understand his or her priorities, direction, and vision. The strategist will then map the proposed solution into that direction and vision, personalizing the approach and beginning the process of building a relationship with the Fox. These are the salespeople who become Trusted Advisors, largely because they operate at both tactical and strategic levels.

In our example, the more tactical IT Solutions Provider is also operating at a strategic level, but he or she is not cognizant of it. While the salesperson's focus is tactical, he or she is unknowingly implementing a *direct* sales strategy, but without an understanding of the implications associated with that class of strategy.

 Going "direct" may make sense, but often it does not.

 Going "direct" requires overwhelming, incontestable superiority; is resource intensive; and is predictable.

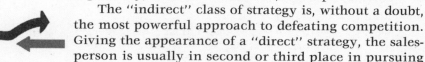 The "indirect" class of strategy is, without a doubt, the most powerful approach to defeating competition. Giving the appearance of a "direct" strategy, the salesperson is usually in second or third place in pursuing

an order. Then, in the eleventh hour, the decision-making criterion is changed, leveraging the relationship with a Fox. It is like pulling the rug out from beneath the competition. They can get up, but do not have time to recover.

A "divisional" strategy is when the salesperson does not have enough competitive advantage to go "direct" or "indirect," so the next best approach may be to partition the business, perhaps even complementing the competition.

If all else fails, a "containment" strategy may be in order, thus delaying a customer decision. Buying time until you can gain additional competitive advantage is a "fall back and regroup" approach.

At Holden International, we recommend that the "indirect" strategy be employed for all "Must Win," very important, and competitive opportunities. Every defense has a vulnerable aspect—that which the competition prepares itself to protect. The key to the "indirect" approach is to identify competitive vulnerability that is unexpected or discounted, and exploit it.

For example, competitive vulnerability can exist in the form of overconfidence. As referenced earlier, when a salesperson implements an "indirect" strategy, he or she is often in second or third competitive position. The competitor is in the lead with the expected business in the 90 percent column of his or her forecast. At that point, where is the competitor's focus? It is likely on deals where he or she is not in the lead, reflecting a false sense of security, and that is vulnerability.

In addition to exploiting existing vulnerability, the "indirect" strategy creates new vulnerability for the competition. When the salesperson is setting the stage to change the ground rules in the eleventh hour of the sales situation, he or she is building relationships and aligning with Foxes and others in the Power Base.

These activities quietly build the salesperson's Support Base, creating vulnerability for the competition that they will not be aware of until the eleventh hour, when it is too late.

World Class Sellers are at the top of their profession, able to formulate Competitive Strategy in order to engage and defeat their competition. They execute an Indirect Strategy by conducting effective Political Alignment. In this way, World-Class Sellers compete based on *how* they sell, rather than *what* they sell.

Name: Ryan Kubacki

Company: Holden International

Web Site: www.holdenintl.com

Biography: Founded in 1979 by Jim Holden, Holden International is a leading sales consulting firm that provides innovative thinking to drive sales achievement for client organizations and sales professionals worldwide.

Specializing in business-to-business selling, Holden helps clients engage and defeat competition in a way that wins customer loyalty and produces the benefits of exceptional sales achievement: increased customer satisfaction, higher revenue growth, increased profit margins, and shorter sales cycles.

Recognized as the pioneer of the sales methodology industry with the introduction of Power Base Selling, Holden has continued to innovate and offers clients an integrated platform of sales training, software, and sales manager coaching.

Selling Philosophy: There is only one reason salespeople lose orders: They are outsold.

Target Industries: All business-to-business sectors, with an emphasis on technology, telecommunications, manufacturing, health care, financial services, and professional services

Best Sellers: Power Base Opportunity Strategy & Management, Power Base Account Strategy & Management, Power Base Territory Strategy & Management, Power Base Sales Manager Coaching, and e-fox software sales solution

Sales Tip One: Ensure that you invest your time with the person who is the most influential person of a decision-making body, one who has the ability to "prewire" decisions before they are actually made. This person typically works behind the scenes and is someone who is the key to unlocking the value of an account: the Fox!

Sales Tip Two: The traditional selling focus of Servicing Demand, such as responding to RFPs (requests for proposals), even with strong selling and value-based offerings, is not sufficient to build a pipeline of quality business. Thus traditional selling is giving way to a new type of selling: Creating Demand.

Sales Tip Three: A sales pipeline is any list of qualified prospects who aren't ready to buy right now. To realize the full potential of a salesperson's pipeline, one must have the discipline to:

• Accurately assess whether the account can be won.

• Determine if the account is "worth winning" with proper margin and business value.

• Understand the investment required to be successful.

Book One: *Power Base Selling: Secrets of an Ivy League Street Fighter*

Book Two: *World Class Selling: The Crossroads of Customer, Sales, Marketing, and Technology*

Book Three: *The Selling Fox: A Field Guide to Dynamic Sales Performance*

Product One: Power Base Interactive

Chapter 33

How to Double Sales in 12 Months Flat

Chet Holmes
Chet Holmes International

Here is the most powerful lesson you will ever learn for doubling sales in the next 12 months.

■ THE BEST BUYER CONCEPT

Completely grasp the power of this:

> **There are always a smaller number of ideal buyers, as compared to all buyers, so ideal buyers are cheaper to market to and yet bring greater rewards.**

A magazine used this strategy to double its sales in 15 months flat. Here's what they did. They had a database of 2,200 advertisers that they sent promotional pieces to each month. After learning this strategy, they did an analysis and found that 167 of those 2,200 advertisers bought 95 percent of the advertising in the competitor's magazine. This concept is called "The Dream 100 Sell," a concept in which you go after your "dream" prospects with a vengeance. This magazine sent the 167 (best buyers) a letter every two weeks and called them four times per month.

Since these were the biggest buyers, the first four months of intensive marketing and selling brought no actual reward. In the fifth month, only *one* of these dream clients bought advertising in the magazine. In the sixth month, 28 of the 167 largest advertisers in the country came into the magazine all at once. And since these are the biggest advertisers, they don't take quarter pages and fractional ads, they take full pages and full-color spreads. These 28 advertisers alone were enough to double the magazine's sales over the previous year. The magazine went from number 15 in the industry to number one in just over a year.

■ LESSONS FOR YOU

Who are your best buyers? If you sell business-to-customer, chances are, your best buyers live in the best neighborhoods. If you are a dentist, accountant, chiropractor, real estate broker, financial advisor, restaurant, or even a multilevel marketer, consistently go after the folks who live in the best neighborhoods. They are the wealthiest buyers who have the money and the greatest sphere of influence. If you send them an offer every single month without fail, within a year you'll have a great reputation among the very wealthy.

If you sell business-to-business, it's usually fairly clear that your best buyers are the biggest companies. So what are you doing, every other week, no matter what, to let these companies know who you are? There's no one you can't get to as long as you constantly market to them, especially after they say they're not interested. People will not only begin to respect your perseverance, they will actually begin to feel obligated.

This doesn't happen right away, but even the most hard-bitten and cynical executive or prospect begins to respect you when you just will not give up. The publication I mentioned earlier went on to double sales two more years in a row. We constantly marketed to the best buyers, and much more aggressively than we did to all buyers.

A company selling to manufacturers used this strategy to target the 100 biggest manufacturers in the country. For the first three months no one responded to any of the calling or phoning. But after three months executives started saying: "I just have to meet you. I've never had anyone continue to call me so many times after I said no." Within six months they had gotten in to see 54 percent of those whom they targeted.

The secret is to *never* give up. Just keep going after those companies again and again. Or if you sell to consumers, commit to sending a promotional piece every single month to those wealthy neighborhoods. Eventually, all the wealthy people in your area will know exactly who you are.

Who are your *dream* prospects? And how committed are you to getting them as clients?

Name: Chet Holmes

Company: Chet Holmes International

Web Site: www.ChetHolmes.com

Biography: Chet Holmes has worked with over 60 of the Fortune 500 companies as America's top marketing executive, trainer, and strategic consultant. Clients include American Express, New York Stock Exchange, Estee Lauder, NBC Television, IBM, Apple Computers, and GNC. Chet wrote the number-one best-selling book, *The Ultimate Sales Machine*, which has been in the top three sales books on Amazon for two years since its release. In his early career, Chet was top producer in every position he ever held. He then moved into management, working for billionaire Charlie Munger. He has developed 65 business growth training products that are selling in 23 countries.

Selling Philosophy: Education-based marketing

Target Industries: Any industry

Best Sellers: *The Ultimate Sales Machine*, Ultimate Business Mastery System with Tony Robbins, Business Growth Masters Series, Guerrilla Marketing Meets Karate Master with Jay Levinson, PEQ with Jay Abraham

Sales Tip One: No matter what else you're doing, you have to have a special effort where you always (no matter how many times they say "no") go after the really huge dream clients. If you are consistent, you will get them and break sales records.

Sales Tip Two: People are way more apt to meet with you if you're offering to teach them something of value rather than just wanting to sell them your product or service.

Sales Tip Three: Sixty-five percent of whether someone is going to buy from you is based upon if they like you and trust you and how well you understand their needs. Put the majority of your focus here.

Book One: *The Ultimate Sales Machine*

Product One: Ultimate Business Mastery System

Chapter 34

Developing the Thank-You Note Habit

Tom Hopkins
Tom Hopkins International

I learned the value and power of thank-you notes early in life. When I was a young child, my parents occasionally went out with friends for dinner. Invariably, when my parents returned from an evening out, I saw my mother sit down at her little desk in the hallway as soon as she got home and begin to write. One night I asked her what she was doing. Her answer came straight out of Emily Post: "We had such a wonderful time with our dear friends this evening that I want to jot them a note to thank them for their friendship and the wonderful dinner." My mother's simple act of gratitude, expressed to people who already knew that she and my father appreciated and enjoyed their friendship, helped to keep my parents' friendships strong for their entire lifetimes.

Because I understood that building relationships is what selling is all about, I began early in my career to send thank-you notes to people. I set a goal to send 10 thank-you notes every day. That goal meant that I had to meet and get the names of at least 10 people every day. I sent thank-you notes to people I met briefly, people I showed properties to, people I talked with on the telephone, and people I actually helped to own new homes. I became a thank-you note fool. And guess what happened? By the end of my third year in sales, my business was 99 percent referrals! The people I had expressed gratitude to were happy to send me new clients as a reward for making them feel appreciated and important.

I understand that you may not be comfortable at first with starting the thank-you note habit, so I took the time to write out 10 situations in which sending a thank-you note is appropriate. Then, to help you even more, I've drafted the notes for you.

1. **Telephone contact.** Thank you for talking with me on the telephone. In today's business world, time is precious. You can rest assured that I will always be respectful of the time you invest as we discuss the possibility of a mutually beneficial business relationship.

2. **In-Person Contact.** Thank you. It was a pleasure meeting you, and my thank-you is for the time we shared. We have been fortunate to serve many happy clients, and it is my wish to some day be able to serve you. If you have any questions, please don't hesitate to call.

3. **After Demonstration or Presentation.** Thank you for giving me the opportunity to discuss with you our association for the mutual benefit of our firms. We believe that quality, blended with excellent service, is the foundation for a successful business.

4. **After Purchase.** Thank you for giving me the opportunity to offer you our finest service. We are confident that you will be happy with this investment toward future growth. My goal is now to offer excellent follow-up service so you will have no reservations about referring others to me who have similar needs as yours.

5. **For a Referral.** Thank you for your kind referral. You may rest assured that anyone you refer to me will receive the highest degree of professional service possible.

6. **After Final Refusal.** Thank you for taking the time to consider letting me serve you. It is with sincere regrets that your immediate plans do not include making the investment at this time. However, if you need further information or have any questions, please feel free to call. I will keep you posted on new developments and changes that may benefit you.

7. **After They Buy from Someone Else.** Thank you for taking your time to analyze my services. I regret being unable, at this time, to prove to you the benefits we have to offer. We keep constantly informed of new developments and changes, so I will keep in touch with the hope that in the years ahead we will be able to do business.

8. **After They Buy from Someone Else, But Offer to Give You Referrals.** Thank you for your gracious offer of giving me referrals. As we discussed, I am enclosing three of my business cards. I thank you in advance for placing them in the hands of three of your friends, acquaintances, or relatives that I might serve. I will keep in touch and be willing to render my services as needed.

9. **To Anyone Who Gives You Service.** Thank you. It is gratifying to meet someone dedicated to doing a good job. Your efforts are sincerely appreciated. If my company or I can serve you in any way, please don't hesitate to call.

10. **Anniversary Thank-You.** Thank you. It is with warm regards that I send this note to say hello and again, thanks for your past

patronage. We are continually changing and improving our products and services. If you would like an update on our latest advancements, please give me a call.

The power of expressed gratitude is immense. Put this tool to work for you today!

Name: Tom Hopkins

Company: Tom Hopkins International, Inc.

Web Site: www.tomhopkins.com

Biography: Tom Hopkins is world-renowned as the Builder of Sales Champions. For over 25 years, he has taught foundational how-to selling skills to over four million sales professionals on five continents.

His proven, effective methods for finding new business, communicating effectively with clients, providing enticing presentations, addressing client concerns, and closing sales have launched or boosted sales volumes of individuals and companies alike.

He has authored 14 books on selling and sales success, including *Selling for Dummies*, *Sales Prospecting for Dummies*, *Sales Closing for Dummies*, and the megahit *"How to Master the Art of Selling,"* and also has numerous audio and video sales training programs.

Selling Philosophy: Effective communication skills

Target Industries: Real estate, financial services, insurance, mortgage

Best Sellers: *Building Sales Champions* DVD system, a complete library of selling skills, and *How to Master the Art of Selling*—a must-have reference for anyone in sales

Sales Tip One: Repetition is the mother of learning. Read or listen to any material that's important to you a minimum of six times to gain maximum retention.

Sales Tip Two: The top salespeople get emotionally involved with the people they serve. Don't build a wall between you and them. People don't care how much you know until you show them how much you care.

Sales Tip Three: Ask questions to gain and maintain control of the conversation. You can't direct anyone toward a purchase that's good for them until you can get them to tell you what they want.

Book One: *How to Master the Art of Selling*

Book Two: *Low Profile Selling: Act Like a Lion, Sell Like a Lamb*

Book Three: *Sell It Today, Sell It Now: The Art of the One-Call Close*

Product One: Achieving Sales Excellence (CD)

Product Two: Building Sales Champions (DVD system)

Product Three: The Highlights of the Perfect Sales Process (DVD)

Chapter 35

Escaping the Price-Driven Sale Selling to Clients at a Premium

John Golden
Huthwaite

How many sales efforts do you know of that don't claim to be about selling "value"? Yet, how many of these sellers actually know what their customers would define as value? Moreover, how many sellers can identify what kind of "value" their customers are willing to pay a premium to receive? If value is defined as something that causes a customer to reduce their price concerns, then effective sellers should be able to answer with a list of specifics. The unfortunate reality is that most will answer with guesses and platitudes.

Huthwaite's recent research has revealed a precise and compelling definition of the overused, yet elusive, concept of value. It is Huthwaite's position that when a seller employs the correct tactics, three enviable outcomes can be achieved:

1. Price will become less important to the customer.

2. In situations where the seller seeks an ongoing relationship with the buyer, the customer will erect barriers to the seller's competition and will redefine the nature of the buyer/seller relationship.

3. The seller will identify areas of the expanding depth and breadth of opportunity available to them from each customer.

This is a critical topic for any company that finds itself increasingly trapped in a commoditized marketplace. It is only through real and individualized value creation that an organization can differentiate itself from the competition and break the barriers of commoditization.

■ WHERE THIS NEW DEFINITION OF VALUE CAME FROM

Huthwaite developed insight into this new definition of client value by assembling data on several thousand transactions that had a curious common characteristic. Huthwaite looked at transactions across a variety of industries that met two criteria:

1. The customer reported that in an effort to purchase a product, service, or bundle of capabilities, they were faced with a group of competitors seeking their business whose offerings all looked the same. The one clear differentiator was price.

2. Despite this apparent similarity, the customer in these transactions did not select the low-cost offering.

It was Huthwaite's contention that if this odd behavior by the customer could be understood, these transactions offered a perfect opportunity to discover what customers meant when they reported receiving "value." Why else would these customers do something so seemingly illogical? Most sellers will find the answer compelling, and one that challenges the current definition of sales excellence.

■ THE FOUR VALUE DRIVERS

At its simplest, what these customers reported receiving was one or more of the "value drivers." That is, these customers were willing to pay a premium, redefine the buyer/seller relationship, erect barriers to the seller's competitors, and establish the seller as a trusted advisor when:

➤ The seller revealed to the buyer an *unrecognized problem* that the buyer or the buyer's organization was experiencing.

➤ The seller established an *unanticipated solution* for the buyer's problems that the buyer or the buyer's organization was experiencing.

➤ The seller created or revealed an *unseen opportunity* for the buyer or the buyer's organization.

➤ The seller served as more than just a vendor of product and services, but instead served as a *broker of strengths,* serving to make available to the buyer the full range of capabilities of the seller's organization in such a way that these capabilities contributed to an expansion or redefinition of the customer's success. At the individual level, this means cross-selling.

As intriguing as these results are at first blush, reflection on their implications reveals that buyers are redefining what professional selling really means. Sellers now need to trade on their *expertise*. Sellers must bring to the benefit of the buyer insights that the buyer cannot achieve on his or her own.

■ HOW IT'S DONE

➤ Part One: You Can't Just Tell 'Em

We have identified the word *expertise* as the key to driving value. This means *bringing the seller's expertise to the benefit of the buyer during the selling process; that is, before the sale is made*. The key is for the seller to employ a particular form of diagnostic questioning.

The word *diagnostic* cannot be overstated in this case. Merely asking questions may be a good way to get the buyer to talk, but in and of themselves, seller questions become nothing more than a polite interrogation if overused.

It is instructive to remember that great selling must be conducted within the constraints of what Huthwaite calls the "boundary conditions" of communication:

> ➤ Customers put a higher value on what they say and what they conclude than they do on what they are told.

> ➤ Customers place a higher value on what they request than they do on what is freely offered.

This is why so many sales calls and sales strategies that focus on description fail to connect in a value-driving way with customers. Bringing the value drivers alive requires conducting calls and strategies that help the customer draw conclusions, establish value expectations, and extend invitations to the seller to describe their offerings and capabilities. The key is asking the right questions.

■ PART TWO: YOU GOTTA KNOW WHERE THE BUYER IS

Another aspect of delivering value is to understand how a customer's view of value changes as they move toward a buying decision. By studying thousands of transactions across multiple industries, Huthwaite built the model of buyer behavior seen in Figure 35.1.

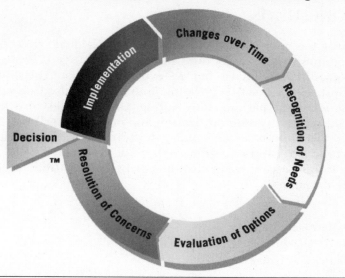

Figure 35.1   Huthwaite

Anyone who has been in sales for very long could tell you that buyers move from recognizing their needs, to evaluating who to buy from, and then through a decision and an implementation phase. What only the exceptional sellers realize, however, is the degree to which a buyer's definition of value changes as they move through a decision cycle. At its most basic, each phase of this cycle has a very different orientation of buyer focus:

➤ **Changes over Time.** The buyer perceives no reason to change from the status quo.

➤ **Recognition of Needs.** The buyer is evaluating whether to make a purchase or to do nothing; they are trying to define what a successful outcome will look like.

➤ **Evaluation of Options.** A decision to make a purchase has been made; the question is, from whom?

➤ **Resolution of Concerns.** The buyer has made a tentative choice of who to do business with, but is examining consequence issues associated with completing the purchase.

➤ **Implementation.** The contract has been signed and the buyer is looking for expected value.

Although these are clearly five very different frames of reference, it is surprising how many sellers adopt the exact same approach to every buyer in every selling situation.

■ CONCLUSION

Painfully few companies, sales forces, or individual sellers have recognized how dramatically their market has changed. There is a bad news/good news scenario here. The bad news about this situation is that most sellers are still operating under the old idea that value *communication* is the path to value selling. Unfortunately for them, this is now the path to commoditization and pure price selling. The good news is that for those who make the transition, there is a unique opportunity to capture a greater share of their market and to do so with a lower percentage of customers who make purely price-driven buying decisions.

Name: John Golden

Company: Huthwaite, Inc.

Web Site: www.huthwaite.com

Biography: Founded on scientifically validated behavioral research, our methodologies, which include the internationally renowned SPIN Selling and the newly enhanced SPIN 2.0 and leading-edge Integrated Learning Experience, guarantee sales success.

For over 30 years Huthwaite has worked with thousands of organizations around the globe, including half of the U.S. Fortune 50, to give them real, proven competitive advantage. Huthwaite is a wholly owned subsidiary of Informa PLC, a leading international provider of specialist information and services for academic, professional, and business communities, and is quoted on the London Stock Exchange (INF).

Selling Philosophy: Value creation

Target Industries: Any industry that suffers price-driven sales, commoditization, and lack of differentiation

Best Sellers: SPIN 2.0 and the Integrated Learning Experience

Sales Tip One: Buyers value more what they say and conclude than what they're told.

Sales Tip Two: Buyers value more what they ask for than what is freely offered.

Sales Tip Three: Great sellers ask questions that help customers make connections.

Book One: *SPIN Selling*

Chapter 36

Creating Client Value

A Practical, Modern Approach to Building Business

Richard Barkey

Imparta

■ EXECUTIVE SUMMARY

What makes a great salesperson, account manager, or business developer? In a world where it's hard to differentiate on the product alone, people buy from people who create value for them—both through the solutions they create, and through the help they provide around the buying process. Rather than being seen as intrusive, great salespeople are seen as trusted business advisors.

Poor salespeople, on the other hand, destroy value—not just through the wasted time and costs of unproductive meetings, but through the hidden costs of leaving problems and real needs unresolved. These salespeople struggle to get meetings, fail to grow accounts, and suffer from long sales cycles.

The sales methodology described below is based on "Creating Client Value" (CCV), an approach that has been helping salespeople to drive revenue growth for the last decade. CCV was developed in a unique collaboration between Imparta and Neil Rackham, the author of SPIN Selling and arguably the world's leading researcher into sales effectiveness. In particular, it reflects Neil's more recent work with McKinsey and the book *Rethinking the Salesforce*, which he coauthored with John de Vincentis.

CCV focuses on the process the customer goes through, rather than on a "sales process." Recognizing where the customer is in their own process is critical in being able to support and influence them through each stage. There are five major stages in any buying decision:

1. Awareness of Needs
2. Assessment of Alternatives
3. Alleviation of Risks
4. Decision and Agreement
5. Achievement of Results

The rest of this article sets out the key sales skills and outcomes at each stage of the buying cycle.

■ AWARENESS OF NEEDS

During this phase, the buyer moves from being happy with the status quo to recognizing the need to change an existing product, service, process, or supplier. The role of the salesperson during this phase is to identify possible opportunities by mapping out the needs of different parts of the customer's business and identifying potential "sweet spots," or overlaps, between those needs and your capabilities. The salesperson also needs to identify an entry point into the organization with whom to test their ideas. A common mistake is to target very senior decision makers first, but they will rarely have the time or inclination to help you understand the organization and its needs, and you may not get a second chance to speak to them.

Once the ingoing hypothesis has been validated, salespeople need to identify the specific individuals who own the problem or opportunities with which you can help, and then to ask them questions to build their sense of urgency around the issues they face. Even that will probably not be enough to secure a commitment to change; you also need to quantify the value that a solution would create, and identify and help to overcome any barriers to change within the customer's organization.

The specific outcomes you can create during the Awareness of Needs stage of the buying cycle include:

➤ Building the sales pipeline though more targeted referral and lead generation activities, and a broader understanding of the different stakeholders in the customer's or prospect's business. This needs to be combined with effective account entry strategies and a sophisticated approach to navigating complex buyer roles.

➤ Reducing cycle time and increasing average account size by building a deep understanding of a customer's or target's business issues and internal performance measures. This allows salespeople and account managers to uncover needs across the wider organization, while allowing issues and benefits to be expressed in the customer's own terms to a range of stakeholders.

➤ Further increasing account size by considering the capabilities your own company has beyond its products and services (from the people it employs to its corporate assets), and mapping these onto the customer's needs in a process of structured creativity.

➤ Improving the rate at which conversations turn into opportunities through questioning skills, a clear understanding of decision roles, and the ability to make a quantified case for change that covers the full range of value created for the customer.

■ ASSESSMENT OF ALTERNATIVES

At this point the customer has decided to act and is evaluating the product or service against competing alternatives (which can include doing nothing). The salesperson or account manager needs to help the buyer to identify and prioritize the criteria against which they are going to assess the alternatives. Then they need to identify how your offer is perceived relative to the alternatives on each of those criteria, and finally to position your offering in the best possible way against these criteria.

Depending on how well the customer thinks you perform against any given criterion, you may try to improve their perception of you, or try to increase or reduce the importance they place on the criterion.

The specific outcomes CCV can create during the Assessment of Alternatives stage of the buying cycle include:

➤ Building trusted relationships by helping to uncover and then clarify the criteria that specific customers (including purchasing departments) will use to assess your solution against those of your competitors.

➤ Improving success rates in competitive situations (one client measured an improvement from 1 in 10 to 3 in 10) by analyzing these criteria and developing strategies to deal with them.

➤ Delivering winning pitches by basing them on this analysis rather than a generic presentation around your strengths.

➤ Improving profitability and maximizing margins by managing the discounting behavior of staff and dealing better with procurement departments.

■ ALLEVIATION OF RISK

During this stage, the customer has narrowed their choice of preferred solution, but begins to think about the personal and business risks that may be involved. The role of the salesperson is to uncover these risks and help them find ways to address them. This can again be a counterintuitive process for salespeople, who need to become comfortable discussing risks as well as alleviating them.

The specific outcomes CCV can help to create during the Alleviation of Risk stage of the buying cycle include:

➤ Reducing the number of stalled opportunities by identifying when risks are blocking progress and uncovering risks at the strategic, tactical, political, and personal levels (each of these may require different interpersonal skills).

➤ Improving the conversion rate by exploring and resolving the obstacles to a decision; this involves different skills depending on the type of risks being experienced: strategic, tactical, political, and individual.

➤ Managing competitive threats by developing a shared, client-focused approach to business development.

■ DECISION

Although a decision flows much more naturally when the principles of CCV are applied, there is still a need to negotiate and finalize contractual agreements.

A good sales process will tend to lead to a good negotiation, since both parties are clear on the value being created and on the issues and interests of the other party. However, there are specific skills and knowledge around the negotiation process that are beyond the scope of CCV, but are covered in depth in other programs covering negotiation and commercial acumen.

■ ACHIEVEMENT OF RESULTS

In this final phase, the decision has been made and the solution is being implemented. The salesperson's role will vary depending on how you handle implementation, but at a minimum it should be to prepare for a successful implementation, help to anticipate potential issues, and look for additional opportunities.

The specific outcomes we aim to create during the Achievement of Results stage of the buying cycle include:

➤ Increasing customer satisfaction by understanding the three phases of implementation that follow a sale—the honeymoon, disenchantment, and success periods—and making sure that value promised is actually delivered, and that new opportunities are identified.

➤ Reducing the costs of acquiring further business through increased confidence from the client.

➤ Identifying new opportunities by being visible during implementation, and in particular by actively managing referrals throughout the Achievement of Results stage.

➤ At this point, the buying cycle kicks off again. For more complex accounts, these buying cycles fall within an overall strategic account plan, which helps to decide where and how you wish to compete within any given account.

■ CHANNEL VERSUS DIRECT

The Buying Cycle is most obviously applicable when dealing with a direct customer or client. However, even when selling through a channel (business-to-business-to-business or business-to-business-to-customer), the Buying Cycle and its associated skills are highly applicable.

➤ There is a buying cycle going on between the manufacturer and the channel:

➤ A full cycle when new products, services, or initiatives are being introduced.

➤ A repeating "Assessment of Alternatives" when products are being promoted, sold, and prioritized by the channel in the normal course of business.

➤ There is also a buying cycle going on between the channel and the end purchaser, and as a manufacturer, you can benefit by coaching and supporting the channel to do this more effectively.

■ TAILORING THE APPROACH

At Imparta we recommend tailoring any training interventions to suit specific market conditions and the different levels of people involved in the sales process. This can include:

➤ Executives involved in selling
➤ Sales leaders and sales managers
➤ Key/global account managers
➤ Channel managers
➤ Sales support and service staff
➤ Marketing staff
➤ Proposition development and product training
➤ Business development managers/account managers/salespeople

➤ Retail sales advisors

➤ Store/branch managers and assistant managers

Of course, the challenge is as much about making new behaviors stick as it is in identifying the right behaviors to build . . . but that is a subject in its own right!

Name: Richard Barkey

Company: Imparta, Ltd.

Web Site: www.imparta.com

Biography: Richard Barkey is founder and CEO of Imparta, a global company that helps companies achieve and sustain significant improvements in sales, service, and marketing performance.

Prior to founding Imparta in 1998, Richard worked at McKinsey & Co., where he was involved in planning and implementing large-scale change management projects and where he pioneered the use of simulation-based training.

Richard is a trainer and consultant in the fields of strategy and consultative selling. He is also a speaker on learning, e-learning, and sales performance improvement.

Richard holds a first-class degree in engineering from Cambridge University and an MBA with distinction from the Harvard Business School.

Selling Philosophy: Customer-centric selling

Target Industries: Technology and communications, professional services, financial services, manufacturing, utilities, retail

Best Sellers: Creating Client Value (best-selling consultative/solution selling program), Negotiating Client Value, Commercial Acumen

Sales Tip One: You will sell more by focusing on the client's agenda than you will by focusing on your own. Closing a deal isn't an event; it's a process of moving clients through their own decisions, finding ways to add value at each stage.

Sales Tip Two: Your best leads will come from referrals and happy customers who move to a new organization, so manage these actively! LinkedIn is a very powerful tool for keeping in touch with people who move jobs and also for engaging new contacts in targeted conversations.

Sales Tip Three: Don't go in at the top, as you won't be prepared and you'll rarely get a second chance. Instead, find yourself a receptive contact to coach you on the issues and needs within an organization, then identify the people who own the key problems, and only then go to the decision maker with a joint proposal.

Book One: *Sales Insights: A Resource for Sales and HR Leaders* (available to current and potential Imparta clients)

Chapter 37

Selling through the Eye of the Buyer

Steve Maul

InfoMentis

Business-to-business selling has changed. However, contrary to what one might believe, the change wasn't a result of someone discovering the secret sauce for better selling or the discovery of some mystical power of persuasion and influence or some archeologist unearthing a set of "best practice sales process" scrolls. It has changed primarily through the introduction, proliferation, and adoption of new technology that has empowered the customer, giving them the ability to do what they've long yearned for—to manage their buying process the way they want. For too long they've felt as though selling was something that was done "to them" rather than "with them." They've been subjected to vendors hoarding information, doling it out in whatever fashion best suited the *vendor*, as well as *vendors* presenting them with plan letters, telling them how to best "manage the evaluation"—methods that were designed for vendors to gain leverage over their customers and competitors.

Today, customers expect more from you than they have in the past, and they have most of the leverage now, and can demand your adherence to *their* processes. If you and your company are not seeing the process through the "eye of the buyer," and prepare yourselves to interact this way, you risk greater difficulty in your sales efforts and in competitive positions.

Certainly the degree to which each of your customers has adopted some of the techniques discussed here will determine the extent of adaptation you will require. But it's rare to find an organization today that is not using their procurement department as a strategic corporate tool, and the more you approach this with the

knowledge I'm sharing here, the better equipped you are to overcome the points of resistance we all face when selling.

■ TECHNOLOGY IS OUR CUSTOMER'S FRIEND (AND OURS, TOO, IF WE USE IT)

The very source of so much change is the technology in use by our
customers, including search engines, blogs, LinkedIn, Facebook,
Twitter, and virtually any other of the Web 2.0 capabilities. Customers are arming themselves with a plethora of information, opinions,
and insights about you, your products, your company, your competition, your successes, and your failures . . . before you even meet
them. Gone are the days where you need a "corporate overview" during your presentation (if you're still doing those, please stop—you're
boring your customers to death). And, while the customers are doing
their homework to learn about you—you should be doing the same
thing. Customers are going to become increasingly intolerant of
"fact-finding" questions during Discovery if the information is available elsewhere. Asking questions to which you can otherwise find
and triangulate the answers not only wastes time with your customer, it lessens your credibility.

If you want to be successful in the new way of selling, you have to
remember that "selling" is what *we* do, but the definitive action in
any transaction is that someone chooses to *buy*. Selling needs to support our customers' buying process, providing them with the information and insight that will ultimately guide them to choose us. We call
this the "Eye of the Buyer" because the more we look at the relationship and activities from the customer's perspective, the more we can
anticipate and respond to their questions and take advantage of the
information they gather on their own. When we consciously and
deliberately recognize that they are going to follow their buying process regardless of how we'd prefer to sell, we demonstrate that we are
focused first and foremost on the customer's success (knowing our
success comes from theirs) and instilling trustworthiness into our
relationship with the customer. If you're interested in seeing through
the Eye of the Buyer, consider the following sections of this article.

■ KNOCK DOWN THE WALLS BETWEEN MARKETING AND SALES

In many organizations these two departments are just that—two separate departments with disparate responsibilities and their own mission to fulfill. Marketing is tasked with everything from corporate
messaging to product competitive intelligence. Sales is tasked with

taking the information provided by marketing and using it to persuade customers to buy. But in so many organizations today, this process is severely broken. It's not just that one hand doesn't always know what the other is doing—it's worse. Because customers are so well equipped with information—good and bad—you need to compensate for their advanced knowledge. Build into your messaging and sales strategy the fact that they can find out so much about you and your company. Vendors no longer control what information can be accessed by customers, so you need to leverage the fact that they have it to your best advantage.

For the sales team to be effective, they need to first find out what the customer already knows and, more important, what the customer is trying to achieve in order to effectively position your products. This means that marketing and sales have to be integrated and interdependent, with a singular mission of helping customers achieve success.

■ QUIT WASTING MONEY ON BROCHURES—WHO NEEDS 'EM?

As mentioned just above, in many instances your brochures—especially if they've been mass produced and shipped to the sales offices by the box-load—are largely useless. Your customers don't care about how your product solves the problems faced by "many firms." They care about one thing only—how it will solve their issues. And they don't need a glossy to make the point. In most cases, they'd rather see your sales team do its homework, ask really smart questions, and speak intelligently about your product or service as it relates specifically to them. Remember a picture is worth a thousand words, so it's better if you can graphically represent your understanding of their situation instead of loading up a PowerPoint with text-filled slides.

■ YOUR SALES PROCESS DOESN'T MATTER

While most companies have some semblance of a sales process (e.g., Identify, Qualify, Discover, Present Solution, Close—or something similar), ostensibly to let them know "where the deal is" in the process, it's useless unless that sales process is aligned to the customer's buying process. You might declare yourself "done" with any given stage in your process because you've done all the activities spelled out in the process guide. However, your customer has a set of activities *they* plan on doing during that stage as well, and if they're not done with those activities, the stage isn't finished. The only way you can know if they're done is if you establish verifiable outcomes— things you can witness the customer say or do that indicates they've completed *their* activities in that stage of their evaluation. This phenomenon of process misalignment represents a major reason that deals in your forecast slip from one period to the next. It's very easy for a sales rep to declare that they've done all the activities they need to start the "negotiation" stage, and forecast the deal for this quarter, but if they fail to realize that the customer is still in the "evaluate options" stage—that is, nowhere near the point of being ready to sign a contract—the deal can't help but slip on the forecast.

■ "SUCCESS" IS MORE IMPORTANT THAN "SOLUTIONS"

Sure, the RFP or evaluation is going to ask for your best approach to solving their problems. Solutions are important to communicate—because the concept of a "solution" gives comfort to the anxiety in a customer organization—and the more they're spending with you, the greater the anxiety. Therefore, we don't want to exclude the conversations around solutions, but they alone are not enough. You have to connect the solution to business results and the ultimate success they're going to realize by the implementation of your solution—and in this case, the more quantifiable, the better.

■ GET BEYOND YOUR CRM

Sales force automation (SFA) and customer relationship management (CRM) tools are critical in today's business environment because they help institutionalize your "corporate memory" of each interaction with the customer—making it easier to add new members to your team, brief your manager on each activity you've performed, and otherwise track a sales opportunity. What most CRM systems do not perform as well as we'd like is the managing and analyzing of information you enter to help you sell better, nor do they provide sales management with meaningful data with which to coach the sales teams on their opportunities. In order to know where you really stand, focus on advancement (in alignment with the customer's buying process) instead of counting activities, and use a tool such as Dealmaker, which works with your CRM, to give you true automation of sales effectiveness, not merely sales activity.

There are more aspects of selling that can benefit from a change in perspective than space allows me to address. But remember, you'll be ahead of the pack if you sit on the customer's side of the table and make it all about what they're trying to achieve, construct your messages to match the opportunity at hand, and give your CRM the ability to help you win.

Name: Steve Maul

Company: InfoMentis, Inc.

Web Site: www.infomentis.com

Biography: Steve Maul is executive vice president and chief learning and strategy officer of InfoMentis. Mr. Maul, with more than 25 years of marketing, sales, and channel experience, became a charter member of InfoMentis in 1996 as the executive vice president of delivery services. He is responsible for managing the curriculum, design, and development process and project management for InfoMentis, including instructor certification (internal and external) for program content and delivery. In addition, he developed and manages the Momentum implementation framework used by InfoMentis principals as solutions are deployed for client organizations.

Selling Philosophy: Customer-collaborative selling

Target Industries: Information technology, telecommunications, financial services, manufacturing, pharmaceutical

Best Sellers: Opportunity Management, Account Planning and Management, Personal Sales Effectiveness, Selling as a Sales Manager

Sales Tip One: Executives want salespeople to provide insight on the prospect's competitors, industry trends, common opinions, and perceptions from the outside world, as well as an unbiased assessment of their people.

Sales Tip Two: The key to team selling is to use other team members to ask questions you have already asked to see if the answer is the same or different.

Sales Tip Three: Many solutions look alike, so be specific about your advantages and their value.

Product One: MentisWare

Product Two: Dealmaker Virtual Learning System

Chapter 38

Building a Bridge between Service and Selling

Walt Zeglinski and Bill Kowalski
Integrity Solutions Holdings

This should not come as a shock . . . *Markets are becoming more competitive and products are rapidly commoditizing.*

Against this backdrop many organizations remain committed to their growth strategies. They have recognized that the success of their growth strategy depends on increasing customer acquisition and loyalty. Therein lies the dilemma: how to acquire new customers and increase the number of products and services purchased per customer, while maintaining the high level of service customers have come to expect. At a time when most consumers feel "like a number," this has great appeal. If your organization can build the bridge between superior service and results-producing selling, you will have created a unique competitive advantage.

■ SERVICE VERSUS SELLING

In a pure service culture, organizational and employee behavior is contingent on your team's skill in responding to customer inquiries. However, in a service-selling culture employees proactively seek to understand customers' wants and needs and increase the value created in every customer experience. Service organizations who have not made this transition will find organic growth difficult.

The most progressive of organizations, across industries, have made significant investments to improve the proactive needs-focused selling behaviors of their service team. Others have chosen to emphasize a more reactive cross-selling approach. Whatever their choice, and despite their best efforts, these investments have generally produced very little in the way of bottom line results. So you may want to know . . .

Why are many service organizations resistant to sales initiatives?

Does service have to suffer in order to develop a sales culture?

Why is it so difficult to build a bridge between service and selling?

■ TRANSFORMATIONAL CHANGE

The successful transformation from a service culture to a service-selling culture is challenging. Many service organizations have struggled with the notion that embracing a sales philosophy is in the best interests of customers and, as a result, both leadership and employees are resistant to adopting a sales philosophy. For decades consumers have been wary of salespeople trying to persuade them to buy their products, since many salespeople are often more concerned with making a sale than fulfilling a customer's needs. This is evident in consumer surveys conducted by the Harris and Gallup organizations that routinely ask consumers to rank the most trusted professionals to give advice. Salespeople typically rank at or near the bottom of the list. This negative view of selling has created a cynical perspective within the leadership teams of many service organizations.

Although leaders may still be committed to growth, they appear to be resigned to the idea that executing a growth strategy will force superior service to take a back seat. Many have come to believe that building the bridge between service and selling is too difficult, too expensive, and/or too traumatic to their cultures.

In our experience, to successfully transform a culture, you must implement solutions that engage the hearts and minds of your employees. To accomplish this, they must learn to embrace the definition of selling and service as one and the same. When "selling" is redefined as doing something for someone, your team may give themselves "permission" to create more value for customers. Once employees believe that selling and service are both noble activities that focus on identifying and fulfilling the needs of customers and creating value for them—you will be on the path to transformational change.

John P. Kotter, the renowned change expert and author of the best-selling book *The Heart of Change*, states that the key factor in a successful change initiative is the behavior of people. As Kotter points out, without changing employees' feelings and beliefs, their behaviors will not be sufficiently altered to overcome the many barriers to large-scale change. It is therefore essential for leaders to implement strategies that will impact their people at the emotive level and help them develop positive beliefs about selling—if you hope to gain their "buy-in." Skill development alone will not produce sustainable behavior change.

■ COMPETITIVE ADVANTAGE

As the competitive landscape becomes more difficult and products look and sound more and more alike, the effectiveness of your service-selling team is still the critical success factor for revenue growth and customer loyalty. Those "moments of truth" with your customers can be your competitive advantage and leveraging them can become the foundation for your growth strategy. If you can build the bridge between service and selling, you will enable your team to find and close sales opportunities while they are delivering extraordinary service.

Once your team consistently approaches service and selling as two sides of the same coin, you will have solidified your commitment to maximizing the value you create for customers. The more value you create for customers, the greater your competitive advantage will be. It's really that simple. Building the bridge between service and selling can be the most significant asset to your growth strategy.

Names: Walt Zeglinski and Bill Kowalski

Company: Integrity Solutions Holdings, LLC

Web Site: www.integritysolutions.com

Biography: Walt Zeglinski is CEO and chief client advocate for Integrity Solutions, a performance improvement company. Walt has over 20 years of experience in the corporate performance industry, diagnosing, planning, and implementing practical solutions for complex business challenges. He has worked with executives and front-line sales and service teams across most industries.

Bill Kowalski is Integrity Solutions senior vice president of client development and consulting. Bill has 15 years of executive management experience in sales, marketing, and customer service, including 7 years in a division of a Fortune 500 company. He has over 10 years of consulting experience in change management and performance improvement.

Selling Philosophy: Customer-centric performance development

Target Industries: Financial services, health care, medical device, pharmaceutical, business-to-business

Best Sellers: Integrity Selling; Integrity Coaching; Integrity Service

Sales Tip One: AID, Inc.: Follow a process from start to finish for success.

Sales Tip Two: Adjust your behavior style to that of your clients and prospects.

Sales Tip Three: Understand and apply the Gap model.

Book One: *Integrity Selling for the 21st Century*

Book Two: *Integrity Service*

Book Three: *The People Principle*

Product One: Integrity Selling

Product Two: Integrity Coaching

Product Three: Integrity Service

Chapter

39

Developing and Implementing
a Structured Sales Process

Justin Zappulla
Janek Performance Group

■ WHY HAVE A STRUCTURED SALES PROCESS?

Structuring a *proven* process for conducting the sale puts your company in a position to define, prepare for, quantify, track, and increase sales success.

Allowing salespeople to "wing-it," be mavericks, or sell in their own "unique" ways is unreliable. You need real data to predict sales with more accuracy, to prepare for a variety of scenarios, to identify areas for improvement, and to make your sales behaviors fit better with your customer's buying behaviors.

Relying on the opinions of salespeople as a source of information is inaccurate and flawed. Consider prospecting—without clear guidelines as to what qualifies as a good prospect, salespeople tend to hold on to the "junk"—they favor the ones that talked to them the most, or maybe they liked the sound of the customer's voice, or they made some personal connection with the customer—they need logical criteria, not their emotions, to guide their actions. We're human—that's why we have structure—it makes us more accurate.

Salespeople, regardless of their years of experience, need a proven process to follow. Even the best, championship-level athletes structure their training to ensure continued levels of performance and success.

Additionally, new resources, new products, and new techniques can be more easily worked in, tracked, and evaluated when you have a solid grasp on how your current sales process is performing. Without an accurate bird's-eye view of your sales process and your sales pipeline, adding new elements into the mix is like throwing stuff at the wall and waiting to see what sticks.

With that in mind, gather together a solid team from many areas and levels of your sales operation to design your structure.

■ DEVELOPING A STRUCTURED SALES PROCESS

Clarify your sales philosophy. It's not the same as your company's mission statement, but instead specifically how you see sales or selling in relation to your buyers or customers. A short example would be "Selling is about identifying the buyer's needs and customizing a solution to fit those needs with our products/services." Your sales philosophy will be your constant guide in developing, implementing, and revising your sales process.

Identify customer profiles. Who is your ideal customer? Who is the typical customer in your existing customer base? What kinds of customers in your existing customer base tend to have the most problems or complaints? What kind of customer needs your products/services? Your customer relationship management (CRM) system, if you have one in place, is a good source for this information.

Describe your most effective sales behaviors. *Based upon your customer profile*, you need to determine:

➤ What your customers need to know, understand, and feel to interact with your salespeople and ultimately purchase.

➤ What your salespeople need to know, understand, and feel to interact with your potential customers and ask for the business.

Do your sales require lots of technical explanations or minitutorials? Or do your sales need minimal, one to two interactions? What can stall sales? What keeps the sales process moving forward? What turns customers on? Off? If you are finding that many potential buyers are putting on the brakes when they feel they don't understand, then you need to structure a sales process that incorporates some solid and user-friendly tutorials. If, on the other hand, you find that buyers back away from sales when they have too much time to decide or too much information, then you need to structure a sales process that remains simple and swift. Will your sales interactions require lots of comparison with competitors? Would visual aids help your buyers?

Develop a model of your sales process. Include a visual aid to map out the behaviors of your sales interactions—a Client Interaction Model. This model should identify certain milestones or marks to help your salespeople know where they are in the sales process. The model will also help show how and where the different parts of your sales process fit together. When should your salespeople be asking questions? Where do your salespeople need preparation time? What kinds of behaviors will your salespeople do on the first interactions? Where do price discussions fit in?

■ IMPLEMENTING A STRUCTURED SALES PROCESS

Implementing your sales process is different from developing your sales process. Implementing is what you will actually do to put your sales process into action and keep it on track. Here's a general checklist:

➤ Communicate your goals to your salespeople and their support team

➤ Define the concepts

➤ Explain the steps and time line of your sales process (using your model)

➤ Describe the actions required

➤ Create documentation (either hard copy or a software system) to track steps and actions

➤ Take measurements and evaluate meaningful data

➤ Provide opportunities to evaluate and give feedback on performance

➤ Solicit feedback from your salespeople

Empower your sales team to succeed in implementing your structured sales process by making the process as clear to perform as possible, by expecting your sales team to follow the process as outlined, and by improving the process with their feedback and hands-on experience.

Name: Justin Zappulla

Company: Janek Performance Group, Inc.

Web Site: www.janek.com

Biography: As corporate vice president of business development at Janek Performance Group, Inc., Justin Zappulla oversees sales across all Janek sales solutions, including corporate sales training, nationwide sales seminars, and sales strategy consulting.

In addition to leading Janek's ongoing efforts to build strong relationships with corporate clients, Zappulla focuses on aligning the company's sales and training philosophies to achieve better client results. His main objectives include expanding the global scale of Janek training offerings, enhancing service levels and client satisfaction, and cultivating a more client-focused environment for the organization. During his career Justin has trained more than 10,000 sales professionals worldwide.

Selling Philosophy: Need-based selling

Target Industries: Business and professional services, consumer goods and retail, energy and utilities, financial and insurance services, health care, hospitality and travel, media and publications, pharmaceutical, real estate and construction, technology and telecommunications

Best Sellers: Customized Corporate Sales Training Services, Several Fundamental and Advanced Sales Training Curricula; Critical Selling, Critical TeleSelling, Critical Sales Coaching and Performance Management, Critical Sales Negotiations, and Strategic Sales Consulting Services

Sales Tip One: Stay committed to exploring your client's full range of needs; you have to be willing to go deeper than what lies at the surface. This will enable you to best position your solution to meet their needs and win the sale.

Sales Tip Two: When selling over the phone it is critical to portray a positive phone presence. Sit up, stand up, use body language, mirror your customer, visualize the person on the other end, and keep a good pace to your call.

Sales Tip Three: The first 30 seconds of a sales call is critical, so don't wing it; instead, be prepared to engage the customer. You'll sound more confident and see better results.

How to Present with Mastery, So People Take Action

Tony Jeary
Tony Jeary International

All professionals need to present well to insure best results in all areas of their professional and personal lives. The following eight simple presentation practices will dramatically increase your impact on making sales, no matter the size of your audience.

1. **Involve Your Audience.** When presenting to an individual or to groups, make sure you involve and engage them. Ask questions, have them write things down, have them talk to each other in a group. Engagement reduces tension and elevates retention.

2. **Prepare Your Audience.** Remember, most audiences spend the first three minutes of the presentation sizing up the presenter. A basic, often overlooked element of working with groups is simply connecting with your audience before your presentation or meeting begins. Warm a few people up and warm yourself up, too.

3. **Research Your Presentation Arsenal.** Build and utilize a Presentation Arsenal. Your arsenal should include quotes, stories, samples, examples, and even statistics. Save them mentally, in hard-copy form, or on your computer.

4. **Explain the "Why."** The single most powerful thing you can do to persuade or convince your audience is to provide a convincing reason why they should do what you suggest (or believe what you say). It's simple: Just tell them why.

5. **State Management.** The mental state of the successful presenter or salesperson must be congruent with the message being delivered. All the techniques you use to get yourself in the proper state of mind can also be used to influence your customers' states of mind.

6. **Eliminate Unknowns and Turn Them into Knowns.** The more you explore all components (such as the room setup, how the audience or customers will react, who will do what and when), the more confident you will be. Strong preparation transforms the unknowns into knowns and reduces nervousness.

7. **Know Your Audience.** Before your presentation, research your audience and plan to address their needs.

8. **Tailor Your Presentation for the Audience.** Your focus must always be on the audience, not only on your agenda. Be flexible and ready to adjust to your audience so they really hear your message.

Here are a few additional ideas to further your Presentation Mastery:

Audience Champions. Having someone else speak not only helps direct attention away from you, but it also changes the dynamic in the room by introducing the power of authority or social proof, depending upon who is doing the speaking. Hearing an authoritative voice in addition to yours can reinforce your message by lending validation to your perspective, and also serves to relax the crowd, which will result in increased receptivity.

Targeted Polling/Verbal Surveying. Ask the audience how you're doing and adjust accordingly; include asking about the speed, the details of the presentation, and so on. This will ensure you are on the mark.

Focus on Continual Self-Improvement. Use the above techniques, and move them into habits. Remember, you're presenting all the time, not just in front of groups and not only when you're trying to make a sale. Life really *is* a series of presentations.

Tony Jeary enjoys advising, coaching, and guiding high achievers to the next level of results and success. Please take the free assessment at www.TonyJeary.com.

Name: Tony Jeary

Company: Tony Jeary International

Web Site: www.tonyjeary.com

Biography: Tony Jeary is about *results*. A sought-after executive coach, strategist and motivational speaker, he is a personal coach to some of the world's top CEOs, including Ford, Wal-Mart, Firestone, and Sam's Club, as well as executives from New York Life, American Airlines, Shell, and many other Fortune 500 companies.

Tony has written 38 books that have been translated into over a dozen languages, including his best sellers *Life Is a Series of Presentations* and *Strategic Acceleration: Succeed at the Speed of Life.*

Over the past 25 years Tony has coached and trained hundreds of thousands of people on how to get results faster.

Selling Philosophy: Strategic Acceleration through Presentation Mastery

Target Industries: All industries

Best Sellers: *Life Is a Series of Presentations* and *Strategic Acceleration: Succeed at the Speed of Life*

Sales Tip One: Speed is the strategic engine needed to compete and win in a rapidly changing marketplace. Results determine if you win or not. Being really, really clear on what you want is step one.

Sales Tip Two: Present Strategically: When presenting/communicating, delivery is only half of the puzzle. Preparing to deliver is equally important.

Sales Tip Three: One of the biggest keys to keeping an audience engaged and buying in to what you're sharing is involvement. Find ways, whether the group size is 1 or 1,000, to get them involved.

Book One: *Strategic Acceleration: Succeed at the Speed of Life*

Book Two: *Life Is a Series of Presentations*

Book Three: *Persuade Any Audience*

Product One: Communication Mastery

41

Biggest Time Wasters for Salespeople

Dave Kahle
The DaCo Corporation

Good time management for salespeople has been an obsession of mine for more than 30 years. In the past decade, I've been involved in helping tens of thousands of salespeople improve their results through more effective use of their time. Over the years, I've seen some regularly occurring patterns develop—tendencies on the part of salespeople to do things that detract from their effective use of time.

Here are the four most common time wasters I've observed. See if any of these apply to you or your salespeople.

■ ALLURE OF THE URGENT/TRIVIAL

Salespeople love to be busy and active. We have visions of ourselves as people who can get things done. No idol dreamers, we're out there making things happen!

A big portion of our sense of worth and our personal identity is dependent on being busy. At some level in our self-image of ourselves, being busy means that we really are important. One of the worst things that can happen to us is to have nothing to do, nowhere to go, and nothing going on. So, we latch onto every task that comes our way, regardless of the importance.

For example, one of our customers calls with a back order problem. "Oh good!" we think, "Something to do! We are needed! We can fix it!" So, we drop everything and spend two hours expediting the back order.

In retrospect, couldn't someone in purchasing or customer service have done that? And couldn't they have done it better than you? And didn't you just allow something that was a little urgent but trivial prevent you from making some sales calls? And wouldn't those potential sales calls be a whole lot better use of your time?

Or, one of our customers hands us a very involved "Request for Quote." "Better schedule a half-day at the office," we think. "Need to look up specifications, calculate prices, compile literature, and so on." We become immediately involved with this task, working on this project for our customer. In retrospect, couldn't we have given the project to an inside salesperson or customer service rep to do the leg work? Couldn't we have simply communicated the guidelines and then reviewed the finished proposal?

Once again, we succumbed to the lure of the present task. That prevented us from making sales calls and siphoned our energy away from the important to the seemingly urgent.

I could go on for pages with examples, but you have the idea. We are so enamored with being busy and feeling needed that we often grab at any task that comes our way, regardless of how unimportant. And each time we do that, we compromise our ability to invest our sales times more effectively.

■ THE COMFORT OF THE STATUS QUO

A lot of salespeople have invested time in developing a comfortable routine. They make enough money and they have established habits that are stable and comfortable. They really don't want to expend the energy it takes to do things in a better way, or to become more successful or effective.

This can be good. Some of the habits and routines that we follow work well for us.

However, our rapidly changing world constantly demands new methods, techniques, habits, and routines. Just because something has been effective for a few years doesn't mean that it will continue to be so. This problem develops when salespeople are so content with the way things are, they have not changed anything in years.

If you haven't changed or challenged some habit or routine in the past few years, chances are that you are not as effective as you could be.

For example, you could still be writing phone messages down on little slips of paper, when entering them into your contact manager would be more effective. This is a simple example of a principle that can be extended toward the most important things that we do. Are we using the same routines for organizing our work week, for determining who to call on, for understanding our customers, for collecting information, and so forth? There is no practical end to the list.

Contentment with the status quo almost always means that salespeople are not as effective as they could be.

My book, *10 Secrets of Time Management for Salespeople*, discusses the use of the "more" mind-set as an alternative to the status quo.

■ LACK OF TRUST IN OTHER PEOPLE IN THE ORGANIZATION

Salespeople have a natural tendency to work alone. After all, we spend most of the day by ourselves. We decide where to go by ourselves, we decide what to do by ourselves, and we are pretty much on our own all day long. It's no wonder, then, we just naturally want to do everything by ourselves.

That's generally a positive personality trait for a salesperson. Unfortunately, when it extends to those tasks that could be done better by other people in our organization, it turns into a real negative.

Instead of soliciting aid from others in the organization, and thereby making much better use of our time, many salespeople insist on doing it themselves, no matter how redundant and time-consuming the task is. The world is full of salespeople who don't trust their own colleagues to write an order, to source a product, to enter an order in the system, to follow up on a back order, to deliver some sample or literature, to research a quote, to deliver a proposal, and so on. Again, the list could go on and on.

The point is that many of these tasks can be done better or cheaper by someone else in the organization. The salespeople don't release the tasks to them because they, the salespeople, don't trust them to do it. Too bad. It's a tremendous waste of good selling time and talent. Chapter 10 of my book *10 Secrets* describes a system to nurture helpful relationships.

■ LACK OF TOUGH-MINDED THOUGHTFULNESS

Ultimately, time management begins with thoughtfulness. That means a sufficient quantity of good-quality thought-energy invested in the process. I like to say that good time management is a result of "thinking about it before you do it."

Good time managers invest sufficiently in this process. They set aside time each year to create annual goals, they invest planning time every quarter and every month to create plans for those times, and they plan every week and every sales call. Poor sales time managers don't dedicate sufficient time to the "thinking about it" phase of their job.

Not only do good sales time managers invest a sufficient quantity of time, but they also are disciplined and tough-minded about how they think. They ask themselves good questions, and answer them with as much objectivity as they can muster.

➤ "What do I really want to accomplish in this account?"

➤ "Why aren't they buying from me?"

➤ "Who is the key decision maker for this account?"

➤ "Am I spending too much time on this account, or not enough in that one?"

➤ "How can I change what I am doing in order to become more effective?"

These are just a few of the tough questions that good time managers consider on a regular basis. They don't allow their emotions or personal comfort zones to dictate the plans. They go where it is smart to go, do what it is smart to do. They do these things because they have spent the quantity and quality of thought-time necessary.

Of course, there are hundreds of other time-wasting habits. These four, however, are the most common. Correct them, and you'll be well on your way to dramatically improved results.

Name: Dave Kahle

Company: The DaCo Corporation

Web Site: www.davekahle.com

Biography: Dave Kahle is one of the country's leading business-to-business sales trainers. He is a world-class speaker, having presented in seven countries and 43 states.

Dave's ability to challenge people to think differently arises from his more than 30 years of sales experience coupled with his educational background. The number-one salesperson in the country for two different companies, he has both a B.Ed. and a master of arts in teaching.

He has written seven books, created dozens of video and CD programs, and has been published over 1,000 times. His *Thinking about Sales* e-zine is received by 30,000 salespeople and sales managers each week.

Selling Philosophy: Selling thoughtfully

Target Industries: Business-to-business, wholesale distribution

Best Sellers: *10 Secrets of Time Management for Salespeople*, The Kahle Way B2B Selling System, and *Question Your Way to Sales Success*

Sales Tip One: The quickest way to improve your sales is to make better decisions about in whom you invest your sales time. "Where to go, who to see, what to do" are the decisions that, more than any other single thing, will impact your performance.

Sales Tip Two: The questions that you ask yourself are just as important as the questions you ask your customers. They prompt your thinking and uncover new ideas.

Sales Tip Three: The ultimate sales tool is a well-constructed series of questions. There is nothing you can do in a sales call that has more power than asking a good question.

Book One: *10 Secrets of Time Management for Salespeople*

Book Two: *Question Your Way to Sales Success*

Book Three: *Transforming Your Sales Force for the 21st Century*

Product One: The Kahle Way B2B Selling System

Product Two: Up-a-Notch Video Series for Outside and Inside Salespeople

Product Three: The Kahle Way Sales Management System

Chapter 42

The Key to Growing
Your Sales

Work on Your Openings, Not Your Closings!

Ron Karr
Karr Associates

CEOs are always looking for ways how to help their salespeople enhance their closing skills. I always tell them that often, it's not the closing skills that are limiting their salespeople's success, it's their opening skills! If the conversation is started properly, the right questions are asked, and the correct value proposition is put forth, closing the deal often becomes the next logical step. Don't get me wrong. You still have to ask for the order. But without the right opening, often the wrong value proposition is put forth, and the close doesn't happen. And that's if the salesperson has managed to keep the customer's attention and arrived at the closing stage to begin with.

Like all effective leaders, top-producing salespeople have to gain their customers' time and attention if they are going to succeed in selling their ideas and products/services. The key to gaining someone's attention is to start the conversation with the outcomes you will produce versus how you will produce them.

Remember, people don't want to be sold in today's economy. They do want help with the acquisition process. As a leader, you must determine the "what" before the "how"—the "how" comes second. Your products and services represent the "how," which means that they are not what you should be starting the conversation with. If you start with the "how" first, the customer will think you are only there to gain a "sale" and will not listen attentively to what you are saying.

Read that again: *You should not begin the conversation on your products and services*—even though you may have received vast amounts of technical training and even though you may know the "how" of your product and service like the back of your hand. If you start the conversation with the "how," you will leave out the most important part of the conversation, namely, the outcomes you are going to produce together.

These may sound like obvious points, but the sad truth is that salespeople routinely ignore them.

Beginning with the "how" guarantees that your conversation will be short and will produce little to no forward movement in the sales process. You may not even be given the opportunity to discuss the prospect's goals or the outcomes you hope to produce with him or her. How many sales meetings have you had that ended abruptly because of some sudden emergency or lack of interest while you were soliloquizing about the many great features you have to offer?

People tend to have very short attention spans these days. They have a lot on their mind, and the higher up they are on the food chain the less time they have for things that don't demonstrate immediate value to them. That's why we must prove in the first few seconds of a conversation that there is a reason someone should give us their undivided attention and their time.

Initiating a conversation by discussing the outcomes—as a leader does—makes all the difference when it comes to winning attention, winning time, closing more deals, expanding the size of the deal, and increasing margins. Launching the conversation in a different way allows you to lay the foundation for a value proposition that is second to none.

Immediately focusing on the "how" limits your conversation with a potential customer strictly to features—features that most customers will think, correctly or incorrectly, that they have heard of and seen elsewhere. This leaves little or no room there for differentiating your product. By leading with the outcome—as a true sales leader would—you can expand the conversation to other issues, issues that involve a larger piece of the pie. As the conversation expands, more and more opportunities will become available. These opportunities can lead to the sale of other goods and services.

For example, let's say that you are selling pool products to a homeowner who wants a new pump. You might be tempted to start talking about the features of your very best pool pump. Suppose you were to ask the homeowner what he or she would want from the new pump that the old pump didn't provide. The homeowner might think for a moment, then answer, "No downtime, better energy efficiency, and lower operating costs."

When you ask the potential customer to explain their reasons for wanting these features, you might hear a story of how the existing pump used to break down—typically on a hot summer day—and how the whole family would have to wait for the service rep to come and repair it. The use of the pool would be interrupted for days, and there would be a hefty repair bill to deal with.

Armed with this information, you can now talk about the ideas and outcomes that are most likely to make a difference to this buyer: Fewer breakdowns and lower bills! You could offer proof of your pump's energy efficiency and reliability, in the form of awards and articles praising its performance in these areas. You could then explain that your company offers a special extended warranty on the pump. This extended warranty is designed to reduce the risk of having downtime in the future, and it will also give the customer automatic top priority on service calls without costing a cent more on the repair bill.

You have just engaged your customer and secured his full, undivided attention; every point you make is now landing with impact. You have just dramatically increased your chances of getting the deal, and you've done so by talking about the outcomes first. You may even have added to the size of the deal by introducing other products that support the outcomes that the customer is trying to attain.

At the end of the day, the customer is not buying a pump at all. The customer is actually buying uninterrupted pool time, reduced energy costs, and a lower cost of operation. Those are outcomes! This is exactly what Hayward Pool Products, the number-one manufacturer of residential pool pumps, trains its dealers to do. And that, along with a great product, is why they are one of the leaders in their industry.

Position yourself at the highest level in your customer's mind by talking first about the big outcomes they will achieve from listening to you and using your products and services. Then get into the details. It is the difference between selling a transaction and selling a bigger solution that involves more product/services and generates greater revenues and profit.

As in real estate, your success in sales all has to do with your positioning!

Name: Ron Karr

Company: Karr Associates, Inc.

Web Site: www.ronkarr.com

Biography: Ron Karr is CEO of Karr Associates, Inc., a firm that specializes in helping organizations build high-performing sales cultures and customer loyalty.

He has conducted seminars and keynote addresses before organizations on three continents. Clients include United Natural Foods, Morgan Stanley, Mass Mutual, Marriott Hotels, UPS, and Hertz.

Karr is the author of *Lead, Sell, or Get Out of the Way* and *The Titan Principle: The Number-One Secret to Sales Success* and coauthor of *The Complete Idiot's Guide to Great Customer Service*.

Ron is an active member of the National Speakers Association and is currently a director of the national board.

Selling Philosophy: Value-added selling, strategic selling, leadership selling

Target Industries: All business-to-business, financial services, manufacturing, service, entrepreneurs

Best Sellers: *Lead, Sell, or Get Out of the Way, The Titan Principle: The Number-One Secret to Sales Success* (book and/or audio), and Titan Sales Boot Camp (consulting)

Sales Tip One: Ground yourself in points of power: your strengths. This is crucial before entering a negotiation. It will help you close the deal and prevent you from giving away unnecessary concessions.

Sales Tip Two: Don't take "no" personally. *No* is the answer of no risk. *Yes* is the answer of risk taking. If you get a no, simply find out what is missing and provide the solution. It often takes several nos to get to a yes. Ninety percent of all salespeople stop after the first no. IF you do everything possible and still get a no, then move on to the next prospect. Concentrate on those who are qualified to buy.

Sales Tip Three: Ask issues-based questions. These are questions about where the customer is trying to go. Then ask about the challenges they have in getting there. This is your moment of opportunity to get the sale.

Book One: *Lead, Sell, or Get Out of the Way*

Book Two: *The Titan Principle: The Number-One Secret to Sales Success*

Book Three: *The Masters of Impact Negotiating: The World's Most Dynamic Negotiators Share Their Passion for Persuasion*

Book Four: *The Complete Idiot's Guide to Great Customer Service*

Chapter 43

How, What, and Why Projects Fail

Dave Allman
Knowledge-Advantage

■ *HOW* PROJECTS FAIL

You just presented your "best and final" proposal in response to one of your customer's major initiatives. They inform you that you have won the business. All they need to do is "get the sign-off" from their senior management. So how is it that six months later you are still waiting for the business?

Customers' initiatives (your opportunities) are expected to improve operational performance and contribute to organizational goals.

McKinsey surveyed CEOs, CFOs, COOs, and CIOs. Their findings: Unless a solution speaks to each of their respective criteria . . . it will not get the sponsorship and follow-through needed to succeed.

A three-step process should be followed to build and sell the case for an initiative. First, stakeholders impacted by the initiative must be categorized (Organizational, Operational, and Infrastructure). Next, business criteria for each category of stakeholder must be determined (ROA, OI, and TCO). Finally, a value proposition must be articulated based on each of the three sets of criteria.

Gartner annually surveys thousands of infrastructure executives. These executives openly admit they do not know how to build and sell the value of their initiatives. Equally important, they are looking for help to build their business acumen and financial selling skills.

Knowing how to identify and articulate a value proposition for each category of stakeholder based on their specific business criteria creates a distinctive advantage.

You have a choice: Let significant sales opportunities stall or vanish, or help your customers to build and communicate compelling value propositions for their initiatives. Don't let their internal challenges impact your sales results.

■ *WHAT* PROJECTS FAIL

They told you what is required to "seal the deal." You provided the best answer in response to their stated requirements. Your solution is clearly the best fit. So what happened?

"Hard factor" requirements (capabilities, speeds, feeds, price, etc.) are much easier to determine than "soft factor" requirements (people, policies, procedures, and politics).

On average, 80 percent of the total time spent to identify requirements is focused on hard factors. Yet repeatedly, survey results highlight that soft factor requirements are the major reason initiatives fail to deliver to expectations (scope, time, and resources).

A solid understanding of organizational, operational, and infrastructure issues is needed to be proficient at gathering soft factor requirements. What is required "of and from" organizational and operational stakeholders determines success or failure.

Customers are not skilled at assessing soft factor requirements and building a road map to ensure the early-on and ongoing success of their initiatives (your opportunities).

Customers will readily accept proven methods and tools to improve their odds of success.

You have a choice. Let significant sales opportunities stall or vanish, or help your customers to ensure the early and ongoing success of their initiatives. Don't let their internal challenges impact your sales results!

■ *WHY* PROJECTS FAIL

Every day, you compete to participate in your customers' initiatives. But the reason why most initiatives fail to be approved will probably surprise you.

Gartner research has found that only one in five major initiatives go forward for senior management approval. And only one in five are actually approved (4 percent odds). Equally alarmingly, it was also found that it takes up to 35 percent of the total acquisition cost simply to reach a final approval decision.

Are your customers' initiatives simply poor ideas? Absolutely not! However, a major reason for their low odds of gaining approval is that they are not aligned with organizational and operational priorities.

For example, consider that *CFO* magazine reports the top CFO priorities to be:

➤ Appropriate use of e-commerce
➤ Prioritizing investments
➤ Return on investments
➤ Opportunity costs of being deficient

In contrast, Gartner found the top CIO priorities to be:

➤ Strategic planning
➤ Aligning IT and business goals
➤ Using IT for competitive breakthrough

Without a framework to drive the alignment of organizational, operational, and infrastructure priorities, a business/IT initiative's relevance is inexact and lacks equal significance to various stakeholders of the same organization.

Organizational priorities must drive operational priorities, which then set the stage for infrastructure initiatives and investments. By demonstrating a strong alignment of priorities, an initiative's odds for approval and ongoing success are dramatically improved.

Helping customers align their priorities helps you to position and sell your offerings. In addition, you are uniquely positioned to separate good opportunities from bad ones, so you can spend your time on the high-odds opportunities that are going to produce sales results.

You have a choice: Let significant sales opportunities stall or vanish, or help your customers to position and sell your offerings. Don't let their internal challenges impact your sales results.

Name: Dave Allman

Company: Knowledge-Advantage

Web Site: www.knowledge-advantage.com

Biography: Dave Allman is founder and CEO of Knowledge-Advantage. He formed the company in 1991 to provide a practical and integrated sales platform to help companies quickly improve sales results.

Dave has nearly 25 years of sales, management, training, and consulting experience, including leadership roles with IBM and KPMG. He codesigned the IBM Sales School and introduced the first commercially available customer collaboration platform.

For nearly two decades, Dave has designed sales training and automation platforms, aimed primarily at the Fortune 500 community. He is dedicated to helping sales organizations improve performance, retain top employees, and satisfy customers. Dave holds an EMBA from Emory University.

Selling Philosophy: Customer Engagement feeds Sales Process; you need both!

Target Industries: Health care and technology

Best Sellers: *The Dimensions of Success*

Sales Tip One: Solutions are the problem: Sales leaders and producers do not understand the difference between "selling solutions" and "solving problems."

Sales Tip Two: Do no harm: Buyers want help to identify and solve their problems; sellers do not know how to help.

Sales Tip Three: Say versus do: Sales leaders are the primary reason for discounting and transactional behavior by salesmen.

Book One: *The Dimensions of Success*

Chapter 44

Making a Difference

Jill Konrath
Selling to Big Companies

"All customers care about today is price. It doesn't matter if your product (service) is better, lasts longer, or enables them to do more things. If you don't have the lowest price, you lose."

Sound familiar? I can't tell you how many times I've heard discouraged sellers say various iterations of that quote in the past couple of years.

No one likes to feel that they might as well be selling wastebaskets or rubber bands. You hate to think your customers could care less about the quality of your products or services. That leaves you feeling empty, like you're wasting your time and your life.

If you're like most people, you want to feel good about the products or services you sell. You want to be proud of your services and capabilities. It's important to believe your product is top-notch and a great value.

Virtually every sales book on the market talks about the importance of being able to enumerate the features, advantages, and benefits of your offering. But in today's market it's just not enough.

To be successful in selling these days, it's imperative for you to go deeper—to understand the difference your product or service makes to your customer. And you must understand it from their perspective, not yours.

■ FINDING THE DIFFERENCE

Use these strategies to better understand the difference your product or service makes to your customers.

1. **Situational Analysis.** Use your critical thinking skills to analyze your customer's world. Ask yourself or brainstorm with colleagues:

➤ To the best of your knowledge, how are customers doing things without your product/service? (Identify the top two to three ways.)

➤ What problems are they likely to be experiencing because of what they're doing/using today? How might their current methods make it difficult for them to achieve their goals and objectives?

➤ How do these problems affect their business? This part is critical. "Feel-good" terms like *lowered morale* or *upset workers* isn't enough. Think in terms of critical business measures such as productivity, operational efficiency, profitability, costs, and time-to-market. How does your offering affect these issues?

2. **Ask Your Customer(s).** This is one of the most important things you can do—and it's much more effective if you do it after you've completed the situation analysis. Ask your customer:

➤ About how they did things before they bought your product or used your service.

➤ To share the problems your offering helped them fix and the goals it helped them achieve.

➤ About the value they realized from using your products or working with you.

This is an invaluable exercise. Have your questions prepared and take good notes. If you don't understand your customer's response, ask for clarification. You're at this meeting to learn as much as you can.

■ QUANTIFY THE DIFFERENCE

If at all possible, quantify the value of your offering. This is what catches the interest of today's business decision makers.

How much was turnover reduced? How much faster did the product come to market? What specific cost savings were achieved? How long did it take to get these results? What percentage increase/decrease was attained? What profits were gained from faster decision making?

Sound like a lot of work? It is . . . but it's worth every ounce of effort you put into it.

➤ When you know the difference you make, developing a strong value proposition is easy.

➤ When you know the difference you make, it's much easier to get your foot in the door.

➤ When you know the difference you make, you can develop great questions that explore customer's needs, issues, and concerns in areas where you have a solution.

➤ When you know the difference you make, it's possible to move a customer from indifference to urgency.

➤ When you know the difference you make, it's much easier to separate yourself from the competition.

➤ When you know the difference you make, it's much easier to keep going when times are rough.

Remember this: Customers could care less about your product or service. They only care about the difference you make!

If you haven't taken time from your busy schedule to find it out, do so right away. Not only will you feel better about yourself and the work you do, but you'll also sell more!

Name: Jill Konrath

Company: Selling to Big Companies

Web Site: www.sellingtobigcompanies.com

Biography: Jill Konrath, author of *SNAP Selling, Get Back to Work Faster*, and *Selling to Big Companies*, is a recognized sales strategist in the business-to-business marketplace. As a frequent speaker at sales meetings and conferences, Jill provides fresh perspectives to sales organizations.

Her Selling to Big Companies training programs are filled with breakthrough strategies, serious provocation, and how-to advice on how salespeople can crack into corporate accounts, speed up their sales cycle, and win more contracts.

Jill is often featured in top business publications like the *New York Times, Success, Inc., Business Journal, Entrepreneur, BusinessWeek*, and *Selling Power* as well as countless online magazines.

Selling Philosophy: Consultative, proactive, and customer-focused

Target Industries: Business-to-business, complex sale

Best Sellers: Selling to Big Companies (workshop), Selling to Crazy-Busy Buyers, Cracking into Corporate Accounts

Sales Tip One: To set up meetings with corporate decision makers, focus on the difference you can make for their business—not on how you're different from competitors.

Sales Tip Two: To shorten your sales cycle, leverage trigger events as a primary account entry strategy.

Sales Tip Three: To differentiate your offerings, become the differentiator. Be the expert that your customers can't live without.

Book One: *SNAP Selling*

Book Two: *Selling to Big Companies*

Book Three: *Get Back to Work Faster*

Book Four: *Winning More Sales Manual*

Product One: Getting into Big Companies self-study CD program

Product Two: Monthly Selling to Big Companies teleseminars

Chapter 45

How to Overachieve

Dave Kurlan
Baseline Selling

One of the questions I get asked most often is "What does it take to succeed?" In response to that question, I wrote the Top Seven Factors that impact your ability to overachieve in sales. I present them here:

1. **Goals.** I'm talking about "raise the bar, stretch, out of the comfort zone, more than the typical 15 percent increase in sales"–type goals here. You must raise your expectations in order to celebrate superior performance. Don't forget two things: (1) that a forecast and plan come from the goals, not the other way around, and (2) goals are derived not from your company but from your income requirements, based on the bills that accompany life's desires and obligations.

2. **Motivation.** This is the combination of goals and incentives. In essence, do you have a strong enough desire and commitment to do whatever it takes—every day—to reach the goals? When you don't, it's your job to motivate yourself by knowing the real reasons why you're doing this selling stuff. I'm not talking income requirements or gross sales here, I'm talking planes, boats, cars, big houses, vacation homes, golf trips, world travel, home theaters, fantasy camps, exclusive events, and so forth. As sales experts since the 1950s have said, the only difference between successful salespeople and their unsuccessful counterparts is that the successful salespeople choose to do the things they don't want to do.

3. **Managing the Pipeline.** A Visual Pipeline makes it significantly easier to manage your opportunities, but the key to managing the pipeline is working with your critical ratios. Think monthly goals, closing percentage, average sale, and length of the sell cycle. If you have a six-month sell cycle, a $100,000 monthly goal, a $20,000 average sale, and a 25 percent closing percentage, then managing the pipeline effectively requires that you put 20 (five $20,000 sales at

25 percent closing) new opportunities worth a total of $400,000 (25 percent of $100,000) into the pipeline six months in advance of the monthly goal (if the goal is for July, then the opportunities must enter the pipeline in February). Get that to work and the outcomes are all but guaranteed.

4. **Self-Starter.** Determine whether you are more effective when working independently or as part of a team, and whether you require supervision or can work without it. Those factors help to determine whether you are a self-starter. If you are not, you must get someone to start you up every day, twice daily, or as often as it takes. If you are a self-starter, you can get started anyplace and anytime.

5. **Skills.** The more the better, but let's focus on the most important skill sets for overachieving. You must be able to hunt for new opportunities, identify the most qualified, and be able to close them. Anything else you can do is a bonus! Baseline Selling provides you with all the skills, tactics, and strategies you'll need to overachieve.

6. **Urgency.** You must have enough urgency to get your opportunities closed, even when your prospects are trying to put you off. You must have a sense of *now*, as in "I have to get this closed now."

7. **Weaknesses.** Unfortunately, there are weaknesses that will neutralize all of the previous factors. There can be dozens of weaknesses that could impact performance, but none are so powerful as these five: Nonsupportive Buy Cycle, in which the way you buy does not support the way you need to sell; Need for Approval, when your need to be liked is stronger than your need to close; Tendency to Become Emotionally Involved, when you get caught by surprise and strategize on the fly, talking to yourself in the process; Money Issues, when you're too uncomfortable to continue a conversation about where the client will find the money; Self-Limiting Record Collection, when your collection of sales beliefs sabotages your outcomes.

This list of factors is not all-inclusive, but it's a good start. You can become an overachiever if you incorporate not some, but all of these factors.

Name: Dave Kurlan

Company: Baseline Selling

Web Site: www.baselineselling.com

Biography: Dave Kurlan is a top-rated speaker and a leading expert on Sales Force Development. He is the founder and CEO of Objective Management Group, Inc., and CEO of Kurlan & Associates, Inc.

Dave hosts the weekly business radio show *Meet the Sales Experts*.

He is the developer of the Dave Kurlan Sales Force Profile, a tool for evaluating the people, systems, and strategies in sales organizations. He has written *Mindless Selling* and his best seller, *Baseline Selling: How to Become a Sales Superstar by Using What*

You Already Know about the Game of Baseball, and is the author of Understanding the Sales Force, a Top 100 Blog.

Selling Philosophy: Baseline selling

Target Industries: Manufacturing, distribution, business services, financial services, high tech

Best Sellers: *Baseline Selling: How to Become a Sales Superstar by Using What You Already Know about the Game of Baseball; How to Get to 1st Base; How to Score; How to Get to 2nd Base; Raising Expectations, Increasing Performance; How to Upgrade Your Sales Force*

Sales Tip One: The Rule of Ratios: The cost of the prospect's problem must be at least twice the cost of your solution.

Sales Tip Two: Closing: You haven't earned the right to close until you've touched first, second, and third base and you've presented a needs and cost appropriate solution.

Sales Tip Three: Closing: Never give options. If you're an expert and you listened effectively, then there is only one ideal solution based on needs and budget. Options cause "think it overs."

Book One: *Baseline Selling: How to Become a Sales Superstar by Using What You Already Know about the Game of Baseball*

Book Two: *Mindless Selling*

How to Make Successful Cold Calls

Ron La Vine
Accelerated Cold Call Training

Are you having a hard time reaching decision makers, setting up well-qualified appointments, getting past gatekeepers, gathering information, or finding if you are calling on a prospect who is an appropriate choice in the first place?

These are big problems today in cold calling on businesses. It is so hard to get a response. The situation is bad, but it really doesn't have to be. This problem often stems from sales training in which reps are trained to start selling *before* they have determined if there is a need to sell. The problem becomes further compounded when sales reps think they are speaking with a decision maker but they really aren't. Add the urge to speak about their solutions rather than asking questions, and all of a sudden cold calling becomes difficult.

Becoming successful at cold calling requires you to switch from the old "If I make enough calls, I'll sell something" to "If I speak with the person who has the authority and need to buy and if I have the right solution to fit their needs, then they will buy" approach. This approach emphasizes finding the decision maker(s); using exploratory questions and active listening to gather information; learning who has the authority to buy, if there is a need to buy, and, if so, what you should be presenting so the prospect will buy.

■ STEP 1: ESTABLISH CALL OBJECTIVES

Your first objective should be to locate what we will call the "who," or decision maker(s). Second, you need to determine if a need exists. Third, suggest a solution based upon the information you've gathered. Fourth, ask for and set up time- and date-specific action steps.

Fifth, summarize and clarify the conversation both verbally and in writing.

■ STEP 2: FIND THE DECISION MAKER(S) FIRST

Before you can find the "who," you must first know how to work your way through the maze of a large organization. It is easy to get sidetracked by someone who says they have the authority to buy, but doesn't.

The easiest approach is the "top-down" approach, using the power of referral from above. Cold calling goes more easily if you always start at the top of an organization and work your way down.

On your initial call, your goal is to discover "who" is responsible for making decisions to buy your type of solution. Start with these questions: "Maybe you can help me? Who is responsible for [your solution]?" "Do you have a [ask for the highest level title responsible for the final decision to acquire your solution]?" "Do you have a CIO or a CFO?"

This isn't the time to talk about your solution. Your goal is to find the "who" first. This set of questions will keep you out of sales mode and help you stay in information mode. These questions will diminish your fear of rejection and build your confidence because people are usually willing and able to answer them. You'll also find that people are less defensive and more helpful when they don't feel like they are being sold.

Start by calling the headquarters receptionist and after confirming the address, ask for the name and correct spelling of the CEO (or president, etc.). Next ask to be transferred to the CEO's assistant.

The advantage of calling the CEO's assistant is twofold. The first reason is that they work and deal with the higher-level people (C-level, VPs, etc.), and second, when they refer you to the person they believe is the "who," that person or their office's gatekeeper will usually take your cold call.

The reason for this is that it is very difficult for a subordinate to refuse a call coming from a superior or a superior's office. Make sure you tell the truth and say you were referred by the CEO's office. This fact alone eliminates many of the roadblocks such as getting return calls or being put through to the decision makers themselves. Remember, you *do not* want to speak with the CEO or president, you want to speak with their assistant.

When you are transferred, the first thing you need to say is that you were referred by the CEO's office (or the CEO, if you speak with them).

Remember to be flexible and continue transferring to different departments to maximize the value of each call. The objective is to find a live person who will speak with you and provide more pieces of the selling puzzle.

Starting from the top and establishing the who's who of the organizational hierarchy eliminates a person at a lower level in the organization who might say, "Don't go above me, you deal only with me." This is because you can mention all the names of the people above.

■ STEP 3: ASK FOR PERMISSION TO SPEAK

From a business perspective, there may be nothing more valuable than our time. Let people know that you respect their time by asking, "Is this a good time to speak?" or "Do you have a few minutes?" before using your opening statement. Not only is this a more professional approach, you'll find people will offer their full attention since you've been given their permission to speak.

If it isn't a convenient time for your prospect to talk, first *confirm* that they are the *who* that you are trying to reach, *schedule a follow-up call*, and then *hang up the phone*. Why waste their time or yours? If they are busy, you certainly will not have their attention. Make a good impression by being polite and respectful of the other person's time.

■ STEP 4: USE DIRECT, OPEN-ENDED QUESTIONS

Start by using direct questions such as: "Who is responsible for . . . ?" or "How do you currently handle . . . ?" or "What are you doing in the area of . . . ?" or "When do you plan to make a decision on . . . ?" or "Why do you think that is?" Direct questions demonstrate you are in control of the conversation and you know what you are doing.

Avoid using weak questions or statements: "Could you possibly . . . ?" or "Might you be able to tell me . . . ?" or "I'm just trying to find out some information," or "I was hoping to find out. . . ." These types of statements imply a lack of confidence.

■ STEP 5: SUMMARIZE YOUR CONVERSATION

At the end and after any conversation involving action items, summarize verbally and in writing important points and clarify time- and date-specific next steps. Follow the verbal summary with a written one in an e-mail, and then call to be sure the information was received.

Use a summary e-mail to help you move forward toward the close of a sale. This e-mail provides a detailed summary of what you heard during the conversation, what it means, and the next steps to be taken, by whom and by when, in order to complete the sale.

In this e-mail, include:

➤ Prospect's company background (describe the past and current company situations).

➤ Current challenges or situation (list the needs, problems, pains, or challenges, and why they are occurring).

➤ Timing (specify the evaluation completion and decision dates you have been told).

➤ Evaluation process (identify who will conduct the evaluation and the criterion that will be used).

➤ Decision process (note who will be involved in making the decision and how they will decide).

➤ Budget (establish that budget has been set aside or to which there is access).

➤ The next step (lay out the process of who will do what and by when).

➤ A signature (include your complete contact information and a tag line explaining the benefits of your solution).

■ SUMMARY

You can make cold calling easier and more effective by starting at the top and by following these five steps:

1. Establish call objectives.
2. Find the decision maker(s) first.
3. Ask permission to speak.
4. Use direct open-ended questions.
5. Summarize your conversation.

Want to remove fear and rejection from cold calling? View cold calling as an informational puzzle. Your goal is to see how many pieces of information you can get on every call. When you gather information you didn't have before, you've gotten a result. If you've gotten a result, then you haven't been rejected. This puzzle approach will allow you to maximize your valuable selling time by calling on the people who can and will buy from you.

Name: Ron La Vine

Company: Accelerated Cold Call Training, Inc.

Web Site: www.coldcalltraining.com

Biography: Ron S. La Vine, MBA, president and founder of Accelerated Cold Call Training, Inc., has been in sales and sales management for over 35 years. Accelerated Sales Training specializes in working with business-to-business salespeople who conduct cold calling over the phone into the Fortune 500 and large organizations.

He works with hundreds of salespeople each year, helping salespeople use the phone more effectively to cold call, prospect, and sell and service accounts, without fear and rejection.

Ron has a bachelor's degree in management theory and practice from California State University, Northridge, and a master's degree in business administration from CLU University.

Selling Philosophy: Polite and respectful persistence using the top-down power of referral methodology

Target Industries: Ninety-five percent technology, 5 percent various other industries

Best Sellers: Top-Down Live Cold Call Training, Mastering the Art of Cold Calling (CDs), *Top-Down Live Cold Calling Workbook*

Sales Tip One: Professional salespeople always ask decision makers for permission to speak. If someone is in a meeting or has people in their office, they will not be listening to what you have to say.

Sales Tip Two: The person who asks the questions drives the direction of the call. Be sure to be in the driver's seat.

Sales Tip Three: Search the career section of a prospect's Web site to see what solutions are in use and what types of projects are being worked on.

Book One: *Creating the Business Breakthrough You Want: Secrets and Strategies from the World's Greatest Mentors*

Product One: Mastering the Art of Cold Calling (CDs)

Chapter 47

Create E-Mail Subject Lines That Draw Prospects In

Kendra Lee
KLA Group

E-mail is now the preferred prospecting tool, far surpassing the phone, to the relief of many sellers who hate cold calling. Yet it hasn't necessarily made prospecting any easier. Response rates are low and many sellers are discouraged by how difficult it is to engage contacts.

Often the culprit is the subject line. It's one of the most important keys to getting people to open your e-mails.

Many sellers love to use fun subject lines like "Enticing Ideas: Kendra Lee, Did You Catch the Wave?" They think that a bit of humor will lighten the recipient's day, prompting them to open it.

Wrong.

Remember who you're writing to and what you're trying to accomplish. Your e-mail is no different than a cold call. You're interrupting the day of an already overworked person.

Picture Steve. He has six meetings and one action item to conquer today. In fly 40, 50, possibly even 100 e-mails throughout the day. While humor is fun, it's a waste of valuable time that Steve doesn't have. Instead of laughing at cute subject lines and enjoying his mail, he's looking for reasons to hit "delete" and avoid another thing landing on his plate. If he doesn't recognize your name immediately, your lighthearted subject line instantly hits the delete barrier.

Regardless of how busy he is, you want your subject line to draw Steve in with a *personal and compelling* message.

If you're attempting to secure an appointment or invite a prospect to a Web event, try:

➤ Shall we meet Tuesday?

➤ Can you talk Wednesday at 2 PM?

➤ Can you attend Friday at 12?

What makes this work when the contact doesn't know you? It feels personal to him.

You're requesting a meeting at a specific date and time. He needs to read enough to determine what you want, then check his calendar to see if he can meet. These subject lines are successful because even though people no longer feel a sense of obligation to return every message, they do *feel more obliged to RSVP* to a meeting invitation.

Another subject-line approach you might use is to *share an insight* or tip you have for the prospect. Try:

➤ A hiring idea

➤ A thought about managing distributed files

➤ An idea about using your IT to grow client satisfaction

People love a new idea related to their job. Don't share the thought in the body of the e-mail, though. Tease your prospect with enough information about it to entice a response and start a conversation. Suggest a time to discuss it in more detail with them.

Bottom line, make it personal to them, but in a way that doesn't sound like a marketing e-mail.

Steer clear of gimmicks such as "Enticing Ideas: Kendra Lee, Did You Catch the Wave?" This didn't have anything to do with me even though it put my name in the subject line. It was clearly a marketing message. No action was required on my part. There was no sense of urgency or compelling reason to open it.

In three seconds it hit my delete barrier. Gone without reading more than the subject line. Don't let that happen to your e-mails.

Name: Kendra Lee

Company: KLA Group

Web Site: www.klagroup.com

Biography: Kendra Lee founded KLA Group in 1995. She is a top IT seller, prospect attraction expert, and president of KLA Group. Ms. Lee wrote the award-winning book *Selling against the Goal*.

Her organization has assisted sellers in increasing referrals more than 328 percent in seven weeks, penetrating SMB markets in six weeks, driving new client acquisition more than 31 percent yearly, and increasing annual revenue.

Articles about or by Ms. Lee have appeared in numerous publications, including *Sales & Marketing Management*, *SalesVantage*, *Sales Dog*, *Selling Power*, *Training*, and EyesOnSales.com.

Ms. Lee has been a featured speaker at various international conferences and channel events.

Selling Philosophy: Prospecting and lead generation; consultative selling

Target Industries: IT, health care, manufacturing, business services

Best Sellers: PowerProspecting Workshop, Selling against the Goal Workshop, Calling Your Way In Workshop, Connecting with Customers Workshop, Developing a Consultative Selling Mind-set Workshop, Delivering Great Customer Service Workshop, Driving Services Revenue Workshop, Custom Development Services, Mentor Coaching Services

Sales Tip One: Follow up! Follow up! Follow up! A majority of leads turn into a sale within one year for somebody. Why shouldn't they be your sales?

Sales Tip Two: Sales is not an art. If you believe in your offerings, have a sincere desire to help your customers, and a genuine willingness to work hard and learn, you can master sales.

Sales Tip Three: Practice consistent lead generation. You can afford to lose one opportunity if you have five more behind it in your pipeline.

Book One: *Selling against the Goal: How Corporate Sales Professionals Generate the Leads They Need*

Chapter 48

The Sales Funnel

Ray Leone
Leone Resource Group

The Sales Funnel is the most copied system in sales, but there is only one true Sales Funnel. I developed it in 1972 and used it to become the top producer in two different industries. If you think you know what it is, you are in for a shock. It has nothing to do with lead generation and everything to do with what happens once you are in front of a client or prospect. It is the psychological process that maximizes your chance of making the sale.

Having said that, let's begin as I begin all of my sales seminars, with the statement that *"You should only present to people that agree to buy first.* If you did that, would your closing average go up?" The look on your face right now is probably the same look that I see in audiences, one of doubt. Well, that is exactly what happens when you use my Sales Funnel system. The foundation upon which the Sales Funnel system is based is that the sale is made before the presentation begins.

The SF has three phases and thirteen steps. The three phases are Research, Education, and Dream Fulfillment, with the sale being made in the Research Phase. The Research Phase is when we are becoming the emotional twin of our prospect, uncovering pains, needs, wants, buying criteria, dominant buying motives, personality types, and potential objection. We are positioning ourselves as problem solvers and increasing our credibility. Most importantly, we are increasing the client's reliance on us for a proper decision. You see, most clients believe they know everything they need to know to make a buying decision before we get there. All they want from us is the price. It is my goal to shatter that belief system as soon as possible during the Research Phase. It is done by asking deficit questions (questions that create a deficit in the client's comfort level). I pride myself on asking powerful questions that create deficit (pain) on the part of a buyer, which is fulfilled by making the sale. For example, when talking to a CEO, I ask, "What are you doing to build a firewall around your customer base against attack by the competition?" or "What is your knowledge asset to book value ratio?" or "What are you doing to create nonrival assets?" or "SHRM (Society of Human Resource Management) says that 29 percent of employees are actively disengaged, causing billions in lost productivity. What is your leadership team doing to eliminate disengagement in your organization?"

Creating deficit means asking Socratic-type questions. It also means getting the prospect to think and respond in new ways. It puts the prospect in a situation where he or she needs, depends on, and has trust in the knowledge of the salesperson, based on the questions he or she has been asked.

I became the top swimming pool salesman in the country, and much of the credit goes to the following question that I would ask when I went into the backyard of the prospect: "Where have you decided to put your primary and secondary focal point?" They never had an answer. That one question accomplished almost every goal I was trying to achieve in the Research Phase.

After I uncover the pain, I ask the client whether, if I can deliver a solution that removes the pain within the budget they have allocated, I will be their vendor. The answer must be yes, or why am I there? And when they say "yes," they have committed to me prior to the presentation.

The Education Phase is what everyone else considers the presentation. This is where you demonstrate your ability to do everything that was agreed to during research. This is where you validate your solution, link it to the client's critical business issue, and obtain agreement that your solution is on target with the customer's expectations and separates you from the competition. You can lose a sale during a presentation, but you cannot win it during the presentation.

The Dream Fulfillment Phase is when the customer takes mental possession of your product. In car sales, it is the test drive. In business-to-business sales, it is the site visit or virtual tour, and of course, it is where the final close is done. You want the customer to visualize reaping the benefit that he attaches to the purchase of your product or service, so that his emotional level is at its highest prior to asking for the final commitment. Don't ask people to buy your product—ask them to fulfill their dominant buying motive (which you determined in the Research Phase).

Most sales training is done on presentation skills and product knowledge (Education Phase), and the remainder on objections and closing techniques (Dream Fulfillment Phase). Almost no time is spent teaching the Research Phase, where the sale is actually made!

The perfect sales presentation is one where you eliminate objections before they occur. By asking questions that lead to a commitment before you present, you can overcome any objection during the presentation. This makes the entire sale nonconfrontational.

I challenge you to review your own process and ask yourself, "Why do I do what I do when I do it?" and justify to yourself that the steps you take to get to a sale are in the right order. I can get the prospect to buy before the presentation is made. The audience may not believe it at first, but when the seminar is completed, I have another group of disciples.

Ask for a commitment during the Research Phase and develop powerful deficit questions, and watch your sales soar.

Name: Ray Leone

Company: Leone Resource Group

Web Site: www.rayleone.com and www.salesfunnel.com

Biography: Beginning in the field of computer science, Ray Leone left to enter sales, becoming the top producer for two international corporations. Ray combined his scientific background with practical field experience to develop his trademark selling program, the Sales Funnel, taught on all five continents. Ray received Target Training International's President's Award for contributions to human development and was recognized by Selling Power Live as an icon of selling.

Corporations that have retained Ray include AT&T, Comcast, Liberty Life, ScanSource, Wachovia, Sprint, and BioLab.

Ray has written *Success Secrets of the Sales Funnel* and hosts the radio program Winning the Game of Life.

Selling Philosophy: My trademarked system The Sales Funnel; uncovering the pain and positioning yourself as a problem solver

Target Industries: Corporate, international, IT, service, real estate, financial

Best Sellers: *Success Secrets of the Sales Funnel* book and CDs, Sales Mastery Continuing Education Series, Sales Leadership Training, developing winning strategies for large deals of corporate clients

Sales Tip One: Always link your solution to the client's critical business issue and dollarize the value of that solution.

Sales Tip Two: You cannot defend a negative, so attack. Always bring up a negative about your company before the client or competition does and you will diffuse it.

Sales Tip Three: Eliminate one step in the sales process by using the fast-forward technique. When someone asks you to do something such as taking them to look at an installation, say "Let's assume that is done; then what?"

Book One: *Success Secrets of the Sales Funnel*

Product One: Sales Mastery (12-CD video series)

Product Two: Success Secrets of the Sales Funnel (12-volume audio CD)

Having a "Great Meeting" Is Not the Objective

Chris Lytle

Sparque

Whenever a salesperson tells the boss that he or she had a great meeting, you can be sure that he or she did not make a sale. If the salesperson had made a sale, he or she would lead with that information: "I got the deal."

The following conversation actually took place. The names have been changed, but I'll let you know that I was the sales manager. A salesperson has just returned to the office from a sales call 102 miles away.

"How was your meeting, Alan?" asks the sales manager.

"It was a great meeting," says the rep.

"You got the order, then? Congratulations," says the manager.

"No, I didn't get the order."

"Oh. Then why did you tell me it was a great meeting?"

"Well, we talked for nearly two hours."

"So, he didn't throw you out."

"And he really likes our product. He says it is the best he's ever seen."

"So what is the next step?" asks the manager.

"He wants me to call him in the spring."

"Spring is six months from now and 91 days long, Alan. Is there a specific date in the spring when you are going to reconnect?"

"No, he just wants me to call him in the spring."

"Let me get this straight. You just drove 204 miles and got put off until spring and you call that a 'great meeting'?"

"Okay, it was a *good* meeting."

"I would call it a continuation and leave it at that, Alan. You had a meeting and have no next step planned."

Using precision language is seemingly a lost art.

Salespeople use terms like "hot prospect" and "great relationship" without really quantifying those things. We tend to be too optimistic for our own good. And this optimism wreaks havoc with projections and drives CFOs crazy.

We want desperately to believe a prospect who says, "I'm very interested. Call me next spring (or next Tuesday)."

Everyone in sales has had the experience of calling that "very interested" prospect and discovering that he or she is very hard to reach. The chase that ensues is frustrating for salespeople and prospects alike.

Here's the "magic phrase" you can use whenever someone says they are interested but need some time.

"I'll be happy to call you. Are you willing to work with me on a calendar basis?"

Real prospects put you on their calendars for a next step. Information seekers act interested, but let you chase them. Salespeople who use the magic phrase have a much more predictable sales funnel. They don't put information seekers into their projections.

If they are *not* willing to work with you on a calendar basis, they are not prospects.

One of the leading indicators of sales success is the number of people who have you on their calendars for a scheduled next step. If you're in a business where there aren't a lot of one-call closes, you have to maintain the momentum by having clear next steps planned.

Here's another thing: In order for complex sales to be made, there will be meetings in the customer's organization when you aren't there. If there's no clear next step in the prospect's mind and on the prospect's calendar, there will be very little thought given to your offering and no action taken internally.

In *The Accidental Salesperson*, I write that you should quit counting sales calls and count the things that count:

1. How many times did you dial the phone?

2. How many prospects did you speak with?

3. How many first meetings did you book?

4. How many first meetings did you complete?

5. How many proposals did you write?

6. How many proposals did you make, and how many dollars did you ask for?

7. How many sales did you close?

The "missing metric" that few measure is the number of prospects in your sales process who have you on their calendars for a scheduled next step.

This is what I call the *engagement metric*. It's important because only engaged prospects become paying customers.

The objective is not to have great meetings. It's to close sales. That means you have to get the order, or get the next step planned, or find a different prospect.

Information seekers may ultimately become real prospects. The marketing department can nurture them and the salesperson can "keep in touch."

Just don't confuse an interested client with someone who will write you a check.

"Are you willing to work with me on a calendar basis?" is a powerful question that will help you identify real prospects and downgrade some "really interested" people to information seekers.

To know and not to do is not to know. How soon do you think you can put this magic phrase into action?

Name: Chris Lytle

Company: Sparque, Inc.

Web Site: http://sparquefuel.com

Biography: Chris Lytle believes that up to 95 percent of salespeople don't choose sales as a career. Sales chooses them—and they end up wondering how to make the most of a profession they were never prepared for.

In *The Accidental Salesperson* Lytle gives readers the road map for excelling in sales. His book and his live presentations are packed with thought-provoking axioms, humorous and instructive anecdotes, specific strategies, and powerful tools to master essential lessons in sales and professionalism.

Lytle offers no dull theories, manipulative methods, or high-pressure tactics. But with his wealth of money-generating, career-building strategies, you won't miss them.

Selling Philosophy: Your clients get better when *you* get better.

Target Industries: Business-to-business sales forces with multiple offices (i.e., broadcast, banking, telecommunications, manufacturing)

Best Sellers: Fuel Web site, a membership site with weekly featured knowledge bites and discussion questions so sales managers can run Instant Sales Meetings. Seminar: Building Relationships Your Competitors Can't Steal

Sales Tip One: Julia Chang interviewed me for an article she wrote for *Sales and Marketing Management* magazine. One question Julia asked really got me thinking: "What do you think is the key skill that separates the A players from the B players?" I told her that "A" players orchestrate the sale while "B" players accommodate the buyer. That is a profoundly simple answer with enormous implications. Do you orchestrate or accommodate? That is the question. There is only one right answer.

Sales Tip Two: To have more productive meetings, ask your prospects and customers to prepare. Send your meeting agenda two or three days ahead and ask them to read it and add any agenda items. Then give them a premeeting assignment. Ask them to do one or two small tasks to prepare for the meeting. Here are seven suggestions for premeeting assignments:

1. Reserve a conference room with an LCD projector.

2. Invite other influencers to the meeting.

3. Read a short article.

4. Bring a specific piece of information to the meeting.

5. Visit your Web site to look at a specific piece of information.

6. Call one of your satisfied customers.

7. Think about the answer to a specific question that you pose in an e-mail or voice mail.

Professional salespeople put a premium on proper preparation. Getting prospects to prepare, too, is part of the process.

Sales Tip Three: "Closing" is the wrong word for it; "order acquisition" is a better term. It reflects the reality that confronts many business-to-business salespeople today. It can take multiple meetings and help from marketing, engineering, finance, and top management to bring in big orders.

Book One: *The Accidental Salesperson: How to Take Control of Your Career and Earn the Respect and Income You Deserve*

Product One: Fuel (www.sparquefuel.com) is loaded with hundreds of audio and video knowledge bites.

Chapter 50

"Referrals" Are a Waste—Introductions Are Golden

Paul McCord
McCord Training

Rick's client was somewhat uncomfortable with his request. The sale had gone well enough—everything considered. There was the matter of the small overcharge on the invoice, but Rick took care of that within minutes of the discovery. And there was, of course, the issue with the programming that required an additional visit by the technician, interrupting another day of work. But, all-in-all, the process was certainly less painful than other installations the company had undergone.

But this last question about referrals was a little uncomfortable. His client was completely caught off guard. He wasn't the least prepared to give a referral and wasn't comfortable giving one. Nevertheless, Rick asked and stood his ground until his client coughed up the name and phone number of one of his vendors that might be able to use his services.

Rick was excited; the referral he received was to a company he had wanted to get into for quite a while. Better yet, it was a referral to Nadia, the company's COO, the exact person he had wanted to reach. He quickly thanked his client and headed to his office to make the call to his new prospect.

As soon as he was in his office, he picked up the phone, called Nadia, and got her assistant, who, despite Rick's insistence that one of Nadia's clients had asked him to call her, refused to put him through. Instead, the assistant demanded that Rick leave his name and number and she would pass the information along to Nadia, who would call if she was interested.

Rick tried several more times to reach her. He called and left messages. He took the liberty of e-mailing her. He sent two letters. Finally, after months of trying, he gave up.

Unfortunately, this scenario is played out thousands of times a day. Salespeople get "referrals," thank their client, rush off to call the prospect, and never have the opportunity to make contact.

Why is this such a common result of "referrals"?

Rick didn't get a referral. He simply got a name and phone number. Certainly, from his perspective, he received a referral. For Rick and most other salespeople, a name and phone number and the permission from the client to use the client's name as the referring party are considered a referral. In reality, it is nothing but a name and phone number.

A real referral isn't simply getting the name and phone number of a potential prospect and the permission of the client to use their name as an introduction.

By simply getting the name and phone number and running off to make the phone call, Rick committed the most common sin salespeople make when they get a referral. He failed to capitalize on the power of the referral and instead turned it into a warm call.

The power of a referral is its potential to open doors, to generate interest, to get an appointment. Seldom can a referral sell for you. That's not the goal of a referral. The goal is to open a door and, it is hoped, begin the relationship from a position of strength and trust.

When you receive a referral, you are hoping to build a relationship with the referred prospect based on their trust and respect of your client. If the prospect trusts and respects your client, a portion of the trust and respect they have for your client is imbued to you because someone they trust referred you.

However, that trust is useless if you fail to connect with the prospect.

In many cases, the fact someone they trust gave you the prospect's name and phone number is not enough by itself to convince them to meet with you. You need something stronger than just your client's name to open the door.

That extra push is a direct introduction from your client to the prospect. A direct introduction is powerful for several reasons:

➤ It is unusual. It isn't often that someone is personally asked by someone they trust to meet a salesperson. The act itself places you in a different category from other salespeople.

➤ It demonstrates trust. A direct introduction demonstrates a high level of trust. Most people will not go to the trouble of taking the time and effort to give a direct introduction unless they have a high degree of trust and respect for the person they are introducing.

➤ It makes it difficult for the prospect to decline a meeting. There is implied pressure on the prospect to meet with you since they don't want to offend the client.

A call using the client's name doesn't have the power of an introduction and gives the prospect an easy out—they simply don't accept your call or decline a meeting. After all, the client wasn't really involved—you simply used the client's name.

On the other hand, a properly executed introduction virtually guarantees a meeting.

In most instances, you have three introduction methods at your disposal:

1. **A letter of introduction written by you for your client's signature.** A letter from the client to the prospect is the most basic form of introduction. Rather than asking the client to write the letter, write it for them on their letterhead for their signature. Let the prospect know what you accomplished for the client; let them know why the client referred you; give a specific time and date to expect your call; and have the client ask them to let the client know their impression of you and your company after the prospect has met with you.

   Mail the letter, and then a day or two after the prospect should have received it, give them a call. Don't introduce yourself first. Rather, introduce the letter and client first, then move on to asking for the appointment.

2. **A phone call from your client to the prospect.** A phone call is stronger than a letter and almost guarantees an appointment, as it is very difficult for the prospect to say no to your appointment request while the client is on the line. The call gives the opportunity for the prospect to ask specific questions of your client and to get detailed information. Do not have your client call unless you are present—you want to know exactly what was said, and you want your client to formally introduce you to your prospect.

3. **A lunch meeting with your client, the prospect, and yourself.** A stronger method than either a letter or a call, a lunch meeting allows you to get to know the prospect as a friend before you get to know them as a salesperson. Like a phone call, it virtually guarantees a private meeting. Also, in a lunch meeting, your client becomes your salesperson, and you're there as the consultant. Although a very powerful introduction format, most clients will only agree to do one lunch meeting, maybe two at the most, so use this method judiciously.

If you want to turn your "referrals" into real referrals, don't settle for just getting names and phone numbers. Learn how to turn those names and phone numbers into real referrals through a direct introduction to the prospect. Not only will the number of appointments you set go up, but your sales will increase, your income will increase, and you'll find selling to be a lot easier.

Name: Paul McCord

Company: McCord Training

Web Site: www.mccordandassociates.com

Biography: Paul McCord has been selling, managing, and training salespeople and managers from dozens of industries around the world for three decades. His sales and management career has been focused on business-to-business sales of high-end services.

Paul is an internationally recognized authority on prospecting, referral selling, and personal marketing; his strategies and processes have not only changed the way referral selling is taught, but are also changing how sellers find and connect with quality prospects. He graduated magna cum laude from Texas A&M University.

Paul is president of McCord Training, a Texas-based sales training, coaching, and sales management consulting firm.

Selling Philosophy: Finding and connecting with high-quality prospects in ways they will respond to

Target Industries: Real estate, insurance, financial planning, securities, computer hardware, software, recruiting, mortgage, consulting

Best Sellers: *Creating a Million Dollar a Year Sales Income: Sales Success through Client Referrals*; How to Become a Referral-Based Salesperson Seminar; Foundations of a Successful Sales Career CD; personal sales coaching

Sales Tip One: Act the part—to become the part. You must act like a successful salesperson to become a successful salesperson.

Sales Tip Two: Clients and customers want to work with experts. Experts don't cold call, plaster the world with fliers, or stick signs on street corners; they generate their business through their image, reputation, and referrals from clients and prospects—learn to do the same.

Sales Tip Three: Take a two-week sabbatical from busy work. For two full weeks, ignore all the busy work you normally do and only concentrate on prospecting, selling, and managing your clients, and your sales will skyrocket.

Book One: *Creating a Million Dollar a Year Sales Income: Sales Success through Client Referrals*

Book Two: *SuperStar Selling: 12 Keys to Becoming a Sales SuperStar*

Product One: How to Become a Referral-Based Salesperson (4-CD set)

Product Two: Foundations of a Successful Sales Career (CD)

Product Three: How to Develop a Public Reputation as an Expert in Your Field CD

Chapter 51

Increasing Sales Quickly

Charles Newby
Mercuri International Group

Are you doing these four things?

1. **Focus on activity rather than results.**

   There is a great temptation to spend all your waking management time thinking about a shortfall in results. This is natural. We all do it! However, it doesn't actually bring in any more business.

   So is there a better area to think about? Well, yes: Sales activity is what drives the result!

   For salespeople and sales managers, the pursuit of the optimum *quantity*, *direction*, and *quality of activity* can improve results generation quickly. How? Well, first, if you have accurate conversion ratios and average order values, then you can calculate with some accuracy how many extra sales prospects you need in order to improve results. Now you are getting some control of the situation.

   The next port of call is to assess how much activity (warm-up letters, mail shots, appointment-making phone calls, and sales visits) you are likely to need in order to convert each prospect into a likely order. This will show you how much extra activity you need, but of course the constraints will be the amount of time that you have and the numbers of salespeople involved.

   With a reasonably well-motivated team, a short, high-profile, and well-planned campaign of extra activity can close many a gap between sales achieved and the target figure.

2. **Select the "right" opportunities and ensure the "right" salespeople approach them.**

   If the above sounds like a recipe for loads of unsuccessful activity, then let's deal with that problem now. Salespeople under pressure will tend to adopt the "Martini Sales Principal: Anytime, Any Place, Anywhere." This is almost always counterproductive. So what can be done differently?

First, call only on companies where there is a real likelihood of success. This means using specific and consistent selection criteria for targeting new business opportunities.

Pursuits are then only started on prospects who have met those criteria. The best place to start is by examining your current "best customers," defining the characteristics that make them the best, and then researching prospects with those specific characteristics.

So you have some good prospects, what then? Develop a prioritized "engagement" plan for each of these opportunities and ensure it's delivered by your best sellers. This will increase your sales conversion and lower your sales costs, as well as contribute to the enhanced motivation of your most effective "players."

3. Make your solution essential rather than merely desirable!

So when you have targeted the best prospects with the most effective activities, what will you sell them when you get there? "The most appropriate solution" is the obvious answer, but doesn't that simply mean the right combination of products and services?

Well, yes and no!

If your salespeople are not defining the decision-making process, criteria, and the time scales for a decision, then it doesn't matter how well constructed your solution is: You are unlikely to get a "yes" when you really need one! So what can be done?

An understanding of the decision-making process together with the prospect's key business drivers gives you the opportunity to link your solution to the business success of the potential customer. Done well, this can persuade the customer to implement your solution as a matter of urgency and hence reduce the sales lead times. In addition, if the prospect sees that you are taking their issues seriously, and not just your own, then a profitable relationship could be the result.

4. Fish where the fishes are!

So now that an effective plan is emerging, what can go wrong?

Well, we mentioned the limiting factors of time and human resources earlier. It is quite possible that it may be impossible to do everything that you would like to do!

So now for the heresy: Deselect some of the prospects!

If time is short and/or tight, then doing a lot of activity of insufficient quality may make the situation worse. It may be time to revisit your selection criteria and make them more demanding.

This will mean that you have developed a set of priority prospects and released some time from potentially unsuccessful pursuits. So you can now focus this released time with your best new prospects and still have time to realize potential from within your existing customer roster. Be demanding about the priorities here, too!

Select the most appropriate existing customers where you believe there is untapped potential (the selection criteria will be more than handy here, too), arrange business review meetings with your main contacts, and agree together what will motivate them to increase how much they'll spend with you in the coming months.

You may be pleasantly surprised, especially if the "account manager" asks the question in the right way!

So finally, are the above factors a guarantee of success?

Well, again the answer is "yes and no." Engaging with these activities will improve your current situation, results, and possibly the morale and motivation of your sales force.

But no, that is not a guarantee!

Name: Charles Newby

Company: Mercuri International Group

Web Site: www.mercuri.net

Biography: Charlie Newby is the global marketing director of Mercuri International Group. He has been with the organization for almost 15 years and has been a consultant, project leader sales director, managing director of a country unit, and with his current role has produced a great deal of in-depth knowledge of the sales improvement marketplace. This kind of profile is reflected throughout the Mercuri organization, with over 300 consultants who focus on the increase in top-line sales with their clients.

Selling Philosophy: Sales and sales management development, sales process consulting, and sales effectiveness analysis

Target Industries: Logistics, telecom and IT, pharmaceutical and health care, fast-moving consumer goods (FMCG), manufacturing and construction, financial and professional services

Best Sellers: International project management, classroom training, Web-based learning, observation and coaching, competitive business simulations

Sales Tip One: What is inspected gets done, what is expected often does not. Sales leaders and managers should regularly work with their salespeople to monitor, analyze, and help plan their quantity, quality, and direction of activity.

Sales Tip Two: If you want your customer to really experience the value you bring to them as a supplier, you must clearly understand the requirements of their situation and their business. Look after your customer in their market and you will win and retain business.

Sales Tip Three: Sales time is crucial. The time spent with customers is often hard-won and sometimes limited. With this in mind, it is imperative that we (1) plan tactics and activities to extend the time with your customer and (2) use the time with customers effectively and with impact.

Book One: *Sales Process Management*
Book Two: *Performance Selling*
Book Three: *Team Selling*
Product One: 3G Selling Pipeline Management
Product Two: 350 E-learning Modules (e.g., consultative selling)
Product Three: Value Selling (the definitive podcast)

Seven Myths and Misconceptions about Top-Performing Salespeople

Sam Reese
Miller Heiman

If there's one profession that's plagued with myths and half-truths, it's sales. And no group is more subject to misunderstanding than your organization's top performers. Below are seven myths and misconceptions about your top sales performers.

Myth One: World-class salespeople just happen to be with the right company at the right time.

Reality: Sales involves thought and action. Like their colleagues in other departments, good salespeople are innovative, coming up with great ideas and strategies for turning those ideas into reality. But at the end of the day, top performers understand sales is about execution and results—and they understand that their ability to do that job well affects everyone in the entire organization, not just the sales team.

Myth Two: The best salespeople are naturals; they just wing it.

Reality: World-class sales performers "train," the same way that world-class athletes do. Our research indicates that, when compared with average performers, the best salespeople are:

➤ 30 percent more likely to prepare for their sales calls.

➤ 30 percent more likely to rely on a well-defined approach to determining which clients to target.

➤ 24 percent more likely to have a standard approach for reviewing existing opportunities.

World-class performers in any field are big on discipline and routine. They're consistent. They're constantly developing new and better systems for getting things done. And they don't wait for breakthroughs—they make breakthroughs happen.

Myth Three: Top-performing salespeople are cutthroat competitors who want to see everyone else fail.

Reality: Like world-class athletes, sales stars don't tie their wins to others' losses. In fact, the best salespeople want everyone else to do well—they just want to do better! After all, in any field, it's more rewarding to beat competitors when they're at the top of their games than to breeze past them when they're down. There's little challenge—in sales or athletics—in beating someone who's a weaker performer or who's having a bad day. And there's no sense of accomplishment at all in winning when there's no competition. Top performers in both disciplines are highly focused and goal oriented. They know exactly what their goals are; they hold themselves accountable for achieving them; and as soon as they've done so, they raise the bar with new, higher goals. Their overall approach can be summed up with the acronym SMART: specific, measurable, achievable, results oriented, and time based.

Myth Four: World-class salespeople care only about making money—after all, that's how they get to the top.

Reality: World-class salespeople believe in what they sell. Jim McCann, founder of 1-800-Flowers.com, the highly successful floral and gift service, puts it this way: He really enjoys hearing how he helped somebody out of a jam at the last second. He gets to help them preserve and honor their most important relationships. Denver real-estate legend Edie Marks cites a similar secret for success: She says she loves "helping good people fulfill their dreams."

Great sales careers are built on relationships, and great salespeople value those relationships above all else. Top performers think about more than selling a house or pushing a product; they genuinely enjoy helping their customers solve problems, meet needs, or move ahead with projects. In a sense, they're "pleasers"; they truly like making customers happy—and they know that involves really understanding what their clients want to fix, accomplish, or avoid.

Myth Five: World-class salespeople are intrusive and pushy.

Reality: World-class salespeople are curious. They like to learn about anything that helps them improve themselves and gain an edge—including knowing as much as possible about their customers. For that reason, they tend to ask a lot of questions. They're curious about what their clients are trying to fix, accomplish, or avoid. In other words, they try to uncover the underlying challenge or problem rather than just make the immediate sale. So, without exception, top performers are good listeners.

In discussing that capability, I'm always reminded of a fellow I know—the heir to a large fortune—who is always changing sales jobs and yet still finds time to golf almost every day. I asked him once why he's got so much leisure time, and he laughed and said, "Sam, you've got to get into sales." He's never once asked what I do; he has no idea that I've been a sales executive for more than 20 years. For his own sake, it's a good thing he's got a trust fund: He'll never be a world-class salesperson because he doesn't ask and doesn't listen. Naturally, good salespeople are persistent. But they don't badger or manipulate people; instead, they come back with one new approach after another. And they do care how people feel about them—after all, they're building long-term relationships.

Myth Six: World-class salespeople are, by definition, self-centered and egotistical.

Reality: Like world-class athletes, top sales performers sometimes appear self-centered or egotistical. Actually, in both cases, it's often more that they're highly efficient. Average performers view time as uncontrollable. By nature, world-class people in any field take the opposite view, avoiding anything that removes time from their control. And they've typically got little patience for time-killing activities. They prefer to trade time only for something else of value. When they sense that their time is being wasted, their guts start churning, and they've got to move on. And in truth, it's the average performers who tend to be more egotistical than their world-class counterparts. When they win, they're often telling themselves: "I'm the best. It's about time somebody recognized that and acknowledged me." Top performers, on the other hand, are always thinking, "Maybe I could have done better. Next time, I'll do better."

Mark H. McCormack, author of *What They Don't Teach You at Harvard Business School: Notes from a Street-Smart Executive*, tells a story about golf greats Arnold Palmer and Jack Nicklaus competing in a tournament. After the third round, McCormack talked individually to both men; each talked about how much better his opponent was doing. In reality, the two were tied. World-class people in any field tend to evaluate themselves honestly, harshly, and constantly. They avoid overconfidence. In fact, they often feel they're lucky when they win and completely to blame when they lose. And they typically feel they've got something to prove—but only to themselves.

Myth Seven: World-class performers are driven by rewards and recognition, and they know that, eventually, they'll be able to coast on their reputations.

Reality: Many superstars don't need acknowledgment. Often, it's enough for them to know that they're the best. They may welcome a little affirmation, but they get uncomfortable with adulation or recognition.

As for resting on their laurels: The best of the best never rest—not when they're ahead and certainly not when they're behind. They fear being viewed as "one-hit wonders," famous for that one big deal. They like to keep going. Like world-class athletes, as soon as they attain their goals, they immediately set higher ones. Not the next year, not the next quarter, not even the next month—but instead, immediately.

Bottom line: World-class salespeople are afraid of complacency. They strive for success, but it's hard to relax and enjoy it once they get there. Remember, top performers constantly strive to improve: It's all about getting better.

Name: Sam Reese

Company: Miller Heiman, Inc.

Web Site: www.millerheiman.com

Biography: Sam Reese is president and CEO for Miller Heiman. During Mr. Reese's tenure, Miller Heiman expanded product offerings and e-learning initiatives and amassed a partner network of world-class sales consultants who implement the company's sales system for clients, which include Fortune 500 companies.

Reese formerly worked for Kinko's, where he transformed sales operations from traditional retail to commercial. As vice president of sales for Corporate Express, he grew the National Accounts Group to over $1 billion.

Mr. Reese is coauthor of *Successful Global Account Management: Key Strategies, Tools for Managing Global Accounts* and *The Seven Keys to Managing Strategic Accounts*.

Sales leaders trust us. We understand their sense of urgency. We don't disrupt their strategy; we give them a foundation to execute and drive results quickly.

Sales managers depend on us. We give them common language and processes to improve revenue predictability, collaboration, and coaching.

Salespeople value us. We respect their natural ability and give them added capability and tools to replicate success and create wealth.

Some Historical Context

From our nearly 30 years' experience and continuous research, we identified that successful selling is based on a fundamental and repeatable process. We defined and documented this process, and refined a systematic approach to manage and implement the process through teaching salespeople, sales managers, and senior corporate management. This culminated in our first programs, *Strategic Selling* and *Conceptual Selling*, which quickly became the gold standards for managing complex sales.

Our experience working shoulder-to-shoulder with the world's leading companies and our comprehensive research has kept us relevant over three decades of change. Bring us your toughest deal or most promising account. We'll gladly prove it.

Selling Philosophy: Strategic Selling, Conceptual Selling, Strategic Selling Government, Large Account Management Process, Channel Partner Management, Executive Impact, Negotiate Success

Target Industries: Health care (products), financial services, manufacturing (industrial), telecommunications, chemicals, business services (HR, staffing, advertising, consulting, etc.)

Best Sellers: Strategic Selling, Conceptual Selling, and Large Account Management Process (philosophies), Sales Excellence Assessment, Predictive Sales Performance, Manager's Coaching, Sales Account Manager, Funnel ScoreCard (adoption and collaboration tools)

Sales Tip One: Top (sales) performers set specific goals, and they always put themselves on the line. They're motivated by continued success, and avoid becoming complacent. Contrary to popular belief, world-class sales performers don't strive for greatness at the expense of everyone else. They want real competition: It's not as exciting to be number one unless the competition is doing well, too.

Sales Tip Two: As we move toward the future of sales, it's important to keep in mind that although technology or innovation can enhance the sales process, salespeople will always need to focus on the customer's buying process.

Sales Tip Three: Many successful companies have dramatically improved their forecasting processes by shifting to a client-centric approach. To forecast correctly requires an enterprise-wide understanding of how the client is advancing through the sales cycle and what specifically needs to happen to move the opportunity forward.

Book One: *Successful Global Account Management: Key Strategies, Tools for Managing Global Accounts* (coauthor with Nick Speare and Kevin Wilson)

Book Two: *The Seven Keys to Managing Strategic Accounts* (coauthor with Sallie Sherman and Joseph Sperry)

Book Three: *The Sales Performance Journal Digest* (coauthor)

Product One: Strategic Selling Fundamentals

Product Two: Various webcasts and video interviews

53

Magic Moments in Selling

Subtle Yet Crucial Actions to Advance the Sale

Anne Miller
Chiron Associates

When your husband or significant other surprises you with flowers and it isn't even your birthday, that is a magic moment in the relationship. When your football-indifferent wife suggests that you stay home and watch the game on television while she takes care of the kids, that is another magic moment in the relationship.

Magic moments are turning points, those little things you do that endear you to the other person and promote the relationship between you.

Alternatively, when your significant other works late on the night of your anniversary or comments, in front of your friends, how inept you are around the house, those are negative magic moments. Those actions weaken, if not totally derail, the relationship.

Relationships in business are similarly affected by magic moments. These magic moments are those subtle, but critical, actions a seller takes that either advance or doom the sale. Sales managers need to ensure that their staffs master those moments.

In my 20-plus years of sales and presentations seminars and coaching work, seven of these turning points continually appear as weaknesses among even the best salespeople. Let me share one of them with you.

■ THE FIRST TWO MINUTES

People generally know a call should be about the client, but the effort to actually engage a prospect to talk openly and comfortably about his business is often poorly executed.

Let me demonstrate. Be yourself. Imagine you are planning a big annual sales conference and you are interviewing speakers (like me).

I am going to open our sales conversation in two different ways. Which one would be the most engaging for you? Which one reflects best on me, the salesperson?

➤ Opening One

After appropriate small talk, I say the following to you: "Mr. Client, thank you for seeing me to talk about the various programs I could offer at your annual meeting, all of which would be highly interactive, entertaining, and valuable to drive sales. May I ask you a few questions?" (You: "Okay.") "How many people will be attending?" (You: "About a hundred.") "Tell me a bit about what you have in mind for this event." (You answer.) "What kinds of programs have you had in the past?" (You answer.) And so on.

➤ Opening Two

Same situation. "Mr. Client, thank you for seeing me to talk about the various programs I could offer at your annual meeting, all of which would be highly interactive, entertaining, and valuable to drive sales. I understand you had a great year last year. Since companies are very different in terms of their staffs, their meeting objectives, and the past programs they've had, I thought a good use of our time would be to review the specifics of what you're seeking, and, then, based on your needs, I can present some relevant ideas. Then, we can talk about the next steps. How does that sound?" (You: "Great.") "What kind of meeting are you looking to run this year?"

I suspect you liked the second opening better for three reasons:

1. Knowing about your account success tells you I did some homework, and that wins initial respect for me.

2. Setting an agenda signals a direction to the conversation. You know the framework for the discussion and what the next step will be.

3. Checking in for agreement or acceptance is a sign of respect for the client's time and interest. You are now prepared for a business discussion about your business as opposed to an interrogation by me, like a seller solely interested in finding my entry point for a sale.

■ MASTER THIS CRITICAL MAGIC MOMENT

If you are a manager, watch your salespeople on your next joint call. How do they establish common ground on which to have a meaningful business discussion with a client or prospect? Are they coming across to buyers as vendors out for the quick hit, or are they presenting themselves as problem solvers, consultants, businesspeople out to provide real solutions to client-specific situations? If you are a seller, try this consultative opening framework on your next call. You will have a much more robust, meaningful, and comfortable conversation with your clients, which will help you win more business more easily.

Name: Anne Miller

Company: Chiron Associates, Inc.

Web Site: www.annemiller.com

Biography: Anne Miller, founder of Chiron Associates, Inc., is a widely respected speaker, seminar leader, author, and consultant. Anne helps salespeople at high-profile firms such as Citigroup, Yahoo!, and Time, Inc., sell millions of dollars' worth of business to their clients. She is the author of *Metaphorically Selling*, *365 Sales Tips for Winning Business*, numerous articles both offline and online, and her own free newsletter, "The Metaphor Minute." Attendees leave her upbeat programs smarter, challenged, and ready to sell the maximum amount of appropriate business for their firms.

Selling Philosophy: People have limited time and attention. Make what you say, *pay*.

Target Industries: Finance, accounting consulting, media, online, technology

Best Sellers: Seminars: Never Run a Marathon Barefoot: Creative Presenting; Make What You Say, Pay!; Your Selling Style: Power or Pitfall?; Command the Room: Women Who Present; Negotiate Like the Pros; Building Client Relationships; Consultative Selling

Sales Tip One: Replace the phrase "in my presentation I will cover . . ." with "in our meeting (discussion) today, we will cover . . ."

Sales Tip Two: The best way to handle confusion or objections is with a metaphor or analogy.

Sales Tip Three: In negotiating, always get something for anything you give.

Book One: *Metaphorically Selling: How to Use the Magic of Metaphors to Sell, Persuade, and Explain Anything to Anyone*

Book Two: *365 Sales Tips for Winning Business*

Book Three: *Presentation Jazz!*

Chapter 54

Truth or Delusion

Busting Networking's Biggest Myths

Dr. Ivan Misner and Mike Macedonio
Referral Institute

Truth or delusion? If you're getting all the referrals you need, you don't need to sell.

Delusion. Anybody who's experienced and successful in referral marketing will tell you that sales skills are absolutely required. They're needed in every part of the process—not only in closing the sale with the prospect.

First, you have to sell yourself to your potential referral source—she has to buy the concept that there's value in introducing you to someone she knows. A referral is not a guaranteed sale; it's the opportunity to do business with someone to whom you have been recommended. You still have to close the deal—most of the time. You have to make it clear that you know how to sell, that you can and will provide the products or services you are expected to provide, and that your customer will be happy with both the process and the result—which will reflect favorably on the provider of the referral. If you can't make that first "sale," your referral provider won't become your referral provider, because she won't be inclined to risk her relationship with the prospect. That is, she won't do her part to sell the referral.

Two separate doctoral studies, one from California in the early 1990s and one from Florida in 2006, found that approximately 34 percent of all business referrals turn into sales. This is an outstanding number, but it's still not 100 percent. Therefore, sales skills are still important in networking. Some people are better at closing sales than others. Having the knowledge and skill to generate the referral, then having the knowledge and skill to close the sale, gives the business person a one-two punch.

208

Second, you have to sell yourself to the prospect in order to get that first appointment. Yes, the referral helps a great deal, but you've still got to convince the prospect that the appointment is worth his or her time and likely to result in a favorable outcome. You should avoid being aggressive, indecisive, or evasive at this point; the prospect, having been in contact with your referral provider, is expecting a high level of respect and professionalism in your approach. You can and should be confident that a mutually beneficial deal is in the works, and you should communicate this to the prospect by your attitude and actions. Strive not to embarrass your referral source.

Third, once you have made the appointment, you have to persuade the prospect to buy your product or service. This is the part that usually comes to mind when one hears the word "sale." Your integrity is paramount at this stage. The prospect should know exactly what to expect—no hidden charges, no unexpected exceptions, and no bait-and-switch.

If you've created a highly efficient system of generating referrals for your business, you will see a steady stream of referrals being funneled to you. This does not guarantee that you will be capable of closing any of them. You'll need sales skills to turn prospects into new clients, customers, or patients.

Note, however, that in referral marketing, closing the deal with your prospect is neither the beginning nor the end of the selling process. In order to get to this point, you will have made at least two other sales, as noted above. And in order to build and maintain the long-term relationships that characterize referral marketing, you have to follow up with both your new customer and your referral provider—again, part of the total sales process.

Remember, the number-one rule in referral marketing is to make your referral provider look good. You need to demonstrate that you know how to sell to the prospect in a way that doesn't embarrass the source of your referral—that you're going to consult with the prospect, discover his needs, offer solutions based on those needs, give him some options, and not force a sale if you know you can't provide a good solution. On the other hand, if your technique is to hold the prospect hostage at his kitchen table until he breaks down and buys, your referral source will not be pleased that you've abused your relationship with him and damaged his relationship with your client. You may get the deal, but you've shut yourself off from further deals with that client—and with any future referrals from your source.

The message about sales in referral marketing is this: *If you're not comfortable in sales or if you haven't been professionally trained, sales training is an investment worth your while.* It will serve you well in every aspect of relationship marketing and referral networking.

Name: Dr. Ivan Misner and Mike Macedonio

Company: Referral Institute

Web Site: www.referralinstitute.com

Biography: Dr. Ivan Misner is a *New York Times* best-selling author and sr. partner for the Referral Institute, an international referral training company. Dr. Misner is also the founder and chairman of BNI (www.bni.com), the world's largest referral organization. His latest *New York Times* best-selling book, *Truth or Delusion: Busting Networking's Biggest Myths*, can be viewed at www.truthordelusion.com.

Mike Macedonio is the coauthor of the *New York Times* best-selling book *Truth or Delusion: Busting Networking's Biggest Myths*. Mike Macedonio is also the president and partner of the Referral Institute, the world's leading referral training organization.

Selling Philosophy: Referral marketing

Target Industries: Financial services, small business owners

Best Sellers: Referrals for Life, Referral Pipeline, Certified Networker

Sales Tip One: Referral marketing: You can't do it alone.

Sales Tip Two: Business networking is about helping other businesspeople as a way of growing your business.

Sales Tip Three: The value that you bring to a referral relationship is directly associated to the quantity and strength of your relationships.

Book One: *Truth or Delusion: Busting Networking's Biggest Myths*

Book Two: *Masters of Sales*

Buying Decisions

What Happens behind the Scenes?

Sharon Drew Morgen
Morgen Facilitations

As sales folks, we like to think that because a buyer's need matches our solution, and because we're professionals who "care," have a "perfect solution," and give "great service," the only thing buyers need to do is choose us.

If only it were that easy, we'd be closing a lot more sales, and we certainly would not lose as many sales as we do. The problem is that the buying decision is so, so much more complex than we realize.

For some reason, sales historically treats an Identified Problem (my term for "need") as if it were an isolated event. It's not: Any Identified Problem is integrated within the buyer's larger, more complex system (defined as the environment of interdependent parts of rules and relationships, policies and people, that make up the culture). When an external solution is considered, it is primarily a Change Management issue, rather than a need-resolution issue, with ramifications and idiosyncratic internal resolutions that only buyers can manage privately and which we can never be privy to.

Indeed, until or unless buyers get appropriate buy-in from within, and until or unless they can be assured that the system itself will not be compromised when something new enters, they cannot risk jeopardizing the integrity of the system and will do nothing.

Herein lies the buyer/seller conundrum: Sellers are managing solution placement, while buyers are managing systems integrity.

Two different outcomes, two different jobs. And the sales model does not address this.

■ WHEN DO BUYERS START FIGURING OUT HOW TO BUY?

Let's look at the problem more thoroughly, so we can begin to recognize how some new skills might enable us to truly assist our buyers better. Let's begin by understanding how an Identified Problem became what it now is.

A buyer's "need" is created over time, by the people, policies, and relationships in the system, which cause and then maintain this "need" through time: It becomes endemic to the system. Workarounds help keep it in place on a daily basis and make it hard to change. All the while, the problem grows larger, involving more people and departments, creating new rules and policies—until it becomes a confusing, yet comfortable, mess that would need to be unraveled and managed prior to any purchase. Indeed, if it were ready to change, it would have already.

Before a buyer seeks a resolution, their first job is to maintain the integrity of the system. That means they must figure out how to manage the very idiosyncratic ramifications of how the system will be affected. They must learn how to cope with Change. What will a solution shift internally? How will the people and policies interact differently if/when they decide to bring in something . . . something different that isn't already there? How can they manage historic problems, or relationships between colleagues that are dysfunctional?

Obviously, the sales model doesn't equip us with the tools to help buyers manage these issues.

As sellers, we don't realize the enormous stake a buyer has in maintaining the congruence and integrity of their status quo: Would you consider purchasing a gym membership before you decided to become a healthy person? Would you consider moving house—even if you needed to move—before you and your spouse chose a neighborhood, or looked into school districts? The vendor might have a great gym; the real estate agent may be the best in her field. But until or unless you have figured out how to manage all of your internal decision issues, you won't make a change.

Until or unless buyers figure out how to discover and manage all of the internal elements that must buy-in to any sort of solution, they will do nothing. Unfortunately they don't start doing the work of figuring out the full scope of the behind-the-scenes issues until they are obliged to (after we've met them), except in cases when buyers call us, ready to buy: When that happens it's because they've made all of the behind-the-scenes buying decisions before they contacted us, and we just got lucky.

■ HOW SALES FAIL

As sellers, we gather and share information quite professionally. But because the sales model focuses on placing solution—the very last thing the buyer needs—we end up coming in at the wrong time, pitching a solution to a small portion of the ultimate Buying Decision Team (it takes a while for the buyer to discern the entire team), and have no tools to help buyers manage the offline decisions necessary for them to get buy-in for change. But we are merely addressing the tip of a very large iceberg; the largest percentage of the total problem is hidden from view.

This is why we have a 90 percent failure rate in sales, why we end up managing objections and have price discussions, why the sales cycle takes 800 percent longer than it should, and why solutions seem similar: until or unless the entire Buying Decision Team has bought into change and the issues that change creates (disruption, job description changes, management issues, implementation issues, technology issues, departmental issues), they will not make a purchase.

And we're stuck with the perfect solution, waiting for a buying decision that has nothing to do with us. Indeed, the time it takes buyers to come up with their own answers is the length of the sales cycle.

As we think about sales, and wonder how to close more sales, more quickly, we must realize that by merely focusing on the solution-placement area, and developing our "understanding"—understanding need, understanding the decision making, understanding the requirements, helping buyers understand the judiciousness of our offering—we are not helping the buyer do their own, critical behind-the-scenes work. Unfortunately, buyers don't know how to do this work easily because it's new to them.

But we can help. We must add another skill set and outcome to our jobs: By becoming decision facilitators, we can use our knowledge of our fields and be virtual GPS systems for the decision issues, guiding them along without bias as to their ultimate destination. Will we end up placing a solution? That depends on how well the buyer's system can manage Change. But we will:

➤ Know on the first call if it's a viable prospect.
➤ Shorten the sales cycle dramatically.
➤ Save the buyer's time and our time.
➤ Differentiate ourselves.

➤ Delay the solution presentation for the right people and the right time.

➤ Greatly enhance the number of buyers who can buy.

Is it sales? No. But since the buyer must do this anyway, and we sit and wait for them to do it, we might as well add a decision facilitation skill set (I call it Buying Facilitation). We will then be true servant leaders, true trusted advisors and relationship managers, guiding them through their systemic, offline buying decision issues.

In this time of economic uncertainty, add Buying Facilitation and differentiate yourself from your competition—and truly help your buyer buy. And save the selling until after the buyer has discovered how.

Name: Sharon Drew Morgen

Company: Morgen Facilitations, Inc.

Web Site: http://newsalesparadigm.com, http://sharondrewmorgen.com, http://buyingfacilitation.com

Biography: Sharon Drew Morgen is the visionary behind the new sales paradigm Buying Facilitation. She is the author of the *New York Times* best seller *Selling with Integrity: Reinventing Sales through Collaboration, Respect, and Serving*, as well as *Dirty Little Secrets: Why Buyers Can't Buy and Sellers Can't Sell and What You Can Do about It*, and over 600 articles on Buying Facilitation, her innovative new model that gives sellers the tools to help buyers navigate their decision issues, so buyers can decide quickly and ethically.

Sharon Drew Morgen speaks, coaches, trains, and consults at global corporations that seek visionary thinking in sales.

Selling Philosophy: Developer of Buying Facilitation

Target Industries: All industries

Best Sellers: Author of *New York Times* best seller *Selling with Integrity*, author of *Dirty Little Secrets: Why Buyers Can't Buy and Sellers Can't Sell and What You Can Do about It*, and developer of the new sales paradigm Buying Facilitation

Sales Tip One: The time it takes buyers to discover their own answers and make the decisions necessary to adopt a solution, with a minimum of disruption to their culture, is the length of the sales cycle. Rather than first gathering data to understand need, help buyers manage their offline decision navigation issues.

Sales Tip Two: Do you want to sell? Or have someone buy? They are two different activities.

Sales Tip Three: Buyers don't need your product, they need to resolve a business problem. They will buy your product when they realize it will be a piece of their problem resolution. How can you stop selling and support the buying process?

Book One: *Dirty Little Secrets: Why Buyers Can't Buy and Sellers Can't Sell and What You Can Do about It*

Book Two: *Buying Facilitation: The New Way to Sell That Expands and Influences Decisions*

Book Three: *Selling with Integrity: Reinventing Sales through Collaboration, Respect, and Serving*

Book Four: *Sales on the Line: Meeting the Business Demand of the 90's through Phone Partnering*

Product One: Hear Sharon Drew Morgen live! Set of three CDs; includes Sharon Drew Morgen making prospecting, qualifying, problem resolution, and fund-raising calls to exhibit the Buying Facilitation method.

Product Two: Guided Study Learn Buying Facilitation. Twenty-six self-guided study sessions that teach the skills behind this innovative decision facilitation model. Starting with learning how to change, and including the skills of Listening for Systems, Formulating Facilitative Questions and Presumptive Summaries, and using interesting experiential homework assignments, this product will teach the material that Sharon Drew teaches in her well-respected three-day live program.

Chapter 56

Your "Needs" May Not Be Your "Rights"*

Napoleon Hill
Napoleon Hill Foundation

Napoleon Hill is the creator of many foundational books that have impacted salespeople over the past 70 years. These have included *Think and Grow Rich* and *Success Unlimited and How to Sell Your Way Through Life*. Although not a sales trainer, we feel Hill's works are too important to ignore. With that in mind, we have included the following excerpt to educate and inspire you in your sales career.

A very brilliant woman recently eliminated herself from a position that offered an opportunity for advancement for which many people would have been willing to render service adequate to help them make the most of that opportunity.

This woman had ability. She had a dynamic personality. She had an excellent education, but what she did not have was a clear understanding of the difference between her "rights" and her "needs."

Her salary was $500 a month. Added to this she received $300 per month in alimony from her former husband. When the alimony payments were ended, she continued to live, as she had been doing for many years, on an $800 per month spending schedule.

Falsely mistaking her "needs" for her "rights," she began needling her employer for more money. Moreover, she worked herself into an irritable state of mind which made her a nuisance to her associate workers. They began to complain about it until, at long last, she was let out of her job.

One's "needs" may be many; one's "rights" are comparatively few. The greatest of all "rights" is the privilege of rendering useful service commensurate with the income one desires to receive, and

---

* Excerpted from *Success Unlimited* by Napoleon Hill, November 1954, p. 12.

this definitely is the only "right" which gives anyone a sound reason for asking for more pay.

The principle of *going the extra mile*—rendering more service and better service than one is paid to render—stands at the head of the list of the things which give one almost unlimited "rights" to receive compensation. And it is a matter of established record that no one ever rises above mediocrity in any calling or circumstance of life without following this profound rule.

Your wife is going to have a baby and you "need" more money. Sorry, but your wife's having a child doesn't increase your value to your employer.

You have sickness in the family and desperately "need" additional money. But, as unfortunate as this may be, it has nothing whatsoever to do with your "rights" to receive more money.

Fellow employees may be earning more than you receive and you feel you are entitled to get as much as they do. Sorry again, but the only person who can possibly up your "rights" is the one person over whom you have complete control, yourself. And, paradoxical as it may seem, the best possible way to improve your own "rights" to receive is by first improving the value of your services, the one thing over which you have complete control.

If you have learned the difference between your "needs" and your "rights," you are wiser by far than nine-tenths of the people of the world, for it is a common error among people to confuse them.

Name: Judith Williamson

Company: Napoleon Hill Foundation

Web Site: www.naphill.org

Biography: Napoleon Hill's Definite Major Purpose was to spread the Philosophy of Achievement (the 17 Principles of Success) worldwide to this and future generations.

Over time, Hill became America's most beloved motivational author. His book *Think and Grow Rich* is the all-time best seller in the field. He uncovered a system of 17 success principles that, when combined, almost universally guaranteed a person's success.

Hill established the Napoleon Hill Foundation (www.naphill.org) as a nonprofit educational institution whose mission is to perpetuate his philosophy of leadership, self-motivation, and individual achievement. The Foundation provides his books, audio cassettes, videotapes, and other motivational products.

Selling Philosophy: Motivational self-help via the 17 Principles of Success

Target Industries: Business, industry, individuals, entrepreneurs, social-service agencies, educators, minority groups, and prison inmates

Best Sellers: *Think and Grow Rich*, *Law of Success*, and PMA Science of Success Course

Sales Tip One: Set your head and heart upon a Definite Major Purpose and go to work, right where you stand, to attain it—and begin *now*.

Sales Tip Two: Adopt and follow the habit of Going the Extra Mile by rendering more service and better service than you are paid for, thus enlarging the space you may occupy in the world.

Sales Tip Three: Control your Mental Attitude and keep it always positive and free from the spirit of defeatism.

Book One: *Think and Grow Rich, Law of Success, The Magic Ladder of Success*

Book Two: *How to Sell Your Way Through Life, Master Key to Riches, Think Your Way to Wealth*

Book Three: *Success through a Positive Mental Attitude, Grow Rich with Peace of Mind, You Can Work Your Own Miracles*

Product One: *Your Right to Be Rich* (audio)

Product Two: *Master Key to Riches* (video)

Chapter 57

The *Real* Secret to Effectively Enrolling and Selling

Michael Oliver
Natural Selling

Having worked with tens of thousands of network marketers and direct salespeople, I've noticed that success, and the money that goes with it, comes to those who have . . .

- ➤ The willingness to learn.
- ➤ The desire to change their present situation.
- ➤ The commitment to take action.

There's also something else that's even more important. And that's making one simple principle the cornerstone of their business: *Putting the needs of their potential partners and customers first, and their own needs second.*

Sounds simple enough, and yet how many distributors and direct sales people really do this, both mentally and practically?

■ ASKING QUESTIONS IS THE KEY TO SUCCESSFUL ENROLLING AND SELLING

Successful and consistent enrolling and selling has little to do with you, your story, your passion, or convincing anyone of anything so that you can get what you want. It's helping people get what *they* value and want the most.

People make changes based on feeling dissatisfied with their present situation. Allow them to talk about *their* thirst, and how it *feels* first, and then offer them your solution, if it's appropriate to do so.

Ask the questions that will uncover whether any dissatisfaction exists. If it does, find out whether they are prepared to do something about it, before even thinking about presenting your solution.

The secret to significantly increasing your results is to *ask for information first* before you give it. After all: *People have the answers. All you need are the right questions!*

■ THE PURPOSE OF YOUR BUSINESS

The path to understanding and then applying this is in the answer to the simple question, "What is the purpose of your business (or any other business at all)?"

Most would answer that it's about making money, being self-fulfilled, or some other self-focused thought.

Nothing wrong in that, except do you think that people will pick up on this self-focused vibration? Of course they will! You give away your thoughts and real intention, both subconsciously and consciously, in the words you use and the way you express them. An indication of this is how you answered that question!

If you answered that the focus is on you, do you think people really care about what you want or think, such as sharing your story and product, or being told that what you're doing will work for them as well, or that your products are like no other, or that they should get in now so as not to miss a wonderful opportunity, and so on?

Do they really want to be externally pressured by having closing and objection-handling techniques used on them, techniques, by the way, that actually cause the resistance every distributor or salesperson is hoping to avoid?

Mostly not—except perhaps for the one in one thousand who just happens to be in the mood to want to listen.

Sadly, however, this approach is still in the mainstream of sales training. It continues to be the main cause of why 90 percent of distributors drop out with less money and self-esteem than when they first started.

It's fascinating to consider why anyone would want to use a sales system that has a high built-in failure rate. It's like getting on an airplane that has a 90 percent chance of not landing in the right place!

■ THE REAL PURPOSE OF A BUSINESS

The real purpose of a business is to *help people solve their problem, or satisfy their needs, wants, and desires.* That's it! (This is also the first of four foundational principles on which the Natural Selling Process is built.)

Here's proof. If your product, service, or income opportunity cannot solve a problem for someone, is there any reason for him or her to get involved with or buy from you? The answer is self-evident!

So who is your business really about and for, then? Other people!

And how do you find out if people have the types of problems you might be able to help them solve? You ask them!

You ask them the right types of questions at the right time. You also listen and respond to what they mean as well as what they say, without attachment to your own agenda. In the process most will tell you (and themselves) everything you need to know. They and you will learn together whether there is a difference between what they have and what they want. If there is, they will also tell you whether they are prepared to do something about it!

Done correctly, the dialogue itself will influence your potential customers and partners to look at and change their present situations, if it's appropriate to do so. No external pressure or manipulation is needed from you!

By the way, making the purpose of your business about others does not mean forgetting about your personal objective or agenda. It's important you achieve your objective. You just put it on the shelf so you can hear the other person and they can hear you.

■ THINKING DIFFERENTLY

Instead of starting the day thinking "In order for me to increase my business today I must prospect as many people as I can and sign them up into my business," think "In order for me to increase my business today I must go out and talk with as many people as I can to discover if they have the types of problems I can help them solve."

Can you *feel* the difference between the two thoughts?

If the second resonates with you more than the first, then follow through with congruent words and actions. Learn to practically apply it so that you can achieve the level of income and success you have set yourself.

Conventional selling is telling. Natural selling is asking, listening, and responding to what is meant, not just what is being said. Listening is the *real* secret to effectively enrolling and selling.

Name: Michael Oliver

Company: Natural Selling, Inc.

Web Site: www.NaturalSelling.com

Biography: Michael Oliver is the founder of Natural Selling, Inc., the only sales training program designed to really eliminate rejection and objections.

He is also the author of the internationally best-selling book *How to Sell Network Marketing without Fear, Anxiety, or Losing Your Friends!*

Every year he helps thousands of salespeople and independent distributors achieve outstanding personal and professional results.

He currently conducts over 100 speeches and workshops a year for a variety of companies worldwide.

He effectively demonstrates how to replace conventional selling techniques that focus on presenting, telling, objection handling, and closing with a pragmatic and natural process that produces positive results every time.

Target Industries: Network marketing

Best Sellers: *How to Sell Network Marketing without Fear, Anxiety, or Losing Your Friends!*

Sales Tip One: Base your sales approach on universal principles, not on techniques. The Four Principles of Natural Selling are:

1. The purpose of your business is to help other people solve their problems.

2. Listen to what is meant, not just what is being said.

3. Ask the right types of questions at the right time.

4. Feed back what you think you heard.

Sales Tip Two: The biggest cause of objections and rejection is presenting your solution too soon. Eliminate this by Discovering first, Presenting second.

Sales Tip Three: The act of listening without judgment, prejudice, or interpretation, and putting your agenda to one side, is so powerful that it will attract people to you like a magnet!

Book One: *How to Sell Network Marketing without Fear, Anxiety, or Losing Your Friends!*

Book Two: *Walking with the Wise—Entrepreneur Edition* (contributing author)

Product One: Best of Michael Oliver's 6-Day Fast Track Teleclasses (audio)

Product Two: 12 Ways to Start Effective Conversations without Fear (audio)

Product Three: Calling Leads (excerpted from the Power Up Your Dialogue series; audio)

Chapter 58

Qualifying Your Sales Process

Rick Page
The Complex Sale

A key to success in business development, as in any strategic endeavor, is picking winnable battles. Realistically, of course, how you qualify prospective customers depends on how many opportunities you have in relation to the resources available to actually do the work. Salespeople with a full pipeline and more prospects than they can handle qualify prospects very differently than those who are just getting into the game at a lesser-known company or in a new territory. There is no universal model for qualifying prospects.

But where is the line between qualification and quitting? Or between a positive attitude and the rookie trait of overly optimistic "happy ears"? Successful selling involves asking some tough questions and being honest about the answers. Enthusiasm is essential to selling, but hope is not a credible sales strategy.

To qualify a prospect, the first question every salesperson should ask is, "Will this business happen for anyone at all?" Experience shows that many customer project evaluations don't ever result in an actual purchase.

When evaluations stall or collapse entirely, one of two things is usually missing: either there isn't a business problem of sufficient magnitude or urgency (pain), or the project lacks political sponsorship (power) to shepherd it to completion. In either case, a deal won't happen no matter how compelling your presentation.

If the prospect's intentions do seem credible, the second question is, is this a good opportunity for us? Sometimes customers will informally pick an integrator for a project without disclosing that fact to the other bidders. There's little you can do to avoid this trap; you just have to trust the customer's integrity. But if, in fact, the playing field is level, then it is best to pursue only those prospects where you have a solution fit and differentiating advantages.

One question traditionally asked by salespeople to determine an opportunity's viability is, is the money in the budget? To some salespeople, this question requires a simple yes or no answer. But if the solution is strategic enough or the sponsor powerful enough, budgets may only be one indicator. Of course, if there is an insufficient budget, there will likely be a longer sales cycle. Also, the salesperson will need to get higher up the sponsorship chain, which adds politics and risk to the sales process.

Ideally, solutions integrators should engage in demand creation, rather than demand-reaction selling. Successful SIs find business problems that need to be solved and create a vision of a solution and a value proposition to drive an engagement, instead of just responding to an RFP.

Of course, there are strategic and intangible reasons that may trump the logical analysis as to why you pursue a particular opportunity. It may be a brand-name customer. You may want to penetrate a new industry or country. You may want to co-develop competencies for use throughout the industry.

An important question to ask that is often neglected is, will this prospect's business be profitable for us? Unfortunately, many SIs measure their salespeople by revenue, not profitability.

The last question to ask is even less obvious: Will this engagement result in a satisfied client and repeat business? If it doesn't, you may get this piece of business and then inoculate the client against doing future business with you.

One other point: The qualification process doesn't always have to culminate in a "go" or "no-go" decision. There is the option to buy another card. This means investing only enough resources to stay in the game for the next step, gather information, and see if you can gain the upper hand later.

If your firm has the capacity and expertise to do a project, there is almost no deal that you can't win with enough effort. But at what cost and what risk? The worst-case scenario is to commit significant resources and then finish second—and there are no silver medals in this business.

Enthusiasm is essential to selling, but hope is not a credible sales strategy.

Name: Rick Page

Company: The Complex Sale, Inc.

Web Site: www.complexsale.com

Biography: A recognized authority in the complex sale arena, Rick Page has trained salespeople from more than 50 countries during his long and distinguished career. One of the foremost experts on sales management and selling, Rick continues to develop innovative sales programs and is the author of sales best sellers *Hope Is Not a Strategy* and *Make Winning a Habit*.

As EVP of Dun & Bradstreet Software (formerly Management Science America), Rick initiated a strategic sales training program for the global sales force. While at the company, Rick also led one of its most successful regions, managing more than 100 consultants and 50 sales reps for a $50 million profit center.

In 1994, Rick founded The Complex Sale, Inc., which has provided sales consulting and training methodologies to more than 100,000 sales reps worldwide in the information technology, consulting, telecommunications, medical, and financial industries.

Rick holds a BS and MBA from the University of North Carolina at Chapel Hill. He contributes numerous articles to leading sales and consulting publications, and is a frequent speaker at sales conferences around the world.

Selling Philosophy: TCS helps you win the sales you can't afford to lose—from speeches and tools to training and coaching to total sales force transformation. TCS helps you create a pipeline, win opportunities, and dominate accounts in the complex selling environment.

Target Industries: Information services, high tech, consulting, health care, finance, and telecommunications

Best Sellers: R.A.D.A.R., Winning Opportunity Strategies, T.otal E.nterprise A.ccount M.anagement (TEAM), BPSC: Best Practices Sales Cycle, CSC: Coaching the Complex Sale, GPS Software Suite

Sales Tip One: Bad news early is good news.

Sales Tip Two: Positioning is the art of saying it first.

Sales Tip Three: Selling technical benefits to executive buyers can be like watching dogs watching TV; they nod, but you know they're really not getting any of it.

Book One: *Hope Is Not a Strategy: The Six Keys to Winning the Complex Sale*

Book Two: *Make Winning a Habit: 20 Best Practices of the World's Greatest Sales Forces*

Chapter 59

Selling to VITOs (Very Important Top Officers)

Anthony Parinello
VITO Selling

VITO is the Very Important Top Officer, the person with the ultimate veto power . . . the CEO, president, or owner . . . the person who cares most about the top, middle, and bottom line, and the person who is most interested in what you and your ideas and solutions can do for their entire enterprise. VITO is the person you need to sell to!

Whether we *like* it or not . . . whether we want to *admit* it or not . . . whether we choose to *do* anything about it or not . . . VITO always has the VETO power over whether your stuff actually gets bought, or gets kicked out the door. No matter what anyone else in the buying enterprise has to say about some salesperson's offering, VITO can (and often will) kill that offering on a moment's notice.

This is a fact of sales life. You are better off accepting it, and adapting to it, sooner than later. If you feel any hesitation about updating your sales process so that it reflects this core selling reality, you should consider these six indisputable reasons why VITO really does equal VETO in your world, and why you *must* contact VITO first.

■ VITO CREATES EVERY IMPORTANT INITIATIVE

By definition, an important initiative at VITO, Inc., only *becomes* important when VITO buys into it. Every critical goal, plan, and objective at VITO, Inc., has VITO's DNA in it. Sure, others in the organization can feed the suggestion box, but VITO decides what's hot and what's not at any given moment. As we have seen, VITO's mind can change on a dime, and may do so without VITO asking a soul anything.

If you want to stay in the know about what's really important at any given moment at VITO, Inc., you'll keep your hand on VITO's pulse throughout your entire relationship with the company.

■ CONSTANT IMPROVEMENT IS VITO'S RESPONSIBILITY

In VITO's world, status quo doesn't go. VITOs are measured on the growth of their organization. Flat, horizontal growth lines just don't compute for them; therefore, they're on a constant lookout for ideas that no one else has brought to their attention. They have an "early adopter" mentality. They are eager to take the risk to have what no one else has, and do what no one else is doing.

In other words, they are likely to be the most receptive people in the entire organization to well-designed sales offerings that actually add value to VITO, Inc.

■ VITO OWNS ALL BUDGETS

When your current contact says "We've got to get the budget approved," who do you think that person goes to for approval? Answer: Either to VITO or to someone who reports, directly or indirectly, to VITO. Depending upon how low on the company totem pole the person is, the budget request may have several levels to travel, but the stream always flows in the same direction. Notice this: Every other person in the organization is told how much they can spend and tries to spend less than they have so they can look like a hero in VITO's eyes. That's why you're always being asked by these underlings to lower your price. VITO, on the other hand, *has* no budget. Or, if you prefer, VITO can say, at any given moment, "Let there be a budget for X"—and suddenly, there's a budget!

If you want to eliminate the price objection from your life (and who doesn't?), I can show you exactly how to do that. Ready? Contact VITO first. Then, during your very first interaction with VITO, state your price clearly and confidently. (I like to pull out my standard agreement and let VITO look it over on the spot.) If there is haggling to be done, you and VITO will do it here, and you'll get it over with before you invest massive amounts of time and energy in the deal. More often than you might expect, you'll name your price and VITO will nod and ask what else there is to talk about. Once VITO decides to work with you, VITO will allocate sufficient funds to the appropriate decision maker. No more "let me get it approved" soap operas!

■ VITO KNOWS WHO'S WHO

VITO not only *knows* everyone of importance on the org chart, but also (most likely) hand-picked, hired, or held on to everyone on that chart. VITO typically has fewer than 10 direct reports. These individuals are VITO's movers and shakers, the people who get done whatever VITO wants done. Investing large amounts of your time with anyone else in the enterprise amounts to sales malpractice.

■ VITO DEFINES THE CRITICAL BUSINESS CRITERIA

At VITO, Inc., there are certain critical business criteria that all partners and suppliers must meet or exceed if they want to exchange their goods for VITO's cold, hard cash. Can you guess who sets those criteria? I thought you could. Some of these criteria are "hard" measurables (expressed in numbers and percentages), and take the form of reliability ratings, performance history, projected savings, and so on. Some of these criteria are "soft" values articulated with descriptive words and phrases such as brand reputation, internal morale, goodwill, prestige among VITO's peers, and so on.

If you and your company can't meet VITO's business criteria, you will be dismissed. If you don't know what the criteria are, you can't meet them.

■ VITO GETS PAID TO MAKE DECISIONS

This one's a no-brainer. You're a salesperson. Your job is to generate positive decisions from qualified people who have the authority to say "yes" to mutually beneficial business propositions. VITO's job is to make decisions that benefit VITO, Inc. It's a match made in heaven!

Some others in the enterprise avoid making decisions, but VITO knows that making a decision is the only sure way to get the ball rolling. VITOs live to get the ball rolling . . . and keep it rolling! So, as the classic film *Ghostbusters* put it many years ago, "Who you gonna call?" Someone who hates making decisions? Or someone who makes decisions for a living?

What's driving those decisions? Glad you asked. The nine values that drive VITO's decisions are as follows:

1. **Competency.** VITO's decision-making actions will typically be based upon experience, reason, and moral principles. There's an emotional component, too, of course, but VITO is too smart a player not to look at the upsides and downsides.

2. **Forward-looking vision.** VITOs set clear goals and envision the future, then make decisions that match that vision. They know where they're going. They habitually pick priorities that support their vision.

3. **Confidence.** VITOs display confidence in all that they do, especially when it comes to making a decision.

4. **Intelligence.** VITOs quickly get access to the background information they need. They are well informed and well connected, and as a result they tend to make good decisions fast.

5. **Fair-mindedness.** VITOs are open-minded and fair. Contrary to popular belief, they are generally sensitive to the feelings, values, interests, and well-being of others. Most of the VITOs I know are the most fair-minded people in the enterprise.

6. **Broad-mindedness.** VITOs instinctively seek out diversity, and in doing so open up their world of possibilities.

7. **Honesty.** VITOs are straight shooters. They will always tell you where you stand.

8. **Imagination.** VITOs know how to make timely and appropriate changes in their thinking, plans, and methods. They are always on the lookout for new and better ideas, and solutions to problems.

9. **Courage.** VITOs don't spook easily, and they have the perseverance necessary to accomplish a goal, regardless of the seemingly insurmountable obstacles they may face. Specifically, they are not frightened of making the "wrong" decision. When this happens, VITOs simply make another decision and move on!

Name: Anthony Parinello

Company: VITO Selling

Web Site: www.vitoselling.com

Biography: In 1995 Tony created his own brand of sales training called Selling to VITO, the Very Important Top Officer. The majority of Fortune 100 and over 2.5 million salespeople in more than 30 countries use his programs. He coaches sales and marketing professionals and entrepreneurs all over the world. He is a *Wall Street Journal* best-selling author and creator of *Selling across America*, a radio talk show dedicated to the art of selling. He is the Marketing and Sales Expert on Entrepreneur.com.

Tony has written eight books, including his massively popular *Selling to VITO, the Very Important Top Officer*.

Tony has delivered more than 3,500 speeches about sales.

Selling Philosophy: Selling to Top Decision Makers

Target Industries: Electronics, components, industrial supplies, computers, software, office equipment, office supplies, medical supplies and electronics, printing/copiers, telecommunications, phone systems, pharmaceuticals. network marketers

Best Sellers: Selling to VITO, the Very Important Top Officer seminars, Club VITO, Sales Mastery Program, Business Builder Program (MLM), The Entrepreneur Mastery Series

Sales Tip One: Ice breakers are for ships, not salespeople! They waste precious time, and they don't help you establish Equal Business Stature with your prospect . . . skip 'em. Instead, present a balanced gain equation that has the critical element of time, such as: "[Five] other [manufacturers] here in [San Diego] trust and rely upon us to [increase revenues] by as much as [2 percent] while [cutting expenses] by up to [14 percent] in just three months." That sure beats "How are you today?"

Sales Tip Two: Ask your "C" suite prospect a question that no one else will ask. Try this: "What's important to you personally about _____?" Make sure you fill in the blank with an issue or situation that your product, service, or solution can solve that's also important to this "C" Suite prospect's industry.

Sales Tip Three: If you're going to give your Top Officer prospect a PowerPoint presentation, I strongly suggest that it be no longer than three slides, each slide should have a maximum of 10 words, and you should never, ever speak for more than 60 seconds without asking a checking question such as "What questions might you have?" or "Where in your operation do you see this idea working the best?" or "What situations do you have to solve in the next 90 days that this idea could help with?" or "Where in your operation/organization would you like to see the biggest improvement in the shortest amount of time?"

Book One: *Getting to VITO, The Very Important Top Officer*

Book Two: *Think and Sell Like a CEO*

Book Three: *Stop Cold Calling Forever: True Confessions of a Serial Cold Caller*

Product One: VITO 101 Sales Course

Product Two: Club VITO, Quota Buster Program

Product Three: Entrepreneur Mastery Series

$$Chapter\ 60$$

The "Book Yourself Solid" Simple Selling System

Michael Port

Enough with the tragic pithy sales prose that is supposed to say something meaningful, but is devoid of any true message, such as "Think outside the box" or "Let's make this a win-win." Or, my personal favorite (imagine this being voiced in an amusing yet slightly cheesy late-night infomercial style), "People hate to be sold, but they love to buy."

Customers can sniff out these cliché sales phrases and tactics from a mile away. They detest them. All people really want to do is to express their values. Plain and simple. After all, isn't that what they are doing every time they reach in their pocket to buy something?

Look at it this way. If you saw a hefty casino tab, Smirnoff bottle service delivery charges, and a Hummer lease payment on my Amex statement, you'd know what I value. However, if my charges included yoga sessions, continuing education in MIT's Birthing of Giants program, and the compost for my backyard vegetable garden, you'd get a different sense of my values.

People don't buy because you want them to. And rarely do they buy because of a sales pitch or something clever you said to convince them.

So if we're kicking the old sales clichés to the curb, then what other options do we have? If you really want to increase sales, first, you've got to earn the proportionate amount of trust required to make the sale. But, how is trust really built? Through commitment making and fulfilling. You make commitments to a potential customer and fulfill them . . . over and over and over again.

So if that's true, then how do we get to show up in front of customers to make these commitments? With the always-have-something-to-invite-people-to offer, of course. Which (aside from pulling prospects out of a burning building) has got to be one of the most effective ways to initiate the trust-building process. It also allows you to:

➤ Continually demonstrate who you are, what you value, and how you can serve customers.

➤ Reduce perceived risk for potential customers by creating a no-barrier-to-entry offer that allows customers to experience you directly.

➤ Extend invitations that add a tremendous amount of value rather than make sales pitches.

Let's say you value eating healthy. You value having readily accessible, yet wholesome food in your home. Let's take it one step further and say you want healthy, balanced meals to show up lovingly prepared and delivered to your doorstep. But perhaps hiring a personal chef five days a week is too great a financial investment. Just because Gourmet Jennie serves your need for nutritious cooking doesn't mean you're ready to give her the keys to your kitchen. You may not know or trust her enough to serve this value. There's still a missing ingredient. Trust is essential.

We've got to slow down the sales cycle and build trust, first. This is what allows prospects to experience your work. And it's also exactly what the always-have-something-to-invite-people-to offer does. It should never come across as a "you show up and then we pitch this thing to you." Instead, these events and experiences are consistent, frequent, and probably even fun. They bring together past, present, and potential customers on an ongoing basis. They are always relevant, but not necessarily exactly what you sell.

A home delivery chef may invite guests to a gathering every other Thursday at 5:30 PM in her home. She may show us how to prepare easy, healthy meals. Or she might serve simple, yet nutritious hors d'oeuvres while teaching us the benefits of cooking with organic versus nonorganic produce. But she's not whipping up some sales pitch. There's no "sales" offering at this event. The entire purpose is to add value, to create an experience that gives potential customers the opportunity to express their values and allows us to demonstrate that we fulfill our commitments. If "guests" want to buy, they will raise their hands. But they never, ever feel pressured.

The Book Yourself Solid selling process is all about your clients' needs. Rarely is it about yours.

If you want to create good customer relationships and ultimately sell more, you need to do these five things:

1. Slow down the sales process.
2. Ask more questions than you answer.

3. Listen more than you speak.

4. Consider the needs and desires of your potential clients before considering your own.

5. Keep the conversation positive and empowering.

Even before you invite potential clients to your always-have-something-to-invite-people-to event, use the following questions in a genuine and sincere conversation. The result is you will be able to guide potential clients through a process where they can learn more about themselves and more about you, and view any dilemma from a positive problem-solving perspective.

➤ What are you working on? What are your goals?

➤ How will you know when you have achieved the results? What results will you see?

➤ What feelings will you have? What feedback will you hear?

➤ What are the benefits of going after this outcome? What will you gain?

➤ If you reach the outcome, will it be worth the invested time, energy, and financial or personal commitment?

➤ Do the benefits outweigh the perceived costs?

You may be asking, "How are those questions actually going to sell anything?" That's the beauty of the Book Yourself Solid simple selling system: you're simply helping potential clients feel better about themselves and their lives by showing them that they can take control and make changes.

Ultimately, the conversation will come full circle back to one very key question, "Would you like a partner to help you achieve these goals?" With that one question you open the door to invite them to your always-have-something-to-invite-people-to gig, and you make yourself available to serve these potential customers and be the solution to their unsolved problems. See how I do this in action at www.bookedsolidu.com.

I'm certain you care about what you do . . . the people you serve, the products you sell, and the reputation you've earned. You wouldn't be reading this if you didn't. And as leader of the Think Big Revolution, I want to encourage you to think bigger about who you are and what you do. Think big (no, bigger!) right now.

When you think big and stay focused on your customers' needs, you begin to know your customers. You build relationships with them. You set yourself apart from the trite sales crowd. And you'll never, ever be put in the same category as those shady, smooth-talking, handlebar-mustache-twirling, sleazeball salesmen.

Be the integrity-based sales professional we all want to know and love.

Name: Michael Port

Biography: Michael Port is called "an uncommonly honest author" by the *Boston Globe* and a "marketing guru" by the *Wall Street Journal*, and is a *New York Times* best-selling author of *Book Yourself Solid, Beyond Booked Solid, The Contrarian Effect,* and *The Think Big Manifesto.*

He writes a monthly sales and marketing column for *Entrepreneur* magazine, is a regular guest on MSNBC and CNBC, and receives the highest overall speaker ratings at conferences around the world. Michael's mission is to make you think bigger about who you are and what you offer . . . and to take typical sales advice and do the opposite.

Chapter 61

Managing Sales Success

10 Critical Performance Factors That Drive Revenue and Sales Team Growth—A System for Improving Both Sales Manager and Sales Team Performance

Warren Kurzrock
Porter Henry & Co

You have probably heard the comment: "Sandy is a great salesperson because she or he _____." Fill in the blank with:

➤ Knows how to sell value.

➤ Is fantastic at prospecting.

➤ Sells strategically at high account levels.

➤ Has super selling skills.

➤ And so forth.

The fact is that few salespeople succeed by performing *one* skill, activity, or behavior well. While the superstars may have a dominant skill or behavior, they usually exceed expectations because they have mastered a variety of the critical sales skills and tactics. Considering that there are a multitude of skills, behaviors, strategies, and actions that make up the "complete salesperson," how does the sales manager know which buttons to push or what actions to take for development purposes? Our research in studying and observing thousands of salespeople on the job has validated that most salespeople have a need/capability to perform about 50 actions (skills, subskills, behaviors, and decisions) on a typical selling day. The bottom line is that the typical sales manager manages 10 people (on average), but also needs to track and monitor their 500 skills and behaviors being used differently on an ongoing basis.

Most sales managers rely on revenue (increase, decline, or flat) to determine who needs help the most, and if they can find time, they try to pinpoint a deficiency and go to the rescue (often too late, focusing on the wrong problem). In today's economy, the situation is compounded by the plethora of demands on the sales manager and the struggle to allocate enough time to supervise 8 to 12 sales-people with varying needs and problems.

What sales managers need is a simple system (with minimum time investment) to organize and monitor activity, predict where the problems will occur, and then focus on the right solution at the right time. To manage sales performance effectively and efficiently, a sales performance system is desperately needed.

■ BENEFITS OF A MANAGING SALES PERFORMANCE SYSTEM

Consider the benefits that a managing performance system will provide. Sales managers will be able to:

➤ Recognize performance "warning signs and symptoms" before they become sales performance problems.

➤ Analyze a wide range of performance indicators that many managers overlook.

➤ Proactively develop their people by identifying gains and gaps in expected performance.

➤ Determine root causes of performance problems and choose from a wide menu of solutions.

➤ Select the most appropriate actions to reinforce gains and eliminate gaps.

➤ Follow a system to drive sales performance and results.

■ OVERVIEW OF THE SALES PERFORMANCE SYSTEM

The system visual below demonstrates the four big-picture logical steps that provide a track to run on. We will start with an overview of this fail-safe process. Later this article will expand the process by offering a detailed model that enables the sales manager to seamlessly manage the sales performance process on an individual sales-person basis.

Sales Performance System

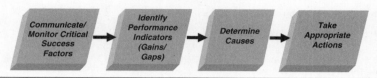

Figure 61.1   Porter Henry

In simple terms, the system involves four steps. The expanded Managing Sales Performance model, which follows on the last page, is comprehensive and provides a detailed map. See Figure 61.1 for a brief description of the key elements and concepts.

■ COMMUNICATE/MONITOR CRITICAL SUCCESS FACTORS

The first challenge is to simplify the sales manager's job by identifying major priorities so that he or she can target what's important and not "get lost in the weeds." As indicated earlier, the problem is that the typical salesperson performs so many actions during a typical period (such as a quarter) that they are impossible to recognize, monitor, or change without consistent tracking. As an analogy, consider watching and coaching a tennis player with dozens of skills and actions involved: forehand strokes, serves, overheads, backhand, net play, and so forth. Each stroke has its own set of subskills: keeping the elbow in, watching the ball, grooving the stroke, and so on. What's needed to create improvement is an effective way to isolate (organize) the major deficiency, and then break it down into small steps for practice. The same guideline applies to sales performance.

That's why we have simplified the Critical Success Factors into a manageable 10 categories or buckets. While they all interact to a degree, it enables the sales manager to start with a level playing field and focus on the priority factors that ultimately define total performance. Once the major categories are defined (there can be more or less than 10 and the Critical Success Factors may differ slightly from company to company), it's essential to communicate expectations for each. Determining expectations for each category sets the stage for the salesperson and indicates "how high he/she is expected to jump."

The 10 interacting Critical Success Factors are:

➤ Account penetration
➤ Administration

➤ Contact activity

➤ General behavior

➤ New business pipeline

➤ Product mix

➤ Sales revenue

➤ Selling skills

➤ Strategy execution

➤ Territory management

Each of the above Critical Success Factors is further defined by the Performance Indicators (next step) that provide key performance measures for each.

In summary, the sales manager can focus systematically on 10 activities, some more important than others, as opposed to randomly examining a myriad of subskills that can drive good or weak performance. For the sales manager, the first step requires (1) setting/communicating expectations for each category and (2) observing and tracking performance (collecting data, critical events, on-the-job observations, interactions with salespeople). While company data are generated on revenue, the balance must be identified from reports, coaching, and observation.

■ IDENTIFY PERFORMANCE INDICATORS (GAINS/GAPS)

In tracking activity for one of the 10 categories (Critical Success Factors) that impact sales performance, the manager notices a shortfall or change in a performance indicator. This should trigger the move to the next step, which is simply getting a more defined or finite fix on the issue or identifying the performance gap. The system provides an inventory of four Performance Indicators for each Critical Success Factor.

For example, the Critical Success Factor for "Selling Skills" identifies four skills as gains or gaps to review:

➤ Call planning

➤ Probing needs/opportunities

➤ Benefits/presentation

➤ Handling resistance/closing

Once the gain or gap is identified, the sales manager can make an informed judgment: Is this a serious gap (i.e., pipeline prospects have dropped 50 percent) or should I just continue to monitor it?

As part of the analysis (for each sales team member), the sales manager has to monitor other Critical Success Factors to see if there are other gaps, since all 10 interact to drive overall performance. Assuming the gap is serious, or there are multiple gaps in other Critical Success Factors, the sales manager can move to the next step with confidence.

■ DETERMINE CAUSES

The rationale for determining causes is simple. The cause can often determine the solution and point to the appropriate sales manager action (or possibly multiple actions). For example, if a sales associate has a skill problem, such as handling objections, the logical and perhaps obvious solution is coaching. But if the same gap or skill deficiency is lack of confidence or aggressiveness, it may be an attitude or motivation and require a different solution. There are no magical answers to every deficiency, but if the cause can be determined (the model provides eight possibilities) it will often point to an appropriate action (or combined actions) that the manager can take to help alleviate the problem and hopefully foster a turnaround.

■ TAKE APPROPRIATE ACTIONS

The final step in the ongoing process is acting on the solution. Many sales managers fall back and assume "one solution fits all" to problems, but they need to have a full menu of solutions and be skilled in their use and application. Our model provides 10 viable solutions, many of which are positive, to offer reinforcement or to create improvement. They range from Appraisal (can improve minor performance gaps) to Training (when knowledge or skills reinforcement are called for), but a full complement must certainly include coaching, counseling, communicating expectations, use of discipline, and so on.

■ IMPLEMENTING THE MANAGING SALES PERFORMANCE SYSTEM

This model is proven and will work with minor customization for any sales force. However, it requires (1) added tools for monitoring and capturing data, and (2) simulated training in the process and application. Of course, the sales manager has to develop the discipline to execute the system on an ongoing basis and avoid the time traps that create a helter-skelter effect on the job. That's where training comes in.

Effective implementation requires the ability to collect data and make notes on critical performance events on a current basis. We recommend a *quarterly review*, which may take a few hours to review and analyze data/notes for the average-size sales team, followed by an accompanying plan for individualized action (accomplished during the next quarter). It should be apparent that major gaps or a serious event should be addressed immediately. With a simple spreadsheet planner, the sales manager can review the entire team's individual performances once a quarter, and develop an action plan for specific salespeople who require reinforcement or need to upgrade their performance in identified areas.

By systemizing the process, the sales manager simply collects or reviews data and individual activity on a constant basis and then puts it into a simple review format so he can determine his focused sales team activity. In the final analysis, the Managing Sales Performance System will provide a method of developing the sales team, separating this productive activity from the abundance of daily actions and interruptions that "come with the territory." In the final analysis, it will provide an organized, time-contained strategy for improving sales and salespeople.

Name: Warren Kurzrock

Company: Porter Henry & Co., Inc.

Web Site: www.porterhenry.com

Biography: Warren Kurzrock, CEO of Porter Henry & Co., has over 25 years of sales force development and consulting experience. He has proven capability in every phase of sales force effectiveness, including strategic selling, sales and management training, analysis, planning, and organization.

Warren is a graduate of Duke University and has a master's degree in marketing from NYU Graduate School of Business. He was a top salesperson in both the steel and photocopy industries, and eventually became a high-level sales manager.

Warren has been a frequent speaker at national sales meetings and large events. He has done training in countries around the globe.

Selling Philosophy: Successful salespeople must be motivated to work hard, need to possess selling skills/strategic know-how, and be able to allocate sales calls for ROI.

Target Industries: Every major industry

Best Sellers: Thirty-three courses include best-selling workshops on topics such as consultative selling, negotiating, strategic business development, value-driven selling, sales coaching, sales leadership, and managing sales performance.

Sales Tip One: In selling, "frequency" is the most vital component, whether in making follow-up sales calls, closing, asking questions, practicing skills, or coaching.

Sales Tip Two: Most salespeople think of price when negotiating, but everything is negotiable. When you give something away, always get equal value in return.

Sales Tip Three: Sales training is wasted unless the sales manager is trained to follow up in the field and reinforce the sales skills on a frequent basis.

Book One: *The Sales Strategist: Six Breakthrough Strategies for Winning New Business*

Chapter 62

Value Clarity

The Optimal Source of Differentiation

Jeff Thull

Prime Resource Group

In today's turbulent and volatile marketplace, even the most experienced professionals are struggling with the rapid commoditization of their complex, high-value solutions. The complexity of the problems to be solved and the competitive threats we face are increasing at an alarming rate. At the same time, customers are wrestling with mission critical decisions and evaluating solutions that all sound the same and come packaged with a high degree of risk and a low probability of success. Your success demands an exceptional strategy, a clarity of value, and a precise execution that must clearly set you apart from your competition.

Business today is not solution constrained. We have the ability to build and offer many solutions that are capable of delivering substantial value to our customers. The issue that creates far more ineffectiveness is that we are more "diagnose"-constrained. There is a great tendency to leap and present our solution before we connect and quantify our value to our customer's world.

Value remains the most sought-after and least-understood factor in the world of complex sales. The challenges in today's marketplace, and the focus of our work, can be summarized in two words: *value clarity*. Companies are finding it increasingly difficult to defend their value because it is increasingly difficult to connect it to their customers' real world and quantify it with an amount their customers believe.

The more complex customers' situations and our solutions become, the more uncertain customers become about the value involved. Customers hesitate to take action when they are uncertain regarding the risks/consequences of a business situation, more so than if they don't understand a value proposition. A simple analogy of the customer's reaction is "I have no doubt that the drug Lipitor can reduce cholesterol, but I am not sure if I have a cholesterol problem." This uncertainty around value manifests in decision paralysis. Sales opportunities ending in *no decision* are running well above 35 percent for most sellers. It is clear that customer uncertainty is consuming a high percentage of companies' resources.

To put it bluntly, because sellers are unable to provide their customers with value clarity, they cannot defend their value. As a result, they have no alternative but to drop their price to match competitors of lesser value, which then requires cutting costs to maintain margins. This can lead to a very dangerous downward spiral, in which the organic growth and profits required to sustain their businesses spin further and further out of their reach.

■ DIAGNOSING COMPLEX PROBLEMS TO ACHIEVE VALUE CLARITY

A core competency of the complex sale is a company's ability—from product development, to marketing, to sales and support—to perform as expert diagnosticians and thoroughly analyze customers' business requirements, and, as experienced advisors, to design and deliver high-value solutions that will uniquely address those requirements.

The Diagnostic Process, and the expertise of your organization, enables you to help customers recognize, analyze, and understand the causes and consequences of their problems. It is critical that the full extent of the customer's problem be measured and connected to their performance metrics. During diagnosis, your focus is more on physical symptoms and the customer's reality, than on your solution's value, which is more speculative. The goal of the diagnosis is to raise customers' awareness of the problems they are experiencing and what it is costing them not to change their current situation. Equally important, the Diagnostic Process allows you to shift the emphasis of your conversations with customers from you and your solutions to their situations and what is truly valuable to them. This is a shift that differentiates your organization via your approach, creates significant clarity for the customer, and builds exceptional levels of trust and credibility.

Companies need a smarter way to connect their value to their market and transform it into profitable growth. They need a platform that is specifically designed for the complex sales arena, one that offers a system across functions, and the skills and mental discipline required to execute it effectively. Diagnostic Business Development converts the conventional solutions-based, seller-first approach into a diagnostic, customer-first approach. It eliminates obsolete sales processes driven by premature presentations, debate, and confrontation, and replaces them with a step-by-step process of mutual confirmation between the sales team and the customer. It transforms the customer's stereotypical impression of salespeople as predators into one in which salespeople are seen as valued business partners who bring credibility, integrity, and dependability to the business relationship.

Sales and marketing engagements become a guided decision process, led by the sales professional, in collaboration with customers, to discover, diagnose, design, and deliver the highest value solutions to their problems. Diagnostic Business Development enables us to:

➤ **Move beyond selling to managing decisions.** We need to set aside confrontational processes and replace them with a high-quality and collaborative decision process, provided by the sales professional.

➤ **Move beyond problem solving to facilitating change.** Change, along with all the attendant risks involved, is the largest area of uncertainty that customers face. We need to help customers navigate the change required to ensure the successful implementation of our solutions, achieve the value they have purchased, and measure the value they have achieved.

➤ **Move beyond meeting needs to managing expectations.** Just because we see a need does not mean that our customers see it or understand it as clearly as we do and will do something about it. We need to clarify our value by connecting it to our customers' performance metrics and quantify our value impact with a number our customers believe. Furthermore, we must clarify our customers' expectations about solutions in a manner that brings them the confidence to invest in our solutions.

➤ **Move beyond transactions to managing relationships.** In the rush to close deals, we too often forget the human factor and squander the long-term opportunity. We need to address the hopes, fears, and aspirations of our customers and create mutually beneficial relationships.

With the proper diagnostic business analysis, your customers will grant you privileged access that will lead to privileged insight. You will be able to achieve value clarity for your customers and create credible and compelling solutions for them. They will decide to buy in a shorter amount of time and will pay a premium price for your value.

Name: Jeff Thull

Company: Prime Resource Group, Inc.

Web Site: www.primeresource.com

Biography: Jeff Thull is a strategist and advisor for executive teams of major companies worldwide. As president and CEO of Prime Resource Group, Inc., he has designed and implemented business transformation and professional development programs for companies including Shell, 3M, Microsoft, Siemens, and Georgia-Pacific.

Thull has delivered over 2,500 speeches and seminars to corporations and professional associations worldwide. He is the author of the best-selling books *Mastering the Complex Sale: How to Compete and Win When the Stakes Are High*, *The Prime Solution: Close the Value Gap, Increase Margins, and Win the Complex Sale*, and *Exceptional Selling: How the Best Connect and Win in High Stakes Sales*.

Selling Philosophy: Sales and marketing strategy, process, and skills development for companies involved in complex sales

Target Industries: Technology, manufacturing, financial services, health care, professional services

Best Sellers: *Mastering the Complex Sale*, Diagnostic Selling, Diagnostic Marketing, Prime Performance Leadership, Diagnostic Business Development, Mastering Executive Relationships, Manager-Led Sales Performance Leadership

Sales Tip One: If you don't have a cost of the problem, you don't have a problem. Until you quantify the value impact, you are dealing with a highly speculative situation. (*Mastering the Complex Sale*, 2nd ed., Hoboken, NJ: John Wiley & Sons, Inc., 2010)

Sales Tip Two: If credibility and trust are established early in an engagement, the decision to change, to buy, and from whom is made during the diagnosis of the customer's business problem. (*Mastering the Complex Sale*, 2nd ed., Hoboken, NJ: John Wiley & Sons, Inc., 2010)

Sales Tip Three: You'll gain more credibility through the questions you ask than the stories you tell. Prime Resource professionals guide their customers to four elemental decisions in the Diagnose phase: They are deciding:

1. A problem does indeed exist

2. They want to participate in a thorough analysis of the problem

3. The problem has a quantifiable cost in their organization

4. Whether that cost dictates they must proceed in the search for a solution
   (*Mastering the Complex Sale*, 2nd ed. Hoboken, NJ: John Wiley & Sons, Inc., 2010)

Book One: *Exceptional Selling: How the Best Connect and Win in High Stakes Sales*

Book Two: *The Prime Solution: Close the Value Gap, Increase Margins, Win the Complex Sale*

Book Three: *Mastering the Complex Sale: How to Compete and Win When the Stakes Are High*

Product One: Mastering the Complex Sale (audiobook, abridged)

Product Two: Connecting at the Level of Power and Decision (CD)

Product Three: Close the Value Gap (CD)

Product Four: Top 10 "Key Thoughts" of Mastering the Complex Sale (CD)

Product Five: Customized audio and video tools

Chapter 63

Selling in Harder Times

Neil Rackham

Here's a scary little factoid. Less than half of the business-to-business salespeople on the planet today have ever sold in an economic downturn. Think about it. One of the penalties of the longest expansion in history is that a whole selling generation has grown up knowing nothing about hard times and how to cope with them. And, for many of those who do remember recession, the memory is now so distant that it's a lurking discomfort rather than a crisp set of coping strategies. Even worse, middle-level sales managers—and sometimes senior management too—are woefully inexperienced when it comes to the tricky task of leading a sales force through difficult economic times.

So how do you handle the present "correction," "soft landing," "temporary economic rebalancing," or whatever other euphemism lets you avoid the dreaded "R" word? I'm already starting to see some companies implementing selling strategies that failed in the last downturn and are likely to have the same spectacular lack of success this time around.

■ WORKING HARDER ISN'T AN ANSWER

The first knee-jerk reaction in hard times is to push salespeople for more activity—more calls, more demos, more proposals. Now there's nothing wrong, in any economy, with working hard to fill the sales pipeline with every qualified opportunity you can find. In fact, studies done in the recession during the 1980s show that for smaller transactional sales, that was all you needed. Pure hustle, hard work, and lots of cold calling was a very effective way to survive. Successful companies selling low-value products managed their call activity ruthlessly and made their people knock on an awful lot of doors. But, the same strategy proved much less productive for the more complex and consultative business sale—and there's no reason to believe that it will be any more successful in the marketplace of today. There are several reasons for this. Buying cycles, in economic downturns, take up to 40 percent longer due to budget freezes and added approval and justification steps. There's very little that sales-people can do to shorten these extended cycles. Attempts to pressure or speed up the buying process will upset customers and make you appear anxious and in trouble, while bringing in very little extra in terms of sales. And diverting sales effort into cold calling in an attempt to generate new business just isn't an economic option in today's world of expensive sales talent. No, just pressing the "more" button won't work.

■ THE "BETTER" BUTTON

So what's the alternative? The first principle for success is to focus sales effort where it counts. During the hard times of the late 1980s my research team carried out a number of studies looking at the differences between successful and less successful salespeople selling in difficult competitive high-end business-to-business markets. We found that less successful people tended to focus on opening up more accounts when times were lean. They chased every opportunity, however small. They created a flurry of activity. They were busy, they were active—but they were in-effective. The average value of each sale fell and their overall sales volume fell, too. In contrast, the successful survivors of those hard times concentrated on their best opportunities. They spent more time in developing call and account strategies rather than rushing out to make extra calls.

Another clear contrast between the survivors and the strugglers was what they did once they came face-to-face with a potential customer. Less successful people were likely to become "talking brochures." In their anxiety to uncover new customer opportunities, they often found themselves pitching product in an attempt to inter-est poorly qualified prospects they had never dealt with before. This way of selling isn't particularly effective in good times, but in bad times it is a recipe for disaster. The tendency of these less successful salespeople to chase every lead—and get rejected most of the time—led them to adopt "tell"-based selling styles that were visibly hurried and communicated an unhelpful sense of desperation to buyers. Their calls became shorter and their hit rate fell even further. The opposite was true for the successful group. Because these salespeople focused their efforts on fewer good prospects, and spent plenty of planning and preparation time, their calls were both longer and deeper. They sold through questions, not through telling. And, unlike their unsuccessful colleagues, they came across to customers as well prepared and confident.

■ A QUESTION OF CONFIDENCE

In our studies, when we interviewed customers to find why they bought from a particular vendor, salesperson confidence was frequently mentioned as a decisive factor in the purchasing decision. Why should confidence be so critically important in an economic downturn? There's a widespread fallacy that in hard times customers buy on price. Nothing could be further from the truth. In hard times, above all else, customers buy *safety*. We carried out research for IBM during the last recession and discovered that, for computer hardware at least, customers actually paid 12 percent more on average for equivalent equipment than they did in easier economic times. Why? There were a couple of answers. First, in hard times decisions are more likely to be taken by committees, and lower-risk options are generally favored in group decision making. Generally, the lower-risk option carries a higher price tag. Second, buyers realized that their decisions would come under more scrutiny and they would personally be blamed if equipment didn't perform. The old slogan "nobody ever got fired for choosing IBM" was a potent selling tool, even if it meant a price premium.

So what's the bottom-line advice for selling in hard times? Put very simply it's this. Focus on the best opportunities; don't go chasing everything that moves. Invest in strategy, planning, and preparation. Be confident. Sell the safety and reliability of your offerings and don't think that you have to compete on price. Come to think of it, that's not bad advice for selling in good times, too.

Name: Neil Rackham

Web Site: www.neilrackham.com

Biography: Neil Rackham is a speaker, writer, and seminal thinker on sales and marketing issues. Three of his books have been on the *New York Times* best seller list, and his works have been translated into over 50 languages.

His book, *SPIN Selling*, is McGraw-Hill's best-selling business book ever.

He has worked with many leading sales forces like IBM, Xerox, AT&T, and Citicorp, and has been an advisor on sales performance to several Fortune 100 companies in the United States.

He currently serves as executive advisor for Go to Market Partners.

Neil's work won him the Instructional Systems Association award for Innovation in Training and Instruction.

Selling Philosophy: Sales and marketing integration

Target Industries: Technology, financial services, professional services

Best Sellers: Three *New York Times* best sellers: *SPIN Selling*, *Major Account Sales Strategy*, and *Rethinking the Sales Force* (coauthored with John DeVincentis) (see *SPIN Selling*, McGraw-Hill, 1987, and *Major Account Sales Strategy*, McGraw-Hill, 1988.)

Sales Tip One: Sales productivity depends more on sales supervision than on salespeople, so invest in sales management.

Sales Tip Two: Teach skills before strategy. This sounds paradoxical, almost illogical, but it works.

Sales Tip Three: Training without coaching is a waste of time and money.

Books: Neil's other books include *Managing Major Sales* and *Getting Partnering Right: How Market Leaders Are Creating Long-Term Competitive Advantage*. His recent book *Rethinking the Sales Force* has received wide acclaim from critics, academics, and salespeople. It is required reading at many leading business schools.

Chapter 64

Advanced Questioning Techniques

Utilization of Questioning Techniques for Consultative Selling

LaVon Koerner
Revenue Storm

■ LISTENING MODES

Following are two general causes for poor questioning practices by sales professionals:

1. The sales professional is a poor listener.
2. The sales professional has a skill deficit in his or her ability to ask questions.

The first cause is often rooted in the natural quality of the person or in the quality of their listening ability. In regard to the former, good questions most often emanate from those who are naturally motivated to listen. They have both the curiosity and patience to listen at a level that others often do not. It's difficult to teach an individual to listen better if they don't care. The human quality of "caring" seeks to find out information. Without that quality, the individual often defaults to a more passive role in their information-gathering activities.

Revenue Storm has identified the following observable listening mode levels of a sales professional. Your "Listening Mode Level" will determine both the type and timing of your questions. It identifies your objective or reason for listening. Your mode of listening answers the question as to "why" you are listening at all. We've all met people who do not listen. They are intent only on being "heard" and do not intend to "hear." But for those realizing that good selling begins with good listening, here are the three Listening Mode levels:

Listening Mode Level #1: *Listen to hear.*   These people are waiting to hear certain "buzz" words pop up in the conversation. Once they do, they pounce on them as if they just got the "green" light to sell something. There is an observable impatience in this type of listener; they want to sell something and move on. And as soon as they hear certain familiar "words" in the emerging conversation, they believe they have just been granted permission to interrupt the conversation and pontificate on their opinions and/or products. As you will see in the Question Classification section, this type of listener will be the most apt to default to Leading Questions to move the buyer in their predetermined direction. There will be more information on this later.

Listening Mode Level #2: *Listen to discern.*   This type of listening is done by an individual who is equally paying attention to what is not being said and what is being stated. They want to go deeper and are not satisfied with the superficiality. They want to know the underlying causes. They want to know the root drivers of the issues being surfaced in the conversation. These people will go the "second mile" in their questioning to uncover information and insight that others would miss. These people resist the urge to prematurely come to conclusions. They know that for every "effect," there is a "cause" and they will not rest until they uncover it. They also know that every situation has a "context" and they refuse to draw a premature conclusion until every piece of the mosaic context has been unearthed and put into its rightful place and the "big" picture can be clearly seen.

Listening Mode Level #3: *Listen to feel.*   This is the deepest kind of listening. It is motivated by empathy and sensitivity for the individual behind the issues being discussed. This sales professional wants to feel what their prospects are feeling. They understand that, ultimately, a person will only end up doing what they "feel" like doing. Therefore, they know that accurate predictions of behavior can only be made when an individual's motivating feelings are known and have been favorably enrolled into the buying equation. They go beyond understanding what the purchase will mean to the company; they know what the purchase will mean to the individual, how it will advance both their personal and professional agendas. They have mastered both the science and art of bringing "real" feelings to the surface. Like a skillful therapist, they evoke and manage a person's feelings. Their individual transparency creates a comfortable environment for their prospects to "open up" and reveal hidden emotions that could have stopped the buying process. This gives the sales professional an opportunity to convert these emotions to positive feelings that advance the pursuit.

■ CLASSIFICATION LIST OF QUESTIONS

If "listening" is the end, then questions are the means. The following is a list of the various types of "questions" that can be used in advancing a sales pursuit.

➤ Closed-Ended Questions

A *closed-ended question* can be answered with a "Yes," "No," or other very simple answer.

For example, if I want to know what happened after I left the meeting, I could ask, "Did you speak to Bob after the meeting?" or "Did Lance leave with Jim to the airport?" or "Did they all stay until the meeting was finished?"

These are closed-ended questions that can all be responded to with very simple answers. A series of *closed-ended questions* can sound like a cross-examination, "putting your contacts on trial."

➤ Open-Ended Questions

The ability to ask *open-ended questions* is very important in consultative selling. An open-ended question is designed to encourage a full, meaningful answer using the subject's own knowledge and/or opinions. It is the opposite of a *closed-ended question*, which encourages a short or single-word answer. Open-ended questions also tend to be more objective and less leading than closed-ended questions.

Open-ended questions typically begin with words such as "Why" and "How", or phrases such as "Tell me about . . ." Often they are not technically a question, but a statement that implicitly asks for a response.

Inexperienced salespeople often find themselves frustrated by client contacts who just won't talk. With experience, they learn how to ask questions that get people to open up. Although you might want a specific piece of information, asking a more general question might elicit a longer, fuller response *that contains the information you really want*.

In the example above, if I wanted to know if you spoke to Bob after I left the meeting, if Lance left with Jim to the airport, or anything else, I can simply ask "What happened after I left?" Chances are I'll hear what I want to know somewhere in your answer. If not, I can follow that up with another *open-ended question*, "What happened with Lance and Jim?"

Examples

Closed-Ended Question	Open-Ended Question
Did you get on well with your last vendor?	Tell me about your relationship with your last vendor.
Whom will you vote for this election?	What do you think about the two candidates in this election?

➤ Leading Questions

Revenue Storm recommends that sales professionals be very careful about using this type of question. It can be seen as manipulative in nature and is not consistent with good relationship-building practices. A *leading question* subtly prompts the respondent to answer in a particular way. *Leading questions* are generally undesirable as they result in false or slanted information. For example:

Did you get along well with your last vendor?	This question prompts the person to question their vendor relationship. In a very subtle way, it raises the issue that the prospect may not get along with their vendor.
Tell me about your relationship with your last vendor.	This question does not seek any judgment and there is less implication that there might be something wrong with the relationship.

The difference in the above example is minor, but in some situations, it can be critical. For example, in a court case:

How fast was the red car going when it smashed into the blue car?	This question implies that the red car was at fault, and the word "smashed" implies a high speed.
How fast was each car going when the accident happened?	This question does not assign any blame or prejudgment.

➤ High-Gain Questions

As you will see later on, all questions can play a role in a consultative conversation, but perhaps no other type of question does a better job at laying a solid foundation than the *high-gain question*.

The *high-gain question* always "gives" before it "takes." It provides specific and relevant value to the listener before it requests information. And by so doing, it positions you as a strategic resource worthy of a conversation. The person being asked a *high-gain question* feels comfortable providing information after they have just received good information deemed valuable.

An example of an *open-ended question* is "Tell me what your organization is planning on doing to make its growth goals in this economy." That is a legitimate question, and the knowledge gained from it would be very helpful in formulating a Value Proposition. But what happens if the client contact does not feel comfortable or compelled to answer your *open-ended question*? This question can be converted into a *high-gain question* that will increase the potential of having a value-rich answer.

Here is the same question in a *high-gain* format. "In our research, we've found that a number of companies in your industry have undertaken some very innovative and unusual steps to accelerate their growth in this economy. One is (list example), and another is (list another example). I'm curious, given these rather unorthodox initiatives other companies are trying, how is your organization going to ensure growth under these economic conditions?"

➤ Reveal Questions

Of all the questions, this question takes both art and skill. Perhaps the most famous Reveal Question is "How did this make you feel?" or some variation thereof. This has become a cliché in therapy circles. The reason it is so widely used is that it's so effective.

In sales campaigns, client stories are all about people and how they are affected by organizational events. People want to experience the emotion. Even though educated clients tend to cringe at this question, it's still so useful that it continues to be a standard tool in relational selling best-in-class practices.

In psychology, feelings and emotions are central to human behavior. Therapists are naturally keen to ask questions about feelings. And for the same reasons, sales professionals should be equally keen to use this question at appropriate times in a sales campaign with the appropriate people.

Show empathy. Often you will need to cover sensitive or distressing topics during the course of a sales campaign. Show some compassion for the subject without getting too emotional. Ask for permission before asking difficult questions, for example, "Is it okay to talk about . . . ?"

From a sales perspective, here is why this type of question is so important. To link to something on the inside of a person by connecting to something on the outside of a person, simply focus on these two areas and utilize reveal questions in getting answers:

1. **Professional Agenda.** What is this person tasked with accomplishing in their specific role or position that will entitle them to either become or stay viewed as being successful?

2. **Personal Agenda.** What obstacles will this individual personally need to eliminate or break through in order to either secure or advance his or her Professional Agenda?

These two agendas are always inextricably linked when the level of interest is elevated to the point whereby a person is sufficiently motivated to take any required action. Another way of saying this is, behind every successful Professional Agenda, there is always a driving and thriving Personal Agenda. And these agendas can usually only be uncovered by asking *Reveal Questions*.

When a sales professional can not only articulate clear answers to both of the Agenda Questions above, but can also link those answers to their solutions, they are in a position to craft a Value Proposition that will result in a potential client being very interested in their solution.

■ THE FOUR-STEP FLOW OF A CONSULTATIVE DISCUSSION

Step One: High-Gain Question. A good consultative conversation can be set up with a good High-Gain Question. It is this question that opens the discussion on a "value" foundation.

Step Two: Open-Ended Questions. Once the client engages in their answer to the High-Gain Question, there will be numerous opportunities to keep the conversation going by asking follow-on Open-Ended Questions. This should be continued until your exploration is complete and you have developed a vision of what your solution needs to include and the business impact it needs to create.

Step Three: Closed-Ended Questions. In the conversation, the client will say a number of important things that you will deem important in putting together your Value Proposition. Because of their importance, it is advised that you validate your listening accuracy by asking Closed-Ended Questions confirming your conclusions.

Step Four: Reveal Questions. Once you've uncovered and validated critical issues around which you can build a compelling Value Proposition, there is one final step left. It is now time to ask Reveal Questions to uncover the individual's professional and personal agendas to which the Value Proposition of your Solution can be linked.

■ MORE QUESTIONING TIPS

These are very general tips that apply differently to different situations. Use your judgment to decide when and how to use them.

➤ **Try to be unique**, so it's not just another sales interview—rehashing the same questions the client has answered many times before. Don't push this too far though—if you try to be cute or disarming it may backfire.

➤ **Be honest.** Sometimes it's tempting to lie or omit important information when securing an appointment. This isn't just unethical; it will damage your career in the long run.

➤ **Don't have an attitude** if you want a quality client discussion. A confrontational approach is less likely to get good information.

➤ **Stay neutral.** Try not to ooze bias. Don't appear to be persuaded by the subject's opinions. Don't judge or directly criticize the subject.

➤ **Don't interrupt.** This can upset the client's train of thought.

➤ **Minimize your own words.** Ask questions clearly and succinctly, and then let the person speak without any more words from you. Learn to react silently as the subject talks—rather than saying things like "uh-huh, right, I see," use nods and facial expressions.

➤ **Don't overdirect.** Try not to give the client too many instructions or be too specific about what you want them to say. In most cases, it's better to let them speak freely.

➤ **It's not about you.** Don't talk about yourself, your company, and your offerings or add your own opinion. There will be time for that *after* the client has completed saying what they need to say.

➤ **Take an interest in psychology.** Conducting client interviewing is very closely associated with psychology. The better you understand how people think, the better you will be able to extract their thoughts from an interview.

➤ **When you finish the meeting**, put your notebook away and have an informal chat. As well as being polite and leaving a good impression, you might be surprised at what additional information flows when the client thinks it's all over and becomes more relaxed.

➤ **If you missed a question** from the client interview, you might be able to call them back later and get the answer. You get one shot at this—call them back twice and you'll probably be out of luck.

➤ **Listen!** Sometimes we are guilty of formulating the next question without paying attention to the answer to the first. You miss great opportunities for follow-up questions if you do this! Make an effort to listen to the answer to the question *you asked!* Become active in your listening approach. Remember to:

➤ **Limit distractions.** Move away from distraction so you can pay full attention to the other person. Yes, that means to silence your BlackBerry and ignore your e-mail.

➤ **Focus on the moment.** Pay attention to what the other person is saying, not what you want to say. Set a goal of being able to repeat the last sentence the other person says. This keeps your attention on each statement. There is nothing more embarrassing than having someone say, "Now where was I?" and having no idea what they just said.

➤ **Be okay with silence.** You don't have to always reply or have a comment. Count to 10 or 20 before replying. The other person may continue after a pause; another person in the room may speak up. A pause in conversation also gives you a chance to collect your thoughts.

➤ **Hold your thoughts.** Encourage the other person to offer ideas and solutions before you give yours. Do 80 percent of the listening and 20 percent of the talking.

➤ **Summarize.** Restate the key points you heard and ask whether they are accurate. "Let me see whether I heard you correctly . . ." is an easy way to shift to your paraphrase.

Name: LaVon Koerner

Company: Revenue Storm

Web Site: www.revenuestorm.com

Biography: LaVon Koerner speaks at hundreds of companies and conferences every year and is seen as an international visionary and industry expert for paving the way of doing business in the future. He and his organization, Revenue Storm, have transformed global companies, resulting in unprecedented growth rates in both down and up markets. His warm and humorous speaking style endears him to conferences around the world, and he is asked to return again and again to address audiences wanting to stay abreast of the latest thinking in the fast-moving and evolving field of business development.

Selling Philosophy: Achieving revenue acceleration through Demand Creation

Target Industries: All industries that involve complex business-to-business sales cycles

Best Sellers: Account Planning, Demand Creation Sales training, psychometric testing of sales personnel, Sales Leadership/Management training, Coaching, Marketing and Sales Alignment

Sales Tip One: Either excite or disturb, but don't ever leave the prospect in the state of emotional neutrality.

Sales Tip Two: Having 1 percent more information one day earlier than the competition is the beginning of competitive advantage.

Sales Tip Three: More sales campaigns are lost at the beginning than at the end, but they only find out they lost at the end.

Product One: Revenue Storm offers a complete online e-learning curriculum.

Product Two: Revenue Storm offers online psychometric testing to uncover competency deficits.

Product Three: Revenue Storm has a complete suite of sales tools and online videos demonstrating their utilization.

Sales Coaching Increases Sales Performance

Linda Richardson
Richardson

No one in a sales organization has a greater opportunity to increase the performance of a sales team than the sales manager. As a sales manager the success of your sales team depends very much on your ability to lead and develop your team members one-on-one and collectively. Yet, a recent Richardson study revealed that 43 percent of salespeople receive little to no coaching. Of the 57 percent who are coached, 97 percent attribute their success to the sales coaching they receive from their managers. The Sales Executive Council's research with 2,000 sales professionals showed that salespeople who are coached for three hours a month, on average, achieve 104 percent of their quota as compared with 83 percent for salespeople who are not coached. A full 75 percent of salespeople feel they could be more productive if they were coached.

Most sales organizations recognize the importance of sales coaching in today's complex and competitive sales environment. Yet, despite understanding the need for sales coaching, sales organizations continue to find the transition from sales manager to sales coach an uphill battle.

Many of the obstacles to sales coaching are cultural. The majority of sales managers are drawn from the pool of high-producing salespeople. As such they are very good at selling and continue to do what has made them successful. Moreover, as much as 80 percent of their remuneration can be based on the revenue generated by their salespeople—a point that does not escape salespeople who ask for and get help in closing deals. To add to that, quarterly goals create an "I can't lose this deal mentality" among sales managers. Fifty percent of sales managers aren't prepared for their new roles with coaching training. And the majority of sales managers are not coached by their managers and, therefore, have few role models.

Rather than developing their salespeople, many sales managers are filling the role of super salesperson on their teams. While it is great that they lead by example, it is more important that they share the secrets of their success.

There simply are not enough sales managers to go around. Sales organizations need sales teams that can qualify, compete, and close. Certainly there are times, such as big deals or developing new recruits, when sales managers should take a lead role, but that is the exception, not the rule. The goal of the sales manager has to be to make sales team members better than they are. It is not okay for the sales manager to remain the best salesperson on the team.

If you are playing the role of super salesperson, it's time to reassess your priorities.

Clearly your plate is full. Becoming a sales coach begins with your making decisions about how to use your time to achieve the greatest gains. The good news is that you have what it takes to build a champion team. Your successful sales background gives you expertise and credibility. Your role places you in the right spot.

As a sales manager, you wear two hats: a manager hat and a coaching hat. The question is, What amount of time should be dedicated to each? Just as the 80/20 rule seems to apply to everything else, it applies to sales coaching. For most sales managers this demands changing, not weakening their priorities. Sales coaching is the catalyst that enables you to reap the rewards of almost everything else you do, from recruitment through to reward, to winning and expanding business. The hard fact is that sales coaching merits 60 to 80   percent of your time.

Sixty to 80 percent may sound daunting. However, you can achieve it using a dual strategy that combines scheduled coaching with curbside day-to-day contact coaching. Certainly, scheduled coaching sessions are essential. But scheduled coaching can consume as little as three hours a month for each of your salespeople, and each session can be accomplished in about 15 minutes. Do the math and you will see that this kind of commitment is achievable. The key is to supplement scheduled coaching sessions with curbside coaching in which you turn an everyday contact into an opportunity to coach by simply asking questions versus giving answers and building coaching into your current activities.

The goal of sales coaching is to improve performance. A misconception is that sales managers are responsible for improving the sales performance of their team members. Salespeople, in fact, are responsible for their own development. The role of sales managers is to create an environment where they support salespeople and help remove obstacles. The way to provide that environment is to coach.

Here are 10 levers you can use to build your champion team:

Proactive, Scheduled Sales Coaching

1. Scheduled Sales Coaching Sessions

   ➤ Plan on a *minimum* of at least three hours of planned coaching with each salesperson each month. This is an average. Spend the majority of your time with middle performers where you have the greatest potential for impact, but don't forget the top and underperformers. For example, two hours per month may be sufficient for top performers and give under/problem performers extra time with measurable objectives and a specific time frame for achieving the objectives, for example, a 90-day plan.

2. Master the Skill of Feedback

   ➤ When you give feedback you share your perceptions of the impact his or her behavior and actions are having. Give specific, balanced feedback. Start with strengths and then explore areas for improvement. Give feedback privately. Limit your feedback to one or possibly two priority points to avoid overload and achieve the exponential power of incremental growth and to coach in 15 minutes or less. Anything the salesperson can change is fair game for clear, honest feedback. Once you provide feedback, check for agreement and/or understanding. If you have information that can help a salesperson improve, it is your job, your obligation, to give feedback.

3. Coaching Using the "Coaching by Asking" Strategy

   ➤ Help salespeople remove their obstacles by asking questions. The mantra of the Coaching by Asking model is "They talk first." It will be much more likely to get buy-in because salespeople will feel heard and respected. It lets you gauge where the salesperson is on the learning curve. It lets you focus on the right things. Use a developmental coaching model (excerpt from *Sales Coaching: Making the Great Leap from Sales Manager to Sales Coach* by Linda Richardson).

   ➤ Open: Begin with brief, *genuine* rapport and neutrally state the purpose. Don't prejudge the situation.

   ➤ Clarify Perceptions: Hold all of your perceptions, feelings, and ideas back until you fully understand the salesperson. Ask the salesperson for his or her perceptions first. Listen, acknowledge, and keep acknowledging and probing the salesperson's perceptions of the situation or problem. Most salespeople will respond with short, fast answers, expecting that you will take over. Don't let that happen. So keep probing. Once you understand the salesperson's perspectives, give your perceptions and check for agreement.

   ➤ Identify the Obstacles: Ask the salesperson what he or she thinks is the obstacle to X (the desired behavior, action, or the problem that needs to be resolved). Probe for other possibilities. Then provide your insights and check for agreement.

➤ Remove the Obstacle: Ask the salesperson for his or her suggestions on how to remove the obstacle. Ask for other possibilities. Then add value and check for agreement. Role-play in appropriate ways, because saying is different from doing.

➤ Close: End every coaching session with a clear, specific action step that spells out what the salesperson will do, the outcome, and time frame.

4. Work on One Priority at a Time

➤ Working on one priority at a time not only is more effective and accelerates development, it also allows you to coach in 15 minutes or less.

5. Debrief Your Coaching Sessions

➤ Ask yourself after every coaching session, "Who did all the work?" If the answer is you, change this dynamic by asking more questions. Probe and drill down. Help the salesperson self-assess.

6. Create Individual Sales Coaching Plans

➤ Create one-page quarterly sales coaching plans for each of your salespeople that defines how much coaching you commit to and what your focus will be.

7. Create a Quarterly Sales Coaching Plan for Yourself

➤ Create a coaching plan for yourself to help you get the input and feedback you need.

8. Follow Up

➤ Demonstrate to your salespeople that you are serious about coaching and about their accomplishing what is agreed to. Make note in your calendar and follow up religiously.

Curbside Coaching

9. Turn the Sales Environment into a Learning Environment

➤ Formal coaching should take up less than a quarter of your coaching time. Turn every interaction into a coaching opportunity. For example, when a salesperson asks you a question, acknowledge and ask, "What do you think?" Probe, then share your expertise, and check for agreement. Build a 10-minute team coaching topic into a sales meeting agenda.

10. Get to Know Your Salespeople on a Personal and Professional Level

➤ You don't have to be best friends with everyone on your team, but it is essential to know them. Show a genuine interest in what is important to them—things such as their aspirations, family members' names, birthdays . . .

Achieving excellence as a coach is a journey. It is within your reach. Think about the best coach you ever had, someone who believed in and supported you. Be *that* coach to your sales team.

Name: Linda Richardson

Company: Richardson

Web Site: www.richardson.com

Biography: Linda Richardson is founder and chairwoman of Richardson, a global sales performance company. She was awarded the Stevie Award for Lifetime Achievement in Sales Excellence for 2006, and in 2007 she was identified by Training Industry, Inc., as one of the "Top 20 Most Influential Training Professionals."

Linda is credited with the movement to Consultative Selling.

She is the author of nine books, including the *New York Times* best seller and winner of the SBA best book of 2009 award *Perfect Selling*. She teaches at Wharton Graduate School of the University of Pennsylvania.

Selling Philosophy: Consultative selling

Target Industries: Across industries, including financial, technology, pharmaceuticals, professional services, retail sales

Best Sellers: Key Richardson Programs: Consultative Selling, Developmental Sales Coaching, Strategic Relationship Management, Strategic Opportunity Management, Consultative Negotiations, Real Deal Coaching, both classroom and Web-based

Sales Tip One: Prepare to maximize calls by setting measurable call objectives. Don't minimize the importance of the relationship. Plan how you will build personal and business rapport.

Sales Tip Two: Begin your need dialogue with strategic, not technical, questions. As your customer answers, acknowledge and probe to drill down to learn more before going on to your next question.

Sales Tip Three: Don't talk about your product capabilities in a generic way. Leverage the customer needs you've identified. Use the customer's language. Position how your capabilities will meet the customer's needs.

Book One: *Perfect Selling*

Book Two: *Sales Coaching: Making the Great Leap from Sales Manager to Sales Coach*

Book Three: *Winning Group Sales Presentations*

Product One: Closing the Sales, NanoSalesBooks series (audio)

Product Two: The Sixty-Second You, NanoSalesBooks series (audio)

Product Product Three: 15 Minutes, Four Steps to Effective Coaching, NanoCoachingBooks series (Audio)

66

Mismanaging Expectations

Are You Preparing Your Sales Team for Change?

Keith Rosen
Profit Builders

Maria was a new sales manager hired by Media Pros, Inc., a sports management consulting firm. She was recently introduced to the coaching model at a seminar for senior managers in her company.

Maria went back to her team pumped up and ready to begin implementing some of the coaching methods. However, it seems that Maria missed the section of the seminar on how critical it is to prepare your team for coaching by managing their expectations.

Compound this with the fact that Maria has only been in her position for less than five weeks. It's difficult enough for a sales team to adjust to a new boss, but further changes without proper preparation and communication will cause a rebellion.

Maria's boss set up a meeting with her and an outside executive coach to discuss the resistance Maria was running up against when attempting to manage and coach her team. Maria told the executive coach that she felt she had assimilated herself into her team and prepared them for any changes she was making. Since Maria's sales team worked remotely, she introduced herself to the team via a conference call and let them all know she was there to support them and help them become even more successful in their careers. Sounds pretty good so far, right? However, after further exploration, the executive coach uncovered the breakdown in Maria's new manager orientation process.

The executive coach asked Maria the following 11 questions to help uncover why Maria failed to manage her team's expectations as well as develop a strategy to communicate her objectives in a way her team would understand and embrace.

1. Did you conduct one-to-one meetings with each salesperson on your team?

2. Did you ask each of them how they like to be managed? Are they coachable?

3. Did you inquire about their prior experience with their past manager? Was it positive or negative?

4. Did you set the expectations of your relationship with them? Did you ask them what they needed and expected from their manager? What changes do they want to see?

5. Did you inform them about how you like to manage and your style of management? This would allow for a discussion regarding how you may manage differently from your predecessor.

6. Did you let them know you just completed a coaching course that would enable you to support them even further and maximize their talents?

7. Did you explain to them the difference between coaching and traditional management?

8. Did you enroll them in the benefits of coaching? That is, what would be in it for them?

9. Did you let them know about your intentions, goals, expectations, and aspirations for each of them and for the team as a whole?

10. How have you gone about learning the ins and outs of the company? Are you familiar with the internal workings, culture, leadership team, and subtleties that make the company unique? Have you considered that your team may be the best source of knowledge and intelligence for this?

11. Did you communicate your willingness and desire to learn from them as well, so that the learning and development process can be mutually reciprocated?

With each question, it became more evident that Maria did not plan or prepare her staff for change. She did not prepare her team for a new boss or for her new approach to management.

At the end of the conversation, it was clear to Maria what she had to do. She would start with a team meeting to address many of the questions posed to her by the executive coach. Maria would use this meeting to explain the changes she wanted to make and the benefits each person on the sales team would realize. Maria also knew that she needed to address any gossip, rumors, or negativity that could poison the team. She would acknowledge that with any change in management, there is an adjustment period. Maria wants her team to know that she is sensitive to what they are going through during this transition, as well as to each of their individual needs. She needs to reinforce her role and the fact that even though her style, personality, and approach may be different from what they are used to, she is there to help them thrive in their careers.

Once Maria finished facilitating this team meeting, she scheduled one-on-one calls with each salesperson on her team to discuss these questions—more specifically, the questions that relate to their specific needs and goals and how they want to be managed and coached. This experience was a huge lesson for Maria and would be for any manager. If you fail to inform your salespeople of your good intentions, they have no idea what they are, thus leaving it up to each salesperson to form his or her own opinion.

A situation where a salesperson had a less than favorable experience with the old manager can be made worse and repeated if the new manager does not take the steps to create a new experience between her and her salespeople.

If management does not break the cycle, they may encounter situations where their salespeople are not engaged at all, especially in the coaching process. New managers would then have to form their own conclusions, thinking that either the coaching doesn't work or it just may be the salesperson who doesn't work. In truth, what isn't working is the exchange of communication and as such, a critical message goes undelivered, perpetuating conflicts, communication breakdowns, distrust, and underperformance.

Ironically, you may be doing everything else right when managing your team. That is, your heart is in the right place, your intentions are pure and sound, and you truly want to be the best coach you can be for your team. But without defusing any faulty assumptions, gossip, or beliefs, resistance from your staff will be imminent and your coaching will be unsuccessful.

Whether you're a new manager or a manager who's a new coach, informing your team about any new initiatives or changes you plan on making and the enrollment process you will use to initiate buy-in needs to happen prior to actually implementing the change.

To recap, first take that step back and assess your team's needs as well as the unique needs of each individual on your team. Let them know how you plan on supporting them. Then manage these expectations with surgical precision. This will foster a strong, healthy relationship that you can build on right from the start, creating the nurturing and open environment that will enable you to earn your salespeople's deeper respect, trust, and commitment to their objectives, even in the face of change.

Name: Keith Rosen

Company: Profit Builders

Web Site: www.ProfitBuilders.com

Biography: Keith Rosen is the executive sales coach that top salespeople and managers call first to attract more prospects, close more sales, and develop a team of top-performing sales champions. An award-winning columnist, speaker, and best-selling author, Keith has written several books including *Coaching Salespeople into Sales Champions*, which was named the 2008 Sales Leadership Book of the Year and one of the World's Best Business Books of 2009.

Keith is the winner of the 2009 Stevie Award and was named The Sales Education Leader of the Year, *Inc.* magazine. *Fast Company* named Keith one of the five most influential executive coaches.

Selling Philosophy: Permission-based selling: a process-driven approach to attracting more qualified prospects and closing more sales, cold calling, presentation skills, coach-the-coach for managers, time management, goal setting, communication

Target Industries: Insurance, financial, health care, real estate, sports management, consulting, accounting, IT, telecom, executive recruiting, automotive/manufacturing, marketing, advertising, direct selling, medical, pharmaceuticals, technology, retail, food service

Best Sellers: *Coaching Salespeople into Sales Champions, Permission-Based Selling, Sales Mojo, Time Management for Sales Professionals, Permission-Based Prospecting, The Complete Idiot's Guide to Cold Calling, The Complete Idiot's Guide to Closing the Sale, How to Hire and Retain a Top Salesperson, Call Me Back, Please!, Build Your Referral Engine*

Sales Tip One: Well-crafted questions, rather than statements, defuse objections.

Sales Tip Two: The greatest salespeople are not the strongest closers. They are actually skilled openers of new selling opportunities.

Sales Tip Three: Selling is the art of creating new possibilities.

Use Social Dynamics to Control Sales Appointments

Frank Rumbauskas

FJR Advisors

Many areas of selling that I've studied and taught to others are rarely, if ever, known and used in the world of professional selling. One of those is the science of social dynamics—before I ever began learning it myself and including it in my training, I'd never before seen it used in sales.

Social dynamics is the science of using nonverbal subcommunication to influence others. What does this include? The primary elements of our nonverbal subcommunication are body language, vocal tone, inflection and volume, eye contact, movement and carriage of the body, and other subtle but important elements.

The consequences of not using proper social dynamics in your sales interactions are severe, and most of us don't even know we're doing anything wrong because we haven't been taught. The situation is much like cold calling—salespeople who cold call only do so because they don't know any alternatives. However, by not paying attention to our social dynamics, we unknowingly give our power away to prospects, let them have control of sales appointments, create an impression that we are not successful, give prospects the "gut feeling" that they should not buy from us . . . all unknowingly.

So, that said, what can we do to make sure we don't short-circuit all of our efforts by using improper social dynamics? Following is a brief and very basic—but highly effective—checklist of things you need to watch out for while selling:

1. Body language. (This isn't easy to explain without pictures, so bear with me!) Be careful not to lean in to prospects when talking with them. Leaning in subcommunicates weakness and submission. Lean

back when you are in front of prospects. This subcommunicates that you are the leader, are in control, and will cause prospects to be more willing to follow your lead and buy. In addition, you should never face a prospect more than they are facing you. In other words, if a prospect is not facing you straight-on while sitting or standing, you should be turned away just a degree more than the prospect is turned away from you. It is okay to face a prospect straight-on only after they have fully turned to face you directly. If you face them directly before they do so to you, you are subcommunicating neediness and submission. However, by allowing the prospect to do so first, they are automatically placed in the submissive role and will be much easier to close.

2. If you cannot hear a prospect, never lean in directly when they repeat themselves. Instead, turn sideways, so that your ear is facing the prospect, but your face is turned away. This allows you to hear the prospect better but without taking a weak stance.

3. Your voice. The single most important thing you can do to be a more effective salesperson is to have a powerful, commanding voice. Like a firm handshake, an impressive vocal presence subcommunicates power and leadership and will cause prospects to be much more willing to buy from you. Practice speaking louder in your everyday communications. You don't want to yell or strain; instead, focus on speaking from your core, your abdomen, which will result in the commanding voice you need to have to be effective.

   Imagine a general who speaks powerfully, but without yelling or straining. This is what you should strive for. I achieved this by simply talking that way all the time. An added benefit is that you will automatically become an excellent public speaker by having this talent, which you can then leverage into more sales by volunteering to speak at networking events, chamber of commerce meetings, and other "target-rich" environments. It will also be a necessary skill should you wish to go into sales training or public speaking later in your career, a choice that is available to all successful salespeople.

4. Your presence. This is closely related to body language, but has more to do with posture than with positioning yourself in front of prospects. For example, weak people are afraid of infringing on others' personal space, so they keep a small presence. Avoid this by standing with your feet at least a foot apart, leaning back slightly, and having your shoulders back and chin up. This is a powerful stance that subcommunicates leadership and confidence. The same rules hold true while sitting—keep your feet flat on the floor (no crossed legs), with your arms spread wide rather than holding them close together. Unless you are sitting with your arms on the desk, lean back in your chair while speaking. Again, you're demonstrating command of the situation by doing so.

What about pacing the movements of your prospect? Don't do it. This is one of those "old, right answers" from the old school of selling that is now wrong. Most prospects can pick up on this because it's been done to them so many times before, and what's worse, why would you want to pace your prospects' mannerisms when you run the risk of reflecting their own weak body language? In addition, it shows a lack of independence, which is the biggest killer of the powerful, confident persona you want to demonstrate in appointments.

Finally, remember that this is not a competition. These suggestions are not given with the intent to rule your prospects. They simply allow you to present yourself as a powerful leader whose advice should be taken, and the end result is that prospects will feel extremely comfortable with entrusting their business to you. Follow these tips, and your close rates will suddenly explode!

Name: Frank Rumbauskas

Company: FJR Advisors, LLC

Biography: *New York Times* best-selling author Frank Rumbauskas began his sales career in failure, cold calling day in and day out on the orders of his sales managers, but with little to show for it. Frank was taught the same outdated sales techniques that most people are still being taught, and those techniques simply don't work in today's Information Age economy. Knowing this, he went from being a total failure to a top sales pro who was consistently over 150 to 200 percent of quota while actually working fewer hours! Frank teaches his secrets to others through his books, CDs, DVDs, and live speaking.

Selling Philosophy: Self-marketing and generating leads without cold calling

Target Industries: All outside sales

Best Sellers: *New York Times* best seller *Never Cold Call Again: Achieve Sales Greatness without Cold Calling*

Sales Tip One: If you're not getting the results you want, the answer isn't to increase your activity and do more of the same. The answer is to change your activity to something that gets results.

Sales Tip Two: Sales is not a numbers game. We all learned in third grade that any number times zero still equals zero, and the same is true for ineffective sales prospecting techniques.

Sales Tip Three: Most salespeople believe that they must "sell" to others, when in reality, the top salespeople in the world understand that the secret is to attract people who are ready to "buy."

Book One: *Selling Sucks: How to Stop Selling and Start Getting Prospects to Buy* (John Wiley & Sons, Inc., 2007)

Book Two: *Never Cold Call Again: Achieve Sales Greatness without Cold Calling* (John Wiley & Sons, Inc., 2006)

Book Three: *The Never Cold Call Again Online Playbook: The Definitive Guide to Internet Marketing Success* (John Wiley & Sons, Inc., 2009)

Product One: *Cold Calling Is a Waste of Time: Sales Success in the Information Age* (book & 2 CDs)

Product Two: The Sales Mastery Program (4-CD set plus guidebook)

Product Three: AdWords Inside Secrets (2-DVD set and 1 CD plus guidebook)

Chapter 68

The Successful Sales Formula

Why 50 Percent of Deals Fail to Close

Keith M. Eades

Sales Performance International

According to the latest survey of sales managers conducted by CSO Insights, less than 50 percent of forecasted sales opportunities fail to close as predicted, as illustrated below. At face value, this number is stunning—how can companies effectively manage their business operations when the ability to predict sales revenues is this unreliable? In addition, more than 20 percent of these sales opportunities result in a decision on the part of the customer to do nothing!

These findings show that too many salespeople are investing in opportunities that they never had a good chance to win. Although

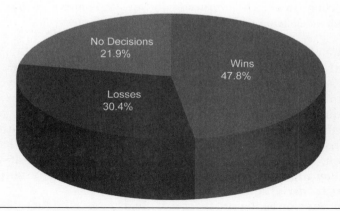

Figure 68.1   Outcome of Forecasted Deals

(Copyright © 2009 CSO Insights, used with permission.)

many managers believe their sales teams have a problem with qualifying new opportunities, we find that most salespeople have a bigger problem—they are increasingly reluctant to disqualify opportunities that they have been working on for a while. That is, many salespeople wait far too long to qualify themselves out of deals that are going sour, especially when their pipelines are lean. As a result, they waste their most precious resource—their time—in bad opportunities that they can't win.

Both qualification and disqualification are important skills for sales professionals to master. The skill of qualification is the ability to help bring an opportunity to an established standard—one where the salesperson has a good chance to win the business. Disqualification is the ability to disengage from an opportunity if it does not meet the standard.

Why do too few salespeople disqualify out of bad deals? We have found that most salespeople don't understand what the standards should be to make a good decision to engage or disengage.

■ THE BIGGEST MYTH OF QUALIFICATION

We often ask salespeople this question: "What elements make an opportunity qualified?" Without too much variance, the answers we hear most often are:

➤ **Budget.** The project is funded.

➤ **Authority.** A decision maker is in place within the prospective buyer's organization.

➤ **Need/fit.** Your offerings match the list of requirements.

➤ **Time frame.** The prospective buyer has identified a date that the purchase decision must be made.

Some people refer to these four elements simply as "BANT." This is useful information, to be sure—BANT elements are very important in any selling engagement. However, using BANT as your sole qualification method may cause you to stay in opportunities that are better qualified for someone else. If a buyer can give you answers to these four elements, then they probably can tell you the answer to the more important fifth question—who they have already decided to buy from. If they already have a clear idea of BANT elements in their head, they must be "down the road a bit" in their buying process, and you are arriving late into the opportunity.

In other words, if a prospect can clearly describe their BANT elements for you, then you are most likely not in first place. In fact, you are probably way behind.

So, should salespeople automatically walk away from deals in which prospects can articulate BANT? Not necessarily. Important information around BANT is critical for a salesperson to discover during a sell cycle, but real opportunity qualification should include some additional criteria as well. BANT only provides some of the picture of a sales opportunity. To qualify in or disqualify out, we need some additional information.

■ THE SUCCESSFUL SALES FORMULA

The formula below expands the basis for qualifying opportunities. In addition to BANT, if you don't have an affirmative answer to each variable, then the chance of a successful sale is zero:

$$Pain \times Power \times Vision \times Value \times Control = Sale$$

Let's examine each of these elements:

➤ **Pain.** The basic principle "no pain, no change" speaks volumes about why this element is so critical to the successful sales formula. Identifying the customer's high-priority business issues, which also include potential missed opportunities, helps answer the question, "*Is the customer likely to take action?*"

➤ **Power.** Simply defined, the person within the buying organization with the ability to make or influence the purchasing decision is power for this opportunity. The questions to ask about power are: "*Do we know who Power is?*" and "*Are we aligned with the Power people?*"

➤ **Vision.** The prospective buyer must understand what your offering will allow them to do, but also be able to visualize themselves doing something different in the future. The question to answer here is: "*Does the buyer have a clear vision of how they can solve their problem with our solution?*"

➤ **Value.** Buyers must grasp the quantifiable value they'll be receiving by making an investment in your offering. The question to answer here is: "*Can the customer articulate the value they will receive from our solution?*"

➤ **Control.** The term *control* might sound a bit heavy-handed, but it is really about guiding your buyer to a good decision, not manipulating them. The question to answer here is: "*Can we influence the buying process?*"

If you don't know the answers to any or all of these PPVVC questions, then you don't know enough to qualify yourself into the opportunity, even if you know all of the BANT elements. Your decision to invest time and effort in the sales opportunity should depend on whether or not you can get these answers, and whether those answers favor you and your solution—or if you can influence the buyer enough to earn their favor before they make a buying decision.

■ THE SALES FORMULA ADDS VALUE FOR THE CUSTOMER

Qualification does not happen just once—it is a continuous process that, if done correctly, adds legitimate value for the customer. This is the case because consistently executing PPVVC ensures the following outcomes in a sales opportunity:

➤ You, with the customer, have identified a legitimate business issue or problem.

➤ You are using the customer's time effectively by identifying a legitimate buying sponsorship.

➤ You are jointly creating a vision for solving a key problem with the customer.

➤ You work with the customer to establish clear, measurable solution value.

➤ You provide clearly delineated accountabilities with the customer to move forward in a successful manner.

The deeper techniques for applying PPVVC are the bedrock of the Solution Selling methodology. Every time you learn new information in an opportunity, reassess using the Successful Sales Formula. You may find a once-qualified opportunity becomes unqualified due to changes within the buying organization or other factors outside of your control. The only thing wrong about being wrong is staying wrong!

Good luck and good selling!

Name: Keith M. Eades

Company: Sales Performance International

Web Site: www.spisales.com

Biography: Keith Eades, chief executive officer of Sales Performance International (SPI), founded the global sales performance improvement firm in 1988. SPI has grown into one of the largest sales improvement companies in the world, doing business in more than 50 countries. Clients include Microsoft, IBM, Manpower, Office Depot, and Bank of America.

He is the best-selling author and coauthor of *The New Solution Selling*, *The Solution Selling Field Book*, and *The Solution-Centric Organization*.

Eades is a graduate of Clemson University, and in 2001, the university recognized him with the Alumni Fellow Award for his outstanding career accomplishments.

Selling Philosophy: Solution selling

Target Industries: Technology, manufacturing, professional services, health care, financial services

Best Sellers: Solution Selling workshops: Sales Execution Workshop, Sales Management and Coaching Workshop, Major Account Selling Workshop, Targeted Territory Selling Workshop, Executive Level Selling Workshop, Strategic Opportunity Selling Workshop, Collaborative Sales Negotiations Workshop, Solution Prospecting Workshop, SolutionSpeak Workshop (presentation skills), Solution Messaging Workshop and Consulting (marketing), Sales Process Design (workshop and consulting), Sales Tool Building Workshop, Sales Management System and Playbook, Structured Account and Opportunity Reviews, CRM/Sales Process Alignment, CRM Accelerators, Solution Selling Software, Management Dashboards

Sales Tip One: No pain, no change: If a person or company doesn't have a problem, critical business issue, or some compelling need or opportunity, then they have no motivation to change (or buy). When pain is admitted and the value of the resolution of the pain is quantified, it provides buyers with a compelling reason to act.

Sales Tip Two: Diagnose before you prescribe: One of the most important selling disciplines is to avoid the tendency to go into the details concerning your product prematurely. The best salespeople follow a structured process focused on diagnosing a customer's problems accurately, and then leading the customer to a vision of the solution that will have a positive, measurable change.

Sales Tip Three: You can't sell to someone who can't buy: If the person you're dealing with doesn't have power, then they *must* provide you with access to someone who does—otherwise you are wasting your time. Many salespeople are uncomfortable approaching power, but the best salespeople work relentlessly to maintain high levels of "situational fluency" about issues important to power sponsors.

Book One: *The New Solution Selling* (McGraw-Hill, 2004)

Book Two: *The Solution Selling Fieldbook* (McGraw-Hill, 2005)

Book Three: *The Solution-Centric Organization* (McGraw-Hill, 2006)

Chapter 69

The Up-Front Contract

Adding Control and Predictability to Your Sales Calls

David H. Sandler
Sandler Training

Has this happened to you?

You schedule an appointment with a prospect who seems to be very interested in your product. You painstakingly prepared a number of questions for the prospect to help you more completely identify and qualify the potential opportunity.

You arrive at the appointment, and before you can ask your first question, the prospect, who was cordial and enthusiastic when you spoke on the phone, assaults you with, "I don't have a lot of time. Show me whatcha got."

What happened?

If you want to add control and predictability to your sales calls and avoid unfulfilled expectations for you and your prospect, you must establish an up-front "contract" with your prospects. The up-front contract is simply an agreement between you and the prospect about what will take place during the meeting. It should describe the objective of the meeting, the amount of time allocated for the meeting, the roles and responsibilities of each party in reaching the objective, and the intended outcome of the meeting. You can think of it as a detailed agenda. It is a guidepost to keep the meeting focused and on track.

Excerpted from *You Can't Teach a Kid to Ride a Bike at a Seminar: Sandler Training's Seven-Step System for Successful Selling*, by David H. Sandler. © 1995 by David H. Sandler. All rights reserved.

Let's examine the up-front contract that could have been established when the appointment was scheduled:

> Mr. Jones, I'd be happy to meet with you and determine what benefit, if any, our solvent recycling equipment can provide for your operation.
>
> I'll have to ask you some questions about your current solvent usage, costs, and disposal procedures. So, it would be helpful if you had those figures available.
>
> I'm sure you'll have some questions for me about space requirements, personnel training, payback periods, and of course the necessary investment. I'll do my best to answer them.
>
> Experience tells me that we will need 90 minutes for the meeting.
>
> By the end of our meeting, we should know whether our equipment represents a good investment for your company and whether we should take the next step, which is to arrange an on-site trial.
>
> Are you comfortable investing an hour and a half with me to determine whether there is a good fit and if we should move to the next step?

With up-front contracts in place, both the salesperson and the prospect know what will take place during the meeting, how long it will take, and what the conclusion will be. No surprises. No unfulfilled expectations. And "show me whatcha got" and promises to "think-it-over" no longer fit.

At Sandler Training, we have developed a seven-step sales system that's more powerful than the prospect's system, and here's how it works. We use a submarine analogy to move the prospect through the seven compartments of the "Sandler Submarine."

> **Step #1: You must establish rapport with your prospect.** In the buyer/ seller "dance," there is a defense "wall" created when you call on a prospect who knows you are "trying to sell something." Help this prospect to know you understand his or her problem from his or her point of view, and make this person comfortable with you so you can begin to establish a relationship.
>
> **Step #2: You must establish an Up-Front Contract with your prospect.** What could be more honest than to establish a set of rules at the beginning of interacting with a prospect? An Up-Front Contract, or better yet, a series of Up-Front Contracts, will save time for both you and the prospect, and help you make more money in sales without offending anyone. By always arriving at an agreement up front, you and the prospect can avoid misunderstandings, as well as the rhetoric and posturing that often occur during the buyer/seller "dance." An Up-Front Contract

improves communications and greatly enhances the profession of sell-ing, as you have read and experienced at the beginning of this chapter.

Step #3: You must uncover your prospect's "pain." People buy emo-tionally, but they make decisions intellectually. What's the most intense emotion? Pain.

Without pain, there's no easy sale. Perhaps there's no sale at all. Without pain, people will continue to do what they've done all their lives until maintaining the status quo becomes so painful that some-thing new is required. Unless you learn to uncover a prospect's pain, you will continue to sell using the most difficult of traditional selling principles: The law of averages!

Step #4: You must get all the money issues out on the table. While you need to discuss the cost of your product or service, it's more important to discuss the cost to your prospects if they do nothing. Deal with money in detail early on. Once you uncover the prospect's pain, and you know money is available to get rid of the pain, you can progress to the fifth step of the Sandler Selling System.

Step #5: You must discover the decision-making process your pros-pect uses when deciding to buy or not buy a product or service. Is the prospect empowered to make the decision alone? Will an associate or spouse be involved in the decision making? Does the prospect like to think things over and decide later? Ultimately, can the prospect make the decision to spend the money to get rid of the pain?

Once you're comfortable that you and the prospect clearly under-stand what it will take to do business together, progress to the sixth step.

Step #6: You must present a solution that will get rid of the prospect's pain. Traditionalists would now say, "Aha, this is where you talk features and benefits." No you don't!

Your sales presentation has little to do with the features and benefits touted by the marketing department and everything to do with showing your prospect that your product or service can eliminate the pain.

Contrary to what the traditionalists say, prospects do not buy features and benefits. They buy ways to help them overcome or avoid pain. Only show those things that will eliminate their pain. It's as simple as that.

Step #7: You must post-sell your sale. How often have your sales slipped away after you've concluded the sale? Perhaps it doesn't happen in your business. But when a salesperson takes business away from a competitor, the competitor usually doesn't surrender. Has your compet-itor ever sent you a congratulatory note that says, "Nice going, George! Good luck with your new client!"

Chances are, the competitor will make a run at saving the business. How? By low-balling your price. Once the gloves are off, the competitor isn't going to be pleasant about it. The final step in the Sandler Selling

System, the Post-Sell Step, deals with buyer's remorse, competitor assaults, and any other potential land mines to eliminate backouts once and for all.

Name: David H. Sandler

Company: Sandler Training

Web Site: www.sandler.com

Biography: Sandler Training has been the leader in sales and management training in the world since 1967, with over 250 Training Centers worldwide. David H. Sandler, founder of Sandler Training, began sales training and developing the Sandler Selling System and Systematic Sales Management in the late 1960s and early 1970s. He created an extraordinary sales training program for small and mid-sized companies, Fortune 500 corporations, global multinationals, and professional service firms. In 1995, David Sandler died, but his legacy lives on through the entrepreneurial spirit of over 250 Sandler Franchises in 32 countries.

Selling Philosophy: Finding power in reinforcement

Target Industries: All industries

Best Sellers: Sandler Training President's Club

Sales Tip One: Today's Sales Meeting Minute: Sales accountability is a misnomer. It's better described as personal accountability. Sales accountability is not about your boss looking over your shoulder, checking in on your behavior numbers in the middle of the week. No, sales accountability is about the personal commitments you make to yourself and tracking those commitments in your "behavior" numbers every day to reach your goals. (© Sandler Training www.sandler.com)

Sales Tip Two: Today's Sales Meeting Minute: "Don't Assume, Ask Questions." The minute an amateur salesperson hears a customer's problem that they probably have heard many times before, they assume they understand the customer's problem and immediately start to solve it by demonstrating their know-how, their product's features, and their company's benefits. Unfortunately, the customer obtains your expertise for free and the salesperson winds up not really understanding the customer's real motivations for making a commitment to buy. Don't assume you know what the customer's real problems are. Let the customer tell you. Don't Assume, Ask Questions. (© Sandler Training www.sandler.com)

Sales Tip Three: Today's Sales Meeting Minute: "Don't Spill Your Candy in the Lobby." Many salespeople call on accounts and are extremely anxious to tell them about their products and services. After the sales call, they walk out bewildered about why they didn't get an order. If you are dropping off information, proposals, or marketing materials without really understanding your customers' buying motives, you are spilling your candy in the lobby. Once they have your information and pricing, do they really need you anymore? Customers are not entitled to your information or demonstration until you understand their buying motives, budget, and how they make decisions. (© Sandler Training www.sandler.com)

Book One: *You Can't Teach a Kid to Ride a Bike at a Seminar* (Bay Head Publishing, 1996)

Chapter 70

How to Write a Winning Proposal

Dr. Tom Sant
The Sant Corporation

In today's economy, salespeople have to write more proposals, and better proposals, than ever before. As the industry has become more competitive and complex, customers have become both more confused and more demanding. As a result, they are likely to listen to a presentation, nod their heads, and mutter those dreaded words, "Sounds good! Why don't you put that in writing for me?"

■ WHY DO CUSTOMERS WANT PROPOSALS?

Writing proposals is about as much fun as having your teeth drilled. And reading them isn't a whole lot better. So why do customers ask for them?

One motivation is that the customer wants to compare offers from various vendors to make sure they buy the highest value solution based on your differentiators and value proposition. At a simpler level, they may simply want to compare prices, clarify complex information, and gather information so that the "decision team" can review it. And let's face it, sometimes they just want to slow down the sales process and they figure that asking for a proposal will keep the sales rep busy for a few weeks.

Whatever the customer's motivation, the fact is that proposal writing has become a common requirement for closing business throughout the entire business world. Today, people who sell everything from garbage collection services to complex information technology installation have to create client-centered, persuasive proposals.

■ WHAT GOES INTO A WINNING PROPOSAL?

Your objective in writing a proposal is to provide your client with enough information—persuasively presented information—to prove your case and motivate the client to buy your services or applications. That sounds pretty straightforward.

So why is it that the vast majority of proposals start out with the vendor's company history? Does the author believe there is something so fundamentally compelling about their origins that clients will immediately be persuaded to buy?

And why is it that a huge number of proposals focus entirely on the vendor's products and services, but never mention how those products and services will help the client solve a business problem or close an important gap? Does the proposal writer believe that facts alone are enough to motivate a prospect to say "yes"?

Winning proposals must be client-centered, not company- or product-centered. Most people buy because they're looking for solutions to pressing problems, additional resources to close gaps, or the means to cope with difficult issues. What this means is that a proposal is *not* a price quote, a bill of materials, or a project plan. Each of those elements may be part of a proposal, but they are not sufficient to make a persuasive, client-centered case.

In our experience, there are four categories of content that proposals *must* contain to maximize your chance of winning:

1. **Evidence that you understand the client's business problem or need.**

   People view major buying decisions with anxiety. The bigger the decision, the greater the anxiety. They know that even a well-intentioned vendor may end up wasting their time or their money, or both. One way to reduce their anxiety and minimize their perception of the risk of moving forward with you is to demonstrate that you clearly understand their problems, issues, needs, opportunities, objectives, or values. Whatever is driving the client's interest, you must show that you understand it and have based your solution on it.

2. **A compelling reason for the client to choose your recommendation over any others.**

   This is your value proposition. Remember that you may write a proposal that is completely compliant with the customer's requirements, that recommends the right solution, that even offers the lowest price, and still lose. Why? Because a competitor made a stronger case that their approach offered a higher return on investment, lower total cost of ownership, faster payback, or some similar measure of value that matters to the customer.

   Note: Most proposals don't contain any value proposition at all. They contain pricing, but no estimation of the rate of return the client will get from choosing you. Failing to address the client's needs and failing to present a compelling value proposition are the most serious mistakes you can make in writing a proposal.

3. **A recommendation for a specific approach, program, system design, or application that will solve the problem and produce positive business results.**

   It may surprise you to learn that most proposals contain no recommendation at all. What they contain instead are descriptions of products or services. What's the difference? A recommendation explicitly links the features of a product or service to the client's needs and shows how the client will obtain positive results. And a recommend contains language that unmistakably shows that the vendor believes in this solution: "We recommend . . ." or "We urge you to implement . . ."

4. **Evidence of your ability to deliver on time and on budget.**

   Most proposals are pretty good in this area. You want to show the substantiating evidence that helps answer the question, "Can they really do this?" Good evidence includes case studies, references, testimonials, and resumes of key personnel. You may also include project plans, management plans, company expertise, and other forms of evidence (white papers, awards, third-party recognition). Avoid throwing in everything. Keep the evidence focused on the areas the customer cares about.

These are the essentials. Every scrap of data, every figure, every paragraph in your proposal must contribute toward providing one or more of them, because they directly address the three key factors on which every proposal is evaluated:

1. **Responsiveness.** Are we getting what we need?

2. **Competence.** Can they really do it?

3. **Value.** Is this the smartest way to spend our money?

Name: Tom Sant

Company: The Sant Corporation

Web Site: www.santcorp.com

Biography: Named one of the top 10 sales trainers in the world by *Selling Power Magazine*, Tom Sant, PhD, is a popular keynote speaker at conferences worldwide, and has written over $30 billion in winning proposals for both private sector and government contracts. Noteworthy clients include Procter & Gamble, AT&T, Microsoft, Johnson Controls, HSBC, Motorola, and General Electric. He is one of the first-ever Fellows of the Association of Proposal Management Professionals.

Tom invented the world's first proposal automation system; the first Web-based content configuration system for producing proposals, letters, and presentations; and the first system for automatically analyzing and responding to complex RFPs.

Selling Philosophy: Strategic selling

Target Industries: Financial services, professional services, high technology, telecommunications

Best Sellers: ProposalMaster and RFPMaster are the world's best-selling software applications for creating client-focused, persuasive sales proposals and RFP responses.

Sales Tip One: Never title your proposal "Proposal." Instead write a title that states a benefit to the client, for example, "Increasing Network Reliability and Convenience through Advanced Online Capabilities."

Sales Tip Two: Focus on your clients' business needs or mission objectives first. Mirror what you have heard from them before offering a solution.

Sales Tip Three: Prioritize your uniqueness factors or competitive advantages. Think about what you have to offer and select a few qualities, prioritized in terms of what your client cares about.

Book One: *Persuasive Business Proposals*

Book Two: *The Language of Success*

Book Three: *The Giants of Sales*

Chapter 71

The 11 Biggest Sales Lies

Stephan Schiffman

Sales professionals have been making concerted effort to improve their image in these "politically correct" times. As a result, they have become more tuned in to their prospects and have developed more honest relationships with their customers. However, salespeople have not really made an effort to be more honest where it counts the most—with themselves.

The following are the 11 most common sales lies that we have seen salespeople use on themselves. These lies that they tell themselves can actually inhibit success and prevent them from achieving their sales goals:

1. **Someday I will not need to prospect.** Salespeople look at veteran successful sales professionals and believe that once they cultivate a few big accounts, they will never have to prospect for new business again. This is the most dangerous sales lie. Without a steady stream of new prospects, a salesperson is putting his or her income stream in jeopardy. All that has to happen is the loss of one major account, and then the salesperson is back to square one.

   It is important for you to prospect regularly to protect your income base so that you are not reliant on the unpredictability of one or several major existing accounts for success.

2. **It's okay to lie—just a little.** Not really. Lies have an interesting way of catching up with you. Whether you are lying to your manager, a coworker, or your prospects, you will find it's really much better to tell the truth—even if you risk losing an account.

   As a salesperson, your reputation and credibility are the keys to success. Be truthful with everyone, even on minor issues, so that you will be trusted throughout your relationships.

3. **People really need our service.** Whether you sell anything from cars to computer systems to insurance to unique engineering

services, nobody really needs you. Prospects have been using or doing something else without you, and they can continue doing that, or something else, indefinitely.

What you do offer your prospects is a means to help them do what they are doing—better. For example, a person whom you think desperately needs a computer can do his or her job manually or hire an outside service. What you offer is a way to get his or her job done more efficiently.

4. **It's business—I don't take it personally.** This is the lie salespeople use to help themselves get over the rejection that occurs often in selling. The problem with this lie is . . . it's not true, and it doesn't work. If a prospect stands you up, it does hurt you—personally. When you've put hours upon hours into a presentation, and the sale doesn't close, it also hurts you personally. The fact is that selling is part of your life. It's your livelihood. When rejection happens, you need to accept it and deal with the blow emotionally, and then move on.

5. **Don't worry about the competition, they'll never reach us, or we really don't have any competitors.** This sales lie has caused great financial damage for major corporations such as GM and IBM. Even if you are in a high tech field selling a breakthrough product or service, you have got to realize someone else is selling, or about to sell, a product or service that may make your product obsolete.

Read your industry and your customers' industry publications regularly. Always seek out information on your existing competition, as well as products that can be used in place of your product.

6. **Someday you will not need to prospect.** Remember, if you want a successful sales career, prospecting must be a part of it for the long term.

7. **People will buy; if they miss an appointment, they owe me.** The fault with this lie is that prospects don't really owe you anything. You are going after prospects for the sale, and whether they feel guilty or not for missing an appointment, or forgetting to return your call, does not affect their buying decisions. Apply your sales skills to the fullest, no matter what you feel your prospect may owe or not owe you.

8. **Sales are really easy to make here.** This is the biggest trap, and too many salespeople fall into it. When sales close easily, it's dangerous to sit back and let them happen. It could be a fluke, or it could be only a temporary phenomenon.

Either way, if sales come easily, it's important to work just as hard as you would if they came with a greater struggle. In the worst case, the hard work will just result in greater success and higher sales income.

9. **This prospect is a sure thing.** Unfortunately, no prospect is a sure thing. Even after a contract is signed, a sale can still fall through. Use something solid to identify the "sure things," such as "freight on dock" for products, or "date of service scheduled" for services.

10. **If you succeed, then I succeed.** This lie is an excuse to sit back and let others take control of your sale. If your prospect is looking into competitors' services and pricing, you must get involved. If your account has been handed over to technical support people, you should still stay involved so you make sure you succeed.

11. **Someday I will not need to prospect.** Keep in mind prospecting is always necessary if you want a fresh business base from which to draw your income.

A sales career is hard work—but it can also be the most financially rewarding career of all the choices open to you. It is crucial to be truthful with yourself as well as your prospects so you can achieve the results you desire based upon trust, solid relationships, and your efforts.

Name: Stephan Schiffman

Web Site: www.steveschiffman.com

Biography: Stephan Schiffman has been a leader in motivational and sales training since 1979. He is a Certified Management Consultant, and has trained and consulted a wide range of corporations, including IBM, AT&T, Motorola, Sprint, and CIGNA. He has trained over 500,000 professionals in over 9,000 companies. Millions more have read his best-selling books internationally. Stephan has developed highly pragmatic sales training and management programs that adapt effectively to many sales environments and industries. He has been rated the number-one sales expert in prospecting by *Personal Selling Power* magazine.

He has appeared on CNBC's *Smart Money, Steals and Deals, Money Talk*, and AP's *Special Assignment*, among others.

Selling Philosophy: Selling is helping people do what they do better, by understanding what they do and how they do it that way.

Target Industries: All industries

Best Sellers: We have conducted nearly 10,000 seminars and speeches in 30 years of doing business.

Sales Tip One: Always get to the next step. No matter how well the sales meeting went, it is not successful unless you have the next step in place.

Sales Tip Two: Remember that your number-one competition is the status quo—meaning that everyone is using something already; the question is why they aren't buying from you.

Sales Tip Three: Never, never, never stop prospecting.

Book One: Stephan has written over 50 best-selling books.

Dan Seidman

Sales Autopsy

Chapter 72

One Great Opening Is Worth 10,000 Closes

■ FOOT-IN-MOUTH KILLS SALESMAN

Rick sells printing services, and he's probably not as good as he is persistent. It took six months of phone calls and mailed literature to finally get into the president's office of a company that the rep wanted to sell very badly. It took less than 30 seconds to undo half a year of time and effort.

Rick had finally nailed this prospect down to an appointment and wanted to make a very good first impression. He figured that this president would look at him as either a strong, persistent salesman or a pest. He would dispose of a pest as quickly as he could, so as Rick walked into the executive's office, he looked for something on the wall or on his desk to use for a little opening small talk.

There it was! "John Madden!" he cried, pointing at a photograph on the prospect's credenza. Every sports fan knows the 300-plus-pound commentator. He's probably the best announcer around, in spite of a face that could stop a bus. "That's a fantastic photo! How did you get a picture of yourself with your arm around John Madden?"

Rick's rapport-building efforts crashed in flames as the shocked company president slowly answered, "That's not John Madden, that's . . . my . . . wife."

■ POSTMORTEM

Our poor salesman, Rick, used an approach that was popular early in the evolution of selling. Are you like this at the initial contact with a prospect? Do you look for that fish on the wall, the trophy on the shelf, the picture on the desk? We're often taught to comment on these items to "break the ice." Can you distinguish yourself by being so ordinary, so predictable? Don't look like, act, or sound like everyone else who sells. This opening performance is wasteful and disrespectful of a buyer's time.

Here's a suggestion for that initial contact that many top-performing sales pros use today: Recognize that your prospects don't have the time to chat like they used to. Simply respect the prospect's time, and review what you agreed upon when you got the appointment. Rick should have said, "Mr. Prospect, I want to respect your commitment to the time we have. When we talked on the phone you said we'd have forty-five minutes to talk. Is that right? Good. What is the most serious concern you were thinking about when you decided to invite me in today?" As a sales pro, you've now honored someone's busy schedule and gotten right to business. Best of all, the prospect is about to do most of the talking.

Name: Dan Seidman

Company: Sales Autopsy

Web Site: www.SalesAutopsy.com

Biography: Dan Seidman of SalesAutopsy.com is the best-selling author of *Sales Autopsy*, which extracts the top seven strategies that distinguish world-class sales professionals from everyone else.

Dan's monthly columns reach over two million business brains each month.

He has been designated "One of the Top 12 Sales Coaches in America" and his creativity, wit, and wisdom are revealed in *The Sales Comic Book* (there is nothing like it on this planet, possibly any planet!) and *Revenge of the Reps*, a video game.

His training experience, Sales Autopsy: A Customized Suite of Strategies to Boost Your Selling Performance, was a *Selling Power Magazine*'s 2006 Awards Program finalist.

Selling Philosophy: Teach with unique and useful strategies that complement the style of today's savvy, experienced buyer.

Target Industries: Financial services, real estate, banking, insurance, printing, health care, pharmaceuticals, manufacturing

Best Sellers: Book: *Sales Autopsy*; video game: *Revenge of the Reps*; comic book: *The Sales Comic Book*; keynote address: *Hilarious Selling Blunders and What You Can Learn!* training program: Sales Autopsy; A Suite of Customizable Strategies to Boost Your Selling Performance

Sales Tip One: DQ your prospects: Disqualify quickly and stop chasing bad business. Don't "qualify" or you'll inject too much hope into your sales funnel.

Sales Tip Two: Find a mentor (to speed up your learning curve). Be a mentor (to build a legacy for others).

Sales Tip Three: When handling objections, *don't get defensive*! Respond by asking how this issue is a concern, so you don't just pitch harder and create a verbal fistfight.

Book One: *Sales Autopsy*

Book Two: *The Sales Comic Book*

Book Three: *The Death of 20th Century Selling*

Product One: Revenge of the Reps (a hilarious video game)

Product Two: Sales Horror Stories (audio CD)

Chapter 73

Life = Sales

Blair Singer
SalesDogs

Every entrepreneur knows that Sales = Income. Ninety-five percent of most businesses fail not because of bad ideas, products, or services, but because the business or people in it either can't sell, don't know how to, don't want to, or refuse to learn how to sell.

It's also why more than 95 percent of most people never become rich. It's because they don't have the ability or confidence to sell their ideas, their dreams, their plans, or even their brilliance. Many think that "sales" is a dirty word—something reserved for a used car lot.

You may claim "I'm not a salesperson" or "That's not me." But I will tell you that if Sales = Income, then Life = Sales: physically, mentally, emotionally, and financially. I defy you to find any arena in your life where someone is not involved in a high-stakes (in their own mind) pitch to gain influence, favor, or action.

The thought "I don't sell'" is not only inaccurate, it is downright debilitating. The more you can instill confidence in others and get them to take action on your notions, the better you sell, the better you lead, and the more income you create. And that's all kinds of income: wealth, money, trust, companionship, and even love.

This is true in business, with your kids, with your significant other, and with everyone you associate with. Politicians are constantly pitching you. Doctors are pitching their prognosis and attorneys are pitching to their clients and for their clients. In pubs, taverns, casinos, sporting arenas, locker rooms, conference rooms, lunch rooms, restaurants, nurseries, and particularly out of the mouths of kids from the moment they are born until they leave the house . . . everyone is selling.

Once you come to grips with the fact that your success in life requires your ability to master sales, communication, persuasion, and influence . . . only then will the world beat the proverbial path to your door.

The biggest reason that Life = Sales is because the toughest and most pivotal sale of all is you selling to yourself. Selling is the "little voice" in your head to take action or not . . . to persevere or not . . . to overcome doubt or not. Ultimately the game of life is won or lost in your own head. We call that "Little Voice Management."

Think about it for a minute . . . You've got to know how to attract interest, to turn "No's" into "Yes's", to pitch, to close, and to follow up. It never ends. Those who do it well not only make a lot of money, but have lots of great friends, awesome teams, great and loving relationships, and happy and healthy bodies. They have the skills to sell themselves on the reasons to take action . . . the ability to overcome the negative little voices in their brains. That is the ultimate sale.

If you are still uncertain about all this, think about sales for a minute. What is the purpose for a sale? Is it to win the battle of persuasion? Is it to get someone else to surrender to your will? Maybe. But for me, it's much bigger than that.

The purpose of a sale is to get an *agreement*. To get that other someone to agree on a mutual point. To agree to listen. To agree to stop fighting. To agree to take another look. To agree to pause for a breath. To agree to take whatever the next step might be.

The reason for the agreement is to gain *cooperation*. To actually get the other party to walk side by side with you in "active agreement." To cocreate a better conversation, to take on a bigger task together, to discover more about each other and our needs . . . to at least look at a journey toward a common goal.

And the ultimate purpose for cooperation is to create a thing called *synergy*. Synergy is a state in which the whole is unpredictably greater than the sum of its individual parts or components. It's where we expand the resources before dividing them, where we cocreate a solution that is greater than anything we individually bring to the table.

It's where magic has a chance to happen. Where each person's individual game gets elevated to a level bigger than either expected. It's where the culmination of coming together results in solutions, artifacts, and resources that could only be imagined before. This is what we call abundance.

So you see that I hold sales to be not only important, but the source of true creation, evolution, and innovation. It's called creating the future. Yet, it starts with you. If you can sell to *you*, to get agreement with yourself, to cooperate with your own best-laid plans, you too can create results beyond the ordinary.

Name: Blair Singer

Company: SalesDogs

Web Site: www.salesdogs.com

Biography: Blair Singer empowers people to achieve peak performance in business, sales, money, teams, relationships, and life. He is cofounder and CEO of SalesPartners Worldwide.

Clients include Singapore Airlines, Deutsche Bank, Redken 5th Avenue NYC, HSBC, IBM, ING Clarion, JP Morgan, Dunkin' Brands, and Westin Hotels.

Singer is the author of three best-selling books: *SalesDogs: You Don't Have to Be an Attack Dog to Be Successful in Sales*; *The ABCs of Building a Business Team That Wins*; and *"Little Voice" Mastery: How to Win the War between Your Ears in 30 Seconds or Less—and Have an Extraordinary Life!*

Selling Philosophy: Objection handling—stand in the heat!

Target Industries: Salespeople, managers, leaders, individuals

Best Sellers: Authentic Sales and Leadership Program; Little Voice Management Systems (English and Spanish); SalesDogs Training School Kit (English and Spanish); Code of Honor; Powerful Sales Presentations, Lead, Teach, and Inspire; High Impact Training; Automatic Lead Generator; Eight Sales and Marketing Steps to Financial Freedom

Sales Tip One: In order to be rich and to succeed in business, your number-one skill is your ability to communicate, sell, and teach others how to sell.

Sales Tip Two: To build a successful business, you have to know how to build a championship team that can win—no matter what.

Sales Tip Three: Listening is a critical skill in sales. Listening well develops more trusting and respectful relationships, which will encourage a positive buying decision.

Book One: *SalesDogs: You Do Not Have to Be an Attack Dog to Be Successful in Sales*

Book Two: *The ABCs of Building a Business Team That Wins*

Product One: Little Voice Management Systems

Product Two: SalesDogs Training School Kit

Product Three: Code of Honor

What Are the Biggest Sales Presentation Mistakes That Professionals Make and How Can You Avoid Them?

Terri L. Sjodin
Sjodin Communications

In today's competitive marketplace, whether selling a product, a service, a philosophy, an idea, or most importantly, yourself, everybody sells something. An individual's success often depends upon his or her ability to deliver a polished and persuasive presentation. Salespeople spend 80 percent of their time verbally communicating; many suffer from common shortcomings in their sales presentations that adversely affect their results. Consider all of the different types of presentations a business professional might deliver: promoting an idea at an office meeting, delivering a three-minute elevator speech at a networking event, giving a sales presentation to a prospect, or selling yourself in a job interview. All require the ability to deliver a solid professional performance!

The following are four of the nine Biggest Sales Presentation Mistakes professionals make. After reviewing this short list, you will be able to do a quick evaluation of your own performance, and then make changes where necessary. Learning to *build* and *deliver* more effective presentations can directly impact your long-term success.

Mistake #1: Winging It. When you "wing it," it's very common for your presentation to "hop and pop" around all over the place, lacking logical, progressive flow. It takes too long to deliver, and prospects may find it hard to follow. Frequently, you may leave out half the points you want to make, including effective illustrations, which bring the presentation to life.

Take time to prepare and practice using a logical outline. Be sure your presentation covers all the points you want to make, clearly and concisely. Don't be afraid to give a copy of the outline to your listener.

Mistake #2: Being Too Informative versus Persuasive. It's very easy to deliver an informative rather than persuasive presentation. The reason? A prospect can't say "no" when you're only disseminating information. Remember, it's a teacher's job to be informative, but a salesperson must be persuasive.

Learn how to build a presentation that *creates needs* rather than just covers the standard needs analysis. Think "proactive" versus "reactive." Design a presentation that anticipates objections and overcomes them before they become reasons not to buy. Think like an attorney, and build arguments for why a client should work with you and your company, and why they should do it now.

Mistake #3: Boring, Boring, Boring. Many professionals do not realize just how boring their presentations are—too many facts, a flat, boring, monotone voice, the same old stories. Sometimes professionals have been giving the same presentation for so long they just slip into autopilot. In today's competitive market, your presentations must be entertaining in order to obtain and maintain the attention of prospects.

Be creative! Put some energy into it! To stay sharp, practice with a tape recorder and listen to the playback to determine where your presentation begins to fall apart. Make improvements accordingly. Be sure to use material that is appropriate for the audience, whether it's made up of 1 or 10 people.

Mistake #4: Relying Too Much on Visual Aids. If brochures, handouts, or slides could sell a product or service on their own, companies would not need salespeople. Depending too much on visual aids can give us a false sense of security. We tend to think it isn't necessary to prepare thoroughly because our props will lead us right through the presentation. We let the visual aid become the star and virtually run the show.

You are the star and the visual is the bit player! It's your job to bring the presentation to life. Strategically place visual aids in your presentation for emphasis of a major point or argument. You must practice with all handouts or aids to insure that they enhance rather than detract from your presentation. Remember who's in charge—you are!

These four points give you a brief overview of some of the most common mistakes salespeople make every day in their presentations. Such mistakes can cost you thousands of dollars every year in lost sales and commissions. Do a simple self-evaluation of your next presentation. Do you make any of these common mistakes when speaking to your clients and prospects? When you can identify the weaknesses in your presentation, you can begin to correct them. As a result, you will become more confident, more polished, more persuasive, and more consistent in delivering effective presentations.

Name: Terri Sjodin

Company: Sjodin Communications

Web Site: www.sjodincommmunications.com

Biography: Terri Sjodin is the principal and founder of Sjodin Communications, a Public Speaking, Sales Training, and Consulting Firm.

She has spoken to and trained thousands of people. She is the author of *New Sales Speak: The Nine Biggest Sales Presentation Mistakes and How to Avoid Them*, and co-author of *Mentoring: A Success Guide for Mentors and Protégés*.

Clients include Fortune 500 companies, industry associations, and academic conferences. She has served as a keynote speaker and consultant for members of Congress at four annual GOP Retreats.

In 2007, Terri was named one of the top five "Women in Business" by the *Orange County Business Journal*.

Selling Philosophy: There is an art to selling and that art takes place in your delivery. As sales professionals we must "build" a great case, employ our own creativity, and deliver our messages in our own authentic voice.

Target Industries: Professional sales organizations that depend on sales presentations to generate business and secure transactions

Best Sellers: Keynote addresses: "New Sales Speak: The Nine Biggest Sales Presentation Mistakes and How to Avoid Them" and "Small Message, Big Impact: How to Put the Power of the Elevator Speech Effect to Work For You!"; One-and-a-half-day workshop: "Persuasive Three-Minute Elevator Speech Workshop" (formally called the "Hell Night Workshop")

Sales Tip One: In today's competitive marketplace, whether selling a product, a service, a philosophy, an idea, or most importantly, yourself . . . everybody sells something. An individual's success often depends upon his or her ability to deliver a polished and persuasive presentation.

Sales Tip Two: Common Pitfall: "Being Too Informative versus Being Persuasive." It's very easy to deliver an informative rather than persuasive presentation. The reason? A prospect can't say "no" when you're only disseminating information. Remember, it's a teacher's job to be informative, but a salesperson must be persuasive.

Sales Tip Three: Common Pitfall: "Providing Inadequate Support." Your prospect won't buy-in to your proposal if you are unable to support your claims. Many people deliver presentations based on opinion rather than logical argument for why a client or prospect should take action. You must be able to prove your case when confronted by the prospect, or you will lose credibility.

Book One: *New Sales Speak: The Nine Biggest Sales Presentation Mistakes and How to Avoid Them* (John Wiley & Sons, Inc.)

Book Two: *Mentoring: A Success Guide for Mentors and Proteges* (cowritten by Terri Sjodin and Floyd Wickman; McGraw-Hill)

Product One: *New Sales Speak: The Nine Biggest Sales Presentation Mistakes and How to Avoid Them* (narrated by the author; 6-CD audio/book combo)

Product Two: "Small Message, Big Impact: How to Put the Power of the Elevator Speech Effect to Work For You!" (audio/CD and data disc set)

It's *Not* a Numbers Game, It's a Game of Numbers

Art Sobczak
Business by Phone

I've long refuted the old saying that "sales is just a numbers game." It's not. It's a quality game, in the sense that you can't just crank out calls and expect success if you're doing the wrong things.

But sales is a game *of* numbers. We use numbers to describe degrees of pain, pleasure, profits, losses, income, and time. And there are smart ways to use numbers on the phone in your sales. Let's look at 10 of them.

1. "Reduce it to the ridiculous." This old technique refers to minimizing your price or the difference in cost between you and a competitor. "Ridiculous" refers to how insignificant the amount really is when you put it in daily terms, for example, "Pat, we're really only talking about a difference of two dollars a day to have the suped-up model." (Or, ridiculous could mean how crazy someone could get with this technique: "Jim, it's only 30 cents per hour difference over the 10-year life of the machine.")

2. "Raise it to the outrageous." Conversely, this is taking a *savings* and extrapolating it over a longer period. It's useful in pointing out how much someone will save, over a greater period of time, by buying from you, for example, "You'll save the shipping cost on every order. On two orders per month at an average of $15 per order, we're looking at $360 for the year."

3. Can you say "dollars"? When you want to maximize the perception of a number, say the word "dollars." "With us, your savings will be over three thousand dollars." Conversely, to minimize it, just say the number: "To upgrade will only be an extra one-fifty."

4. Use exact numbers. Stating exact numbers adds more credibility to your statements than using rounded numbers. For example, "Our program is in place at 358 dealerships," sounds authoritative. "Our program is in about 400 dealerships," leaves a feeling that the number might be fudged a bit. Likewise, if you want to minimize the importance of a number, you could use a rounded figure, for example, "We're only looking at a figure for customization somewhere in the 200 range."

5. Put price in a different perspective. You probably can recall those hair-pulling situations where you've established the savings or additional profits you could help someone realize, but yet, they don't act on it. It's normally because they don't see the number as being significant enough. So put it in terms they can understand. "Paul, you're right, we're only talking about $400 a month savings here. But I bet that would make the monthly payment on one of your delivery vans." Another example would be: "The $200 cost reduction might not seem like a lot, but let's look at it a different way. You said your profit margin is about 10 percent. You'd need to do another $2,000 in sales per month just to make the $200 I'm basically offering you, for free."

6. Investment versus cost. Use the word "investment" when talking about the price of your product or service (unless, of course, it would be inappropriate or inane to do so in your industry). For example, "Your investment in this new unit is only $23,500." Use "cost" or "expense" when referring to the competition. "The expense they're quoting you is $25,800."

7. Minimize the next-level amount. You can upsell more by presenting the higher level in a more attractive way. For example, instead of saying, "The next price break is at 150 units," which can seem large, instead say "You need only 10 more units to get to the next break."

8. Question to attach numbers to circumstances. When the prospect/customer shares that they have a problem, are wasting money or time, or are missing out on opportunities or profits, question them to quantify their statements.

➤ "How often does that happen?"

➤ "What does that cost you?"

➤ "How much time, specifically, would you say you spend on that?"

➤ "How many times did that occur?"

9. Have them do the math. Ask questions designed to have them figure the calculations. "Okay, let's figure this up. You're paying how much, now, for the setup? Okay, now, how many of those orders do you have per month? Now, let's take that multiplied by 12 to get a yearly cost. What did you come up with? Wow! You're paying that much just for setup on a yearly basis?"

10. The theory of contrast. Very simple . . . probably one of the easiest ways to dramatically increase your sales. Ask for more than you ultimately expect, or offer less than you expect to pay (or give as a concession). The rationale is that by starting with an extreme number, the next counteroffer doesn't seem so extreme in comparison, although it's more (or less, depending on the circumstance) than what would have been arrived at otherwise.

For example, let's say they could use 1,000 units, but likely wouldn't volunteer that order, and alluded to maybe . . . 200 or so. You suggest they go with the 1,000. Their idea of 200 now seems small in comparison. So you end up with 400 or 500. Not bad!

Master your use of numbers in sales, and you'll see the number on your own paycheck getting larger.

Name: Art Sobczak

Company: Business by Phone, Inc.

Web Site: www.BusinessByPhone.com

Biography: Art Sobczak, president of Business by Phone, Inc., provides real-world how-to ideas and techniques that help business-to-business salespeople use the phone more effectively to prospect, sell, and service, without morale-killing "rejection." He has produced and delivered over 1,200 training sessions over the past 26 years for companies and associations in virtually all business-to-business industries. For over 25 years, Art has written and published the how-to tips newsletter, "Telephone Prospecting and Selling Report," and he has written several books and numerous audio and video programs, including his newest, "Smart Calling: Eliminate the Fear, Failure, and Rejection from Cold Calling."

Selling Philosophy: Helping people buy

Target Industries: Whatever business uses this method of sales communication: Using the phone

Best Sellers: *How to Sell More, in Less Time, with No Rejection, Using Common Sense Telephone Techniques* (vols. 1 and 2), also available on audio CD; Telesales College two-day training workshop, also available on audio CD; "Telephone Prospecting and Selling Report," a monthly sales tips newsletter

Sales Tip One: Never place a cold call. Always know something about the person/organization you call so that you can customize your call to their world, therefore sparking interest and setting you apart from most other prospectors.

Sales Tip Two: Never talk about products or services in your opening statement or voice mail message. People buy *results*, so hint at the results you might be able to provide.

Sales Tip Three: Get information before you give it. Otherwise you are giving a "pitch" that actually creates objections, rather than a recommendation that is tailored to their needs, desires, problems, and pains.

Book One: *How to Sell More, in Less Time, with No Rejection, Using Common Sense Telephone Techniques* (vols. 1 and 2)

Book Two: *How to Place the Successful Sales and Prospecting Call*

Book Three: *Smart Calling: Eliminate the Fear, Failure, and Rejection from Cold Calling*

Product One: Telesales College (audio CD)

Product Two: Hello Success: Everything You Need for an Entire Year's Worth of Training

Product Three: Telesales TV video series

Chapter 76

Optimizing Sales Leads

Moving Quickly from Inquiry to Lead to Closure

Drew Stevens
Stevens Consulting Group

A growing concern for many sales and marketing managers is optimization of sales leads. Each year selling professionals get a plethora of business development leads, but unfortunately unearth less than 47 percent. Worse, over 50 percent remain dormant. Managers postulate, but to no avail. The numbers barely move. In recent research for this article, several clients utilized the Internet for sales leads, but with less than 5 percent reaching closure. To develop and optimize a productive lead-generation program, sales and marketing leaders must formulate a business-to-business (B2B) strategic plan. The following information is meant to initiate dialogue.

■ CONTENT IS KING

Since the dawn of the Internet, information has proliferated in our society. Current clients can obtain more information about your organization than you realize. Press releases, news stories, earnings, even advertisements all provide data for an analysis of the organization. When a lead finally does reach a selling professional, research illustrates that 87 percent of selling professionals merely repeat known content.

Solution: Sales and marketing must develop strategic client questions that provide client value. Rather than rehash features and claims, new leads are taken through an analysis to better understand needs. An exemplar might provide competitive product samples or packaging. Competitive firms can then provide alternative means and find gaps.

■ MOM ALWAYS LIKED YOU BEST

Clients today report to all representatives that they lack time and interest. In fact, according to CSO Insights, the quality of leads is positively impacting the conversion rate of leads to first calls. Marketing and sales must collaborate on lead-completion strategies. These are plans that assist in collecting a myriad of data for lead movement through the pipeline. Marketing instructors always discuss the "-phics" when discussing the Four Ps, and so must sales.

To help lead movement, organizational strategies must be developed to understand demographic, geographic, psychographic, and behavioral issues. This tool provides sales representatives with a better initial call to comprehend issues. Similar to an archeologist trying to unearth the past, a selling professional has more data to motivate the lead to a next step.

Solution: Provide sales representatives with enough data to move the lead through the management system. Have marketing work closely with sales to establish the type of content required for your organization. Additionally, clients today require multiple "touch points." Produce value for prospective leads with white papers, analysis, industry trends, market data reports, Environmental Protection Agency (EPA) analysis, and so on. Acquire an e-mail address or physical address to send updates to prospects. Constant contact with leads will help convert them into future sales.

■ TECHNOLOGY FOR TECHNOLOGY'S SAKE

People are becoming overwhelmed by electronic commerce. Even though it is faster and least expensive, it is still intrusive.

Solution: Work with marketing to develop a paper and a paperless campaign. Direct mail is on the rise. B2B lead generation techniques need to follow this trend. Conversion rates must increase and the alternative is to remain in contact with leads in a plethora of ways that capture attention. Personalize pieces for maximum benefit. Sales and marketing might work together to develop a cover letter that discusses previous conversations and outlines plans for future action.

■ ANALYSIS, NOT PARALYSIS

One client recently indicated that over 87 percent of their leads came through the Internet. However, when seeking additional information, we uncovered that fewer than 10 percent of leads closed. There are a number of reasons for this, from questions to demographic data to disinterest in the lead. Some representatives have problems in discerning what is a good lead.

Solution: What is needed is not more leads. Sales and marketing need to work together to discern what constitutes a qualified lead as well as how to execute the lead to the next step. Each B2B process is different; ensure success by truly understanding how your organizational process works from beginning to end. Do not overanalyze; instead, try different scenarios to identify what works best.

■ NO PAIN, NO GAIN

Face it: Selling professionals can get quite frivolous with leads and inquiries in the system. Blame is easily cast on marketing for poor execution and comprehension. Yet this is a team effort. One does not blame the running back for poor running if the line does not block. Inquiry management is a team effort.

Solution: Provide incentives for both sales and marketing professionals. Additionally, performance reviews for selling professionals must include the quality of inquiry management information. Exemplars provide full disclosure of prospective clients, not simply names and addresses. Key individuals consistently provide information used by marketing that is critically analyzed and used to optimize the lead equation.

Present B2B companies use services such as Six Sigma, Balanced Scorecard, and a cadre of services to develop, qualify, and optimize the business. For many years a division existed between the worlds of sales and marketing, encouraging territorial behavior. In a shifting global economy, a competitive industrial environment, and the knowledge explosion, it does take a village to raise a lead and close a lead. Rather than count the leads, we need to move them. New methods need to be employed to keep the pipeline flowing.

To book Dr. Drew for a workshop or keynote address or to obtain his Secrets of Ultimate Business Success, e-mail him today at www .drewstevensconsulting.com/contact.

Name: Drew Stevens

Company: Stevens Consulting Group

Web Site: www.stevensconsultinggroup.com

Biography: Drew Stevens, PhD, is a leading expert in sales and sales skills. He is the author of the best seller *Split Second Selling* and the upcoming *Ultimate Business Bible: 12 Strategies for Ultimate Success*. Dr. Drew has over 25 years of experience in helping entrepreneurs and selling professionals experience higher efficiency and effectiveness.

He has been featured in *Selling Power*, the *Chicago Tribune*, *Entrepreneur* magazine, and the *New York Times*. Drew provides over 50 workshops and keynotes annually. He is an adjunct instructor in marketing and entrepreneurial studies at several graduate universities and is the founder of the Sales Leadership Institute at St. Louis University.

Selling Philosophy: Sales skills, sales techniques, sales training, sales expertise, strategic selling

Target Industries: Real estate, legal, physician practices, entrepreneurial

Best Sellers: *Split Second Selling*, *Split Second Customer Service*, Pump Up Your Productivity, Sales Acceleration Skill-Based Workshops, and *Ultimate Business Bible*

Sales Tip One: Great sellers forget about commissions and revenue and focus all their attention and energy on providing great customer service. Sellers realize that good service leads to referrals, additional sales, and customers for life. Being service-savvy provides sales not only for today but also for tomorrow in both good and bad times.

Sales Tip Two: Review your organization's mission, vision, and value statement. Create a list of benefits that align your products and services with them. Create statements to prepare for client presentations that help those statements focus on your objective and value.

Sales Tip Three: Write down five adjectives that you hear customers state about you. Develop a sentence that depicts the value you provide to your clients.

Book One: *Split Second Selling*

Book Two: *Split Second Customer Service*

Book Three: *Ultimate Business Bible*

Product One: Grand Slam Customer Service

Product Two: Negotiation Secrets

Chapter 77

Unmanaged, Telling Tensions Cost You Sales

Conrad Elnes
STI International

Telling Tension develops whenever someone feels a strong emotion about a situation: The stronger the emotion, the more compelling the desire to express it. This need to talk is like walking with a sharp rock in your shoe. It's hard to think of anything else until you get rid of it!

When either you or a buyer feels high Telling Tension, a condition called LO/LO sets in; LO/LO stands for Lock On/Lock Out. Since the human mind cannot think two thoughts simultaneously, it "Locks On" to its own thought and "Locks Out" other ideas. In highly emotional situations, the "Lock Out" can be complete, thus preventing you and the buyer from listening to one another.

■ TELLING TENSION: THE COMPELLING NEED TO TALK

Those who become skilled at managing Telling Tension create many allies who help them increase their sales. Those who don't learn to manage it suffer the penalty of lost opportunities.

Your skill at managing Telling Tension will help both you and your buyers be more receptive. "Managing" begins with bridling your own Telling Tension and listening as buyers talk about a concern that is important to them. As they express their concerns, their Telling Tension diminishes rapidly, leaving them with open minds and open ears. Then it's your turn to talk.

➤ Causes of Telling Tension

Three causes of Telling Tension are encountered frequently during sales and service interviews:

1. Strong emotions such as anger, defensiveness, enthusiasm, and helpfulness

2. Questions

3. Silence

When a buyer says something with which you disagree, or if a statement makes you angry, you may feel compelled to cut him or her off in order to express your own feelings. Anger can reduce receptivity to zero.

Another cause of Telling Tension is the defensiveness you may feel when you encounter objections or complaints. Since you may be reluctant to let an objection go unchallenged, you're likely to try to "overcome" it by talking faster and louder. Those who express objections usually have high Telling Tension of their own and are not receptive to what you say while trying to "overcome" their concern. As both parties feel a need to talk, they Lock On to their own point of view and Lock Out new information from the other, and the issue remains unresolved.

Their enthusiasm for their products, a temporarily discounted price, or a new feature may cause salespeople to launch a pitch with little regard for the buyers' needs. Having failed to learn the needs, they have little idea which product or service features or benefits to stress. Unless they're lucky and quickly touch on an area of interest, buyers are likely to become bored and turn them off. If the seller does happen to present something of interest, perhaps solving a major problem, enthusiasm will quickly drive up the buyer's Telling Tension. The seller's continuing desire to talk will conflict with the buyer's, and this clash of Telling Tensions will have a chilling effect on the relationship.

Managing your own Telling Tension in such a situation can yield great rewards.

As you become more experienced and knowledgeable, it's increasingly likely that your desire to be helpful as quickly as possible will lead you to talk about an obvious solution without completing a thorough diagnosis. Since the buyer talked very little, he or she may be left with unreleased Telling Tension, causing LO/LO.

Another cause of Telling Tension, questions, is doubly dangerous. When a buyer asks a question, it is nearly impossible not to answer quickly. The question drives up your Telling Tension and you may begin talking without considering the implication behind the question. However, it is important to remember that nearly 70 percent of buyer questions have a hidden agenda; that is, they are loaded questions, and "correct" information may not be the "right" answer from the buyer's point of view. Questions containing a negative contraction, such as can't or don't, are nearly always motivated by a hidden agenda. Also, remember that the questions you ask buyers drive up their Telling Tension, allowing them to describe their needs and wants.

Finally, any extended period of silence is certain to drive up your desire to talk. For instance, when you ask a closing question and the buyer remains silent while considering whether or not to agree, you may feel compelled to say something within a few seconds. If you talk to break the silence, you are likely to lose the sale.

➤ Symptoms of Telling Tension

Let's examine some obvious symptoms that can guide you in managing high Telling Tension in others and yourself. The most obvious symptom is talking. Many prospects and a high percentage of salespeople are viewed by others as being primarily interested in talking. Interestingly, studies show that more than 50 percent of the skills associated with high-performance salespeople are actually related to their ability and desire to listen and ask questions rather than talk.

As noted earlier, spoken objections and complaints are two signals that a potential buyer may feel high Telling Tension. Also, anyone who interrupts and those who express a strong bias, such as "I'd never buy a foreign-made car," are likely to feel a strong desire to express the rest of their opinion.

In addition to these obvious signals, prospects may use more subtle means. For example, while you are talking, prospects may clear their throat as they prepare to talk. Also, those who shift in their chair from leaning back to leaning forward may be signaling that they're preparing to talk. Finally, if a buyer's eyes seem to glaze over and he or she becomes unresponsive, you may have said something to which he or she wishes to reply. When any of these occur, quickly wind up what you are saying and ask a question that invites them to speak.

■ CONCLUSION

You add great value and create many allies when you're willing to listen to buyers as they express themselves. The four steps required to manage Telling Tension are:

1. Be aware of the causes and symptoms, so you are prepared to recognize it.

2. Stop talking as soon as possible after you receive the buyer's signals. This may be difficult because of your own need to talk.

3. Listen responsively and fully to the buyer.

4. Avoid presenting information for longer than two minutes without asking the buyer a question. If the buyer is enthusiastic, he or she will want to talk about it. If what you've said hasn't caused enthusiasm, it is likely that he or she is bored. Your question will help re-involve the buyer in the presentation.

Since buyers can coach you only when they talk and you listen, use questions to increase their Telling Tension while you focus on their answers.

Name: Conrad Elnes

Company: STI International

Web Site: www.salesinstitute.com

Biography: Conrad Elnes is Chairman of STI International, an author and speaker, and a member of Who's Who of Sales Thought Leaders. Conrad's analysis of the research being performed to learn the secrets of highly successful salespeople inspired his book, *Inside Secrets of Outstanding Salespeople*.

After Conrad earned his master of arts in training (M.A.T.) degree from Washington State University, he authored STI's QUAD-TRAK Consultative Selling Program, Major Account Selling Strategies, PHONE-TRAK Tele-Prospecting Program, and Advanced Listening Skills Program. His Customer Satisfaction PLUS program is employed by many leading companies. His programs have established STI as a national leader in the contemporary training scene.

Selling Philosophy: Research validated, consultative sales skills

Target Industries: Manufacturing and distribution companies

Best Sellers: QUAD-TRAK Consultative Sales Program, Customer Satisfaction PLUS, Essential Skills for Creating Allies

Sales Tip One: Customer objections and complaints are a form of coaching for you. "Resolve" them rather than "overcome" or "handle" them.

Sales Tip Two: Whenever you are confronted with buyer resistance, transition back to Fact Finding to learn "the rest of the story." (Apologies to Paul Harvey.)

Sales Tip Three: Every ally you create is a force multiplier in your effort to make the sale. Creating Allies Is Job #1.

Book One: *Inside Secrets of Outstanding Salespeople* (Prentice-Hall)

Product One: QUAD-TRAK Consultative Sales for Insurance (DVD)

Product Two: 12 Secrets for Closing Sales (CD)

Product Three: Resolve Objections, Close More Sales (CD)

Twelve Things Your Buyers Want Other Than Lowest Price[1]

Bill Brooks
The Books Group

There's an old quotation that says, "The bitterness of poor quality remains long after the sweetness of low price is forgotten."

It's still around because it's unquestionably true! Of course your prospects would like a low price. But 9 times out of 10, they know that "low price" can often translate into "poor quality." In fact, your prospects value many things other than a low price . . . and some of these other things can be just as persuasive as a low price in getting them to buy from you, whether you sell products to individual end users or services to major corporations.

There are countless other reasons people buy, but let's take a look at 12 of the most basic things that will encourage your prospects to buy from you, even if your price is higher than your competitors'.

1. An Easy, "No-Brainer" Relationship. When it's easy to do business with you, your customer's life is easier. If you can provide your prospects and customers with a relationship in which they get what they want, when they need it, on time and in good shape, you'll most likely find it easier to sell to them at full price, rate, or fee.

2. Reliability and Dependability. It's simple. People must know that they can rely on you. It is a foolish (and rare) customer who will drop a known provider to save a few pennies buying from an unknown source. If

---

[1]Excerpted from *How to Sell at Margins Higher Than Your Competitors*, by Dr. Lawrence L. Steinmetz and William T. Brooks.

you have a solid history of reliability and dependability, you are in the position to remind your customers that they can rely on you when they are considering buying what you sell from one of your competitors.

3. Predictability. Customers not only like reliability, they like predictability. Most people who study behavior know this—what someone has done in the past likely indicates what they'll do in the future. So if all of your actions and behaviors have been consistently professional and your sales are always handled effectively and efficiently, your customers will be able to say you are "predictable" based on your past relationship and reputation.

4. Reaction to Their Needs. "You don't understand: Our business is different from those other guys" is a very common refrain I hear from our prospects. Most people like to think of themselves as being a little bit different from everyone else; and, to some degree, they are right. If you can find ways to acknowledge your customer's uniqueness, and be flexible and responsive to their specialized needs, you will almost always earn a purchase order, even if your price is higher than your competitor's.

5. Short Delivery Times. Even those prospects and customers who do not say they need "just-in-time" delivery still like short delivery times; that is true no matter what the product or service is. Everybody wants it yesterday, and if you can provide it sooner than your competitor, you can charge a higher price for it. In fact, this is one of the *best* ways to sell at premium prices (or rates or fees).

6. Breadth and Depth in Quality. You stand a much better chance of building a valuable, long-term relationship with your customers if you do everything you can to provide not only a quality product or service, but also ensure that your customers achieve maximum utilization of the product or service they're buying from you. Your customers are hoping to use your product or service to achieve a goal. So they want to know that you have depth in your understanding of the things they're trying to accomplish—and are not just out to sell them more.

7. Knowledge, Competence, and Follow-Up. We all like to know that we're in good hands. Salespeople who are serious about following up on orders, making sure that everything's right, are thorough in processing and expediting requests and being available after the sale is made find that these activities give them an opportunity to sell at a premium price . . . and the opportunity to make more sales to their existing accounts.

8. Your Willingness to "Go to Bat" for the Customer When Problems Arise. All customers like to have somebody on their side. Your customers will appreciate—and likely pay a premium price for—genuine help if and when any kind of problem arises. Even though your employer is the one who pays your commission or salary, your customers should be able to expect you to advocate for them with your employer, if necessary. You can win customers for life when you are willing to help them in crisis situations.

9. Salespeople Who Know Their Product Line. Your customers expect you to know a lot about what you're selling. If you do, they will believe that you can assist them in making the best choice in buying what it is that they want or expect to buy from you. If you don't know your own product line, you're not going to be very convincing to a customer as to why he or she should buy from you—particularly at a premium price, rate, or fee.

10. Ease of Interpretation of Your Price Lists and/or Quotes. If you can point out to your prospect exactly what the price is in simple, understandable terms, you're more apt to get the order. It's this simple: A confused prospect buys nothing! If prospects have to sort through a lot of paperwork or ask you a million questions to ascertain the real (or total) price, they're apt to give their business to a competitor who gives them a simple, quick, clean, and easy-to-understand quotation.

11. Early Notice of Shipment or Product Problems. If you ever see that shipping or product problems are coming up, let your customers know about them as far in advance as possible, and let them know up front how you are going to help them get through the difficulty. If there's nothing you can do to help them, you've got to give your customers the opportunity to find some other source of the product or materials so that your delay doesn't cause *them* a delay. Of course, it's hard to maintain customers when you force them to look for other sources . . . but it's probably impossible to retain them when you give them too many nasty surprises.

12. Advance Warning of Discontinuance of Items. Again, people don't like surprises. If you are going to discontinue a product or service that your customer has been using, they'd like to know in ample time to cover their own self-interests relative to the unavailability of that product or service. Can they phase it out of their inventory? Can they avoid building an expensive marketing campaign around a product that isn't going to be available for them to resell? Can they avoid the expense of designing your software into their offering and then discovering that it's no longer available for them to use in making their system work? How about a financial product that is factored into a business's benefit package and is then suddenly taken off the market?

The bottom line? Your prospects are realistic enough—and smart enough—to know that they are, in the final analysis, going to get what they pay for. They know that if they buy from your lower-priced competitor, they will probably be setting themselves up for problems, some of which ultimately will be intolerable. So you should never compete on low price. Instead, you must concentrate all of your efforts on providing your customers with what they want and need—when they want it—and on charging them a premium price for it.

Name: Jeb Brooks

Company: The Brooks Group

Web Site: www.brooksgroup.com

Biography: Author of 19 books, hundreds of audio programs, and countless articles, Bill Brooks has personally trained more than one million salespeople worldwide. Prior to his death in 2007, he appeared on television and radio shows nationwide and was featured in the *Wall Street Journal*, the *Los Angeles Times*, *USA Today*, the *New York Times*, and *Investors Business Daily*.

Bill founded The Brooks Group, which helps organizations anticipate and manage their critical business development and strategic growth challenges. The firm was named the most outstanding sales consulting organization in the world by *Selling Power* magazine and is one of the world's top 20 sales methodology training companies.

Selling Philosophy: Application-based selling

Target Industries: Insurance/financial services, industrial distribution, medical/health care, technology, and high-level sales

Best Sellers: *Sales Techniques*, *The New Science of Selling and Persuasion*, *Perfect Phrases for the Sales Call*, TriMetrix Assessments, IMPACT Selling Program, Sales Management Symposium

Sales Tip One: The secret to selling is rarely in the selling. Rather, it is about accurate prospecting, proper positioning, and solid precall planning.

Sales Tip Two: Forget about needs-based selling because people don't always buy what they need. Instead, they always buy what they want.

Sales Tip Three: Strong brands can create weak salespeople. So don't rely on your brand—no matter how strong it may be—to carry the sale.

Book One: *Sales Techniques*

Book Two: *The New Science of Selling and Persuasion*

Book Three: *Perfect Phrases for the Sales Call*

Product One: Sales Techniques Book (CD)

Product Two: The New Science of Selling and Persuasion Book (CD)

Product Three: Playing Bigger Than You Are: How to Sell Big Accounts Even If You're David in a World of Goliaths (audio)

Chapter 79

No Thanks, I'm Just Looking!

Professional Retail Sales Techniques for Turning Shoppers into Buyers

Harry J. Friedman
The Friedman Group

■ THE PRIMARY GOAL OF OPENING THE SALE IS TO GET PAST RESISTANCE

What happens when a salesperson greets a customer in a retail store? Do you think you can predict the response in 90 percent of all these contacts? You bet you can: It's "No thanks, I'm just looking." It's amazing how many salespeople hear this and never seem to figure out how to get beyond that reply. I'm not talking about how to handle it once you have heard it—I mean how to avoid getting that response to begin with. I was in a store recently where the salesperson asked, "Are you looking for anything in particular, or are you just looking?" Talk about sleeping on the job! I had the irresistible desire to smack him and tell him to wake up!

■ ESTABLISH A PERSON-TO-PERSON RELATIONSHIP RATHER THAN A SALESPERSON-TO-CUSTOMER RELATIONSHIP

A person-to-person relationship is the opposite of what I refer to as "clerking." Think of the last time you were in a store. Can you remember the kind of relationship you had with the salesperson? Or how about doing this exercise: Write down the stores and the salespeople you can name that you go back to time and time again because of the personal relationship and the terrific service.

This entire process begins in the opening of the sale. Take the few extra seconds in the beginning and you will have a customer who not only enjoys the process, but might spend a lot more money.

■ OPENING LINES

If you greet a customer with a business line, then you will get a reactive and resistant response such as "I'm just looking," or something similar. What is even more amazing is that most of the time customers don't even know they are saying it. It's a spontaneous reaction—but customers also know that it works and sends salespeople away. I'm sure you would agree it would be nice if we could go up to customers and be helpful and say, "What can I do for you?" or "How can I be of assistance?" Well, folks, here's the truth. It does work . . . with 3 out of 10 customers who know what they want, or with people who go to McDonald's. But not if you want to sell to the majority of the people you talk to in a retail store, where people really don't need what you have. Therefore, rule number one in creating an opening dialogue would be: Opening lines must have nothing to do with business.

■ OPENING LINES MUST HAVE NOTHING TO DO WITH BUSINESS

You really shouldn't go any further in this chapter until you understand that your opening salutation cannot be about business. It's as if you have a neon sign over your head that reads, "Don't trust me, I'm a salesperson." If your opening cannot be business-related to be effective, then it holds true that the most used and written-about technique, the "merchandise approach," would also be ineffective.

■ THE MERCHANDISE APPROACH IS INEFFECTIVE AND RUDE

My brother calls me on the phone and tells me that he has just purchased a $500 tennis racquet. I think, "That's reasonable—for someone who is nuts!" I don't like tennis, and I find what he is telling me a little difficult to understand, particularly since he isn't that great a tennis player. I am, however, a scuba diver, and I need a new mask and snorkel. As I enter the sporting goods store all excited about getting a new mask, what is on display in the front of the store?

You've got it—tennis racquets. I stop and pick up . . . guess which one? You've got it again. The $500 racquet, just like the one my brother purchased. As I'm looking to see if it has a motor or some built-in parts to help his game, out of nowhere a salesperson comes over and says, "It just came in, isn't it a beauty? I'm sure that no matter how well you play the game now, it will help improve your game." Any guesses about what I'm thinking? "Get off my back, you idiot. I don't want a racquet."

A very talented salesperson in Florida told me about the first time she was on the selling floor. She had just been promoted to the floor from a clerical job. She eyed a customer coming in and started the long journey of making her first presentation. The customer had his head buried in a ring showcase in the front of the store. She walked over and started the conversation by saying, "I see that you are interested in our beautiful rings." His simple reply? "No, I'm the carpenter and I was told the case needed repair."

First off, how could you possibly determine what customers want or why they have come in by what catches their eye, or where they just happen to stop? Second, it's rude to have someone come into your store, where you spend a major portion of your life, and not even say "Hello" to them before you start your presentation. The merchandise approach is lazy and can ruin more relationships than it helps.

However, if you are inclined to sell only 2 or 3 out of the 10 people who come in, use it because there will always be 2 or 3 who know what they want and won't let even you deter them—no matter how hard you try and mess things up.

■ OPENING LINES SHOULD BE QUESTIONS TO ENCOURAGE CONVERSATION

Person-to-person conversations are the key ingredient in the process of breaking down resistance. Short and quick statements do not get you anywhere. Have some fun. Make your questions interesting. But don't forget to make your initial greeting a question.

It must have been 15 years or so ago that a lady came into the store with a child in a stroller. You might think I would have said, "What a beautiful baby!" Sound good? No way. It's not a question and doesn't get you past the resistance that may be there. This is what I did say. "That's a beautiful little baby. Where did you get it?" Now I know you might be laughing, but the truth is that I used the line then and have been using it ever since. It has never, ever failed to get a terrific response.

Name: Harry J. Friedman

Company: The Friedman Group

Web Site: www.thefriedmangroup.com

Biography: Harry J. Friedman, founder and CEO of The Friedman Group, is an internationally acclaimed consultant, trainer, speaker, and author, specializing in retail sales and management. As retail's most sought-after consultant, his techniques on High Performance Retailing have been used by over 500,000 retailers worldwide.

His book *No Thanks, I'm Just Looking!* is a retail best seller.

Mr. Friedman has also developed retail's most heavily attended store management seminars and Project Gold Star, a series of monthly meetings for retail owners and executives focused on developing a high-performance, sales-driven retail organization, and maximizing the performance of staff and stores.

Selling Philosophy: Creating an unforgettable "shopping experience" that generates customer loyalty and referrals

Target Industries: Retail, manufacturers, trade associations

Best Sellers: Public and private retail management seminars; on-site retail consulting and training; Project Gold Star: High Performance Retailing program; customized retail training programs; retail sales, customer service, and management training books, manuals, DVDs, CDs; public speakers; manufacturer's dealer training on sales, product knowledge, and management

Sales Tip One: Passion in your heart and a smile on your face go a long way in building a sales career.

Sales Tip Two: If your conversion rate is less than 50 percent, it's time to work on "Why?"

Sales Tip Three: Each month your number of repeat customers has to increase in order to ensure long-term success.

Book One: *No Thanks, I'm Just Looking!*

Book Two: *The Retailer's Complete Book of Selling Games and Contests*

Book Three: *The Retail Policies Manual*

Product One: Gold Star Selling, the world's #1 retail sales training course (DVD)

Product Two: Retail Management Training Camp, live seminar recording (CD)

Product Three: Multiple Store Supervision Camp, live seminar recording (CD)

Chapter 80

The Keys to Successful Pipeline Management

Donal Daly
The TAS Group

During consultations, some common challenges in pipeline management have surfaced, in particular whether to focus on pipeline volume or pipeline velocity. Also, we've been asked frequently to explain the "secret sauce" that can identify pipeline risks or potential breakdown. Here are four of the best practices lessons that we've shared with our customers.

■ BEST PRACTICE #1: MAP THE PIPELINE STRUCTURE TO A SALES PROCESS

It is often difficult to decide how many stages you should have in your sales pipeline. We have seen different companies with their pipelines segmented into anything between 3 and 12 stages (we recommend no more than 5 or 6) in the pipeline. Every week, or month, sales managers then "manage" the sales force by working through each individual's sales pipeline to determine how many opportunities are at each stage, and what probability to apply to each opportunity. More often than not, this is a fruitless exercise for two main reasons.

First, subjectivity plays a large part. In most cases, the interpretation of how to categorize the opportunity is left to the salesperson's discretion. The buying cycle is often ignored, and there is usually little linkage between the key qualification questions used, and the stage of the process. One of the benefits of a standardized sales process is that everyone in the company involved in the sale adopts a common language.

Second, it is futile to determine the value of a pipeline by multiplying the value of each opportunity by the probability of it closing. There is no prize for second or third place in selling. You either win the deal or you lose. Having 10 opportunities at 10 percent probability mathematically may be the equivalent of one full opportunity—but it is not the same as having a signed contract. We are constantly amazed at how seasoned sales managers continue to value their pipelines in this manner. Having a standardized sales process, and a fully documented and formally defined pipeline, with well-understood rules, results in everyone having the same, realistic view of the forecast.

You should design your sales process to incorporate stages in the pipeline that reflect the customer's buying cycle. If you link the selling cycle to the customer's buying cycle, the selling actions that you have to plan become self-apparent. You understand the concerns of the buyer at each stage of the buying cycle, and your pipeline management becomes a summary sales action plan. In addition, you can now link and layer the qualification process to the overall sales process to help determine which qualification questions need to be answered at each stage in the process.

■ BEST PRACTICE #2: KEEP THE FUNNEL FULL

Sometimes you're going to have to generate your own leads. Getting appropriately targeted customers into the top of your sales funnel is the source of your raw material. Without that raw material, you can't build a pipeline. When there are gaps in your pipeline, pressure builds on the few opportunities you have. You're tempted to try to progress a specific deal too aggressively. Your state of anxiety over this quarter's revenue is heightened by the fact that you are looking into a void for next quarter. It may be the stated role of the marketing department to deliver qualified leads to the sales team, and you might be one of the fortunate few who is adequately served in this manner, but if you don't recognize the need to look constantly for new opportunities yourself, you lose control over your destiny.

The likelihood of finding a good opportunity is dependent on the type of activity you undertake. If you've got your act together, you have a broad network of contacts who are potential customers. Your existing customers can provide you with further business within their company, and referrals to their counterparts in similar companies. Strong relationships with industry consultants and analysts are a good source of recommendations for new business opportunities.

Your own market assessment and development activities will always provide the best quality of sales leads, but be sure that the folks in marketing aren't working in a vacuum. Help them understand what's exciting the customers. Together, you can craft effective seminar programs, social media campaigns, e-marketing, or other campaigns for your territory. Marketing people often bemoan the fact that they generate leads and the sales team ignores them. Get them on your side by telling them what you need, and then by showing them how you are responding to the good work that they do.

■ BEST PRACTICE #3: ROCKS AND STONES AND PEBBLES

If you want to fill a barrel with rocks and maximize the capacity of the barrel, you have to fill the gaps between the rocks with stones or pebbles. Have you ever been in the situation where you're dependent on that *one big deal*? Our customers say that highlighting risks in the funnel mix—by identifying when there is an imbalance in deal sizes—is one of the things that delivers the most value to them.

Experienced sales professionals understand that relying on a small number of big deals is risky: big deals inevitably take longer to close than originally envisioned. You need to be working on a mix of large deals and smaller opportunities. While waiting for the big deal, no one is making any money and desperation levels increase if there isn't a backup plan. Your negotiation position weakens, and that major opportunity turns into a minor profit deal. Rocks and stones and pebbles make for a full barrel.

■ BEST PRACTICE #4: KNOW HOW MUCH YOU NEED IN THE FUNNEL

There are four factors that determine the health of a sales pipeline:

➤ Integrity of data

➤ Deal value

➤ Number of deals

➤ Balance across pipeline stages

Your pipeline must be continually updated to reflect progress. Everyone must understand the language being used, and the salesperson must constrain their normal unbridled optimism and not allow themselves to overstate the potential value or closure probability of a deal. Every person entering or viewing the data must have a common understanding of the rules being applied to determine where an opportunity sits.

■ SUMMARY

Pipeline management is complex, but if you adhere to the guiding principles above, you'll do better than most in building and managing your pipeline. Also, contemplate how you can use your CRM system and the plethora of Sale 2.0 tools available in the marketplace to help you automate your pipeline management and analytics to ensure that you not only start off on the right path, but stay on it.

Name: Donal Daly

Company: The TAS Group

Web Site: www.thetasgroup.com

Biography: The TAS Group helps companies achieve predictable, profitable, and consistent revenue growth through the combination of sales methodology, sales process, and enterprise-class technology. The TAS Group has helped over 400,000 sales professionals succeed and serves companies in all major global economies with native language speaking, culturally attuned, sales effectiveness experts. The TAS Group solutions are available in up to 14 languages. The TAS Group integrates proven sales methodologies with Dealmaker, the most advanced technology platform for sales effectiveness, and is the only sales effectiveness company with a continuous multi-million-dollar investment in our own dedicated sales effectiveness methodology and technology R&D center.

Selling Philosophy: The TAS Group enhances sales effectiveness for companies involved in longer, complex sales

Target Industries: Technology, services

Best Sellers: Target Account Selling (TAS), TAS Select Live!, Dealmaker, Enterprise Selling Process (ESP), Channel and Alliance Management Process (CHAMP), Create & Win (C&W)

Sales Tip One: Continually assess your competitive position in any sale you are involved in.

Sales Tip Two: Know your customer and the customer's business, and understand what unique business value your product or solution represents to them. It's their perception that counts.

Sales Tip Three: It's a buying process, not a selling process; always understand your client's need to buy.

Book One: *The Select Selling Sales Field Book*

Chapter 81

Superior Sales Management

Brian Tracy
Brian Tracy International

■ THE PIVOTAL ROLE IN THE SALES TEAM

You are a sales manager. Your job is the pivotal skill in the sales organization. What you do and how well you do it has more of an impact on sales results than any other factor.

Of all your responsibilities, your ability to get the very most out of the salespeople you manage is the area where you can make the greatest contribution to your company. Every skill or behavior that you learn and practice that motivates your sales team will increase and improve sales activity, and boost sales volume.

According to Columbia University, the average salesperson works only 20 percent of the time, about one-and-a-half hours per day. The rest of his or her time is spent preparing for sales work, warming up or gearing down, coming in late or leaving early, drinking coffee or eating lunch, taking care of personal business, chatting with coworkers, and surfing the Internet.

When is a salesperson actually working? Only when he or she is involved in the direct process of generating sales. And when is this? It is only when the salesperson is face to face or ear to ear with a prospect, defined as "someone who can and will buy and pay within a reasonable period of time."

All other activities are secondary to those specific actions that are responsible for generating the sales upon which your company depends. Your job is to keep your salespeople focused on doing these things more and more often all day long.

The three most important activities of the sales professional are prospecting, presenting, and closing sales. And salespeople do this only 20 percent of the time.

In my seminars, I teach the "Minutes Principle" of sales success. It says simply that "If you are making all the sales that you are making today with the number of minutes that you are spending face to face with prospects today, if you double that number of minutes, you must double your level of sales, holding all other factors constant."

Salespeople are always astonished when they double their sales by doubling the number of minutes they spend in direct contact with customer.

■ THE KEY TO SALES SUCCESS

Many thousands of salespeople have been interviewed over the years. These studies show that the number-one reason that a salesperson takes a job is because of the sales manager. The number-one reason that the salesperson stays at that particular job is because of the sales manager. The number-one reason that salespeople become demotivated or discouraged and leave the job is because of the sales manager. All other factors are secondary.

In the "Interaction Model of Performance," we teach that it is the point at which the sales manager and the salesperson interact personally on a day-to-day basis that has more of an impact on sales performance than any other factor.

Because you are the boss, everything that you say or do, positive or negative, raises or lowers motivation and sales performance. Nothing is neutral. Everything counts.

You can dramatically improve the energy, enthusiasm, and commitment of your salespeople, and motivate them to spend more time prospecting, presenting, and closing, by practicing the following five simple behaviors regularly and systematically with each member of your sales team.

1. **Communicate clear expectations.** Make sure that each salesperson knows exactly what he is expected to do all day long, day in and day out. The primary demotivator in the rule of work is unclear expectations or fuzzy instructions.

2. **Practice participative management.** Salespeople need to feel that they are involved in the decisions that affect their lives and their incomes. Take the time to sit down with your salespeople, as individuals or in groups, and talk about the market, the customers, the products or services, and the activities necessary to fulfill sales quotas. Ask for their input and listen carefully to them when they speak. Don't interrupt.

3. **Praise them regularly.** Most salespeople have what psychologists call "insecurity of status." This means that, no matter how well they do, they never feel completely secure. If they win the award for the top

salesperson for the month or the year, the very next day they begin to question their ability and doubt their performance.

For this reason, salespeople need a continuous flow of praise and encouragement from their managers. Praise them for small efforts as well as for large results. Continually look for any reason to praise people.

The closest correlation between a sales success and any other factor has to do with the self-esteem of the salesperson. The more he likes himself, the better he will perform, under any conditions. And one of the definitions of self-esteem is "the degree to which a person feels praise-worthy."

When you praise people, you raise their self-esteem, build their self-confidence, improve their self-image, and make them feel like going out and breaking down doors for you.

One additional point: Praise in public, but appraise in private. When you praise a person in front of other people, especially higher-ups or their peers, the praise is multiplied in its impact on the future performance of that person. Always begin every sales meeting with a period of praise for the accomplishments of one or more people in the meeting.

4. **Keep them informed.** Salespeople need to know what is going on in the company and in the market. Hold weekly meetings with your sales team. Prepare an agenda that consists of a list of all your team members. Go around the table and have each person explain what they are doing and how it is going out there. Invite questions and comments.

Each person has a deep need to feel that he is a part of something bigger than himself. By bringing your people together to talk, discuss, and share experiences each week, they realize that they are not alone. They feel more committed and loyal to you and the company. And they become more determined to have something positive to report at the next meeting.

5. **Finally, practice the three Cs of motivation: Concern, Consideration, and Courtesy.** Practice the Golden Rule and treat each person as you would like to be treated if your situations were reversed.

Remember, selling is difficult work. Your salespeople face rejection and disappointment every day. They are continually being bruised, mentally and emotionally. The way that you help them to overcome discouragement and disappointment is by treating them with value and respect. This behavior on your part builds loyalty, commitment, and motivation. It turns average people into top performers.

Name: Brian Tracy

Company: Brian Tracy International

Web Site: www.briantracy.com

Biography: Brian Tracy, president of Brian Tracy International, is the top sales speaker, trainer, and consultant in the world today. He addresses more than 250,000 men and women each year in public and private seminars.

Brian has worked with over 500 companies since he began teaching and training in 1981. He has developed a series of high-impact audio and video sales training programs that have been translated into 16 languages and are used in 23 countries.

Brian has written 24 books and has given more than 1,000 radio and television interviews on the subjects of personal and professional success.

Sales Tip One: Get serious! Make a decision to go all the way to the top of your field. Make a decision today to join the top 10 percent. There is no one and nothing that can hold you back from being the best except yourself.

Sales Tip Two: Identify your limiting skill to sales success. Identify your weakest single skill and make a plan to become absolutely excellent in that area.

Sales Tip Three: Get around the right people. Acquaint yourself with positive, successful people. Associate with men and women who are going somewhere with their lives. And get away from negative, critical, complaining people.

Book One: *Maximum Achievement*

Book Two: *Speak to Win*

Book Three: *Eat That Frog!*

Jump-Starting a Stalled Sales Opportunity

Julie Thomas
ValueSelling Associates

It seems that you have done everything right: Your prospect has clearly explained his business and relevant personal issues; you've connected to those issues with a solution only you can provide; you are working directly with the person who has the authority and ability to make the decision; and you've agreed, in writing, to what you and the prospect will do together to initiate a business relationship. The only thing that you haven't been able to do is get them to sign on the dotted line.

If you are like most salespeople, between 30 and 50 percent of the sales in your pipeline will result in no decision. In a tough market, one of the biggest productivity returns you can reap is to reduce the impact of stalled decisions by identifying them early in the sales cycle; however, in order to jump-start a stalled sale, you must first diagnose the reasons behind it. The problem isn't that the sale stalls out in process, the problem is that often we don't recognize it soon enough and expend the necessary time and resources on these dead-end opportunities.

One of the most common complaints or challenges we hear from our clients has to do with stalled opportunities. The scenario typically goes something like this: A sales cycle is progressing with an individual—all the buying signals are being observed—and then . . . nothing happens! No return phone calls, no return e-mails, and no communication at all!

What do you do?

After reviewing thousands of stalled sales cycles with our clients over the years, we have identified the five most common explanations for a sale in limbo.

1. Lack of Connection to a Critical Business Issue. Unless your solution has increased revenue, time to market, cost management, improved quality, competitive differentiation, or some other looming business issue tied to it, you can expect a stall. Senior executives spend time only on matters that directly impact their business.

There are only three questions a sales rep has to ask to uncover business issues . . . Why? Why? and Why?

➤ Why do you want this solution?

➤ Why are those problems important to solve?

➤ Why would that matter to you or any other executive?

2. Lack of Perceived Value. Most people can only juggle five or six critical issues at a time. We prioritize these issues in order of their "value"—the benefit tied to solving the issue. If value isn't identified, an issue will quickly fall to the bottom of the list. Can your prospect articulate the "value" or impact of addressing their business issue? If your solution, from their perspective, doesn't have enough value to get in their top five or six issues, you are stalled or put on the back burner. Ask the prospect to quantify the impact of resolving the business issue. And better yet, ask them how the solution will impact them personally.

3. Lack of Differentiation. Lack of differentiation will cause the prospect to spend more time evaluating, which translates to a stall. If you are unable to differentiate on capabilities and solving problems, you will be forced to differentiate on price. Please look up the previous article on differentiation for more on this subject.

4. Decision Authority. Decision authority is one of the most common causes of a stalled decision. The buying frenzy of the last decade all but eliminated the need to call on the real decision makers for everyday purchases. Those days are over. In order to avoid a stall caused by lack of authority, you need to ask your prospect key questions such as, "Have you made this type of decision before?" and "When and how?" Triangulate your information by asking these questions to multiple people in the organization in order to find out who really has the decision-making power in the organization.

5. Risk. Selecting a new vendor or a new solution involves risk for your prospect. The prospect's perception of risk can span business impacts, such as lost time or money, or personal ramifications, such as career or reputation. As a prospect gets closer to making a decision, the risk becomes greater in his or her mind. Common tools for alleviating risk include supplying references, trial usage, demonstrating credibility with iron-clad implementation plans, guarantees, and your executive backing.

Once you identify the likely cause of your stall, you can craft a strategy to reenergize the sales cycle by focusing on the missing link or underdeveloped component.

Name: Julie Thomas

Company: ValueSelling Associates

Web Site: www.valueselling.com

Biography: Julie Thomas, president and CEO of ValueSelling Associates, is a public speaker, author, and consultant.

Her experience applying, coaching, and reinforcing the ValueSelling Framework began in 1991 as the foundation of her own personal success. In 1999, she became vice president of Gartner Inc.'s Sales Training for the Americas.

In 2005, Julie was awarded the Entrepreneurial Star Award from Business Women's Network and Microsoft. She speaks at events such as the Selling Power Sales Leadership Conferences and Strategic Account Management Association (SAMA) Annual Conference. In 2006, Julie published her first book, *ValueSelling: Driving Up Sales One Conversation at a Time.*

Selling Philosophy: People buy from people; the key to successful sales, whether you are selling a product or solution, is your ability to connect to the buyer.

Target Industries: Technology, health care devices and high-end services, business-to-business services

Best Sellers: The ValueSelling Framework, the sales methodology preferred by sales executives around the globe. With the ValueSelling Framework, sales teams of all sizes learn the secret to qualifying prospects and turning them into sales successes. Inside and outside sales teams alike will benefit from flexible training, consultation, and a customizable toolset that can be adapted and implemented to drive business performance up.

Sales Tip One: Selling isn't telling: The difference between being perceived as a solution provider or a trusted business consultant lies in how you manage the conversation about those capabilities with your prospect.

Sales Tip Two: Invest the time to profile what your ideal customer looks like. Think about who is most likely to do business with you and why.

Sales Tip Three: The product is in the mind of the buyer—it doesn't matter what you do; it matters what the prospect *thinks* you do.

Book One: *ValueSelling: Driving Up Sales One Conversation at a Time*

Product One: ValueSelling Essentials

Chapter 83

All Salespeople Use Scripts

Wendy Weiss
Weiss Communications

When you are speaking with a prospect, do you use a script? The Queen of Cold Calling says, "yes." Find out why . . .

Many sales professionals claim that they never use scripts and never would. Many take issue with the entire idea of scripting, saying that scripts are "phony," "don't work," "make you sound like a telemarketer," or that "every call is different, so it's impossible to use a script."

The reality is that all salespeople use scripts. Here is why . . .

You probably hear certain questions from your prospects over and over and over and over. If you've been in sales for even a very short time, you probably have fairly standard answers to those questions. If you are more or less repeating the same answers every time you hear particular questions, those answers are your script.

You probably also hear the same objections from prospects over and over again, and probably have developed fairly standard responses to those objections. If you are responding to a particular objection over and over again with more or less the same counterargument, those responses are also lines in your script.

You also probably have a fairly standard way you introduce yourself to new prospects. Sometimes this is called an "elevator speech"—a brief introduction you could make to a prospect in an elevator that would be finished and understood by the time the elevator reaches your floor. If you have been in sales even just a little while, you are most likely repeating, more or less, the same "elevator speech" over and over again to prospects: by another name, this is a script.

You see, it doesn't matter that your consistent responses are not written down or that there are slight variations in the way you deliver them each time. If you are repeating the same language with different prospects or customers over time, then you are using a script.

The question is *not*: Should you use a script? The *real* question is: Does your script work? Does your script work to get you the results that you want? And if it does not, shouldn't you be saying something else?

If you are calling prospects to make appointments, does what you say get you the appointment? If it doesn't, your script doesn't work. If your entire sales process happens over the telephone, does what you say get you the sale? If it doesn't, your script doesn't work.

If you are making prospecting calls to schedule appointments and you are in fact making many appointments, why would you ever want to say anything other than what works? And if your entire sale happens over the telephone and you are in fact closing many sales, why would you ever want to say anything else?

Sales professionals who are extremely successful have scripts that they use regularly and that they have honed over the years. They know what to say and know when and how to say it. Many of these successful professionals do not think of what they are saying as a script, but if you pay attention you will hear them use the same introductions, talking points, and responses over and over again. The really successful salespeople are not winging it.

Bottom line: all sales professionals use scripts; not all sales professionals use good scripts.

Name: Wendy Weiss

Company: Weiss Communications

Web Site: www.wendyweiss.com, www.thequeenscards.com

Biography: Wendy Weiss, "The Queen of Cold Calling," is an author, speaker, sales trainer, and sales coach. She is recognized as one of the leading authorities on lead generation, cold calling, and new business development, and she helps clients speed up their sales cycle, reach more prospects directly, and generate more sales revenue. Her clients include Avon Products, ADP, Sprint, and thousands of entrepreneurs throughout the country.

Ms. Weiss has been featured in the *New York Times*, *BusinessWeek*, *Entrepreneur Magazine*, *Selling Power*, *Sales & Marketing Management*, and various other business and sales publications. She is also a featured author in two recently released books, *Masters of Sales* and *Top Dog Sales Secrets*.

Ms. Weiss is the author of the book *Cold Calling for Women* and the recently released *101 Cold Calling Tips for Building New Business in a Down Economy*. Her latest book is *The Sales Winner's Handbook: Essential Scripts and Strategies to Skyrocket Sales Performance*.

Wendy is also a former ballet dancer who believes that everything she knows in life she learned in ballet class.

Selling Philosophy: Sell with integrity. Follow up, follow up, follow up.

Target Industries: Cold calling, prospecting, lead generation, and new business development, appointment setting

Best Sellers: Seminars: "Prospecting University"

Products: *The Sales Winner's Handbook: Essential Scripts and Strategies to Skyrocket Sales Performance, Cold Calling for Women, 101 Cold Calling Tips for Building New Customers in a Down Economy, The Miracle Appointment-Setting Script, Getting Past the Palace Guard,* Cold Calling College (home study), The Queens Cards, an automated follow-up and referral marketing system, are available at www.thequeenscards.com

Sales Tip One: Make prospecting calls: No one will buy from you if they do not know of you or your company/products/services.

Sales Tip Two: Make a lot of prospecting calls: If you have only one prospect to pursue, that prospect becomes overwhelmingly important. If you have hundreds of leads, no one prospect can make or break you.

Sales Tip Three: Target your market: Out of every one in the entire world who might possibly buy what you are selling, who is most likely to buy? Create your "ideal customer profile."

Book One: *The Sales Winner's Handbook, Essential Scripts and Strategies to Skyrocket Sales Performance*

Book Two: *Cold Calling for Women: Opening Doors and Closing Sales*

Book Three: *101 Cold Calling Tips for Building New Customers in a Down Economy*

Top 10 Reasons Sales Managers Fail and What to Do about It

Jacques Werth
High Probability Selling

Two primary causes of sales managers failing: (1) They don't know how to manage their people and (2) they don't rigorously implement effective selling processes.

Just as an engineering manager needs to be a pretty competent engineer, a sales manager needs to be a pretty competent salesperson. In both cases, their essential responsibility is to manage staff performance for optimum productivity. Understanding basic management principles is crucial.

Most engineering managers know that technology is evolving too quickly for them to keep up at the level of a functioning engineer. However, they do know enough about the latest technology to manage the engineers deploying it.

In contrast to engineers, most sales managers believe that very little has changed in the "Sales Game" since they became a manager. Therefore, they tend to manage their people in the same way that they used to sell. However, the markets for every product and service have changed dramatically in the last 20 years. Information overload, the Internet, increased competition, better informed prospects, brain science, and new sales channels have affected all businesses.

Top salespeople have developed new sales processes to address and exploit these changing market conditions. Here are 10 trends that most sales managers should know about.

1. Most sales managers don't know how to use highly effective tools to recruit and train salespeople that will perform well specifically in their organization. Therefore, they often hire salespeople who are incompatible with their company's culture and lack the appropriate sales aptitudes and behavioral traits for their industry.

Solution: Contract with a service agency that will benchmark you and your best salespeople. Find candidates with similar aptitudes and behavioral traits. Select salespeople most compatible with your management style.

2. Most sales managers don't have a highly effective, uniform sales process for their company's products and services. They advocate "best sales practices" based upon past market conditions and obsolete sales strategies. Therefore, they focus on the wrong metrics, which inevitably are flawed.

Solution: Develop or acquire a simple linear sales process that is customized to your products, services, and markets.

3. Most sales managers don't know how to train, supervise, and track their salespeople's performance to optimize their sales effectiveness.

Solution: Maintain a uniform and consistent process, monitoring and benchmarking all sales activity throughout the sales process.

4. Most sales managers lack skills in target marketing and prospecting. Therefore, their salespeople waste most of their time with prospects who will not buy.

Solution: Set demographic standards for the type of prospects that are most likely to buy. Develop criteria based upon booked business and competitive information.

5. Most sales managers believe that "you can't close if you don't get in front of prospects." Their salespeople go on as many appointments as possible, spending far more time with prospects who *will not buy* than with those who will buy.

Solution: Insist that salespeople find and make appointments *only* with high-probability prospects.

6. Most sales managers believe that salespeople should be able to convince prospects to buy. Therefore, they expect their salespeople to persuade prospects to buy when they are merely "interested." They don't realize that their salespeople cannot convince people to do anything they don't already want to do.

Solution: Abandon the "Persuasion Game": There is no way to consistently win at it. Insist that your salespeople treat prospects with trust and respect. Utilize an effective sales process that eliminates all forms of persuasion and manipulation.

7. Most sales managers don't know how to shorten the sales cycle. Their salespeople rush into appointments and create sales resistance by selling to prospects who are not yet ready to buy. That lengthens the sales cycle and decreases closing rates.

Solution: Insist that salespeople make appointments only with prospects who are ready to buy or specify. Closing rates will increase dramatically.

8. Most sales managers don't understand how the human mind works, and how it accepts or rejects information. Salespeople typically talk up features and benefits in terms of industry jargon.

Solution: Use words that prospects can readily understand. They'll feel motivated to keep listening, they'll absorb and retain more information, and they'll be more actively engaged in the sales process.

9. Most sales managers believe that prospects make logical buying decisions. If that were true, enrolling in logic courses would be the path to success in sales.

Solution: Engage prospects emotionally. Recent studies in brain science have revealed that most important decisions are made in the part of the brain that deals with emotions. Learn how to connect at an intuitive level.

10. Most sales managers don't know how to get salespeople past their fears. Therefore, most of their salespeople stay in their comfort zones and underperform. The cost of this problem is enormous.

Solution: Your sales forces can operate at optimum effectiveness. It is an entirely reachable goal. Almost all salespeople can learn how to get past their fears and avoid slumps or burnout. It just requires specialized coaching.

Name: Jacques Werth

Company: High Probability Selling, Inc.

Web Site: www.highprobsell.com

Biography: Jacques Werth, MBA, is president of High Probability Selling, Inc., an international sales training and consulting firm. He has conducted research into the sales practices of hundreds of the top 1 percent of salespeople in 23 different industries.

Werth has turned around failing companies in various industries.

He discovered that most of that top 1 percent have intuitively developed new methods to create immediate Relationships of Mutual Trust and Respect with almost all prospects. That is one of the features that make the High Probability Selling process unique.

High Probability Selling has trained thousands of people in over 70 industries.

Selling Philosophy: Mutual trust, mutual respect, and mutual commitments

Target Industries: Financial services, high-tech hardware and software, real estate, capital equipment, transportation, and consultants of all types

Best Sellers: Sales training workshops; sales management training and consulting; books, MP3s, and CDs

Sales Tip One: Interested prospects seldom buy. Learn how to find prospects who already want to buy the benefits of your products and services.

Sales Tip Two: Don't waste time building rapport. Learn how to develop deep relationships of mutual trust and respect.

Sales Tip Three: Closing is based on mutual agreements and mutual commitments. Learn how to quickly arrive at 25 mutual commitments in a one-hour sales visit.

Book One: *High Probability Selling* (book or CD)

Product One: Selling beyond Fear (CD)

Product Two: Overcoming Suspicion and Distrust (CD)

Product Three: How to Turn Cold Calling into Warm Calling (CD)

Chapter 85

Become the Duke or Duchess of Dialogue

Three Keys to Successful Dialogue Selling

Floyd Wickman
Floyd Wickman Team

Need more sales? Why not become a Duke or Duchess of Dialogue?

At one point or another, you'll have to deliver a persuasive presentation. You know the one—that face-to-face method of conveying the features of your product to another person or persons to convince them to buy.

So, what can you say to "sell" your prospect? Hang on to your hat—because I propose that it's not really *what* you say, but *how* you say it that makes the sale. How effective you are during your presentation will depend very much on your ability to deliver the three keys of successful dialogue selling.

Anyone who knows me knows that I'm not a big fan of "scripts" alone. I believe that scripts by themselves only work if you hand your prospect their copy of the script and say "Go ahead and study this and I'll be back in a couple of hours for our presentation!" Just kidding, of course! However, with or without scripts you must become effective at presenting your product or service if you want to be successful in sales.

That's where truly mastering the keys of dialogue selling comes into play.

What is dialogue selling? Dialogue selling is the interaction between a salesperson and a prospect that helps cause the prospect to *want* to buy. After all, people want to buy, they just don't want to be *sold*.

Let's dissect the three keys to dialogue selling: Words, Methods, and Delivery

1. The Right Words. Well, of course you need words—right? If a scripted set of words suits you, then by all means use the words. But words can't do the work all by themselves. In fact, one study even showed that sales persuasion is 55 percent voice inflection, 38 percent body language, and only 7 percent the actual words you use. So, choosing those words wisely is extremely important. What's the secret? Consider these four components:

➤ **Use their names.** This personalizes everything you do and helps you to draw people in. After all, everyone loves to hear their name.

➤ **Make your words your own.** I'll give you an example: Early on in my real estate career, listing doctors, attorneys, or professors was difficult because I mistakenly thought I had to come off sounding as if I had some sort of advanced degree. My natural style and educational level caused me to use words like "gonna," "wanna," and "geez." I'm sure it was because I was trying to use words that I was not comfortable with, and sounding phony, that caused them to not want to do business with me! After I realized I just had to be myself, I ended up doing very well in those markets. People know when you're trying to be something you're not, so be yourself. Use the words you are comfortable with.

➤ **Use power words.** What I mean by power words are those kinds of words or phrases that refer back to what your product or service can ultimately do for your client. Lacing your conversation with their names (the ultimate power word) and those words that touch on the thoughts, concerns, expectations, and emotions of your clients helps you keep them engaged and connected to you and your presentation. Let me give you a few examples:

> ➤ I care about your . . .
> ➤ You'll be happy with . . .
> ➤ This is a great return on investment.
> ➤ . . . help you avoid complications.
> ➤ The help you're looking for.
> ➤ Peace of mind.
> ➤ Saves you heartache.
> ➤ Then you can avoid mistakes.
> ➤ . . . protecting your family.

➤ **Use as few words as possible.** You know I've never met a great speaker, communicator, or salesperson that was a "talker." Your skill as a salesperson isn't the ability to recite long narratives or drone on and on. A great rule of thumb I've always taught is *"Never* sell with blah-blah-blah what you can sell with blah." If you're ever in doubt during your presentation, stop and ask your prospect this question: "Well, are you sold or should I tell you more?" You get the picture.

2. Methods of Persuasion. Methodology can be a little tricky. Just remember that you are almost always selling to more than one person, such as spouses or business and/or personal partners. When you understand that opposites attract and that there's also a good chance that one is an "Analytical Al or Ella" and one is an "Emotional Ed or Ellie," then you realize that you have to be able to communicate effectively with both. How?

➤ **Use facts with emotional words.** The analytical person needs to see and hear the facts and numbers, while the emotional person needs to connect to your words. For example, "That should give you both an 18 percent return on your investment and provide you with the peace of mind you're looking for."

➤ **Use visuals.** My motto is: Never tell a prospect something you can show them, because a picture is worth a thousand . . . dollars! Sure, it's worth a thousand "words" to most people, but when it comes to selling, a visual or picture is worth a lot more than that. Using visuals such as brochures, articles, special reports, graphs, newspaper clippings, and so on, with the right corresponding words allows you to communicate with both the visual person who needs to see and the auditory person who needs to hear the details. When you are selling both of these prospects at the same time, your success ratio increases. For example: "Having seen this presentation, you can see how you can get both the 18 percent return on your investment and how it will provide you with the peace of mind you're looking for."

➤ **Use questions often.** Asking questions throughout your presentation is a perfect way to keep the prospect's interest. Both analytical and emotional people need to participate in the process. For example, when you're communicating great facts and figures, and the emotional person is clearly in over his or her head, questions such as "Would that provide peace of mind?" or "Are there any questions?" are great ways to keep them in the conversation. Also, questions are the surest way to test their buying temperature. For example: "Having been shown the facts, can you see how you can get both the 18 percent return on your investment and the peace of mind you're looking for? Would you agree?"

➤ **Create a fear of loss.** Remember always that "fear of loss is a greater motivator than opportunity to gain." If you want someone to *want* something, talk about the benefits of ownership, but if you want them to *act*, and act now, talk about what they will lose if they don't buy, and you'll sell more. Whenever you point out a benefit to someone, bring up the alternative as well. For example: "Having been shown the facts, can you see how you can get both the 18 percent return on your investment and the peace of mind you're looking for? And knowing there are only limited shares available at this time, wouldn't it make sense to take advantage of this now?"

➤ **Break it down into numbers.** Breaking your presentation down by the numbers makes it easier for the emotional person to understand, and makes the process "complete" to the analytical person (for example, refer to the "three-step process" or "six major benefits"). Again, you sell both prospects at once. For example: "Having been shown the four features of this plan, can you see how you can get both the 18 percent return on your investment and the peace of mind you're looking for? Knowing there are only limited shares available at this time, wouldn't it make sense to take advantage of this now?"

3. Showmanship of Delivery. Successful delivery lies in facial expression, body language, and voice inflection. All three need to match the mood of the conversation. In other words, if you're talking about something sad, don't plaster a huge smile on your face. If your topic is serious, ensure that your expression matches that emotion. Always remember to look people directly in the eye. You then demonstrate caring and a genuine interest in them.

Many of the top stars in the entertainment industries got there because of their ability to use their voice and body language to engage the audience. Practice your voice inflection by adding pauses, slowing your pace in some areas, speeding it up in others, or raising and lowering your pitch.

If you really want to see how effective someone is at selling, video them and then play it back *without sound*. You'll see how effective they are just by watching their face and body gestures and their prospect's reaction. It's an eye-opener!

The bottom line is this. *Be* yourself. Believe in your product. Become a Duke or Duchess of Dialogue Selling and *be* successful!

Name: Floyd Wickman

Company: Floyd Wickman Team

Web Site: www.floydwickman.com

Biography: Floyd Wickman can teach anyone how to succeed in real estate regardless of their background.

Floyd Wickman is synonymous with the Sweathogs training program. He has helped more than half a million agents to realize their potential and fulfill their dreams.

Wickman has spoken to over 3,000 audiences, authored six top-selling books, and sold over 1,000,000 audio programs. He was elected as CSP, CPAE, and a Hall of Fame member of the National Speakers Association. The National Association of Realtors and *Realtor Magazine* named Floyd Wickman one of the 25 Most Influential People in Real Estate.

Selling Philosophy: Building a Book of Business Referral Base

Target Industries: Real estate

Best Sellers: S.M.A.R.T. Program, Short Sales Seminars, 101 Greatest Dialogues (DVDs), Letters to Linda, Straight Talk Series (audio CDs)

Sales Tip One: Great results are the sum of *small things*, done well, repeatedly.

Sales Tip Two: It takes no more pain to succeed than it does to fail . . . *choose success*.

Sales Tip Three: We are more apt to do what is *inspected* than what is *expected*.

Book One: *Mentoring*

Chapter 86

Is Your Customer Base at Risk?

Protecting Your Existing Business in Tough Times

Ed Emde
Wilson Learning

In a challenging economic climate, you may be finding that prospective customers are strongly focused on downsizing and cost cutting rather than on expanding their business or acquiring the latest new product features. Companies that may have been in growth mode last year are putting projects on hold, reducing capital budgets, and paying renewed attention to cash management.

In the face of retrenchment, it is increasingly costly and time consuming to develop new business. Now, more than ever, it makes sense to keep your existing customers close and invest in expanding business with companies that are already buying from you. But how long has it been since you took a serious look at the loyalty of your current customers—their loyalty to your sales reps, your solutions, and your company? Have you earned that loyalty by consistently focusing on how to deliver value with each meeting? Have you checked in on how they feel you have serviced their needs? Or have you been taking their business for granted? If you aren't sure of the answers to these questions, your current business may be more at risk than you think. In challenging economic times, your key customers may be far more vulnerable to lower-priced offers and discounting than they were when times were good.

Regardless of how long you have done business together, it is critical to understand and protect your relationship with your best customers—the ones that you count on to meet your goals for a stable stream of revenue and a healthy balance sheet for your company.

What can you do to protect your base from price cutters, and continue to expand your business, even in these hard times?

The first step is to reassess your relationship with each of your major accounts and determine how likely they are to consider changing suppliers in the near future. The second critical step is to develop strategies to shore up your defenses and reduce the risk of losing customers to predatory competitors.

■ WHAT ARE THEY BUYING AND WHY?

To better understand your relationship with your key customers, answer the following true-or-false questions:

1. Our products/services are critical to how the customer does business.	T or F
2. Our products/services are interconnected with the customer's business processes or procedures.	T or F
3. The customer has invested in lasting assets (equipment/products) we provide.	T or F
4. Price has not historically been a primary concern in this relationship.	T or F
5. Execution of delivery, restocking, and other aspects of how we do business are important, but not primary reasons to buy from us.	T or F
6. The customer sees great value in unique benefits we provide, such as consulting, sharing information about our technology direction, access to special services, and so forth.	T or F

If you answered "true" to the above questions about key customers, you are fortunate in having strong relationships with customers who will experience high "switching costs" if they consider changing to another supplier. These are costs incurred when a buyer changes from one vendor to another. Types of switching costs include tangible costs such as dollars, people, equipment, and procedures, as well as less tangible costs like potential business disruption or increased personal risk to the decision maker. Switching costs may also include the loss of "added value" benefits that the company receives from its current supplier.

Customers facing relatively high switching costs are less likely to change suppliers lightly. Still, even they may feel forced to make that choice if they are downsizing or under strong pressure to cut back on capital investments and find lower-cost, long-term solutions.

On the other hand, if you have important customers for whom the answers were "false," you have a business that is potentially at higher immediate risk. If your customers see themselves as buying a commodity that is not highly critical to their business, they probably care most about factors that are not hard to duplicate, such as price, delivery, and product specifications. They find it relatively easy to change suppliers because their switching costs are low. They will experience few business disruptions, and are not concerned about having to make new long-term investments or about losing highly valued benefits that are only available through your company.

■ STRATEGIES FOR PROTECTING YOUR BASE

Regardless of where you feel your current customers are today, you can protect against erosion of your existing relationships, and even expand your share of business. The key is to focus on how you can increase switching costs and reduce the probability of engaging in unprofitable price wars just to keep your current customers.

➤ **Look at how customers use your product or service offering.** If customers view your offering as a "commodity," consider how they buy it, use it, and dispose of it or reorder at the end of the usage cycle. Can you link to the customer's ordering and purchasing procedures? Can you offer innovative solutions for replacing or recycling? These kinds of links can be developed with any customer, whether their current switching costs are higher or lower.

➤ **Make sure you are performing at the highest level to meet customer requirements.** Consider not only whether your customers have invested in dollars, equipment, procedures, and so on, but also what other sources of value you are providing. If they care about delivery, conformity to specifications, and quality, is your company aligned with what they need and want to buy? Make sure your company is performing in all areas to the highest standards. If it is not, identify ways to enhance and improve performance on all critical factors.

➤ **Make sure the customer is aware of your value.** Don't assume the customer understands the extent to which your company is meeting and surpassing their requirements with every interaction or order. Arrange a meeting with customer executives to provide an update on what you are doing to help them meet their business requirements.

➤ **Look for new ways to address the customer's current business issues and concerns.** Ask how you can provide additional value and benefits that will help the customer's business succeed. Consider the expertise of your sales representatives. Since they are the first line of customer contact, can they serve as genuine business partners in solving problems and advancing the customer's goals? Developing innovative approaches that impact business results will differentiate you and your product or service, and will create unexpected value to the customer's organization. Perhaps your company can offer financial arrangements that will provide a solution to a cash-flow problem. You might be able to improve how you are delivering products or services to help your customers gain competitive advantage in their own markets.

Consider this: Most sales representatives spend far more time researching and preparing for calls with new customers than they do on preparing for calls with existing customers. This is because they believe they "know their customers" and that they have already won their loyalty. In fact, rapidly changing conditions are affecting your existing base just as strongly as they are affecting prospective customers. Maintaining a keen awareness of your current customers' issues and concerns and taking steps to strengthen your relationships can make the difference between falling behind and continuing to thrive, even in the current hard times.

Name: Ed Emde

Company: Wilson Learning

Web Site: www.wilsonlearning-americas.com

Biography: As a leader in sales force development, Wilson Learning has been helping Global 2000 clients for more than 45 years to advance their sales capabilities and competitiveness. Wilson Learning offers a comprehensive approach to sales force competitiveness that includes assessing the organization's readiness, ensuring developmental efforts are aligned with strategy, and creating an environment that supports high performance. The research-based programs, innovative custom solutions, and the use of technology to enhance, reinforce, and sustain learning experiences assist client organizations to improve the performance of their sales force to achieve sales and revenue goals.

Selling Philosophy: Consultative and strategic selling, and sales management and leadership

Target Industries: High tech, telecommunications, manufacturing, life sciences and pharmaceutical, and financial services

Best Sellers: The Counselor Salesperson, The Versatile Salesperson, Negotiating to Yes, Sales Advantage Series, Consulting with Clients, Turning Information into Sales, The Sales Leader-Manager, Lighthouse Coaching

Sales Tip One: To stand out from the competition, become a true business consultant by asking questions about the customer's core business processes, and use the information to improve key metrics for the customer.

Sales Tip Two: If your offering is viewed as a commodity, analyze all aspects of the customer's experience, from how they buy your product or service through how they use and dispose of it. Use the information to add unique value to your offering.

Sales Tip Three: To build and sustain open, trusting relationships with a wide variety of different prospects and customers, learn how to be versatile in your communication style to better adapt to each individual's preferred interpersonal style.

Book One: *Versatile Selling: Adapting Your Style So Customers Say "YES!"*

Book Two: *The Social Styles Handbook: Find Your Comfort Zone and Make Your Partner, Family, Friends, and Co-Workers Comfortable with You*

Book Three: *Getting to Yes: Negotiating Agreement without Giving In*

Product One: Many of the face-to-face and virtual-seminar-based programs include video components to reinforce, illustrate, and provide right way and wrong way examples.

Chapter 87

Become a Champion Performer

Dirk Zeller
Sales Champions and Real Estate Champions

Do you have the desire to receive recognition from your peers, to be recognized as one of the top agents in the country? If you do, you need to start by taking dead aim daily. It is the disciplines we do each day that make the difference between being on top or being part of the crowd.

Start each day focused on the success of your business. You want to begin each day by reviewing your business plan. Focus in on the activities that will lead you to the successful result you have set forth in your plan. Long-term success is built on top of achieving daily performance standards for weeks and months at a time. If your business plan is not broken down to the daily activities or daily performance standard, you should take the time to do so now. I call these daily activities "The Disciplines of a Champion." We each have activities that, if left undone daily, will cause our business to suffer.

Some of the "Disciplines of a Champion" could be:

➤ Prospecting for a specific time period.
➤ Doing lead follow-up.
➤ Contacting a certain number of past clients.
➤ Spending time in personal development.
➤ Practicing scripts and dialogs.

The "Disciplines of a Champion" are quantifiable and trackable. They consist of a specific amount of time or a specific number that must be achieved. To have power, the disciplines must set the time frame or the quantity. It is too easy for us to opt out and not accomplish our goals when we don't have concrete parameters.

Next, you need to evaluate whether you are ahead or behind for this week. Then create the strategy to catch up if you are behind, or focus on maintaining the current strategy and direction that has kept you on plan or even ahead of schedule. Too often, we know we are behind and let it go for too long without a change. You must react and change quickly to catch up. We often do not raise the level of our intensity or increase our work output until it is too late. If you get too far behind and are spending tremendous amounts of time inflicting wounds on yourself, change the plan.

Always have a Plan B. There is no embarrassment in working a Plan B. Often, Plan B is the better plan because you can invest the mistakes you made in Plan A in Plan B. Edison tried over 10,000 different elements in his lightbulb before one worked. What would have happened had he stopped after Plan A?

Zero in on your area of success. People are paid very well for the few things they do very well. That is one of the best things about the field of selling real estate. There are so many ways to earn an outstanding income. Do what you do very well. We coach our clients to develop three to four areas of specialization in the real estate field and work to project their skills in these areas. Do not be a generalist in a specialized world. The "jack of all trades" is also the master of none. You are highly skilled in a few specific areas of real estate sales. If you have only one or two areas, you need to begin to learn and add another area or two to give yourself balance. The possibilities are truly endless when you become a specialist. Here are some ideas of specialization:

There is an endless supply of opportunities to let your ability lead you to become the recognized expert in your area in a few categories. I could list three pages of categories, but you get the idea.

Your success in your real estate career must be built from the ground up. Pour a solid foundation of daily disciplined goals and activities. These daily disciplines or "Disciplines of a Champion" will set you on the path to success in your career. Review and analyze your progress daily. Do not be afraid to adopt a Plan B if needed. Create a few areas of specialty. Decide what you enjoy doing and do well. Then zero in and take dead aim for the target of being the recognized expert in your area.

Name: Dirk Zeller

Company: Sales Champions and Real Estate Champions

Web Site: www.saleschampions.com, www.realestatechampions.com

Biography: As a salesperson who rose to the top of the sales field quickly, Dirk has set new standards for sales and sales performance.

Throughout his real estate career, Dirk was recognized numerous times as one of the leading real estate sales agents in North America.

Dirk is now one of the most published authors in success, time management, and sales training in the sales field. His *Coaches Corner* weekly newsletter has over 200,000 subscribers. His programs, coaching, and training systems are used in 97 different countries. Dirk has been a featured sales representative in conferences on five continents. He is the author of six best-selling books.

Selling Philosophy: Four Day Work Week, Stewardship Selling, Sales 2 Systems

Target Industries: Real estate, financial services, insurance

Best Sellers: Success Trio: Lead Mastery, How to Create and Deliver a Dynamic Listing Presentation, Convert and Commit the Buyer . . . Every Time!

Sales Tip One: Invest in your time and resources. You must be willing to invest time in larger amounts than other agents in direct income-producing activities (DIPA).

Sales Tip Two: Invest in your personal development: A champion has the passion and invests the time in improving his or her mind-set, skills, and business system. Invest time in reading, seminars, training CDs, coaching, and any other form of personal development.

Sales Tip Three: Invest in your selling skills: One of the key investments of your time resource needs to be in the sales skills development area. How effective are your scripts and dialogues that generate the lead and drive the lead to a sales appointment? What are your conversion ratios? How strong is your listing presentation? Do you close the client at the end of every presentation or do they close themselves? Can you get buyers to come to your office for a consultation?

Book One: *Successful Time Management for Dummies*

Book Two: *Success as a Real Estate Agent for Dummies*

Book Three: *The Champion Real Estate Agent*

Book Four: *Your First Year in Real Estate*

Book Five: *Telephone Sales for Dummies*

Product One: The Success Trio (audio CD set)

Chapter 88

Timeless Truths in a 2.0 Sales World

Ownership, Integrity, and Amplification

Zig Ziglar and Tom Ziglar

Ziglar

■ OWNERSHIP

Do you believe you sell a pretty good product or service? *Do you believe* you sell an extraordinarily good product or service? Do you sell a product or service that solves a problem? *Do you believe* that when you sell a product or service that solves a problem that you deserve a profit? Do you still have every dime you've ever earned in the profession of selling? Do you have customers that are still using and benefiting from what you sold them a year ago, 2 years ago, 10 years ago, or even longer? Then who is the big winner? The customer!

So many questions, but the big one is: *Do you believe* in your product or service? Are you "cooking in your own cookware"? The following story is from Zig's early sales career:

"I was in the cookware business in Columbia, South Carolina, working for the Saladmaster Corporation out of Dallas, Texas, and my friend Bill was struggling. We sold the same product but we were in different organizations and we were friends and we'd frequently get together just to chat. I was over at his house and I was really all excited and he was singin' the blues! I mean, things were tough. And as I got to talking to him, I said, 'Well, Bill, I know what your problem is.'"

He said, "What's my problem, man? Tell me quick!"

I said, "You're trying to sell something you don't believe in."

Well, he about exploded. He said, "What do you mean, I don't believe in it? We've got the greatest set of cookware on the American market!"

I said, "I know that, Bill! But it's obvious you don't know it!"

He said, "What do you mean I don't believe it? I left the company I'd been with for four years; I was a manager there, I came aboard here as a salesman, I believe in this product! But, Zig, you know what my situation has been. I wrecked my car and for about a month there I had to depend on the bus and cabs in order to go make calls, and you can't operate like that!" And then he said, "You know my wife has been in the hospital! She was there for ten days. We didn't have any insurance; the bill was horrendous! Now it looks like we're going to have to put the boys in the hospital and get their tonsils out, and I still don't have any insurance." He said, "But I'm going to get that set of cookware, Zig!"

I said, "Bill, how long have you been with us?"

He said, "Well, five years."

I said, "What was your excuse last year and the year before and the year before that?" I said, "Bill, let me tell you the thought process that takes place when you're in the closing situation. The prospect says to you, 'Bill, I'd love to buy the set of cookware! It is really neat! But, you see, I can't. I wrecked my car a month ago, and man, you can't sell and operate unless you've got transportation and buses and taxis, that just won't get it! My wife's been in the hospital for ten days; I don't have any insurance, and man, that just stripped us bare. Now it looks like we're going to have to put the boys in the hospital and get their tonsils out!'"

I said, "Now, Bill, you and I both know nobody's gonna come up with exactly the same excuses that you come up with. But when they give you any excuse at all, you're sitting there saying to yourself quietly, 'Now think positive, Bill, think positive!' But deep down what you're thinking is, 'Yeah! I know exactly what you mean! That's the reason I don't have a set of the stuff myself!'

"Bill, let me tell you something. You need to buy a set of the cookware from yourself today, before you go out on your call."

He said, "You really think it'll make a difference?"

I said, "No, I don't think it'll make a difference—I *know* it will make a difference. Write your order; send it in. Do it before you go out to make your first call." I persuaded him to do that. I said, "Bill, if you do you will sell enough extra cookware this week to pay for your own set of cookware."

Later he told me he earned more than enough to pay for his own set of cookware and acknowledged as he went on in his career that the best investment he ever made was the investment in his own product. Owners are closers.

"Selling is a *transference of feeling*," in the words of Zig Ziglar.

◼ INTEGRITY

Belief in your product or service is essential, but not enough unless you build this belief on the foundation of integrity. No matter how much a prospect believes that you believe in your product, they will not do business with you if they do not trust you, and trust begins with integrity.

"The number-one tool in your sales arsenal is integrity," in the words of Zig Ziglar.

It works like this: Values determine behavior. Behavior determines reputation. Reputation determines advantages. In today's Sales 2.0 world you need every advantage you can get. Long-term sales success is absolutely dependent on your integrity.

With integrity you do the right thing. Since you do the right thing, there is no guilt involved. With integrity you have nothing to fear because you have nothing to hide. You can talk to customers whom you sold yesterday, you can talk to them tomorrow, next week, next year, because you know in your heart that they made the best deal, and that's where the integrity comes in.

Integrity in sales is built in two primary ways:

1. Your word is your bond.

2. You understand that the sale is not complete until the order has been signed, the goods or services are delivered, and the customer is completely satisfied with the transaction.

◼ AMPLIFICATION

In the Sales 2.0 world, amplification is the great multiplier or divider—the choice is yours. Your belief in what you do, and the integrity that you have, are both now immediately amplified by the Internet and social media. Today, in only a matter of seconds, thousands and thousands of people can instantly know if you kept your word and if the customer was completely satisfied with the transaction.

Amplification through social media, if you harness it, can really grow your reputation of belief and integrity and lead to referrals and repeat business. Here are three keys to consider:

1. Everything online is public and permanent. Post with the assumption that your best customers and prospects will read it.

2. Write your own blog and/or post on Facebook, Twitter, LinkedIn, and industry-specific Web sites examples of your expertise, integrity, and reputation.

3. Critical! Whenever you post, always include knowledge or information that is valuable to the reader, even if they never contact you!

Selling is a transference of feeling: Do you believe in your product? Reputation is based on integrity: Work on your integrity and your reputation will follow. How many prospects know about your belief and your integrity? Amplification is the key!

Remember this: Sales success in a 2.0 world starts with the foundation of integrity, is fueled by your passionate "ownership" belief in your product or service, and is then amplified through social media to accelerate and multiply your success.

Name: Zig Ziglar and Tom Ziglar

Company: Ziglar, Inc.

Web Site: www.ziglar.com

Biography: Since 1970, Zig Ziglar has traveled over five million miles across the world delivering powerful life improvement messages and cultivating the energy of change.

Ziglar offers public seminars, customized educational programs, workshops, and keynote speakers focused on personal and professional development.

He has written 29 books. Nine titles have been on the best-seller lists; his books and tapes have been translated into over 38 languages and dialects.

Tom Ziglar is the CEO of Ziglar and works to continue the legacy of his father's message. Tom specializes in creating relationships through social media and using technology to bring state-of-the-art service to his customers.

Selling Philosophy: TRUST Selling: Maximizing Customer Relationships through a Trust Centered Approach

Target Industries: All industries

Best Sellers: Ziglar Sales Systems, Effective Presentation Skills, Strategies for Success, Top Performance Leadership

Sales Tip One: Selling is a process, not an event. Selling is something you do with a customer, not to a customer.

Sales Tip Two: Lead with need, establish trust, and be sincere in trying to provide a solution. We make more money as sales professionals by solving problems, not selling products.

Sales Tip Three: Focus more on what the customer is buying, and not on what you are selling.

Book One: *Secrets of Closing the Sale*

Book Two: *See You at the Top*

Book Three: *Top Performance: How to Develop Excellence in Yourself and Others*

Product One: Secrets of Closing the Sale

Product Two: Closes, Closes, Closes

Product Three: How to Stay Motivated

Chapter 89

Your Best Sales Year Ever!

Eric Taylor and David Riklan

Mastering the world of selling doesn't happen in a day. It happens day by day. For you to have your best sales year *ever,* you have to put together 365 days of focus, self-discipline, and commitment, and strive to give your personal best to everything you do.

Since you've gotten to this point in the book, you have probably invested some time and energy and studied *Mastering the World of Selling.* You've read about many different sales philosophies, methodologies, strategies, tactics, tips, and secrets from the "Best of the Best" in the world of professional selling.

You now have a wealth of the necessary sales tools at your disposal or, at the very least, unprecedented access to them.

But are sales tools alone enough?

Challenge: Imagine having your best sales year *ever!*

➤ What would it look like in terms of rewards and recognition?

➤ How would it make you feel?

➤ What would you be thinking?

➤ How confident and self-assured would you be about your ability to achieve even more in the upcoming year?

➤ What would you be saying to yourself?

➤ How much would you have grown, improved, and perfected your sales skills, networking skills, and relationship-building skills?

➤ How much money would you have made, and how many clients would have given you repeat business or the coveted unsolicited referrals?

While there is so much in this book that will enable you to move your sales skills forward in the quest to achieve your goals, it's unlikely that sales skills alone will raise you to, and keep you continually at, the top of your game.

Here's why: Beyond mastering the craft of selling, you must embrace the continuing process of all-around self-improvement. You must continue to strive to reach championship levels of mastery of the fundamentals of *life*.

There's no doubt you can follow a sales process, memorize the language and syntax, and even intellectualize the philosophies to move ahead in the world of selling. But it takes more to move ahead—and stay ahead—and know true success in *life*.

All of the sophisticated and even simple sales tools at your disposal won't work if you don't commit to working on *you*—becoming a better you and having your own *personal* best year ever, as well as your best sales year *ever!*

You've only just begun. The process doesn't end when you have become an elite athlete in the game of selling. The air is rare at the top, because winners do what losers choose not to do.

One of our mentors, the late, great Jim Rohn, said, "They put the good books on the higher shelf so you have to reach for them."

The same s-t-r-e-t-c-h thinking holds true for the elite sales professional who wants the most from life. The big awards . . . the big money . . . the *big life* comes from setting and reaching goals that are higher than others even dare to think about, and employing success secrets and strategies that move beyond the realm of selling alone.

All of the resources to become the best, to become elite, to have your best year *ever,* as well as your best sales year *ever,* are available to you. Hundreds, perhaps thousands, of resources are offered in this book. Some are free. And some may require you to make an additional investment of time, money, and effort.

But, for all that, remember . . .

YOUR MOST IMPORTANT RESOURCE
IS *YOU* !

For your consideration: Here are five additional Critical Components we encourage you to think about and work at developing when you commit to becoming the undisputed leader in your field, your *life*, and have your best year *ever*:

1. Your personal energy.

2. Your belief system.

3. Your goals.

4. Your time.

5. Your ability to communicate with purpose, clarity, and confidence.

Not just lip service: Here are a few challenges to get you pointed in the right direction and have you take a quick, closer look at a few strategies to jump-start the process.

■ CHALLENGE #1: EVALUATE YOUR PERSONAL ENERGY

Challenge: What is your personal energy level throughout the day on a scale of 1 to 10?

When we talk about *boundless personal energy*, we use the acronym D.R.E.A.M.S. to remind us of what's critical to our success.

> **D.** = **Diet:** World-class athletes use food like it's fuel. What are you running on?
>
> **R.** = **Rest:** Get your required amount of sleep. Some say "I'll sleep when I'm dead." Good night!
>
> **E.** = **Exercise:** You know this: "Winners do what losers choose not to do." Remember?
>
> **A.** = **Attitude:** You can't have a positive mental attitude if you're hung over!
>
> **M.** = **Mental Focus:** You will attract and become what you think about most of the time.
>
> **S.** = **Success:** We all define it differently. What's your definition? Write it down.

■ CHALLENGE #2: EVALUATE YOUR SELF-BELIEF

Challenge: How would you rate yourself on a scale of 1 to 10?

➤ Do you truly believe in yourself and your self-worth?

➤ Do you work on building your self-esteem and self-confidence daily?

Selling is the noblest profession one could ever be blessed to choose. But also know that, if you are in sales, you need to do more than the average person to protect your self-confidence and your self-esteem.

You need to feed it . . . build it . . . and make it stronger every day. You need to . . .

Build an unstoppable belief system. Not one that is cocky or arrogant—one that is certain; certain that you are worthy of everything you have and desire.

Building your belief system is similar to going to the gym. You can't exercise for one day and be fit for life. You can't read a motivational quote and be jacked for the next 25 years.

Surround yourself with people, places, and things that inspire you to become more and make you feel good about you. Building an unstoppable belief system requires daily exercise, daily positive input both external and internal.

➤ Do the right thing.

➤ Be honest.

➤ Have integrity.

➤ Be grateful and thankful.

All of these personal attributes produce a tremendous positive impact on your belief system. When you do what you say you will do, you begin to trust yourself. And Self-Trust increases Self-Esteem and Self-Confidence.

■ CHALLENGE #3: EVALUATE YOUR GOALS

Challenge: Do you have personal and professional goals?
Of course you do! But . . .

➤ Are they written down?

➤ Have you established a date when you are going to achieve them?

➤ Do you have a detailed outline of how you will achieve them?

➤ Have you written down *why* you must achieve them and how you will feel if you don't?

➤ Do you carry your goals with you and review them daily?

Your goals are your M.A.P.—your *Massive Action Plan*. Don't take goal setting lightly.

Achieving your goals is about facing the truth of what you deserve to become and what you're scared of becoming.

If you build your self-worth and eliminate self-sabotaging behaviors (procrastination, to name one of the most destructive), you will reach your goals.

■ CHALLENGE #4: EVALUATE YOUR TIME

Challenge: On a scale of 1 to 10, how proficient are you at being efficient? Speaking of procrastination, time is your greatest challenge and your biggest trap.

Are you *spending* . . . or *killing* . . . or *wasting* valuable selling time?

The honest answer is probably "Yes."

Time is an investment. Are you *investing* your time in revenue-generating activities?

If you were paid by the hour for a 50-hour workweek, what would you be making per hour? Take your current income (and don't overlook the value of perks and benefits), and figure out what your hourly rate is.

$100.00?

$500.00?

$2,500.00 an hour?

Money time is your rainmaking time! If you know the activities that, at your hourly rate, make you money, then . . .

Why aren't you doing those activities—full tilt—all day? The simple, sometimes painful, truth of the matter is: If you are doing any activity during "money time" that doesn't equal your hourly rate . . . Stop doing it!

Easy example: If there is an administrative activity that you could hire someone to do for $10 an hour, why are *you* doing it? Stop!

■ CHALLENGE #5: EVALUATE HOW YOU COMMUNICATE

Challenge: Have you ever seriously evaluated how you communicate?

Unless you're a hermit, living in a cave or under a rock, you're communicating virtually every waking hour of every day. In sales, or in any activity, the level of your communication will often equate to the level of your success. It's critical to assess the clarity, likeability, and effectiveness of your messages.

Consider all of the mediums your communication is now exposed to.

➤ You are speaking to prospects, clients, service providers, internal customers, tech support, and administrative assistants, all day, every day.

➤ You are communicating face-to-face, over the phone, by e-mail, text messaging, and fax. Hopefully, you are using social media platforms like LinkedIn, Facebook, Twitter, YouTube, and more. And remember, it's not just words. A look or a gesture "communicates" volumes.

It's endless. And your ability to communicate effectively, with confidence, cuts both ways. The great challenge, and the tremendous opportunity, is that you express your personal brand to others 24/7/365.

So how successfully do you communicate throughout every day? Do you know the perception of your personal brand in the marketplace? How are you being perceived and received by everyone you communicate with in the global market?

And beyond work: How about at home with your spouse or kids? How about at the town hall meeting? With your leisure-time friends and neighbors? With the folks who repair your car? With strangers?

"How you spend your days, is how you spend your life." When you consider this statement, evaluate how you communicate.

This might hurt . . . but try it anyway. Ask the people who are closest to you to appraise the effectiveness of your communication. What is their opinion? Insist that they give it to you straight and honest. Tell them that your future success is hinging on their feedback and that you appreciate positive and constructive criticism.

Ask them to write their thoughts down when they are alone and have time to think. Ask them to look at every medium where you communicate. Is your message and personal brand clear? Do you come across as confident and credible? Do they think you are likeable?

Accept the feedback and evaluate what you are willing to change without compromising your self-beliefs.

Putting it all together: Of course, these Quick 5 Challenges and the steps we've shared in this limited space are just the tip of the iceberg.

There's more. There's much more to be investigated, studied, implemented, mastered, and revised in our rapidly changing and challenging world.

So are you ready to continue the process of lifelong learning that goes into having your own, personal best year *ever* year after year?

We're confident you are. A commitment to *Mastering the World of Selling* suggests that you have the right attitude and approach to make it happen. And without doing one thing more, you may experience short-term success. But . . .

Short-term success is everywhere. It's often referred to as a flash-in-the-pan, a one-hit wonder, or "here today, gone tomorrow."

And that's not enough for you, we're **sure!** Elite Champions prepare for long-term success, back-to-back championships, year after year, decade after decade—a lifetime of winning.

Success in *life* is not something the Elite Champion experiences at only one time. He or she does it *all* the time. It's a Way of Life.

And it's expected. The intrinsic things you can't fake, *internal motivation, boundless personal energy,* and *an unstoppable belief system*, all transfer to a client's belief and trust in you.

This might prove to be one of the greatest sales- and skill-building exercises you have ever experienced.

Thanks for buying and reading *Mastering the World of Selling*!

Go out and make this Your Best Sales Year *Ever*!

Chapter 90

More World-Class Sales Training Resources

DAN ADAMS is a popular professional speaker, award-winning author, and consultant who draws upon 28 years of experience in the field of sales and marketing. Having honed his sales skills selling multimillion-dollar solutions for Fortune 500 and high technology companies, Dan founded a profitable sales consulting company called Adams & Associates. Utilizing his own strategic selling principles, he created the Trust Triangle Selling sales training methodology, and now the Selling Power Sales Strategizer.

Trust Triangle Selling offers sales education for the study and application of advanced selling skills. With a mind-set to "Pay It Forward," Dan created the Selling Power Sales Strategizer to enable accessibility to the consultative sales theories embodied by Trust Triangle Selling. www.trusttriangleselling.com

MITCH AXELROD is creator and CEO (Chief Encouragement Officer) of "The NEW Game" and author of both *The NEW Game of Business* and *The NEW Game of Selling*, which have generated $2.5 billion of new sales for thousands of companies and individuals in 35 countries. Mitch is featured in hundreds of radio appearances, in publications including *American Express, Fast Company, Selling Advantage, Executive Sales Briefing, Selling Power, National Underwriter*, and *Professional Speaker*, and his cable TV show was seen by 250,000 people. Brian Tracy says, "Mitch Axelrod is responsible for boosting more professionals into the top 10 percent than almost any trainer alive." www.thenewgame.com

THE BARON GROUP, with Founder and CEO Eric R. Baron, offers sales process consultations. Baron is a special events speaker and has spent more than 30 years in sales, sales management, and sales training. His diverse background further includes significant experience in sales, sales training, creative problem solving, and motivational team building. He regularly conducts programs ranging from small group training sessions to large group presentations. He is widely featured as a motivating keynote speaker, and routinely provides salespeople with insights that create a distinct edge over the competition by demonstrating how every sales call can be transformed into a problem-solving opportunity. Eric is an adjunct professor at the Columbia University Business School, where he teaches "Entrepreneurial Selling" to MBA students. www.barongroup.com

CHUCK BAUER is known as America's most innovative coach. His up-to-the minute industry information and knowledge base from two decades of sales coaching help his clients increase their revenue.

His most notable clients include Chase Health Advance, Thomson Reuters, Nationwide, and Mass Mutual. He currently works with approximately 25 students from across the country and does one-on-one consulting with many sales managers, sales VPs, and CEOs.

He is an acclaimed speaker and his writing can be found in print and Internet publications. He is also an instrument-rated private pilot, committed body builder, and mountain biker. www.chuckbauer.com

HAL BECKER is a nationally known expert on sales, customer service, and negotiating. He conducts seminars or consults to more than 140 organizations a year. His client list includes IBM, Disney, New York Life, Continental Airlines, Verizon, Terminix, AT&T, Pearle Vision, Cintas, and hundreds of other companies and associations.

At the age of 22, he became the number-one salesperson among a national sales force of 11,000 for the Xerox Corporation. Hal is the author of *Can I Have 5 Minutes of Your Time?* which is now in its 18th printing and is used by many corporations as their "Sales Bible." www.halbecker.com

JOANNE BLACK is a leading authority on referral selling. She is the author of *No More Cold Calling: The Breakthrough System That Will Leave Your Competition in the Dust* (Warner Business Books). Joanne's proven No More Cold Calling system works: Referral selling generates revenue faster than any other business development method—while decreasing costs, aceing-out the competition, and gaining new clients more than 50 percent of the time. A captivating speaker, Joanne is a member of the National Speakers Association and regularly speaks at sales and incentive meetings, sales conferences, and association meetings. www.nomorecoldcalling.com

TOM BLACK founded the Tom Black Center for Selling. Based in Nashville, Tennessee, the Tom Black Center for Selling, a member of the National Speakers Association (NSA), offers customized sales training services to national clients of all sizes in a wide range of fields. Areas of specialization include basic sales skills, key account strategies, sales management training, and keynote speeches.

Tom has also partnered with Mark Victor Hansen, author of *Chicken Soup for the Soul*, to form Mega Success. These one-day seminars in major markets feature Mark Victor Hansen, Art Linkletter, Tom, and other entrepreneurs, authors, and personal success trainers. www.tomblackcenter.com

ROBERT CALVIN teaches the Fundamentals of Effective Sales Management Executive Education course at the Booth Graduate School of Business at the University of Chicago. He is the author of three best-selling McGraw-Hill books: *Sales Management* and *Entrepreneurial Management*, both of which are titles in the McGraw-Hill Executive MBA Series, and *Sales Management Demystified*. He also teaches courses in sales management and entrepreneurship at the Bank of China, Xiamen University, and the Chinese European International Business School in the People's Republic of China.

As a salesperson, sales manager, vice president of sales, and company president, Mr. Calvin has rebuilt sales forces and trained many sales teams.

He is the president of Management Dimensions, Inc, an international consulting firm specializing in sales and sales management training. Clients range from Fortune 500 to the Inc. 100. www .salesmanagementdemystified.com

SUSAN CARNAHAN, as one of the leading speakers today on gender selling, has been retained by these clients and other top companies worldwide to help understand, evolve, and change their sales training and marketing approach when it comes to selling to the opposite sex. Susan is also a trainer, consultant, and coach on communication, leadership, and self-empowerment. An entrepreneur who has been in business for 21 years, she has appeared on CNN Live speaking on communication between the sexes. She is also the author of *Motivational Leaders* and producer of the learning programs Lessons in Leadership and What's Sex Got To Do with It? www .CarnahanPresents.com.

BRIAN CARROLL is CEO of InTouch, Inc., and author of the popular book *Lead Generation for the Complex Sale* (McGraw-Hill). Brian is a popular speaker and leading expert in lead generation. He's profiled and regularly quoted in numerous publications. His acclaimed B2B Lead Generation Blog (blog.startwithalead.com) is read by thousands each week.

Since 1995, InTouch has been executing lead generation programs designed to profile sales prospects, uncover viable opportunities, and create demand. Core services include teleprospecting, lead qualification, lead nurturing, and lead management.

InTouch has years of experience working in complex selling environments and has cultivated the people, processes, and technologies needed to give you measurable results and ROI. www .startwithalead.com

PAUL CHERRY is founder of Performance Based Results and is recognized as the leading authority on how to ask the right questions to win in business, in sales, and in life. He is the author of *Questions That Sell: The Powerful Process for Discovering What Your Customer Really Wants* (AMACOM). His next book, *Questions That Lead: How to Empower Your Team to Take Action*, will be published in 2011. His partial list of clients include Philips, Wells Fargo, Blue Cross, Stryker, Hilton, Moody's, Johnson & Johnson, and the U.S. Department of Energy. www.pbresults.com

JACK DALY delivers explosive keynote and general session presentations, interactive workshops, in-depth seminars, and lively training sessions that inspire audiences to take action in the areas of sales, sales management, customer loyalty, and personal motivation. A nationally known speaker, Jack leads with content, delivers with contagious enthusiasm, and leaves his audiences both wanting more and committed to taking action.

Jack has spoken to companies of all sizes, including Fortune 500 companies, Inc. 500 companies, Young Presidents' Organization (YPO), Young Entrepreneurs' Organization (YEO), TEC, trade associations, conventions, nonprofits, and schools. www.JackDaly.net

KEVIN DAVIS is president of TopLine Leadership, Inc., a company that provides systematic, proven, and customizable seminars for both salespeople and sales managers. Kevin's ideas are the result of more than 30 years of corporate sales, sales management, and training experience. A former executive with Lanier Worldwide, he is the author of the highly acclaimed book *Getting into Your Customer's Head*. Kevin's second book on sales effectiveness will be published in September 2010 by AMACOM Books. TopLine Leadership also provides an "open enrollment" Sales Management Leadership workshop. www.toplineleadership.com

ROGER DAWSON is one of this country's top experts in the art of negotiating. Businesspeople around the world respect him for his ability to improve their bottom line profits by teaching them and their people how to Power Negotiate. He has a unique ability to translate lessons gained in international and corporate negotiations into skills that can be quickly learned and easily used by executives and salespeople. *Success Magazine* calls him "America's premier business negotiator." He has been awarded the National Speakers Association "Certified Speaking Professional" designation. He was inducted into the Speaker Hall of Fame in 1991. www.rdawson.com

DR. ROBERT DEGROOT is founder and president of Sales Training International. He is an author, counselor, consultant, sales professional, and trainer with over 30 years of experience in the fields of sales and psychology. He holds a bachelor's in psychology, master of education in school psychology, and a doctorate in clinical hypnotherapy.

Sales Training International offers Web-based courses blended with live coaching for the professions of sales, sales management, and customer service.

He is the author of *Psychology for Successful Selling* (Branden Publishing, 1988) and has designed and developed over 70 Web-based training programs. www.SalesHelp.com

KIM DUKE is CEO and founder of The Sales Divas. She's an international sales expert who provides savvy, sassy sales training for entrepreneurs (with a twist!).

She is a national award-winning salesperson—and was the second youngest sales manager in Canada for CBC Television (Canada's oldest network). Now Kim is a successful entrepreneur, providing training for companies internationally.

She's an author and speaker who's had numerous interviews for international and national television, as well as radio and print across North America. (She was recently featured on NBC Television!) Kim also writes hundreds of articles for newsletters and Web sites internationally. Ten thousand entrepreneurs from 54 countries around the world eagerly await her sales tips each week. www.salesdivas.com

ROXANNE EMMERICH is America's most sought-after workplace transformation expert. She is listed by *Sales and Marketing Management* magazine as one of the 12 most requested speakers in the country for her ability to transform negative workplace performance and environments into "bring it on" results-oriented cultures.

A *New York Times*, *Wall Street Journal*, and *BusinessWeek* best-selling author, her many books include *Profit-Rich Sales*, *Profit-Growth Banking*, which has been called "the bible of successful business," and her newest book, *Thank God It's Monday! How to Create a Workplace You and Your Customers Love*. www.ThankGoditsMonday.com

DAVE FELLMAN has had broad and successful personal experience in sales, sales management, and marketing management. Prior to founding DF/A in March 1989, he held positions as vice president of sales and marketing for Spectra Graphics, director of marketing for Paris Business Forms, director of marketing for Keuffel & Esser Company, and a series of increasingly important positions while moving "up the ladder" with Moore Business Forms.

As the principal of DF/A, Dave is a popular speaker and seminar leader, and a frequent contributor to trade publications in a number of industries. His speaking credits range from seminars presented in conjunction with trade shows and association conferences to keynote presentations at a variety of events. www.davefellman.com

ENCORE CONSULTING designs and delivers customized sales training solutions that are 100 percent tailored to your unique value proposition. Their sessions are 40 to 50 percent interactive, integrating role-playing, group activities, and discussion forums. Encore Consulting offer both foundational and advanced sales training.

Clients include Johnson & Johnson, AT&T, The Cleveland Clinic, Georgia-Pacific, Six Flags, Rinnai, Marriott, and SAIC. Contact John Naples, Managing Partner, at www.encoreconsulting.net

NANCY FRIEDMAN and her husband, Dick, have owned two radio stations over the years, in San Diego, California, and St. Louis, Missouri. It was in St. Louis that her career as Telephone Doctor was born.

Telephone Doctor Customer Service Training has helped thousands of companies and associations communicate better with their customers. It's the salesperson who bleeds when a situation is mishandled, and through Telephone Doctor training, employees learn how to handle the event.

Nancy is the spokesperson in the popular Telephone Doctor training DVDs and a speaker at conferences around the world. She's a two-time featured speaker at the Top Hopkins Sales Boot Camp and the author of six customer service books. www.telephonedoctor.com

JOSH GORDON works to improve the performance of organizations and sales teams with research-based training and consulting services. Gordon is the author of four books on selling and has been on CNN, CNBC, and National Public Radio. His books have been translated for publication in Germany, China, Korea, and Taiwan. www.Selling2.com

DIANE HELBIG is an author, business development coach, and speaker. As president of Seize This Day Coaching, Diane helps businesses and organizations operate more constructively and profitably. She evaluates, encourages, and guides her clients. Working with as few as one person to as many as 100-plus, Diane creates an environment that is cooperative and interactive. She is also cofounder of Seize True Success, Coaching for Franchisees.

Diane is the author of *Lemonade Stand Selling* and a contributing author to *Chicken Soup for the Soul: Power Moms*. www.seizethisday-coaching.com

KEVIN HOGAN is the author of 19 books. He is best known for his international best-selling book *The Psychology of Persuasion: How to Persuade Others to Your Way of Thinking*. In the past decade he has become the Body Language Expert and Unconscious Influence Expert to ABC, Fox, the BBC, the *New York Times*, the *New York Post*, and dozens of popular magazines like *Forbes*, *Investors Business Daily*, *InTouch*, *First for Women*, *Success!*, and *Cosmopolitan*. He has become the go-to resource for analyzing key White House figures. www.KevinHogan.com

MARK HUNTER, "The Sales Hunter," helps individuals and companies identify better prospects, close more sales, and profitably build more long-term customer relationships. He spent more than 18 years working in the sales and marketing divisions of three Fortune 100 companies. He is best known for custom-tailoring his programs for an individual client's needs. Thousands of sales professionals benefit from his daily blog and weekly sales tip. Mark not only has consultative sales expertise, but also knows how to communicate it to others. He is a member of the National Speakers Association, the premier speaking organization recognized around the world for its top-notch communicators. www.TheSalesHunter.com

KERRY L. JOHNSON, MBA, PhD, is a best-selling author and speaker who speaks at least eight times a month, in locations ranging from Hong Kong to Halifax, and from New Zealand to New York. Traveling 8,000 miles each week, he speaks on such topics as "How to Read Your Customer's Mind," "Marketing to the Affluent," and "How to Increase Your Business by 80 Percent within 8 Weeks."

In addition to speaking, Kerry heads a personal coaching company. Peak Performance Coaching guarantees an 80 percent increase in sales production within just a few weeks. Professionals around the world use Dr. Johnson and his coaches to increase business, usually by 300 percent or more within only weeks. www.kerryjohnson.com

JOHN KLYMSHYN is a sales management and creativity coach. He is a lifelong student of the art of communication, and spends his time developing experts in Moving Conversations Forward, his trademarked process for sales, parenting, leadership, management, and communication skills.

John Klymshyn's professional selling career (which spans more than 25 years) includes stints as a recruiter, corporate sales trainer, sales manager, regional manager, and production salesperson. He has sold (and taught others to sell) services (commercial real estate, recruiting, telecommunications, and advertising), products (computer products, office furniture), and intangibles (consulting, outplacement, staffing). www.johnklymshyn.com

GERRY LAYO is one of the nation's most dynamic and sought-after speakers, trainers, authors, and coaches. Gerry delivers energizing and innovative world-class keynote addresses, seminars, and workshops. He draws upon over 20 years of street-tested, no-nonsense sales and management experience.

Before founding Sales Coach International, Gerry cofounded and ran three companies, building sales organizations from 5 to 1,500 people. As head coach and visionary for SCI, Gerry uses his unique approach to dramatically increase growth and profits for companies thoughout North America. Gerry is the author of the top-selling book *Smart Selling Strategies to Reinvent the Sales Process*. www.GerryLayo .com

ERIC LOFHOLM is a master sales trainer who has trained tens of thousands of sales professionals nationwide. He is president and

CEO of Eric Lofholm International, Inc., an organization he founded to serve the needs of sales professionals worldwide.

Eric began his career as a top-producing sales representative for three different sales organizations.

Many of America's top companies hire Eric regularly to train, motivate, and inspire their sales teams. Eric has delivered over 1,500 public and private presentations. www.ericlofholm.com

PAUL KARASIK is one of America's leading sales and management consultants. He is president of The Business Institute, a sales and management training and consulting organization. He is the creator of eight sales and management programs.

Paul's client list reads like a *Who's Who* of American business.

Paul is the author of eight all-time business classics, *Sweet Persuasion* and *Sweet Persuasion for Managers* (Simon and Schuster), and *22 Keys to Sales Success* (Bloomberg Press). His most recent books are *Brilliant Thoughts* and *How to Market to High-Net-Worth Households*. Paul is a frequent speaker and seminar leader at conferences, sales rallies, and advanced sales and marketing programs, both nationally and internationally. www.paulkarasik.com

SAM MANFER is a leading authority for selling to C-level executives and other powerful people. He is the author of *Take Me to Your Leader$: The Complete Guide for Establishing Executive Relationships*. Sam is an expert salesperson, as well as a keynote speaker and seminar leader. He uses his personal experiences along with humor and stories to show salespeople how to connect with influential people to generate quality leads and become 70 percent–plus closers. His client list is a *Who's Who* of all types of businesses in various industries, such as Emerson, Marriott, Apple, Kemper, Texas Instruments, and Medtronic. www.sammanfer.com

DON MCNAMARA, CMC, has over 30 years of sales experience, from the field level to executive sales management with firms ranging in size from start-ups to divisions of Fortune organizations. In his career he has been an individual contributor, corporate sales training manager, regional manager, national sales manager, and vice president of sales. During this span he recruited, hired, trained, and supervised over 1,200 salespersons and their managers. He is the award-winning author of *Visionary Sales Leadership: How Senior Executives Can Erase Status Quo Myths and Build Superior Sales Organizations*. www.heritage-associates.net

JIM MEISENHEIMER is a former U.S. army officer and vice president of Sales and Marketing for a division of Baxter Healthcare. He shows salespeople and entrepreneurs how to increase sales, earn more money, have more fun, and how to do it all in less time, with common-sense ideas that get immediate results. He is the creator of the Sales Trailblazer V.I.P. Selling Club, which provides sales tips and proven selling strategies in 24 lessons spread over 24 weeks. He has been in business 21.5 years . . . has 525 corporate customers . . . and last year had 72.7 percent repeat business. www.startsellingmore.com

JOE NUNZIATA is an internationally known speaker/trainer and best-selling author of *Spiritual Selling, Finding Your Purpose*, and *No More 9 to 5*. He has been delivering his life-changing message at seminars and events since 1992. His unique blend of psychology, philosophy, spirituality, and the power of energy resulted in revolutionary new programs and seminars. Joe specializes in helping people break through the unconscious barriers that are holding them back. He is dedicated to helping you become empowered in all areas of your life. www.spiritualselling.com

JIM PANCERO has been directly involved in business-to-business selling for over 35 years. Six of those years were spent successfully selling the largest computer systems for the Data Processing Division of the IBM Corporation. During Jim's prestigious IBM career he earned several awards, including the coveted "Golden Circle" designation annually awarded to the top 5 percent of their international sales force.

In 1982, Jim founded his advanced sales training and consulting company. Since then, Jim has conducted over 2,500 presentations or consulting days for 500 companies, providing a career average of five events per client. Over 90 percent of Jim's clients utilize his services more than once. www.pancero.com

BOB POTTER helps top-producing service providers win more in competition without competing on price. He is the managing principal of RA Potter Advisors LLC and author of *Selling Real Estate Services: Third Level Secrets of Top Producers* and *Winning in the Invisible Market: A Guide to Selling Professional Services in Turbulent Times*. Bob spent 25 years in business development for IBM, McGraw-Hill, Dean Witter, and MBIA. He has opened new markets in the United States, Mexico, Australia, and Asia. In 2000 he started RA Potter Advisors to help others develop and communicate differentiated value propositions and accelerate business relationships to win and retain committed clients. Bob received his BA degree from Santa Clara University and his MBA from University of California, Berkeley. www.rapotter.com

SAM RICHTER is an internationally recognized expert on sales intelligence. He has more than 25 years of experience in advertising, public relations, and e-commerce, creating and managing award-winning technology, sales, and marketing programs for start-up companies and some of the world's most famous brands. His top-selling book, *Take the Cold out of Cold Calling* (www.takethecold.com), is in multiple editions and has won numerous awards. Sam is an internationally sought-after presenter and is founder of the Know More! sales improvement program. Sam was formerly president of a national business research organization and was a finalist for *Inc.* magazine's Entrepreneur of the Year. www.samrichter.com

ALAN RIGG has helped business owners, executives, and managers at hundreds of companies build and manage top-performing sales teams. A 23-year student of selling and sales management, Alan is the author of *How to Beat the 80/20 Rule in Sales Team Performance*, *How to Beat the 80/20 Rule in Selling*, and the 80/20 Selling System Home Study Course. A past president of the Arizona chapter of the National Speakers Association, Alan specializes in delivering his unique insights into sales and sales management via highly interactive seminars, workshops, webinars, and teleconferences. For more information and *free* sales and sales management tips, visit his Web site. www.8020sales.com

STEVEN ROSEN, MBA, is Canada's Sales Leadership Coach and the founder of STAR Results.

Steven helps companies transform sales managers into great sales coaches. He works with sales executives to develop high-performance sales organizations. Through his Focused Leadership Coaching, Steven has helped his clients achieve greater personal and professional success.

Steven is an authority in the area of sales management and has authored many articles in the area of sales management coaching and on driving sales performance. He was awarded the Top Sales Article in 2009 by Top 10 Sales Articles. Contact Steven at steven@staresults.com, call 905-737-4548, or visit his Web site. www.starresults.com

LEE B. SALZ is a sales management strategist who specializes in helping companies build scalable, high-performance sales organizations through hiring the right salespeople, on-boarding them effectively and efficiently, and aligning their sales activity with business objectives using his Sales Architecture methodology. He is the president of Sales Architects, the CEO of Business Expert Webinars, and author of the award-winning book *Soar Despite Your Dodo Sales Manager*. Lee is a member of the Editorial Advisory Board and featured columnist with *Sales and Marketing Management* magazine. He is a results-driven sales management consultant and a passionate, dynamic speaker. Lee can be reached at lsalz@SalesArchitects.net or 763-416-4321. www.salesarchitect.com

TIBOR SHANTO is the founder and president of Renbor Sales Solutions, Inc., and creator of Objective Based Selling. Renbor enables companies to sell better and achieve sustained growth, by focusing on decisive strategies, activities, and metrics at the most critical points along the sales cycle.

Renbor's measure of success is to help you sell better by educating your team to execute and deliver results rather than just complete tasks. He is coauthor of the book *How to Harvest Trigger Events to Close More Deals*. www.sellbetter.ca

ERIC SLIFE is president of Slife Sales Training, Inc. Since 1998 they have been a leader in utilizing the Internet to make sales training programs more easily accessible.

Although they have programs fully capable of training larger sales forces, their real niche is in providing small businesses comprehensive sales training programs that can accommodate even the smallest of budgets. www.salestrainingcentral.com

GREGORY STEBBINS is an internationally recognized authority on sales psychology. He is a master at improving the greatest asset of any business—its people. With more than 30 years of business experience, he applies a wealth of knowledge, street smarts, and high-impact ideas to the challenges his clients have.

As a trainer, Greg has designed and delivered numerous corporate sales, management, and human resource development programs. Over 20,000 sales professionals have benefited from Greg's expertise and training. He has consulted on strategic planning, leadership development, and organizational culture for dozens of organizations, large and small, profit and not-for-profit. www.peoplesavvy.com

BILL STINNETT of Sales Excellence, Inc., is a global training and consulting organization focused on helping companies of all sizes grow their client base, increase revenue, and keep more profit. We offer custom-tailored sales and sales management training delivered as onsite workshops, instructor-led web workshops (webinars), and computer-based e-workshops (e-learning) programs, as well as strategic consulting services for sales professionals, marketing professionals, telesales, pre-sales (technical) professionals, sales and marketing managers, and business executives. www.salesexcellence.com

THE WATERHOUSE GROUP founder and CEO, Mr. Steve Waterhouse, is the author of *The Team Selling Solution: Creating and Managing Teams that Win the Complex Sale* (McGraw-Hill, 2003) and *Ending the Blame Game: 20 Rules to Live By* (Englander Press, 2000). A consultant and sales trainer, Mr. Waterhouse's TeamSelling process helps companies involved in complex sales cut both costs and selling cycle time by learning to coordinate their internal assets. Steve has appeared in *Sales & Marketing* magazine, *Selling Power*, *PC Week*, *Investors Business Daily*, *B2B*, *Entrepreneur Magazine*, *Washington Technology*, *Smart Partner* magazine, and numerous local publications and business journals. www.waterhousegroup.com

ED WALLACE, throughout his 25-year career as a number-one sales producer and vice president of business development for a firm that grew from $1 million to over $120 million in revenue, has learned that creating outstanding business relationships is the true secret to success.

Ed founded The Relational Capital Group so he could bring his relationship-building principles to corporations and their client-facing professionals. The firm provides professional development and consulting services to help organizations and individuals develop the key relationships that most impact their business performance—

leading to improved profitability and sustainability in the global marketplace. www.relationalcapitalgroup.com

■ ONLINE SALES TRAINING RESOURCES

JUSTSELL.COM has provided the sales world with free sales tools, tips, and inspiration since 1998. The people there are obsessed with delivering authentic and no-fluff content to their more than 100,000 active e-mail subscribers. If you consider yourself SalesTough (or want to be), these people are all about serving you. www.justsell.com

THE SALES ASSOCIATION is the premier association for sales and business development professionals from all industries worldwide. Our mission is to provide members a powerful and strategic means to connect with one another at events and online, grow professionally, and drive profits within their organizations. www.sales association.org

SALESBLOGCAST.COM's Founder, Doyle Slayton, is an internationally recognized Sales and Leadership Strategist, Speaker, and Blogger. He created SalesBlogCast.com to be an online community where business professionals network, share best practices, and make each other better! www.salesblogcast.com

SalesGravy.com's founder and publisher, Jeb Blount, is considered one of the leading authorities on sales and sales leadership in the world. He is the best-selling author of *Power Principles*, *Seven Rules for Outselling the Recession*, and *People Buy You*. His sales audio programs have been downloaded more than three million times.

SalesGravy.com is the most popular sales content Web site in the world (source: Quantcast, Alexa, and Compete). Often called the "Facebook of the sales profession," SalesGravy.com offers sales professionals and leaders more than 30,000 pages of articles, blogs, videos, audio programs, and sales training materials.

In 2008 Jeb launched Sales Gravy Jobs. In just 10 months Sales Gravy became the number-one ranked Sales Niche Job Board in North America. Today Sales Gravy Jobs dominates the sales recruiting marketplace. www.SalesGravy.com

SellingPower.com provides senior sales managers high-quality content delivered through print, audio, video, webinars, and sales leadership conferences. Its offerings include best practices, tactical solutions, and proven strategies to help sales leaders create a more efficient and effective sales organization. www.sellingpower.com

About the Authors

■ ERIC TAYLOR

Eric Taylor is the president of Empowerment Group International and the chief inspiration officer of SelfGrowth.com. Since 1988, he has inspired, educated, and entertained over 1,600 audiences on the topics of sales, leadership, customer service, and personal development. He has been invited to speak at annual conventions, tradeshows, private seminars, workshops, and colleges.

Taylor is the author of *The Energy Passport* and cocreator of the 12-volume program *Best Year Ever! Secrets and Strategies for Unlimited Success,* and contributing author to the book series 101 Great Ways to Improve Your Life.

Since 2001, Taylor and Empowerment Group International has produced and promoted public business seminars featuring best-selling authors, speakers, and celebrities such as Christopher Reeve, Brian Tracy, Jeffrey Gitomer, Bryan Dodge, Tony Jeary, and Dr. Bob Nelson.

In 2003, Taylor was named second runner-up in the EAS Body for Life International Fitness Challenge. He went from 18.5 percent to 8 percent body fat and lost 28 pounds in 84 days. Taylor shares his physical transformation success strategies in seminars and workshops across North America.

Taylor is happily married to Clare and is a devoted father to Kelly, Mark, Zachary, Luke, and Jake. He spends his time at the Jersey Shore, his horse farm, and driving his kids to play at some basketball court or soccer field somewhere in New Jersey.

■ DAVID RIKLAN

David Riklan is the founder and president of Self-Improvement Online, Inc. His company specializes in publishing information on self-improvement, business, and natural health on the Internet. The company manages multiple Web sites including SelfGrowth.com, which is the number-one ranked Web site for self-improvement on the Internet.

Riklan's career started in sales and marketing, working for well-respected companies including Hewlett Packard and Dale Carnegie. After years in corporate America, he found his true calling: "Providing good quality self-improvement and personal growth information on the Internet." His first vehicle to do that was SelfGrowth.com.

SelfGrowth.com is the largest online self-improvement community, bringing together experts, articles, videos, products, events, discussions, and links to other Web sites. Riklan has integrated the capabilities of Wikipedia, Amazon.com, Facebook, Google, and Ticketmaster for the self-improvement community.

The SelfGrowth.com expert community includes over 15,000 experts with profiles and information about their companies and their services. The expert community includes many of the leaders in the sales training world, including Tom Hopkins, Zig Ziglar, and Tony Allesandra.

David has also published books on the topics of self-improvement and health, including *Self Improvement: The Top 101 Experts Who Help Us Improve Our Lives*, and the 101 Great Ways to Improve Your Life series.

During David's career, he developed expertise in the areas of e-books, search engine optimization, list building, and social media. He first applied his expertise to building up his own business. His first book, *Self Improvement: The Top 101 Experts Who Help Us Improve Our Lives*, was originally published as an e-book and sold $108,142 worth of e-books in one 24-hour campaign.

David later took his expertise and created four powerful Internet marketing and training programs on e-book marketing, search engine optimization, e-mail marketing, and social media. He has thousands of successful graduates using his programs.

Riklan lives and works in New Jersey with his wife and business partner, Michelle Riklan. Together, they founded SelfGrowth.com and Self Improvement Online, Inc., and are raising three wonderful children: Joshua, Jonathan, and Rachel.

Index

Aberdeen Group, 9
Accelerated Cold Call Training, 177, 181
"Accidental Salesperson, The" (Lytle), 189
Acclivus R3 Solutions, 1–3
Account size, increasing, 139
AchieveGlohal, 4, 7
Achievement of Results buying stage, 140–141
Action Selling, 8, 12
Activity, focus on, 196
Adams, Dan, 352
Administration, versus sales management, 64–67
Advanced questioning techniques, 249–256
Agreements, 288
Alessandra, Tony, 13, 14
Alleviation of Risk buying stage, 139–140
Allman, Dave, 167, 169
Always-have-something-to-invite-people-to offer, 231, 232, 233
Amplification, 343–344
Anniversaries, thank-you notes for, 130–131
As is category, xxviii–xxix
Ask Sam Deep, 72, 75
Assessment of Alternatives buying stage, 139
Assumptive questions, 41
At-Leaster image, reversing, 18–20
"At-Leaster" phenomenon, 16–21
Attitude, 82
Audience
 analyzing, 72

involving and preparing, 156
persuading, 156
researching, 157
"wowing," 72–75
Audience champions, 157
Audience questions, handling, 74–75
Audiovisual aids, effective, 74
Authority, going along with, 50
Authority principle, 53
Awareness of Needs buying stage, 138–139
Axelrod, Mitch, 352
Azar, Brian, 16, 20

B2B Lead Generation Blog, 354
B2B lead generation techniques, 298. See also Business-to-business (B2B) strategic plan
Baker Communications, 22, 25
BANT (Budget, Authority, Need, Timeframe) elements, 270–271
Barkey, Richard, 137, 142
Baron Group, 352–353
Baseline Selling, 174, 175
Bauer, Chuck, 353
Becker, Hal, 353
Behavior, telephone, 13–14
Behavioral knowledge, 18
Belief system, unstoppable, 347
Benchmarking, 82
Best buyer concept, 126–127
"Best customers," 197
 relationship with, 334–335
Best opportunities, focusing on, 246
Best practices, 83–84

Best prospects, targeting, 47
Best salespersons, characteristics of, 112–114
Best sales year, 345–351
Black, Joanne, 353
Black, Tom, 353–354
Blount, Jeb, 363
Body language
    influential, 73–74
    while selling, 266–267
"Book Yourself Solid" selling system, 231–234
Boring presentations, 291
Bosworth, Mike, 26, 29
Brand identity, 47
Breakthrough Selling System, 32
Brenny, Nancy, 337
Brian Tracy International, 316, 318–319
Broad-mindedness, 229
Brochures, 145
Brodie, Ian, 30, 34
Brodow, Ed, 35, 38
Brodow's Law, 36
Broker of strengths, 133
Brooks, Bill, 304, 307
Brooks, Jeb, 307
Brooks, Mike, 40, 41
Budgets, 224
    approval of, 227
Burg, Bob, 43, 45
Burg Communications, 43, 45
Business
    expanding, 334
    modern approach to building, 137–142
    profitability of, 224
    protecting in tough times, 334–337
    purpose of, 220–221
    relationships in, 205
Business by Phone, 293, 295
Business consultant role, 83–84
Business criteria, critical, 228
Business development, success in, 223
Business discussions, common ground in, 206–207
Business Institute, The, 359
Business review meetings, 198

Business-to-business (B2B) strategic plan, 296. *See also* B2B entries
Business-to-business selling, 143
Business-to-business sales, 127
Buyer behavior model, 134–135
Buyers
    convincing to pay more, 35–39
    requirements of, 304–307
    selling through the eye of, 143–147
    turning shoppers into, 308–311
Buyer/seller conundrum, 211
Buyer/seller dynamics, 27
Buyer/seller relationship, 46
    as a critical selling skill, 9
    trust in, 95
Buyer's "needs," 212
    awareness of, 138–139
Buyer tactics, 37–38
Buy Gitomer, 112, 114
Buying
    persuasion and, 209
    reasons for, 94–95
    thank-you notes related to, 130
Buying cycles
    in economic downturns, 246
    linking selling cycles to, 313
    major stages in, 138–141
Buying decisions, 61, 211–215, 283
    logical, 328
Buying Decision Team, 213
Buying Facilitation, 214
Buying motives, understanding, 41
Buying process, 117

Calculations, questions related to, 294
Call objectives, establishing, 177–178
Calvin, Robert, 354
Can be category, xxix
Carnahan, Susan, 354
Carnegie, Dale, 68–70
Carroll, Brian, 354
Cathcart Institute, 46, 48–49
Cathcart, Jim, 46, 48–49
Causes, determining, 239
Centers of Influence, 69
CEO assistant, calling, 178
Champion performers, 338–340
Champions
    audience, 157

as sources of business
opportunities, 69–70
Change
champions of, 52–53
facilitating, 243
ramifications of, 212
Change Management issues, 211
Cherry, Paul, 355
Chet Holmes International, 126, 128
Chiron Associates, 205, 207
Cialdini, Robert, 50, 53–54
Circumstances, attaching numbers
to, 294
Client-centered proposals, 279
Client conversation, 102
Client needs, focus on, 232, 233
Clients, helping to succeed, 93–97
Client success, facilitating, 95–96
Client testimonials, asking for, 90
Client update meeting, 69
Client value, 132–133
creating, 137–142
Closed-ended questions, 251, 252,
254
Closing. *See also* Inquiry-Lead-
Closure progression
criteria for, 60
effective, 33
Closing skills, 163
Closing strategy, effective, 60–63
Closing techniques, 220
Coaching, preparation for, 262
"Coaching by Asking" Strategy,
259–260
Coaching sessions
debriefing, 260
scheduled, 258, 259
Cold calling, as an informational
puzzle, 180
Cold-calling secrets, 105–109
Cold calls, successful, 177–181
Collaboration, 1–3
Comfort zones, 17–18
getting past, 328
Commitment
gaining, 10
importance of, 53
Commitment objective, 9
Communication
boundary conditions of, 134

evaluating, 349–350
testimonials as, 89–90
Communispond, 55, 59
Compensation, reasonable, 35
Competency, 228, 305
Competition, xxv, 283
customer relationships and, 4
engaging and defeating, 122–125
Competitive advantage, 46, 150
Competitive mind-set, 122
Competitive strategy, advancing,
123
Competitive threats, managing, 140
Competitive vulnerability, 124
Complacency, fear of, 203
Complex problems, diagnosing,
242–243
Complex Sale, The (TCS), 223–225
Concessions, making buyers work
for, 37
Conferencing, Web-based, 56–59
Confidence, 229
for closing, 33
during economic downturns, 247
Connor, Tim, 60, 63
Connor Resource Group, 60, 63
Constant improvement, 227
Consultative discussion, four-step
flow of, 254
Consultative salespersons, roles of,
83–85
Consultative selling, questioning
techniques for, 249–256
Containment sales strategy, 124
Contracts, up-front, 274–277
Contrast, theory of, 294–295
Control, as an element of the
successful sales formula, 271
Conversation, summarizing,
179–180
Cooperation, 288
Core problem, identifying, 106–107
Core problem question, 107–108
Corporate overview, 144
Cost, versus investment, 294
Courage, 229
Courtesy, telephone, 13–14
Creating Client Value (CCV)
approach, 137–142
Critical business criteria, 228

Critical business issues, lack of connection to, 321

Critical components, developing, 346

Critical sales/selling skills, 9–10, 235–236

Critical success factors, monitoring, 237–238

CRM processes, 24. *See also* Customer relationship management (CRM)

Curbside Coaching, 260

Curiosity, strategic, 47

Customer acquisition, increasing, 148

Customer base
conditions affecting, 337
risk related to, 334–337
strategies for protecting, 336–337

Customer business issues, addressing, 336–337

Customer business value, delivering, 122

Customer buying process, support of, 144

Customer centric selling, 26, 64, 66–67

Customer-first approach, 243

Customer initiatives, organizational priorities and, 168–169

Customer loyalty, 334

Customer needs, reaction to, 305

Customer needs principle, 219

Customer perception, 6, 48

Customer process, 137–138

Customer profiles, identifying, 153

Customer project evaluations, 223

Customer referrals, 69

Customer relationship management (CRM), beyond, 146. *See also* CRM processes

Customer relationship management challenge, 22–25

Customer relationship management software, 5, 6

Customer relationship management system, 153

Customer relationships, weakening, 5

Customer response exercise, 172

Customers
empowerment of, 143
gaining the attention of, 163–164
influence of dialogue on, 221
knowing, 14
technology in use by, 144–145
willingness to "go to bat" for, 305

Customer satisfaction, 38

Customer uncertainty, 241–242

DaCo Corporation, 162

Dale Carnegie & Associates, 68, 70

Daly, Donal, 312, 315

Daly, Jack, 355

Daniels, Sharon, 7

Davis, Kevin, 355

Dawson, Roger, 355

Dealmaker, 146

Deals, failed, 269–273

Decision buying stage, 140

Decision facilitation, 213–214

Decision makers, finding, 178–179

Decision making, by Very Important Top Officers, 228–229

Decision-making process, 276
understanding, 197

Decision management, 243

Decision paralysis, 242

Decisions, values that drive, 228–229

Deep, Sam, 72, 75

Deficit questions, 185–186

Degroot, Robert, 355–356

Delivery, successful, 332

Delivery times, 305

Demand creation, 224

Dependability, 304–305

DF/A, 356

Diagnostic Business Development, 242–243

Diagnostic Process, 242

Diagnostic questioning, 134

Dialogue, in cold calling, 107

Dialogue selling
components of, 330–332
successful, 329–333

Differentiation
lack of, 321
optimal source of, 241–244

Direct introductions, power of, 193–194
Direct sales strategy, 123
"Disciplines of a Champion," 338–339
Divisional sales strategy, 124
Dodge, Bryan J., 76, 77
Dodge Development, 76, 77
"Dream 100 Sell, The," 126
Dream Fulfillment phase, of The Sales Funnel, 186
D.R.E.A.M.S. strategy, 347
Duke, Kim, 356

Eades, Keith M., 269, 272–273
"Early adopter" mentality, 227
Economic downturns, selling in, 245–248
Education, xxviii–xxix
Education phase, of The Sales Funnel, 186
Effective closing, 33
Effective closing strategy, 60–63
Effective sales training, vision for, 11–12
Effective training, failure to deliver, 24–25
80/20 rule, 17, 27, 258
80/20 Selling System Home Study Course, 361
Electronic commerce, 298
Electronic communication, 51
"Elevator speech," 323
Elite Champions, 350
Elnes, Conrad, 300, 303
E-mails
  as a prospecting tool, 182
  to summarize conversations, 179–180
E-mail subject lines, prospect-drawing, 182–184
Emde, Ed, 334
Emmerich, Roxanne, 356
Emotional connection, in presentations, 102–103
Employee behaviors, altering, 149–150
Employees, guiding toward winning goals, 19–20. See also Staff entries

Empowerment Group International, 365
Encore Consulting, J56–357
Endless referral business, cultivating a network of, 43
Engagement metric, 190
Engage Selling Solutions, 89, 92
Enrolling and selling, effective, 219–222
Eric Lofholm International, Inc., 359
Etiquette, telephone, 13–14
Excelling, preparing for, 46
Executing Political Alignment method, 122, 123, 124
Executive leadership/sponsorship, CRM and, 23
Expectation management, 243
Expectations
  communicating, 317
  mismanaging, 262–265
Experience, giving samples of, 48
Expertise
  credible, 96
  as the key to driving value, 134

Fair-mindedness, 229
Farber, Barry, 79, 80–81
Farber Training Systems, 79, 80
Farrington, Jonathan, 82, 85–86
Fear of loss, 331–332
Feedback, 259
  customer, 90
Fellman, Dave, 356
"50 Percenters," 17
Final refusals, thank-you notes related to, 130
"Fit," determining, 108
Five critical selling skills, 9–10
FJR Advisors, 266, 268
Floyd Wickman Team, 329, 332
Focused Leadership Coaching, 361
Forecasted sales opportunities, failure of, 269–270
Formulating Competitive Strategy method, 123
Forward-looking vision, 229
Fox, Jeffrey, 87, 88
Fox & Co., 87, 88
Francis, Colleen, 89, 92

FranklinCovey Sales Performance Solutions, 93, 96–97
Freese, Thomas A., 98, 99–100
Friedman, Harry J., 308, 311
Friedman, Nancy, 357
Friedman Group, 308, 311
Fripp, Patricia, 101, 103
Funnel mix, risks in, 314. *See also* Sales funnel entries
Future, key to, xxvii–xxviii

Gaining commitment, as a critical selling skill, 10
Galper, Ari, 105, 109
General Physics Corporation, 110, 111
Gitomer, Jeffrey, xxiv, xxx, 112, 114
Global employee survey, 51–52
Goals
  evaluating, 348
  role in success, 174
  setting and reaching, 346
  for virtual meetings, 57
"Going the extra mile" principle, 217
Golden, John, 132, 136
Good life rules, 76–78
Gordon, Josh, 357
Gratitude
  acts of, 129–131
  power of, 131
"Great Meetings," 188–191
Great sales leaders, five traits of, 79–81
Green, Charles H., 115, 119
Growth strategies, 148, 149

Habits, changing, 12
"Hard factor" requirements, 168
Harding, Ford, 120, 121
Harding & Company, 120, 121
Healthy company environment, 19
Heart of Change, The (Kotter), 149
Helbig, Diane, 357
Help, asking for, 20
Hidden pressures, recognizing and diffusing, 108
High-gain questions, 252–253, 254
High performers, investment in, 87–88

High-performing salespeople, 117
High Probability Selling, 326, 328
Hill, Napoleon, 216
Hogan, Kevin, 357
Holden, Jim, 124–125
Holden International, 122, 125
Holland, John, 64, 66–67
Holmes, Chet, 126, 128
Holt, Matt, xxiii–xxiv
Homoly, Paul, xxix
Honesty, 229
Hopkins, Tom, 129, 131
"How," initiating a conversation with, 163
Hunter, Mark, 357–358
Huthwaite, 132, 136

Ideal buyers, 126–127
Ideas, expressing, 27
Identified Problems, 211, 212
Imagination, 229
Imparta, 137, 142
Improvement, constant, 227
Independent professionals, selling for, 30–34
Indirect sales strategy, 123–124
Industry jargon, 328
Influence at Work, 50, 53–54
InfoMentis, 143, 147
Information, importance of, 110–111
Information technology, 110–111
Informative presentations, 291
Infrastructure executives, 167
Initiatives, important, 226–227
Inner resources, importance of, 18
In-person contacts, thank-you notes for, 130
Inquiry-Lead-Closure progression, 296–299
Inquiry management, 298–299
"Insecurity of status," 317–318
Integrity, 343
Integrity Solutions, 148, 150
Intelligence, 229
Intentions, honest, 95–96
"Interaction Model of Performance," 317–318
Interdependent needs, 1–2

Internet, transformational effects of, 55. *See also* Web-based entries
Internet leads, 298
InTouch, Inc., 354
Introduction methods, 194
Introductions, 72
    versus referrals, 192–195
"Invest in performance" rule, 87–88
Investment, versus cost, 294

Janek Performance Group, 152, 154, 155
Jargon, 328
Jeary, Tony, 156, 157
JF Consultancy, 82, 85
Job interviews, 98–100
Johnson, Kerry L., 358

Kahle, Dave, 159, 162
Karasik, Paul, 359
Karr, Ron, 163, 165–166
Karr Associates, 163, 165
Key customers, relationship with, 335–336
Khalsa, Mahan, 93, 96
KLA Group, 182, 183
Klymshyn, John, 358
Knowledge, 83, 305
Knowledge-Advantage, 167, 169
Know More! sales improvement program, 360
Koerner, LaVon, 249, 256
Konrath, Jill, 171, 173
Kotter, John P., 149
Kowalski, Bill, 148, 150
Kubacki, Ryan, 124
Kurlan, Dave, 174, 175
Kurzrock, Warren, 235, 240

Language, correct, appropriate, and eloquent, 73
La Vine, Ron, 177, 181
Layo, Gerry, 358
Leaders, persuasion advice for, 52
Leading by example, 80
Leading questions, 252
Lead movement organizational strategies, 297

Leads
    generating, 313–314
    qualifying, 298
Learning, role in sales, 110–111
Lee, Kendra, 182, 183
Left brain/right brain functions, 28
Leone, Ray, 185, 187
Leone Resource Group, 185, 187
Letter of introduction, 194
Life = Sales concept, 287–289
Life history, xxiii
Listening, importance of, 118
Listening mode levels, 249–251
Listening to discern, 250
Listening to feel, 250–251
Listening to hear, 250
Little Red Book of Selling, The (Gitomer), xxx
"Little Voice Management," 288
Lock On/Lock Out (LO/LO) condition, 300
Lofholm, Eric, 358–359
Long-term ally role, 84–8!
Long-term customer relationships, 1, 5
Long-term relationships
    building, 1
    sales organization and, 6
"Loser" salespeople, 17–18
Losing, fear of, 16, 331–332
Low performers, 87
Loyal customers, cultivating, 48
Lunch meetings, 194
Lunsford, Seleste, 4
Lying, 282
Lytle, Chris, 188, 190

Macedonio, Mike, 208, 210
"Magic phrase," 189
Making a difference, 171–173
Management
    availability of, 20
    guiding employees toward winning goals, 19–20
    of salespeople, 87–88
Management Dimensions, Inc., 354
Manager orientation process, 262–264
Managing Sales Performance system, 236
    implementing, 239–240

Manfer, Sam, 359
Manipulation, versus persuasion, 50–50
Manufacturers, selling to, 127
Marketing, connection to sales, 144
"Marketing Bridge," 43
Market profile, 47
Market trends, awareness of, 326–328
Massive action plan (M.A.P.), 348
Maul, Steve, 143, 147
McCann, Jim, 201
McCord, Paul, 192, 195
McCord Training, 192, 195
McCormack, Mark H., 202
McNamara, Don, 359
Meaning, consciousness of, 48
"Measurable results," 17
Mediocrity, 17–18
Mega Success, 354
Meisenheimer, Jim, 359–360
Memorable stories, in presentations, 102
Mental objective, changing, 105–106
Merchandise approach, 309–310
Mercuri International, 196, 198
Miller, Anne, 205, 207
Miller, Daniel, 110, 111
Miller Heiman, 200, 203
Mind-set, understanding, 106
"Minutes Principle," 317
Misner, Ivan, 208, 210
"Missing metric," 189
Money issues, 276
Morgen, Sharon Drew, 211, 214
Morgen Facilitations, 211, 214
Motivation
    role in success, 174
    three Cs of, 318
Motley, Arthur H., xxv
Moving Conversations Forward, 358
Mr. Inside Sales, 40, 41
Murphy, Randall K., 1
"Must Win" opportunities, 124
Mutual understanding, 6

Napoleon Hill Foundation, 216, 217
Natural Selling, 219, 221
Natural Selling Process, 220–221
Needs, versus rights, 216–218

Negotiating, tips for, 35–38
Negotiation Boot Camp, 35, 38
Negotiation process, 2
Nervousness, controlled, 74
Networking, 43–44
    effective, 70
Networking myths, 208–210
"Never give up" strategy, 127
Newby, Charles, 196, 198
New customers, testimonials from, 90
NEW Game, The, 352
"No-brainer" relationship, 304
No More Cold Calling system, 353
Nonsales facing functions, 24
Nonverbal subcommunication, 266–268
Norton, Michael, 344
Nunziata, Joe, 360

Objection-handling techniques, 220
Objective Based Selling, 361
Obstacles, removing, 260
Oliver, Michael, 219, 221
Once was category, xxvii
Online profiles, 110
Online sales training resources, 363
Open-ended questions, 251–252, 254
    in cold calling, 179
Opening lines, 309
    questions as, 310
Openings
    importance of, 285–286
    primary goal of, 308
Opportunities
    looking for, 47
    "right," 196–197
    unseen, 133
    viability of, 224
Opportunity Chart, 69
Optimization, of sales leads, 296–299
Orders, asking for, 48
Organizational priorities, 168–169
Organizations, relationship between, 85
Outcomes, value of discussing, 164–165
Overachievement, 174–176

Page, Rick, 223–225
Pain
  as an element of the successful
    sales formula, 271
  uncovering, 276
Pancero, Jim, 360
Parinello, Anthony, 226, 229
Participative management, 317
Peak Performance Coaching, 358
Pencil selling, 40–41
Perceived value, lack of, 321. *See also*
    Value
Performance
  impact of weaknesses on, 175
  improving, 336
  tracking, 327
Performance Based Results, 355
Performance factors, critical,
    235–240
Performance indicators, identifying,
    238–239
Performance reviews, 298–299
Performance standards, daily, 338
Performers, champion, 338–340
Permission to speak, asking for, 179
Personal Agenda, 254
Personal energy, evaluating, 347
"Personal Walking Ambassadors,"
    43
Person-to-person conversations, 310
Person-to-person relationship,
    versus salesperson-to-customer
    relationship, 308–309
Persuasion
  methods of, 331–332
  psychology of, 50–54
Persuasive presentations, 291
Philosophy, xxix–xxx. *See also*
    Selling philosophy
Phone calls, unreturned, 120–121
Phone introductions, 194
Pipeline gaps, 313
Pipeline management, 315
  role in success, 174–175
  successful, 312–315
Pipeline structure, mapping,
    312–313
Pitching, 40, 41
Plan B, 339
Planning, of telephone calls, 14

Platinum Rule Group, 13–15
Poe, Edgar Allan, writing formula of,
    58
Points of view, managing, 47–48
Port, Michael, 231, 234
Porter Henry & Co., 235, 240
Positive interaction, 19
Positive mind-set, developing, 31–32
Positive thinking, 19
Post-selling, 276–277
Potter, Bob, 360
Power, as an element of the
    successful sales formula, 271
Powerful customers, alignment
    with, 123
Power Negotiation, 355
Power Point, 74
Power words, 330
Predictability, 305
Presence, while selling, 267
Presentation arsenal, researching,
    156
Presentation practices, 156–158
Presentations
  breaking down by the numbers,
    332
  effective, 329
  informative versus persuasive,
    291
  mistakes in, 101–104, 290–292
  preparing for, 58, 157
  strong opening and closing in, 103
  tailoring for the audience, 157
  thank-you notes related to, 130
  virtual, 55–59
Presentation skills, 10
Presenters, mental state of, 156
Price
  apologizing for, 36
  different perspective on, 294
  justifying, 36
  minimizing, 293
  versus quality, 304
  when to negotiate, 36–37
Price-driven sales, 132–136
Price lists, 306
Price negotiation tips, 35–38
Price structure, 35
Prime Resource Group, 241, 243–244
Priority prospects, developing, 198

Proactive sales management, 66
Problems
 early notice of, 306
 unrecognized, 133
Problem-solving perspective, 233
Process, defined, 82
Product-centered value proposition, 4
Product discontinuance, advance warning of, 306
Product information, 110, 111
Product line, knowledge of, 305
Product mastery, 14
Products, xxix
 belief in, 341–344
 customer use of, 336
Product sales, 40–42
Product/service provider, reasons for selecting, 94
Product/service quality, understanding differences in, 171–173
Professional Agenda, 253, 254
Professional retail sales techniques, 308–311
Professionals
 independent, 30–34
 trustworthiness of, 118
Professional services
 best selling in, 117
 selling, 115–119
Profitability, 122
 improving, 139
Profit Builders, 262, 265
Project failure, 167–170
Proposal pipelines, 65
Proposals
 content of, 279–280
 why customers want, 278
 withdrawing, 65
 writing, 278–281
Prospecting, 43, 68, 152
 need for, 282, 283, 284
Prospecting skills, 327
Prospective buyers, qualifying, 37
Prospects
 deselecting, 197–198
 e-mail subject lines that draw, 182–184
 high probability, 327

initial contact with, 285–286
 persuading, 327
 psychological needs of, 47
 qualifying, 223–224
 rapport with, 275
 serious, 189
 as a sure thing, 284
Psychology of persuasion, 50–54
PTVVC. See Control; Pain; Power; Value; Vision
Public seminar promoters, xxiii–xxiv
Purchasing decisions, testimonials and, 89–90
Pushbacks, handling, 96

QBS Research, 98, 99–100
Qualification, myth of, 270–271
Quality, breadth and depth in, 305
Quarterly review, 240
Questioning
 as the key to selling, 32
 role in selling, 41
 tips for, 254–256
Questioning skills, 10
Questioning techniques, advanced, 249–256
Questions
 as a cause of Telling Tension, 301–302
 core-problem, 107–108
 direct, open-ended, 179
 handling, 74–75
 as the key to enrolling and selling, 219–220
 in presentations, 331
 opening lines as, 310
 sales-related, 61–63
 types of, 251–254
 from world-class salespeople, 201–202
Quotas, xxvii
Quotes, 306

Rackham, Neil, 137, 245, 247
RA Potter Advisors, 360
Rapport, 26
Real estate champions, 338–340
Recession, selling during, 245–248
Recruiting, 79
Recruitment/training tools, 326–327

Reese, Sam, 200, 203
Referral business, 129
Referral Institute, 208, 210
Referral marketing, 209
Referral provider, 209
Referrals, 69
    cultivating, 43–45
    power of, 193
    specific, 47
    thank-you notes for, 130
    versus introductions, 192–195
Rejection, 283
Relational Capital Group, The, 362
Relationship process, defining, 5
Relationship management, 243
Relationships
    collaborative, 1–3
    cultivating, 47
    person-to-person versus
        salesperson-to-customer, 308–
        309
    win/win, 44
    in the workplace, 2
Reliability, 304–305
Renboor Sales Solutions, Inc., 361
Repeat customers, testimonials
    from, 90
Reps. See also Sales reps
    assessing the sales skills of, 40–41
    problematic, 87
    strengths and weaknesses of, 80
    trusting, 80
Request for proposal (RFP) trap,
    66
Research phase, of The Sales
    Funnel, 185–186
Results, noticing, 46
Retail sales techniques, 308–311
Rethinking the Salesforce (Rackham
    & McKinsey), 137
Reveal questions, 253–254
Revenue generation, focus on, 23
Revenue Storm, 249, 256
Richardson, Linda, 257, 261
Richardson Company, 257, 261
Richter, Sam, 360
Rigg, Alan, 361
Right brain/left brain functions, 28
Right customers, finding, 4
Rights, versus needs, 216–218

Riklan, David, xxiv, 345–351,
    365–366
Risk, xxix, 16
    customer-related, 334–337
    for prospects, 321
"Rock star" sales, 112–114
Rogers, Walter, 22, 25
Rohn, Jim, 346
Rosen, Keith, 262, 265
Rosen, Steven, 361
Rosenthal, Bill, 55, 59
Routines, comfortable, 160–161
Rules, for a good life, 76–78
Rumbauskas, Frank, 266, 268

Sales. See also Cold-calling secrets;
        Retail sales techniques; Selling
        entries
    actions to advance, 205–207
    choosing, 76–77
    connection to marketing, 144–145
    disassociation from, 19–20
    doubling, 126–128, 317
    easy, 283
    effect of telling tensions on,
        300–303
    failure rate of, 213–214
    as a game of numbers, 293–295
    increasing, 93–97, 110–111,
        196–199
    key to growing, 163–166
    key to success in, 77
    mastering the use of numbers in,
        293–295
    price-driven, 132–136
    purpose of, 288
    in referral marketing, 209
    right questions related to, 61–63
    trust and, 118–119
    twenty-one ways to increase,
        46–49
    walking away from, 36
Sales 2.0 revolution, 22
Sales 2.0 world, timeless truths in,
    341–344
Sales activity
    focus on, 196
    quality of, 65
Sales appointments, controlling,
    266–268

Sales Architecture methodology, 361
Sales articles, xxv
Sales Association, The, 363
Sales Autopsy, 285, 286
SalesBlogCast.com, 363
Sales books, xxiii
Sales call planning, as a critical selling skill, 9
Sales calls
adding control and predictability to, 274–277
as job interviews, 98
opening, 285–286
Sales careers, great, 201
Sales Catalyst, The, 16, 20–21
Sales Champions and Real Estate Champions, 338, 339
Sales clichés, 231
Sales closing methods, traditional, 61
Sales coaching, 257–261
goal of, 258
obstacles to, 257
Sales Coaching Plan, 260
Sales Coach International, 358
Sales Competence Evaluation and Assessment Tool, The, 62–63
Sales conversations, opening, 206
Sales culture, 5
Sales cycle
length of, 213
shortening, 327
Sales Divas, The, 356
SalesDogs, 287, 289
Sales effort, focus of, 246–247
Sales = Income concept, 287
Sales Excellence, Inc., 362
Sales Force Automation (SFA), 22, 146
Sales force automation software, 5, 6
Sales force training
effective, 11–12
failure of, 8–12
providing, 8–9
reasons for failure of, 9–11
Sales formula, successful, 269–273
Sales funnel, 313–314
Sales Funnel, The, 185–187
SalesGravy.com, 363

Sales Gravy Jobs, 363
Sales Hunter, The, 357–358
Sales leaders
five traits of, 79–81
traits of, 79
Sales leads
optimizing, 296–299
quality of, 297
Sales lies, 282–284
Sales management
focus on, 23
proactive, 66
superior, 316–319
versus administration, 64–67
Sales manager performance, 235–240
Sales managers
importance of, 317
responsibilities of, 316
role in performance, 257–258
top 10 reasons for failure of, 326–328
Sales meetings, 68
Sales methodology, becoming skilled at, 32–33
Sales models, traditional, 116–117
Sales opportunities
jump-starting, 320–322
stalling of, 167–169
uncovering, 68–71
Sales organization roles, 6–7
Salespeople. *See also* Salesperson entries
accountability of, 11
defining, 17–18
experienced, 8
high-performing, 117
improving, 317–318
informing, 318
knowledgeable, 6
lack of trust in, 161
managing, 87–88
as "naturals," 200–201
one-to-one meetings with, 263, 264
praising, 317
preparing for training, 10
presentation mistakes by, 101–104
recruiting, 79
"right," 196–197

structured sales process for, 152–153
supervising, 236
teaching to fail, 20
time wasters for, 159–162
top-performing, 200–204
as trusted business advisors, 137
Sales performance
benchmarking, 82
sales coaching and, 257–261
Sales Performance International, 269, 272
Sales Performance System, 236–240
Salesperson confidence, as a factor in purchasing decisions, 247. *See also* Salespeople
"Salesperson" stereotype, 106
Sales philosophy, 149
clarifying, 153
Sales pipeline
building, 138
health of, 314
stages in, 312
Sales presentation mistakes, avoiding, 290–292
Sales presentations, perfect, 187
Sales process, 118
designing, 313
number of prospects in, 189
qualifying, 223–225
standardized, 312–313
structured, 152–155
tension management during, 48
uniform, 327
Sales process checklist, 154
Sales process misalignment, 145–146
Sales process model, 153–154
Sales profession, freedom of, 76
Sales professionals
important activities of, 316
listening mode levels of, 249–251
Sales programs, good, 76
Sales Psychology, 362
Sales puzzle, reconstructing the pieces of, 82–86
Sales reps, CRM and, 25. *See also* Reps
Sales reputation, managing, 47
Sales rock stars, 112–114
Sales scripts, 41, 323–325

Sales skills, 345
building, xxv
importance of, 208
improving, 46
learning, xxiii
Sales strengths, 48
Sales success
key to, 317–318
managing, 235–240
"Minutes Principle" of, 317
Sales success storytelling, 26–29
Sales team
empowering, 154
preparing for change, 262–265
performance of, 235–240
Sales team processes, 24
Sales times, effective investment of, 159–160
Sales tips, xxv. *See also* Telephone tips
Accelerated Cold Call Training, 181
Acclivus R3 Solutions, 3
AchieveGlobal, 7
Action Selling, 12
Ask Sam Deep, 75
Baker Communications, 25
Baseline Selling, 176
Brian Tracy International, 319
Brooks Group, 307
Burg Communications, 45
Business by Phone, 295
Buy Gitomer, 114
Cathcart Institute, 49
Chet Holmes International, 128
Chiron Associates, 207
Communispond, 59
The Complex Sale, 225
Connor Resource Group, 63
Customer Centric Selling, 67
DaCo Corporation, 162
Dale Carnegie & Associates, 70–71
Dodge Development, 78
Engage Selling Solutions, 92
Farber Training Systems, 81
FJR Advisors, 268
Floyd Wickman Team, 333
Fox & Co., 88
FranklinCovey Sales Performance Solutions, 97

Sales tips (*continued*)
   Friedman Group, 311
   General Physics Corporation, 111
   Harding & Company, 121
   High Probability Selling, 328
   Holden International, 125
   Huthwaite, 132–136
   Ian Brodie, 34
   Imparta, 142
   Influence at Work, 54
   InfoMentis, 147
   Integrity Solutions, 150–151
   Janek Performance Group, 155
   JF Consultancy, 86
   Karr Associates, 166
   KLA Group, 184
   Knowledge-Advantage, 170
   Leone Resource Group, 187
   McCord Training, 195
   Mercuri International, 198
   Miller Heiman, 204
   Morgen Facilitations, 214
   Mr. Inside Sales, 42
   Napoleon Hill Foundation,
     217–218
   Natural Selling, 222
   Negotiation Boot Camp, 38
   Neil Rackham, 248
   Platinum Rule Group, 15
   Porter Henry & Co., 240
   Prime Resource Group, 244
   Profit Builders, 265
   QBS Research, 100
   Referral Institute, 210
   Revenue Storm, 256
   Richardson Company, 261
   Sales Autopsy, 286
   The Sales Catalyst, 20–21
   Sales Champions and Real Estate
     Champions, 340
   SalesDogs, 289
   Sales Performance International,
     273
   Sandler Training, 277
   Sant Corporation, 281
   Selling to Big Companies, 173
   Sjodin Communications, 292
   Sparque, 190–191
   Speaker for All Reasons, 104
   Stephan Schiffman, 284
   Stevens Consulting Group, 299
   STI International, 303
   Story Leaders, 29
   TAS Group, 315
   Tom Hopkins International, 131
   Tony Jeary International, 158
   Trusted Advisor Associates, 119
   Unlock the Game, 109
   ValueSelling Associates, 322
   VITO Selling, 230
   Weiss Communications, 325
   Wilson Learning, 337
   Ziglar, 344
SalesTough, 363
Sales Trailblazer V.I.P. Selling Club,
   359
Sales training companies, 12
Sales Training International,
   355–356
Sales training resources, xxv
   online, 363
   world-class, 352–363
Sales train wrecks, avoiding, 64
Sales year, best, 345–351
Salz, Lee B., 361
Sandler, David H., 274, 277
Sandler Training, 274, 277
Sant, Tom, 278, 280
Sant Corporation, 278, 280
Savings, maximizing, 293
Scarcity principle, 52
Scheduled Sales Coaching Sessions,
   258, 259
Schedules, honoring, 286
Schiffman, Stephan, 282, 284
Scripts, 329
"Seal the deal" requirements, 168
Seidman, Dan, 285, 286
Seize This Day Coaching, 357
Self
   as an important resource, 346–347
   selling, 98–99, 116, 208–209
Self-belief, evaluating, 347–348
Self-esteem, 17, 318
SelfGrowth.com, xxiii, 365, 366
Self-growth workshops, 19
Self-improvement
   continual, 157, 346
   value of, xxv
Self-Improvement Online, Inc., 365

Self-knowledge, importance of, 62–63
Self-motivation, 18–19
Self-starting, role in success, 175
Selling, xxv–xxvi. *See also* Dialogue selling; Sales entries
  channel versus direct, 141
  effective, 219–222
  through the eye of the buyer, 143–147
  in harder times, 245–248
  for the independent professional, 30–34
  magic moments in, 205–207
  negative view of, 149
  positive mind-set about, 31–32
  of professional services, 115–119
  purpose of, 118–119
  redefining, 149
  science of, xxii
  service and, 148–151
  as a skill, 33–34
  social dynamics checklist for, 266–268
  as a transference of feeling, 342, 344
  trust-based, 118
  versus service, 148–149
  world-class, 122–125
Selling philosophy
  Accelerated Cold Call Training, 181
  Acclivus R3 Solutions, 3
  AchieveGlobal, 7
  Action Selling, 12
  Ask Sam Deep, 75
  Baker Communications, 25
  Baseline Selling, 176
  Brooks Group, 307
  Burg Communications, 45
  Business by Phone, 295
  Buy Gitomer, 114
  Cathcart Institute, 49
  Chet Holmes International, 126, 128
  Chiron Associates, 207
  Communispond, 59
  The Complex Sale and, 225
  Connor Resource Group, 63
  Customer Centric Selling, 67

DaCo Corporation, 162
Dodge Development, 77
Engage Selling Solutions, 92
Farber Training Systems, 81
FJR Advisors, 268
Floyd Wickman Team, 332
Fox & Co., 88
FranklinCovey Sales Performance Solutions, 96
Friedman Group, 311
General Physics Corporation, 111
Harding & Company, 121
High Probability Selling, 328
Holden International, 125
Huthwaite, 136
Ian Brodie, 34
Imparta, 142
Influence at Work, 54
InfoMentis, 147
Integrity Solutions, 150
Janek Performance Group, 154
JF Consultancy, 86
Karr Associates, 166
KLA Group, 184
Knowledge-Advantage, 169
Leone Resource Group, 187
McCord Training, 195
Mercuri International, 198
Miller Heiman, 204
Morgen Facilitations, 214
Mr. Inside Sales, 42
Napoleon Hill Foundation, 217
Negotiation Boot Camp, 38
Neil Rackham, 247
Platinum Rule Group, 15
Porter Henry & Co., 240
Prime Resource Group, 244
Profit Builders, 265
QBS Research, 100
Referral Institute, 210
Revenue Storm, 256
Richardson Company, 261
Sales Autopsy, 286
The Sales Catalyst, 20
Sales Champions and Real Estate Champions, 340
SalesDogs, 289
Sales Performance International, 273
Sandler Training, 277

Selling philosophy (*continued*)
  Sant Corporation, 280
  Selling to Big Companies, 173
  Sjodin Communications, 292
  Sparque, 190
  Speaker for All Reasons, 103
  Stephan Schiffman, 284
  Stevens Consulting Group, 299
  STI International, 303
  Story Leaders, 29
  TAS Group, 315
  Tom Hopkins International, 131
  Tony Jeary International, 158
  Trusted Advisor Associates, 119
  Unlock the Game, 109
  ValueSelling Associates, 322
  VITO Selling, 229
  Weiss Communications, 324
  Wilson Learning, 337
  Ziglar, 344
SellingPower.com, 363
Selling systems, 26
Selling time, wasting, 161
Selling to Big Companies, 171, 173
Selling yourself short, 35–36
Service, selling and, 148–151. *See also* Services
Service-centered value proposition, 4
Services, xxv. *See also* Service
  belief in, 341–344
  need for, 282–283
  professional, 115–119
  thank-you notes for, 130
Service sales, 40–42
Service-selling culture, transformation to, 149–150
Service value, improving, 217
Shanto, Tibor, 361
Shoppers, turning into buyers, 308–311
Singer, Blair, 287, 289
Situational analysis, 171–172
Sjodin, Terri L., 290, 292
Sjodin Communications, 290, 292
Skill of Feedback, 259
Skills
  development of, 82
  monitoring, 236
  role in success, 175

Slayton, Doyle, 363
Slife, Eric, 361–362
Slife Sales Training, Inc., 361
Smart questions, 32
Sobczak, Art, 293, 295
Social dynamics, using to control sales appointments, 266–268
Social media, amplification through, 343
"Soft factor" requirements, 168
Software, customer relationship management/sales force automation, 5, 6
Software applications, 22–23
Sole practitioners, selling for, 30–34
Solutions
  acting on, 239
  essential, 197
  presenting, 276
  unanticipated, 133
  versus success, 146
Solution selling, 26
Solution Selling methodology, 272
Sparks, Duane, 8
Sparque, 188, 190
Speaker for All Reasons, 101, 103
Speaking, wowing audience while, 72–75
Specialization, areas of, 339
Speech, clear and distinct, 73. *See also* Speeches
Speeches
  closing, 75
  direction and content of, 73
  purpose of, 72
SPIN Selling, 137
Staff, resistance from, 264. *See also* Employee entries
Staff performance, managing, 326
Stalled opportunities, reducing the number of, 140
Stalled sales opportunities, jump-starting, 320–322
Standardized sales process, 312–313
STAR Results, 361
Status quo, contentment with, 160–161
Stebbins, Gregory, 362
Stevens, Drew, 296, 299
Stevens Consulting Group, 296, 299

STI International, 300, 303
Stinnett, Bill, 362
Stone, W. Clement, 89
Story Leaders, 26, 29
Storytelling, 26–29
Strategic client questions, 296–297
Strategic orchestrator role, 84
S-t-r-e-t-c-h thinking, 346
Structure, of presentations, 101–102
Structured sales process, developing
    and implementing, 152–155
Success
    focus on, 338
    importance of, 146
    impressions and, 99
    short-term, 350
Success equation, 82, 85
Successful cold calls, 177–181
Successful dialogue selling, 329–333
Successful sales formula, 269–273
    customer value and, 272
    elements of, 271–272
Summary e-mails, 179–180
Super salesperson role, 258
Superstar salespeople, investment
    in, 87–88
Support base, 124
Support group, 19
"Switching costs," 335–336
Synergy, 288
Systemic obstacles, 5–6
System users
    buy-in from, 24
    including in design/deployment,
    23

"Talking brochures," 246
Targeted polling, 157
Target marketing skills, 327
TAS Group, 312, 315
Taylor, Eric, xxii–xxiii, 345, 365
TeamSelling process, 362
Technology, overwhelming aspect
    of, 297–298
Technology misuse, in
    presentations, 103
Telephone contacts, thank-you notes
    for, 130
Telephone Doctor Customer Service
    Training, 357

Telephone tips, 13–15
"Tell"-based selling styles, 246
Telling Tension, 300–303
    causes of, 300–302
    managing, 301, 302–303
    symptoms of, 302
10 Secrets of Time Management for
    Salespeople (Kahle), 161
Testimonials
    making noticeable, 91
    power of, 89–92
    writing, 91
Thank-you note habit, 129–131
Thinking, unclear, 101
Third-person endorsements, in
    presentations, 102
Thomas, Julie, 320, 322
Thoughtfulness, tough-minded,
    161–162
Three Cs of motivation, 318
Thull, Jeff, 241, 243–244
Time, evaluating, 348–349
Timeless truths, in a 2.0 sales world,
    341–344
Time management, for salespeople,
    159–162
Time wasters, for salespeople,
    159–162
Tom Black Center for Selling, 353
Tom Hopkins International, 129,
    131
Tony Jeary International, 156, 157
"Top-down" cold calling approach,
    178–179
TopLine Leadership, Inc., 355
Top-performing salespeople
    as competitors, 201
    myths and misconceptions about,
    200–204
Tracy, Brian, 316, 318–319
Training, sales-force, 8–12
Training interventions, tailoring,
    141–142
Training problems, solutions for,
    11–12
Training process, involvement in,
    11
Training programs
    content of, 9–10
    reasons for failure of, 9–11

Transfer, critical elements of, 10–11
Trust
  building, 231–232
  client, 94–95
  direct introductions and, 193
  with the sales team, 24
Trust-based selling, 118
Trusted Advisor Associates, 115, 119
Trusted advisors, 123
Trusted relationships, building, 139
Trust Equation, 118
Trust Triangle Selling, 352
Twain, Mark, writing formula of, 58
Twain/Poe rule, 58

Unlock the Game, 105, 106–107, 109
Unreturned phone calls, 120–121
Up-front contract, 274–277
Urgency, role in success, 175

Value. *See also* Perceived value; Values
  changes in customer view of, 134–135
  customer awareness of, 336
  as an element of the successful sales formula, 271
  new definition of, 133
  quantifying, 172–173
Value clarity, 241–244
  diagnosing complex problems to achieve, 242–243
Value communication, 136
Valued customers, retaining, 7
Value drivers, 133–134
Value proposition, 167
Values, expressing, 231
ValueSelling Associates, 320, 322
Very Important Top Officers (VITOs), selling to, 226–230
"Very interested" prospects, 189
Victory, risk involved in, 16
Virtual meetings, Twain/Poe rule for, 58
Virtual meeting technology, 56–59
Virtual presentations, 55–59

Virtual presenting, skills related to, 59
Vision, as an element of the successful sales formula, 271
Visual aids, 291. *See also* Visuals
Visual pipeline, 174
Visuals, use of, 331. *See also* Visual aids
VITO Selling, 226, 229. *See also* Very Important Top Officers (VITOs)
Voice
  impact on listeners, 73
  while selling, 267
Voice of change, 52–53
Vows, in a whirlwind economy, 4–7

"Wall, The," 106, 107
Wallace, Ed, 362–363
Waterhouse, Steve, 362
Waterhouse Group, 362
Wealthy buyers, 127
Web-based events, hosting, 57. *See also* Internet entries
Web-based technology, 55–56
Weiss, Wendy, 323, 324
Weiss Communications, 323, 324
Welcoming home, building, 5
Werth, Jacques, 326, 328
Whirlwind economy, living vows in, 4–7
Wickman, Floyd, 329, 332
Will become category, xxix–xxx
Williamson, Judith, 217
Wilson Learning, 334, 337
"Winging it," 290–291
Winner profile, 18–19
"Winner" salespeople, 17–18
Winning, risk involved in, 16
Winning proposals
  content of, 279–280
  writing, 278–281
Words
  choosing, 14
  choosing wisely, 330–331
  emotional, 331
Workshops, self-growth, 19
Workstreams, failure to integrate, 24

World-class salespeople,
  characteristics of, 200–203
World-class sales training resources,
  352–363
World-class selling, 122–125
Writing, xxv

Zappulla, Justin, 152, 154
Zeglinski, Walt, 148, 150
Zeller, Dirk, 338, 339–340
Ziglar, 341, 344
Ziglar, Tom, 341, 344
Ziglar, Zig, 341, 344